It is not possible to find in the annals of criminal jurisprudence, a more deliberate and cold blood villain than the central figure of this story...
Detective Frank P. Geyer

MURDER BY GASLIGHT

MURDER, MAGIC & MADNESS AT THE FAIR THAT CHANGED AMERICA

TROY TAYLOR

AN AMERICAN HAUNTINGS INK BOOK

MURDER BY GASLIGHT

Murder, Magic & Madness at the Fair That Changed America

© Copyright 2025 by Troy Taylor

All Rights Reserved.
ISBN: 1-892523-86-8
Second Edition

Published by American Hauntings Ink
301 East Broadway – Alton IL – 62002
www.americanhauntingsink.com

Publisher's Note:
No part of this publication may be reproduced, distributed, or transmitted in any form or by any means, including photocopying, recording, or other electronic or mechanical methods, without the prior written consent of the publisher, except in case of brief quotations embodied in critical reviews or other noncommercial uses permitted by copyright law.

Cover Design by April Slaughter
Interior Design by Troy Taylor
Author Photo by Stephanie Susie

Printed in the United States of America

INTRODUCTION

IN 1893, THE WORLD CAME TO CHICAGO.

Plans began to be made for a World's Columbian Exposition to celebrate the 400th Anniversary of Christopher Columbus' arrival in America a few years earlier. Chicago, New York, Washington, D.C., and St. Louis all began competing vigorously for the honor of hosting the fair. It was during the jockeying for first place in the melee that followed that Chicago gained the nickname of the "Windy City" – which, by the way, had nothing to do with blustery days along Lake Michigan.

As delegates from Chicago were boasting about the city's landscapes, people, transportation, streets, and amenities, the editors of newspapers in competing cities were doing all they could to boost their own image – and take the shine off a city that had completely rebuilt itself in just two decades after the devastating Great Chicago Fire.

Charles Dana, then editor of the *New York Sun*, advised his readers to ignore what he called the "nonsensical claims of that windy city." It was the first use of the term, referring to the bragging and wild claims by the city's lobbyists.

But the World's Fair board did listen, and Chicago won the prize. On April 25, 1890, President Benjamin Harrison designated the city as the site of the exposition – and the frantic preparations began. A virtual city had to be built from scratch from the mud and swamp of Chicago's South Side. There would be no time to waste.

To the elitists in New York and Washington, Chicago was a backwater town. St. Louis might have been worse, but Chicago was a symbol of the nation's raw, commercial industries, a colossal but crude "hog butcher to the world," as officials like to brag about the sprawling stockyards on the city's edge. The cynics predicted the worst – a world's fair that reflected not only the host city's crude and colorful image but also was an embarrassing display of American vulgarity.

But the organizers quickly silenced their critics. They called on the nation's most eminent architects, painters, sculptors, and engineers to design the exposition grounds. This elite group of creators would dazzle the world and fashion the greatest event to ever occur in the history of Chicago.

The completed fairgrounds became known as the "White City" – a shining beacon of transformation, science, and change. Massive pavilions were constructed, lakes were created, miles of walks were built, and the nation was permanently changed by what happened along Lake Michigan during one short year.

But not everything that happened at the World's Fair was wonderful.

The fairgrounds were a prime target for confidence men and pickpockets. There were robberies, muggings, and assaults, and

The statue of Columbia overlooks the great lagoon at the center of the fairgrounds, which had been dubbed "The White City."

just a short distance away was Chicago's notorious Red Light District, which did a booming business during the Fair.

And there was worse. On the evening of the "Chicago Day" event, the city's five-term Mayor Carter Harrison was shot to death in his home by a disgruntled office-seeker, which, as you might imagine, put a bit of a damper on the celebration.

In the wake of the Fair, the list of those who never made it back to the small town or city they traveled from was a long one, and, for many of those folks, foul play was suspected. Were they murdered, kidnapped, or sold into the city's brothels – a fate so many preachers warned about could happen in the big city – who knows? All we do know is that many of those who attended the Fair simply never returned home.

When efforts were made to track down some of the missing, it was discovered that their trails went cold somewhere on the south side of Chicago.

There's a good chance this wasn't a coincidence.

Daniel Burnham

DANIEL BURNHAM WAS THE MAN CHOSEN TO TAKE ON THE daunting task of turning a patch of sand, mud, and wild oak into a wonderland that was worthy of being visited by the world.

Burnham had already created some of Chicago's most acclaimed buildings. He and his partner, John W. Root, had started working together just two years after the Great Fire of 1871. They were both in their early twenties at the time. Their offices began as a single room and slowly grew along with their reputation. When the era of the skyscraper arrived, Burnham and Root designed the Montauk, which was "described as a 10-story monster."

The partners were selected to construct the White City in 1891, but John Root never had the chance to bask in its success. He died from pneumonia at the age of 41 that same year, leaving Burnham to bear the burden alone. Even while mourning the loss of his friend, though, he rose to the challenge of organizing the construction of the fairgrounds. He fought and won a battle with a large, stubborn group of Chicago businessmen who insisted on telling him how to create the committees and collect the designs for the grounds. They wanted architects to compete for the open design slots, but Burnham convinced them he did not have time for that.

He ended up choosing the architects he wanted to work with, and they were among the best in the country. His first recruit was Frederick Law Olmstead, who had created Central Park in New York and was considered America's foremost landscape architect. Others, equally distinguished, included Henry Ives Cobb, Richard Morris Hunt, George B. Post, and Louis B. Sullivan. Sophie Hayden,

Construction on the grounds and on the massive pavilions that became centerpieces for the exposition began two years before the gates opened.

the first woman awarded a degree in architecture from the Massachusetts Institute of Technology, designed the famous Women's Building.

The Columbian Exposition grounds took shape on a stretch of boggy shoreline that, for the moment, was mud, windblown sand, and trees. It was about seven miles south of downtown Chicago. Work officially began in February 1891. The land had to be cleared, filled, and leveled before anything could be built. Over time, the work crew would grow into a team of 7,000 men, all toiling heroically to finish the fairgrounds on time.

Frederick Olmstead tackled a swampy area that was prone to flooding and turned it into what would be called Jackson Park. Businessman and nature lover James W. Ellsworth, a member of the World's Fair board, privately donated $15 million so that he could give Olmstead a free hand to create whatever he liked within the grounds. The park would not only serve the Fair but would be a place of permanent beauty still in use today. The transformation required slicing acres of sand from the surface and replacing them with train cars filled with soil and importing thousands of flowers, plants, and shrubs to beautify the lagoon and wooded island in the center of it.

Burnham recruited the eccentric sculptor August Saint-Gaudens, and he brought other sculptors with him, like Daniel C. French, Paul Bartlett, and many others. All of them, like Chicago's own Lorado Taft, were eager to work with Saint-Gaudens and provided Burnham with scores of ideas and designs for the White City.

But don't be fooled into thinking everything went smoothly.

Burnham was constantly fighting with his architects. The planners had selected a classical theme for the fair buildings, over the strong objections of the more innovative architects. Burnham got it. He wanted to take risks, too, but they couldn't. That was not what they had been asked to do. There were constant complaints. Louis Sullivan pronounced the Greek and Roman temples they were being told to build old-fashioned and outdated and predicted that the damage to modern design caused by the Fair would last for 50 years or more.

But none of them would be around that long. In fact, they'd be destroyed when the Fair ended. The buildings were meant to be amazing, both for their beauty and size, but they were never meant to be permanent. They were built from a material called "staff," a mixture of plaster and wood fibers that, when hardened, could be cut like wood. By pouring staff into glue molds, many ornamental pieces, which appeared to be handmade, could be achieved in a short time. The structure underneath the material was steel or wood, so the buildings wouldn't collapse, but they weren't meant to last longer than the duration of the Fair.

One did, though. Out of the 200 buildings constructed, only the former Palace of Fine Arts remains today. It was also built using staff, but it housed the Field Columbian Museum at the Fair, and that remained open until 1920. A few years later, the building was reduced to its steel skeleton and was rebuilt using stone and solid materials. It re-opened in 1931 and remains today as the Museum of Science and Industry.

Despite the valiant efforts of Daniel Burnham, though, the construction of the White City fell months behind schedule. The fairgrounds would eventually be dedicated in October 1892 – the anniversary of Columbus' landing – but it happened with the gathered dignitaries standing in a muddy field, looking off into the distance at half-completed buildings, unfinished walkways, and partially dug canals and ponds.

Even so, these preliminary ceremonies were a huge success. The festivities began with a 10-mile-long military parade from downtown to the fairgrounds. An estimated 80,000 people turned out to cheer as marching bands played, soldiers passed on horseback, and fair officials and dignitaries waved from carriages decked out with flags and banners.

The dedication itself took place inside one of the exposition's few completed buildings – the massive Manufacturers and Liberal Arts Building. The spectators packed into the cavernous structure heard several hours of speeches from fair officials, Chicago politicians, and other notable windbags. Luckily, there was also some music added to the mix. Other highlights included an awards presentation by Harlow N. Higginbotham, the head of the World's

The Manufacturers and Liberal Arts building

The "surging sea of humanity" at the opening of the World's Columbian Exposition on May 1, 1893.

Columbian Exposition Corporation, and a "light luncheon" for the assembled crowd – only half of whom managed to get anything to eat in the mad scramble for food.

It was an exciting day, but it didn't hide the fact that the fair was still not ready to open. That wouldn't happen for more than six months, on May 1, 1893.

On opening day, President Grover Cleveland was on hand to cut the ribbon, and nearly 400,000 people came to cheer him on. Between May 1 and October 31, the fair attracted more than 25 million visitors – a number that equaled half the American population at the time. They came to see the palaces, the Midway, the rides, shows, and the immense white buildings, which were electrically illuminated at night and gleamed so brightly in the sunshine that the fair was dubbed the "White City."

President Cleveland arrived at the front of a procession of 23 carriages that conveyed Chicago's most influential citizens. Thousands of ordinary folks pushed into an area near the main reviewing stand to get a look. Their cheers and shouts were drowned out when an orchestra began to play – which meant that no one could hear their cries and screams when the crowd surged, crushing people against the stage. Children wept, and women cried out as they were smashed, jostled, and shoved. Dresses were torn, people fainted, and many had to be rescued from being stomped into the muddy lawn.

Out of reach of the chaos, President Cleveland opened the fair by pressing an electric switch – the very modern version of

ribbon cutting was how the organizers saw it. The president then made a speech – which no one could have possibly heard – and the flags of the United States and Spain were run up their respective flagpoles.

Nearby fountains came to life and sent water spurting into the air. The thunder of guns could be heard coming from warships on the lake and, throughout the fairgrounds, large and mysterious machines began to hum, rotate, and turn.

The 1893 World's Columbian Exposition was finally open.

From among the assembled crowd, thousands braved a heavy rain shower to be the first to roam the soggy fairgrounds. When the rain finally cleared off that morning, the view that stretched out before the surging crowd was almost overwhelming.

In the huge buildings were exhibits that matched the theme of each structure, from Arts to Science, Agriculture, Electricity, and much more. Within those buildings, though, the most popular exhibits were the curiosities, not the serious displays of technology. Among them was a stuffed whale that attendees could walk through, a 1,500-pound replica of the Venus de Milo made from

chocolate, a 70-foot-tall tower of light bulbs, an 11-ton block of cheese, and a cotton exhibit where miniature bales of cotton could be purchased as souvenirs from the ex-slaves who had once grown and picked it.

There were buildings dedicated to each of the states, showing off their history, archaeology, and their products and industries. The Louisiana building showcased a Creole kitchen, staffed by appropriately dressed workers of color and supervised by ladies who were white, of course. Florida's building was constructed to look like the old fort in St. Augustine. Virginia's display was built to look like Washington's Mount Vernon. Massachusetts' building was a reproduction of John Hancock's home on Beacon Hill, and so on.

At the heart of the fair was what was designated the Court of Honor. From its center, fair attendees could take in a breathtaking vista of glittering palaces, soaring arches, and gleaming domes, all flanking a formal basin that was 2,500 feet long. Colossal statues rose from the water at either end of the basin. To the east stood Daniel Chester French's "Statue of the Republic," a towering, robed female figure that some wit had nicknamed "Big Mary."

The famous – and overwhelming – "Grand Barge of State that drew admiring crowds.

The fountain at the opposite end was dominated by the "Grand Barge of State." This sculpture was over the top, even for the late nineteenth century, when such designs were greatly admired. It was a huge, monumental depiction of Columbia – the goddess-like female personification of the United States and of liberty itself -- sailing triumphantly over the water, enthroned atop a great barge with Father Time clutching a trumpet at the helm. At the oars were eight sturdy maidens representing Music, Painting, Architecture, Sculpture, Science, Industry, Agriculture, and Commerce.

You can see what I mean when I say, "over the top."

But these were not all the wonders the fair had to offer. There were always sights guaranteed to amaze a visitor, whether they came from the city or the farm. There were:

- Movable sidewalks
- Elevators
- Replicas of Columbus' three ships, which were sailed from Spain for the Fair.
- An Irish Village, complete with a replica of Blarney Castle and an inappropriately fake Blarney stone to kiss that was actually a piece of a Chicago sidewalk.

The authentic Irish Village, which had a Blarney Stone made from a piece of Chicago sidewalk.

- A high-current wire devised by Nicola Tesla that powered a long-distance telephone line to New York.
- The Liberty Bell was on display.
- Visitors could also meet and listen to Susan B. Anthony, who held what seemed then like a curious belief that women should be allowed to vote.

There were also the innovations and products first introduced to the world at the 1983 fair. They included:

- Thomas Edison's Kinetoscope, an electrically driven peepshow-like device that showed moving pictures.
- Zippers were first introduced for clothing
- A souvenir item was first offered that continues to delight young and old to this day -- the squashed penny.
- A salty-sweet concoction called Cracker Jacks was first sold at the fair.

Nancy Green – the first "Aunt Jemima" – demonstrated a new self-rising flour for pancakes.

- There was a former slave named Nancy Green who, as Aunt Jemima, sang songs, told stories, and offered cooking demonstrations during which pancakes were made from a new kind of self-rising flour that could be purchased in a box with her picture on it.

- Other food products introduced at the fair included Cream of Wheat, the first hamburgers, Juicy Fruit gum, and Shredded Wheat, which some fairgoers referred to as "shredded doormat."

- Pabst Beer from Milwaukee won a blue ribbon in a competition, hence the name change.

- A fairgoer named Hershey from Pennsylvania was so excited about the German chocolate-making machinery that he saw at the Fair that he bought it, took it home with him, and started his own line of candy.

THE WORLD'S COLUMBIAN EXPOSITION WAS ALSO THE FIRST event of its kind to feature a separate amusement and entertainment area. It was dubbed the Midway, and the noisy and light-hearted attractions found there were concentrated in an area that wouldn't disturb the park-like setting of the rest of the exposition. The fair was meant to be dedicated to the high-minded principles of progress, patriotism, and culture, but Daniel Burnham knew that attendees would also be looking for loud, rowdy, raucous fun, so, he gave it to them with this slightly segregated, mile-long sideshow filled with thrilling attractions.

There were Japanese and Indian bazaars, a Moorish palace, South Seas and Chinese villages, a Lapland village, complete with reindeer, a Tunisian village with a Bedouin encampment, and a concert hall for musical, juggling, and dancing performances.

The Midway at the World's Fair was the first separate amusement area to be featured at this kind of event. It would soon be copied by carnivals and fairgrounds across the nation.

There were also German and Austrian villages with restaurants and shops staffed by respective nationals, as well as a cider press, where French villagers demonstrated how the drink was made.

There was a giant painted panorama of the Swiss Alps, models of the Blue Grotto of Capris, St. Peters in Rome, the Eiffel Tower, a Hawaiian volcano, and a Colorado gold mine.

If all of this sounds vaguely familiar, then you can understand where the idea for the World Showcase at Disney's Epcot park came from.

Although, there was a very un-Disney-like ethnic display that included a Dahomey village, where 100 native Africans demonstrated their cultural and religious customs – or were supposed to anyway. First, the Dahomey people were late to arrive, so local African Americans were hired to portray them, next to a giant banner of a man in a loincloth, holding up the severed head of his enemy. When the Dahomey arrived from West Africa, the peace-loving people refused to work until the banner was removed.

A man from California operated an ostrich farm and offered guests ostrich omelets to eat, while the Fleishman's Yeast Company hired famed boxer John Corbett to give demonstrations on how he had defeated the great John Sullivan. I have no idea what they had to do with yeast, but I suppose it was a celebrity endorsement.

Other wonders of the Midway included the World Congress of Beauties, which advertised "40 Ladies from 40 Nations," hot food, cold beer, and a recreated street from Cairo, Egypt.

It was here, in what was called the "Streets of Cairo" exhibit, that fairgoers were entertained by an attraction that became the most popular -- and the most controversial -- of the fair.

This was the first venue to introduce the art of exotic dancing to America. While shocking to many, the exhibit proved to be the most successful Midway attraction, and its backers made more than double back on their investment.

Without a doubt, the sensation of the exhibit was Fahreda Mahzar, better known as "Little Egypt." Fahreda was a practitioner of what Americans began to call "belly dancing."

The diamonds on her garter, her colorful brassiere, and her body contortions either fascinated or scandalized everyone who saw her perform, and she easily became the must-see attraction of the fair for men and women alike. The music to accompany her dance, the familiar "snake charmer" tune that pops into everyone's head when they think of belly dancing, was composed in a flash of inspiration at a press preview by the Midway's manager, 23-year-old Sol Bloom.

The notorious "Streets of Cairo" exhibit, which was located on the Midway, became one of the most famous sections of the Fair.

(Below) The scandalous "Little Egypt"

As exotic as she was then, her costume seems tame by modern standards. Even so, she was remembered for years as the most beautiful and wondrous attraction of the entire exposition.

The world's first Ferris Wheel was designed and built for the Columbian Exposition.

Even those scandalized by Little Egypt still didn't miss the Midway's other attractions, like the captive balloon ride that took visitors 1,500 feet above the fairgrounds and, of course, the world's first Ferris Wheel.

The giant, rotating wheel of steel, which eventually became a staple of amusement parks was named for its inventor, George Washington Gale Ferris, a bridge-builder from Galesburg, Illinois, who created it specifically for the 1893 Columbian Exposition.

The wheel was 264 feet in height, 250 feet in diameter, and 825 feet in circumference. The axle was the largest piece of forged steel in the world at that time, weighing more than 142,000 pounds. This was heavier than anything that had ever been lifted and had to be mounted on top of eight towers. The Ferris wheel held 36 wooden cars that were the size of small railroad coaches, and each could hold 60 people.

No one had ever seen a contraption like it. It looked very fragile and very dangerous. Nothing like it could exist today because no company would dream of insuring it. But on every day of the fair, thrill-seekers paid 50-cents -- equal to about $17 today

-- to climb into the cars and soar for 22 minutes above the fairgrounds.

Rumors spread about suicides, but the company denied these allegations. The cars had barred windows to keep people from jumping out, although some passengers discovered their fear of heights a little too late. One man panicked and hurled himself against the bars with such force that he shattered the glass and bent the iron bars. He pushed away everyone who tried to hold him back until a woman -- to the mixed shock and delight of onlookers -- lifted her skirt and placed it over the man's head until he calmed down. It was a method that worked with panicked horses, she later said, and it worked equally well with a panicked man.

The Ferris Wheel was unquestionably the fair's most popular attraction, and the ride, along with the entire Midway, would soon be copied all over the world.

The unrestrained atmosphere of the Midway provided a much-needed escape from the harsh realities of day-to-day living. For those millions of people who came and enjoyed their time there, it became their most cherished memory of the fair. Americans, especially Chicagoans, it was said allowed themselves a little time in their busy and often unhappy lives for simple enjoyment. The Midway taught America to be happy for reasons that had nothing to do with family, work, religion, education, or business. It was fun for fun's sake.

As one newspaperman wrote, "The first time that America turned out for an unrestrained good time was in Chicago and that properly gives the city a strong claim to distinction, as well as to gratitude."

But not everything about the Columbian Exposition was pristine, beautiful, and fun. Behind the shining mask of the White City was a darkness both terrifying and deadly.

It was a place where monsters lurked.

THE WORLD'S COLUMBIAN EXPOSITION CAME TO AN END AT sunset on October 31, 1893. It closed, perhaps fittingly, to the strains of "Funeral March" by Beethoven. Grand ceremonies, like the ones that had opened the fair, were planned for this occasion, too, but were canceled at the last minute.

A short time earlier, the fair celebrated "Chicago Day," during which the city's five-term mayor Carter Harrison predicted a great future for Chicago.

His future, though, was not so great.

That evening, the mayor was resting at home in his robe and slippers when the doorbell rang. When Harrison answered, he was shot to death by a man named Patrick Eugene Prendergast.

Prendergast was a Chicago newspaper distributor, and in 1893, he supported Harrison's re-election campaign. Unfortunately for the mayor, Prendergast was also more than a little unhinged. He was under the delusion that if Harrison won the election, he would receive an important role in the mayor's cabinet. When his appointment

Chicago Mayor Carter Harrison

didn't come, Prendergast went to Harrison's home and shot the mayor four times.

When news of the assassination spread throughout the city, the flags at the fair were lowered to half-staff, and, on the Midway, rioting broke out. The city was in shock. Not since the arrival of Abraham Lincoln's funeral train in 1865 had there been such a weeping and grief-stricken horde of mourners on the streets as when the mayor lay in state at City Hall. It was, some have said, a fitting climax to the twilight days of the fair.

It seemed that after the summer heyday of the exposition, a dark cloud had settled over what should have been a celebration.

It was hard to ignore the fact that the last months of the fair took place during a major panic on Wall Street and a serious depression that severely affected the city of Chicago and the rest of the nation. The Chemical National Bank, with a branch at the fair, failed just eight days after the exposition opened.

The fair's Jewelry Exhibition, a supposedly impregnable repository, was robbed, and two large diamonds were stolen, along with a riding crop that was owned by King Leopold II of Belgium.

As grim as the final weeks of the fair were, that time likely saved Chicago. If not for the exposition, the local economy would have been hit even harder than it was by the depression of the day. The gate receipts brought in more than $10 million, and the concession receipts garnered at least $4 million more. This did not include millions of dollars made from souvenir books, commemorative coins, and other items that were sold. It was thought that at least $3 million was left over to divide between the investors. This was a sum equal to about $90 million today.

But the glory of the Columbian Exposition was a transient one for Chicago. The White City was gone, except for the great buildings, which some were now calling "white elephants" for which no purchasers could be found.

On January 8, 1894, a fire destroyed three major Exposition buildings – the Casino, the Peristyle, and the Music Hall. Six months later, an even more devastating blaze burned the most glorious structures on the fairgrounds, including the magnificent Manufacturers and Liberal Arts Building, which was the largest building ever constructed at the time. At the height of the fair, few visitors would have believed just how fragile those stately white structures were.

The depression that was affecting the rest of the nation finally settled on Chicago and late fall and winter brought misery to scores of the city's residents. As the winds grew colder, the effects of the closed factories, stores running with reduced workforces, and the scores of men and women laid off from their jobs started to show.

At City Hall, the stone corridors were filled with sleepers at night, trying to stay warm. Police stations throughout the city sheltered between 60 and 100 transients every night. In the Harrison Street station, cells were packed, and men crowded the floors of the hallway. Reporters stated that the hallways, where the shrieks of prisoners could be heard, were packed with men sleeping elbow-to-elbow, sometimes with rats running over them. Mothers and children slept in stations and jails, too, usually in the women's section.

That winter was terrible for children. Babies were given to overcrowded orphanages. Thousands of older children were turned out on the street with parents who no longer had work. There were hundreds of evictions every day – mostly because rents had been raised so high during the Fair. Jane Addams, and other social workers, worked hard to keep mothers and children from the poorhouse, but there were just too many to care for.

The streets were filled with people begging for a handout. Some of them were stranded fair vendors, who now found their Armenian rugs and glittering fake jewelry impossible to sell. On every corner, poor outcasts, who had profited during the days of plenty, now cried for help but received very little.

But even with hundreds of thousands of people out of work, Chicago was still the "city of big shoulders," as Carl Sandburg would later call it.

Money was donated to rent vacant stores where soup kitchens could be opened. Merchants stocked them with food. In slum districts, aldermen distributed food and clothing to the needy, who, of course, immediately became loyal voters. Saloon operators and brothel owners sheltered and cared for hundreds of people, and "free lunches" in taverns saved many from starvation. It was later reported that during the worst of the crisis, 60,000 men were fed each day for free by saloonkeepers.

Chicago was not defeated by mere financial setbacks. It was a city that had completely rebuilt itself after a devastating fire and a place that had created the world's most dazzling fair out of a few miles of sand and barren lakefront. The crisis of the middle 1890s passed, and Chicago moved on to embrace another century.

But it wouldn't do so without a lot of blood being spilled.

Even during the glittering days of the fair, the White City was considered easy pickings for con men, pea-shell and three-card monte men, thieves, pickpockets, and strong-arm robbers of every kind.

They were the darkness that lurked behind the shiny mask.

Newspapers – all of them from out of town, of course – wrote sensationally of muggings, beatings, and brawls at the fair. They warned of country yokels who were conned by loaded dice, marked cards, gin joints, and prostitutes, who plied their trade a stone's throw from the fairgrounds.

But these cautionary tales did little to deter the countless people who dreamed of making the trip to Chicago for the fair. Ordinary people mortgaged their farms and dipped into their life savings to attend the once-in-a-lifetime event.

For the travelers who came from all over the country – and from countries around the world -- Chicago offered them every sort of accommodation possible. Visitors with large bank accounts

Englewood, then a separate city south of Chicago, in the early 1900s.

could stay at a luxury hotel downtown, while those on smaller budgets were happy to settle for a well-kept boardinghouse. The demand was so great for decent lodging -- especially within walking distance of the fairgrounds -- that anyone with a clean room to spare could pick up a few extra dollars by renting the room to a desperate tourist. A landlord with even a few empty apartments could make a nice profit in a very short amount of time.

In Englewood, which was then a separate community on Chicago's south side, travelers had several options when it came to places to stay during the fair. There were a few small hotels and several boarding houses along 69th Street, and at the spot where the street intersected with Wallace Avenue was a commercial building that contained a few shops, including a pharmacy and a jewelry store. Two of the upper floors of the building had been converted into what the owner was advertising as his "World's Fair Hotel."

He had been making plans for years to make money off travelers to the fair, almost as soon as it was announced that Chicago had been chosen as the site for the exposition. He had purchased a large amount of furniture and linens for the rooms, and when the fair's opening day finally arrived, he began placing advertisements for the hotel in newspapers and periodicals.

No one can say how many fairgoers stayed at the hotel between May and October 1893, but stories say it may have been filled to capacity on most nights, especially during the busy summer season. If that's the case, then possibly hundreds of visitors slept within those walls. But we'll never know the exact number – any more than we'll ever know just how many of those guests checked in but never checked out of the hotel.

The list of those who never returned home after the fair ended is a long one. You likely won't be surprised to learn that foul play was suspected for many on that list. But just how many vanished under suspicious circumstances is unknown.

And how many of them fell prey to the owner of the so-called World's Fair Hotel is also a mystery. But if he did kill anyone at the hotel, it would later be discovered that he had the perfect facility for murder.

By using control valves that were hidden in his private quarters, the owner could fill many of the rooms on the second and third floors of the building with gas. Anyone asleep in those rooms would have simply never awakened. For the rooms not hooked up to the gas lines, chloroform served as an effective tool. The owner had a master key that allowed him access to any room. A sleeper could be dispatched without much effort.

Disposing of the bodies of slain travelers was as simple as dropping them down a chute that led to the basement. There were trapdoors that hid those chutes on both floors.

Although many of the owner's victims later became medical specimens, others were burned in his make-shift crematorium or dissolved in the basement acid vat, along with whatever personal effects he had no use for.

The owner did not kill for any deviant sexual need. He had no morals and no conscience, so he murdered for convenience. When someone outlived their usefulness or became a threat, he killed them without a second thought. He had no moral compass and thought nothing of killing guests who wouldn't be missed. The owner had a ferocious greed. His desire for money was insatiable, and he was simply incapable of having enough money to satisfy his needs.

Travelers who brought valuables to his hotel were nothing more than easy targets. They had something he wanted, and it never crossed his mind that he shouldn't have it. Murder was simply a way of trying to satisfy his greed – which is why the true number of people he killed – including those who stayed at his hotel during the fair -- will never be known.

He would eventually confess to only a single murder of a fairgoer, but the owner of the hotel was known for never letting the truth get in the way or a self-serving story.

It seems too much of a coincidence that there were many people who went missing after the fair and were traced as far as Englewood before their trail went cold.

After the thousands of reports of robberies, picked pockets, and assaults, that came in during the exposition, the police breathed a sigh of relief when the lights went dark on the fairground. They hoped the bad element that had been attracted to the fair would finally move on from Chicago to somewhere – anywhere else.

But, of course, the worst element would not. He would remain in the city for a little while longer and would continue to use it as the perfect hunting ground.

H.H. Holmes was only just beginning to discover the darkness that Chicago had to offer.

They called themselves "resurrectionists," but really, it was just a fancy word for "grave robber." But they were not common thieves, skulking about in cemeteries, unearthing caskets, and stealing valuables buried with the dead. They were respectable men, doctors and surgeons, who weren't looking for gold rings and diamonds. They were digging up graves for something far more valuable – the bodies of the dead.

By the middle of the nineteenth century, American medicine had come a long way. Doctors weren't root healers or performing crude operations in barber shops anymore. This was because of their newfound knowledge of human anatomy – knowledge gained by dissecting the bodies of the dead.

Human cadavers were essential for medical schools. The students needed corpses so they could learn the essentials and practice their skills.

In other words, if you're going to start cutting on someone, you may want to know where all the various parts are located.

But since few people were willing to donate their bodies to medical schools when they died, doctors and medical students had no choice but to find their own bodies to work on. Sneaking into a graveyard in the dead of night as a resurrectionist became a rite of passage and even showed a little school pride.

But as the uneducated public began to realize that every medical school was either robbing graves or hiring men to do it, doctors started to be both feared and reviled by their communities, and medical schools were regarded as being even lower than a brothel or saloon.

Soon, laws began to be passed that restricted doctors from claiming the dead for dissection. The only exceptions were the bodies of criminals who were sentenced to death. As you might imagine, though, the demand for corpses far outweighed the number of dead criminals, so the resurrectionist activities of otherwise eminent medical schools continued. The professors who taught the next generation of doctors and surgeons continued to do what was necessary.

One such man was Dr. Nahum Wight of Gilmanton, New Hampshire. He was a professor of anatomy, and as early as 1846, he was said to own a collection of anatomical specimens that violated pretty much every law you can think of when it comes to storing body parts. He also maintained a dissection room for his students to use, which was later mentioned in his obituary. It read:

He maintained a dissection room for the benefit of his students and himself when such an enterprise was made difficult and sometimes perilous by prejudice, and by the law, at a time when one might be sent to state prison for having possession of a dead human body. He defended human dissection and taught the public its necessity.

Many of Dr. Wight's students were live-in apprentices who worked and studied at the doctor's home, where his offices were located. One of those students, Rueben Price, became a field surgeon for the First New Hampshire Heavy Artillery during the Civil War.

Reuben didn't often return to New Hampshire after the war, but when he did, it's likely that he often told stories about the things he saw on the battlefields to his young nephew, who listened to his bloody stories with wide-eyed fascination.

Dr. Nahum Wight

His young nephew, probably no more than 10 years old at the time, was his sister's son, a little boy named Herman, who would later study anatomy with Dr. Wight himself. Much of what he learned there would be put into practice in ways that would shock the entire country.

WHILE THE DEVIL MAY NOT HAVE BEEN STANDING NEXT TO THE bed in which Herman Mudgett was born – as stories said he'd later claim – he was the fourth child of Levi Mudgett, a house painter and later a postmaster, and his wife, Theodate, in Gilmanton, New Hampshire, on May 16, 1860. He had one sister, Ellen, and two brothers, Clarence and Arthur.

The Mudgetts were ordinary people. There was nothing all that interesting about them, and if they were anything other than upright, respected members of the community, no one at the time wrote it down.

By all accounts – other than his own – Holmes' childhood was almost entirely normal. When the Mudgett family and their neighbors were later interviewed by newspapers, no one in town had a bad thing to say about Herman or his parents. Herman was a good student and an agreeable, if unremarkable, young man.

Gilmanton, New Hampshire in the 1870s

The only bad thing anyone recalled was that Herman seemed "too fond of money." A schoolmate later remembered that Herman had once stolen 43 cents from his vest pocket, tried to get paid twice for cutting some wood, and claimed he'd mailed a payment for a shoe repair that he'd never actually sent.

If only those had been the worst crimes he'd committed.

Herman told a much different story of his early life, though. He told that story in an autobiography that he would later write while sitting in prison with nothing else to do. I'll refer to it often throughout, but keep in mind that it has little value as literature and even less value as a true source about H.H. Holmes. It's likely that a large chunk of the book is fiction, written by a reporter without Holmes' permission. The reporter also likely "enhanced" sections that Holmes did write to make them more exciting.

The home in which Herman Mudgett was born and grew up in Gilmanton.

And even if we believe he wrote the whole thing himself, it doesn't matter. Holmes was an unrepentant, chronic liar, and nothing he wrote can be taken at face value.

According to Herman, his mother, Theodate, was a harsh woman with sharp, severe features, a cool demeanor, and a lack of fondness for children – both other people's and her own. Married life had not been kind to her. Her husband Levi was an often-violent man, Herman said, who never hesitated to discipline his children or his wife. Levi ran a successful farm, but the fact that he was a good provider likely offered little relief to his family when he was doling out punishments.

Herman would recall that whenever one of the children had a toothache, Levi pulled the offending tooth himself. If the child cried, a cloth reeking of kerosene was roughly held over their nose and mouth, causing them to become unconscious so the dental work could be done without a struggle. He also used the kerosene-soaked cloth as a punishment, too.

If this sounds to you a lot like the commonly used technique for subduing the victim of a robbery or murder with chloroform, you'd be correct. It was a rather strange family, if this was true, but since Holmes tells the story, it's impossible to say if it was.

Although neighbors' recollections stated simply that the Mudgetts attended church, Herman claimed his parents were devout, almost fanatical, Christians. They drug the children to church services and prayer meetings several times a week, and the pastor preached that children should be harshly disciplined to learn the strict rules of faith and conduct – advice they happily followed.

Herman also recalled that he was one of the brightest children at Gilmanton Academy, a respected school that was close to the Mudgett home. Teachers and other adults often remarked on how smart he was, but despite his intelligence – or perhaps because of it – he was often

Gilmanton Academy, where Herman Mudgett attended school as a boy in New Hampshire.

bullied and teased by older boys in town.

He was smaller than average as a boy, thin, with dark brown hair, and bright blue eyes. He often spoke above the heads of other boys in his grade, which earned him some resentment, but it was his small size that made him a target for bullies.

A bullying incident when Herman was only five haunted him for the rest of his life. His route home from school each day took him past the office of Dr. Nahum Wight, his uncle's former anatomy professor. The office doors were rarely closed, likely because of the sharp medicinal odors from inside – a smell that reminded Herman of the cloth his father pushed over his face when he wanted him to behave. This caused him to fear the office, as did the stories other boys told at school about what the doctor kept inside. They whispered about amputated limbs, preserved human heads, and deformed babies in jars. Herman was terrified of the place.

One day, after some boys learned about Herman's fear of the office, they grabbed him while Dr. Wight was out running an errand and tugged him inside. Struggling and weeping, Herman was left on the office floor by himself. When Dr. Wight returned, he discovered the boy weeping at the feet of an articulated skeleton, nearly catatonic with terror.

We can doubt most of the stories that Holmes wrote about his life, but that one has a ring of truth to it. He later attributed his interest in anatomy and his side career with skeletal remains to this traumatic experience. As a teenager, Herman studied with Dr. Wight, just as his uncle had and always claimed to have a deep respect for him.

Dr. Wight may have been one of the few childhood friends that Herman had, although there are claims that another was an older boy named Tom who rumors say died under mysterious circumstances. One day, the two boys were exploring an old house outside of town, and during this adventure, Tom fell down some stairs and broke his neck.

Years later, community residents would suggest that Herman had killed him – just as he allegedly did an old man named Beck, who died in London, New Hampshire. Beck, who had married the widow of one of Herman's uncles, was found in his home, the victim of a possible suicide. A rope was around his neck, but his legs were bent at the knees. Rumors had long claimed Beck was murdered, and by the time Herman gained infamy as H.H. Holmes, fingers were pointing directly at the teenaged boy that he'd been at the time.

THERE IS NO RECORD OF HERMAN'S LIFE BETWEEN THE AGES of 16 and 18. No one knows what secrets those years hold. His autobiography – that document of lies, half-truths, and nonsense – made no mention of that time in his life, his first and only legal marriage, or the birth of his son, Robert.

Nothing about his everyday life was very interesting to Holmes. Perhaps he just considered it too boring, or too much at odds with the portrayal of the "criminal mastermind" that appeared in newspapers.

Herman Mudgett as a young man

No matter what Holmes did or didn't want people to know, records state that Herman graduated from Gilmanton Academy and became a teacher at the local elementary school. We know that he also studied with Dr. Wight and expressed an interest in becoming a doctor. The only problem was that he didn't have the money to pay for medical school. But, as Herman would do for the rest of his life, he came up with a plan.

Clara Lovering, Holmes's first (and only legal) wife. She was also the mother of Holmes' only son, Robert.

Herman was only 16 when he started teaching at elementary school, and it was during that time, he later said, that he met and fell in love with Clara Lovering of New London, New Hampshire.

There are a couple of different versions of how the two of them met. One said that Herman met her while working on her father's farm. Another claimed they became a couple at a church social. Clara had been flirting with another boy, and Herman became jealous. He told the boy that if he didn't stop paying so much attention to Clara, there would be trouble. The other boy left the social early, and Herman left with Clara on his arm.

Clara seemed to be well-liked and admired in the community. A neighbor would later describe her as "a very pretty little woman," although I'm not convinced that Clara's looks mattered much to Herman. What mattered to him was her father's substantial farm and his large income, which he knew she would inherit someday. Even before that, Clara would have access to her father's money, allowing him to comfortably attend medical school – or so he initially believed.

For the next year, Herman was a constant presence at the Lovering home. Then, on July 4, 1878, the two 17-year-olds eloped and were married in front of a justice of the peace in Alton, New Hampshire.

The marriage was kept secret from their parents at first, and the couple lived separately. When their parents did find out they'd eloped, none were thrilled by the news. Herman's mother allegedly told her son: "She couldn't have done worse. She'll probably have to support you."

Clara's family wasn't happy either, but her father arranged to have Herman start work as a clerk in her uncle's grocery store in East Concord. Herman and Clara were living there when she gave birth to their son, Robert.

We'll never know what finally caused Herman to take the next step toward becoming a doctor. It may have been his memories of his uncle's stories, being an apprentice to Dr. Wight, or those terrifying moments locked in a room with a grinning skeleton, but he soon decided that he deserved more out of life than working as a clerk in a country store. Being a doctor would make him an illustrious man – and a rich one if he could invent one of those patent medicines he'd been reading about.

These elixirs – which earned the name "snake oil," thanks to the charlatans that sold them – were advertised to cure pretty much anything and everything using exotic ingredients. They consisted of pills, liquids, and balms sold to consumers through misleading advertising claims, taking advantage of the fact that doctors of the era usually lacked the knowledge to treat their patient's ailments.

Most patent medicines were nothing more than bad-tasting water, but some of them did deliver the promised results by using some very dangerous ingredients. For example, medicines advertised as "infant soothers" contained opium, which would have the effect of soothing infants to the point of unconsciousness. Then there were those advertised as "mood lifters," which contained the mood-lifting ingredient of cocaine.

People desperately wanted a cure for things like cancer, cholera, epilepsy, scarlet fever, body pains, headaches, and female complaints. Aspirin hadn't yet been invented, and doctors were helpless, so people turned to anything that might work. Patent medicines seemed to be miracle drugs, and it would still be many years before they would be exposed for the fraudulent potions they were.

Herman undoubtedly knew how phony the medicines were, but he didn't care. As his old schoolmates later described him, "he loved money a little too much."

He quit working at the store, moved home to Gilmanton, and returned to his apprenticeship with Dr. Wight. He wanted the older man to teach him everything he needed to know to get his medical career off the ground.

After a year with Dr. Wight, Herman spent a term studying medicine more formally at the University of Vermont in Burlington. He rented a room from Mrs. Thomas Brew, sharing the space with another student, Fred Ingalls. The two did not get along well. Herman asked his roommate not to tell anyone he was married, and Ingalls agreed on the condition that Herman conducted himself like a married man and did not chase other women around. But when Herman began flirting with Mrs. Brew's daughter – so much flirting that people thought they were engaged – Ingalls told her Herman had a

Medicine was studied at Pomeroy Hall at the University of Vermont in Burlington.

wife, straining the relationship between the two men.

According to Mrs. Brew, though, their worst disagreement was when Ingalls used some of Herman's mustache wax without permission. The argument turned violent, and Ingalls was left badly beaten with two black eyes.

Mrs. Brew would recall other things about her tenant, too:

He was wild about chemistry. All the time, he was experimenting with liquids in his room, mixing up this one with that and littering the room with his concoctions. I was afraid that he'd do some damage, but he never had a mishap.

Herman had hired a private tutor after he decided that the chemistry department at the school was lacking. He turned his side of the room into a lab with test tubes and unlabeled bottles that Mrs. Brew feared would kill them all.

She also recalled that Herman seemed particularly eager about dissecting bodies at school. He often told stories about working on them around the boarding house and, once, even brought his work home with him. Mrs. Brew discovered a jar containing a dead baby under his bed when she was cleaning one day. He was sternly told not to bring home anything else, and she added that it was weeks before she had recovered enough to clean his room again.

But Herman's money didn't last in Vermont, and he returned home to Gilmanton to teach school again while he saved up for a return to his studies. He did well as a teacher, but there is one story about this period that must be told, although there's a good chance that it's not true. Even so, I couldn't resist including it.

Herman kept up with his medical studies while teaching grade school, and he even assisted a local doctor named Gray. One night, Dr. Gray had to amputate a man's frozen foot, and Herman, never squeamish, convinced Dr. Gray to let him keep the foot so that he could show it to his students the next day. When the class began, he brought out the foot and started to explain its

The University of Michigan Medical School at Ann Arbor in the 1880s when Herman was enrolled there.

anatomical features. The children were horrified. They told their mothers, who complained to the school's superintendent, E. H. Shannon, who hadn't wanted to hire Herman in the first place. That, according to the story, allegedly marked the end of his teaching career.

Herman left Gilmanton again in 1882 and he enrolled at the University of Michigan Medical School at Ann Arbor. Since Clara's father had provided the money so he could continue his studies, he felt obligated to take Clara and the baby to Michigan with him, even though their marriage was already troubled.

In Ann Arbor, they lived in a rooming house along with other students and their families. Clara covered the family's basic expenses by working as a dressmaker, but others in the house heard the couple arguing frequently. Clara was even seen around the house with bruises and black eyes. Divorce was very uncommon in those days, though, and a terrible social stigma for a woman. Besides that, women were regarded as the property of their husbands, and there were no laws against domestic violence.

But at some point, Clara decided she'd had enough, packed her bags, and moved back home with Robert. She stayed with her family for a time and then moved to Tilton, New Hampshire, where she again worked as a dressmaker.

Herman would see her again someday, but in his mind, she was part of his past, not his bright and brilliant future. She was largely forgotten.

Excerpted from an 1880 bird's-eye map of Ann Arbor, Michigan. Holmes lived at 15 Cemetery, at the corner of Cemetery and Observatory. The cemetery was located on the right side of the map, while the medical school is directly across from it on the middle left.

And that was the best thing that could have happened to Clara. If they'd stayed together and she'd ended up in Chicago with him, it's almost guaranteed that her life would have been much shorter.

HERMAN CONTINUED HIS MEDICAL STUDIES IN ANN ARBOR, moving into a house on Cemetery Street with several other medical students. The location of this house near the cemetery turned out to be convenient.

The medical school was generally supplied in those days by bodies on their way to pauper's graves. By the 1880s, laws were in place that specified that such bodies would first be given to the schools, then buried. But these laws rarely stopped grave robbing. Schools needed more cadavers than the state could provide, and, anyway, cadavers were too valuable in cities where such laws weren't in effect, so grave robbers continued to pilfer local cemeteries so they could sell the corpses and ship them elsewhere.

Herman, by all accounts of everyone who knew him, was at his best when dissecting bodies – to such a degree that even other medical students took notice of it. John Madden, a fellow student, later recalled:

He seemed to take a great deal of pleasure in the uncanny things of the dissecting room. One afternoon's conversation I remember distinctly. He talked a great deal about what he'd done in the dissecting room with, what appeared to me at the time to be unnecessary gusto and told me the professor of anatomy was to permit him to take the body of an infant home with him for dissection during the spring vacation, which was to begin the following day. I asked where he would find a place to carry on his work without offending his neighbors, and he replied with something to the effect that he would find a place. He seemed completely unconcerned about what they might think.

Herman's comfort around corpses led to his employment by Dr. William J. Herdman, an anatomy professor at the college. He began spending most of his time in the dissecting rooms, for which Dr. Herdman had given him the keys. He also hitched up the doctor's horses when needed for nighttime calls, took charge of the coat room, rented out drawers for dissecting tools, and prepared the bodies for the classes.

Dr. William J. Herdman

Herman took credit for the often mysterious arrival of cadavers for dissecting, and most of the students believed he was accompanying Dr. Herdman during his "night trips" to the local graveyards. The doctor had long been an advocate for resurrectionist activities.

But despite Herman's aptitude for cutting up bodies, he was a poor student. His grades were below average, and some even believed his professors graduated him out of pity. But even those who criticized him admitted that he was exceptionally clever and recalled his attention to detail in his class work. Dissecting a body, though, was different than doing well on a test.

Herman would later state several times that it was in college when he and a friend named Robert Leacock came up with an idea that he would use many times in his life.

The idea was to pay for an insurance policy on someone and then claim the money by producing the corpse of the insured – or rather, a convenient body from the dissecting lab to which Herman had the keys. Despite rumors, there is no evidence that Herman followed through on this idea while still in college, but if he did, it might explain how he managed to live well during the latter days of his time at the university.

But even if Herman didn't use this idea while in college, he certainly would later – and it would lead to his downfall.

He was never caught stealing bodies from the medical school, but his days at Ann Arbor were not without scandal. In March 1884, he was caught up in a case of what was called "breach of promise," which means Herman had promised to marry someone and then backed out. At the time, promising to marry a young woman was almost a surefire way of getting her into bed. Sex was not indulged in lightly by proper ladies at the time, but a promise of marriage became an acceptable excuse for doing so – and that's exactly what Herman did.

Although still married, he had been courting a young hairdresser who lived in the same boarding house that he did. He had promised they'd get married, so she'd sleep with him, but then she found a letter in his room that he'd written to his wife, Clara. Realizing she'd been deceived, she went before the faculty of the medical school, claiming breach of promise. Herman was called to a hearing before the faculty to defend himself. If the stories the young woman told were confirmed, he would be expelled just weeks before graduation.

During the hearing, though, Dr. Herdman defended him in front of the rest of the faculty, having been assured by Herman that the stories were lies. Herman was quickly acquitted.

However, on the afternoon of graduation, Herman walked up to Dr. Herman with his diploma in his hand and, with a slight smile on his face, said: "Doctor, those things that woman said about me were true."

Dr. Herdman was enraged. He later wrote:

It was the first positive evidence I had received up until that time that the fellow was a scoundrel, and I told him so at the time. I subsequently learned, however, that he made two attempts to enter my house in the character of a burglar and also that he had, while occupying a room in a portion of my house, attempted to force a drawer in my library in which I had been in the habit of keeping some valuables.

Of course, Dr. Herdman would later learn about much worse things that his star pupil had accomplished. He was likely very thankful then that Herman had only lied to him and had stolen a few petty things from his house.

AFTER GRADUATION, HERMAN RETURNED TO NEW HAMPSHIRE and his family for a time. He only stayed in Gilmanton for a short time, though. He had little interest in his wife and his child, and if I had to guess, I'd say they didn't have much interest in him either.

Things are a bit hazy after that. He apparently worked doing several things in several different towns before ending up as a physician and schoolteacher in the small upstate New York town of Mooers Forks.

According to later accounts, the people in the village quickly began to think of Herman as a queer fellow, mostly because he never bothered paying off his debts.

His record as a teacher was never mentioned, but he left behind stories about his work as a doctor – and about his romantic life. Herman told people he was single and even proposed marriage to a couple of women, including one whose father died rather suspiciously.

He was also reported to have been friendly with Minnie Everett, a fellow schoolteacher who Herman hired to tutor him in French. But Minnie stopped the lessons soon after they started. She told a friend:

The school where Herman Mudgett taught while living in Mooers Forks, New York.

> *There is something lurking in that man's character that time will reveal. I do not like him. I firmly believe that he will commit murder.*

Herman also came up with a money-making scheme during this time in Mooers Forks. When a minor smallpox scare broke out, Herman managed to get a supply of vaccines and traveled the area, telling people that he was from the Board of Health and that vaccines were mandatory – and cost 25-cents. That's only about $8 today, but money went much further then, especially for farm folks who probably didn't have it to spare.

With the money from the scheme, Herman rented an office from Ed Steele and apparently used it as a laboratory in which he tried to invent a patent medicine. He never came up with a mixture that he liked, but Ed Steele admired him for trying. Steele mostly spoke highly of Herman, but he even admitted:

> *I never saw a man who was a more accomplished liar than the Doc. He could look you right in the eye and tell as beautiful a*

lie as you ever heard, and you would have hard work to bring yourself to doubt him.

When Herman eventually left Mooers Forks, he did so suddenly and in the dead of night. He also, not surprisingly, left a lot of unpaid bills and rents behind. He even swindled Ed Steele out of the price of his train ticket.

Herman landed next in Philadelphia, where he spent a short time working at the Norristown Asylum for the Insane. His recollections of this time were not pleasant. He later wrote:

This was my first experience with insane persons, and so terrible was it that for years afterward, even now, sometimes, I see their faces in my sleep.

Herman left the asylum job after only a few days and later told police that, soon after, he "perfected" the insurance scheme that he developed in medical school.

According to the story, Herman contacted Robert Leacock, who had helped him think up the scheme. They updated the plan to include a friend of Leacock's, who would take out a large insurance policy on his wife and child. Then, later, the friend would send his family to stay out west, write a confession saying that he had killed them in a drunken rage, dismembered their bodies, and then committed suicide.

A fake corpse would be dressed in the friend's clothes and bodies would be substituted for the wife and child. The money would go to Leacock, posing as a relative, and then the spoils would be divided. Later, the friend could rejoin his wife and child to start a new life.

It was a convoluted plan, and it seems hard to believe it would work. Finding one body would be difficult, but finding three seems much harder. Regardless, each person involved in the plan was supposed to supply one corpse, so they all split up.

Herman ended up in Minneapolis, where he found work as a drug clerk over the winter of 1885 and spring of 1886. During that time, Herman found his body – at a medical school, he claimed – and sealed it in a barrel that he shipped to McCoy's Hotel in Chicago. The other men found their bodies, too. One was shipped to the Fidelity Storage Warehouse, also in Chicago and close to the hotel, and the third was sent to New York. Herman followed it to New York by train, but he later told police he decided to call off the plan when he read an article during the trip about how well-equipped insurance companies were at detecting fraud.

Was there any truth to this story? No one knows. Herman told the story to the police soon after he was arrested in 1894, and he added to it later when bones were found buried in the basement of a building he owned. He told the police they weren't murder victims – although they almost definitely were – but the bones of two bodies that had been placed in barrels during the botched scheme.

The next time Herman detailed this plot, he changed so many details in the second version of it that it was difficult to believe any of it was true – but honestly, who knows? We do know that Herman went on to defraud a lot of insurance companies, so it's not impossible that he tried to carry out the plan he cooked up in college for the first time after leaving Philadelphia.

We'll never know for sure, but we do know what Herman did next – he boarded a train and headed west to Chicago. He arrived there in 1886 with a new scheme on his mind. He opened an office – posing as an inventor – in the 400 block of South Dearborn Street. He planned to get investors for what was called the ABC Copier, a machine for duplicating documents.

No one knows if this contraption was real, but if it was, it might have been the only honest business Herman ever ran. But it quickly failed, and the machine's investors and creditors were left holding $9,000 in worthless stock and unpaid bills and rent. Herman skipped town with the equivalent of about $281,000 today and rode off into the sunset.

But he wouldn't stay away for long. He couldn't. The opportunities offered to him in Chicago were too good to pass up. This was a city that pulsed with crime, corruption, vice, con men, prostitutes, and killers. It was an exciting city that had rebuilt itself after its destruction – a place where anything was possible. Chicago may not have created Herman, but it certainly shaped him into the monster that he became.

At the moment he stepped off the train in Chicago, Herman Mudgett ceased to exist. A new man took his place – one he called Dr. Henry Howard Holmes.

Where the name came from is unknown. It seemed to have no special meaning. For all we know, it might have been a random name that Herman came up with, as most of his aliases were. He'd use many others over the next decade, but he would never abandon H.H. Holmes.

As he stood there that day on the railway platform, one of the most terrifying killers in American history was born and it was in Chicago where his story truly begins.

BEFORE THERE WERE PHARMACIES IN AMERICA, THERE WERE apothecaries. Such places could be operated by anyone. You didn't have to know much about medicine or treating patients or anything else that kept people from dying under your care.

But that began to change in the 1820s, when Louis Dufilho, Jr., became the country's first licensed pharmacist. He'd studied and knew something about the basics of medicine. Also, his pharmacy was in New Orleans, a city that frequently battled devastating epidemics and needed those skilled in science to help save lives.

Of course, "science" didn't have a lot to do with medicine in those days. Louis' pharmacy was stocked with *some* of the same things you'd find in one today, as well as leeches, opium, Voodoo spells, home remedies, and a soda fountain that offered sugary drinks.

The years that followed marked a turning point for American medicine, though. Surgical anesthesia was discovered, and a new respect for germs allowed patients to start surviving routine surgeries that might have killed them before. Pharmacies changed along with medicine, becoming less "anything goes apothecaries" and more professional and in tune with the way that medicine was developing.

Soon, licenses began to be required to own and operate a pharmacy. The reason for this was that a pharmacist was more like a general practitioner doctor today. People went to them to diagnose their ailments and treat them accordingly.

They mixed medicines from scratch using plants, minerals, animals, and even insects as ingredients. Mortars and pestles were used to crush and blend dried herbs, which were made into pills, liquids, plasters, and injectable medicines. Passers-by had no doubt that a pharmacy was located behind the window glass. The front windows displayed multi-tiered bottles of colored water, which were called "show globes." The bottles became a symbol of a pharmacy, just as a barber's pole became a symbol of a place for a shave and a haircut.

Soda fountains were also an integral part of pharmacies in the late nineteenth century. According to the saying, a spoonful of sugar helps the medicine go down, but it was also believed that sugary soda had curative powers. By the 1880s, the drugstore soda fountain had become an American institution. Drinks we still enjoy today – like Pepsi. Dr. Pepper, and 7-UP – originally had medicinal purposes and were invented by pharmacists. And yes, it's true that the original formula for Coca-Cola had

cocaine in it, which is how it got its name.

One of the most prescribed medicines of the era was opium – and it was used for many everyday purposes. Morphine, laudanum, and even heroin – all derived from opium – were used as painkillers, sedatives, for calming nerves, and even as an anti-diarrhea medicine, and all were readily available over the counter.

And, of course, there were many poisons available, too. Strychnine and arsenic had many common uses, including killing rodents and removing stains, as did other medicines that were freely distributed to anyone who asked for them.

It was a different time, and it seems almost impossible for us to believe that a man with no legitimate history could simply open a shop and start handing out narcotics and poisons to his customers – but that's exactly what H.H. Holmes did when he came to Chicago in the late 1880s.

EVEN THOUGH HOLMES FLED THE CITY AFTER HIS EARLIER swindle, he learned a lot during his time in Chicago. Not only was it a place where men of genius like himself could make a lot of money, but he also discovered how important his past studies would turn out to be. Holmes had a medical degree from Michigan, but he had no desire to be a physician. Instead, he would turn his knowledge of medicine into a more lucrative career as a pharmacist.

In the state of Illinois, though, a license was required to be a pharmacist, so Holmes went to the state capital of Springfield to get one. On July 15, 1886, it was posted in the newspaper that Harry H. Holmes was among 22 candidates who passed a three-day exam to become a licensed pharmacist. Soon after that, he returned to Chicago – or at least to the southside community of Englewood, which became his home.

Today, Englewood is a poverty-stricken neighborhood with a crime rate that is among the highest in the nation, but in the 1880s, it was a prosperous and pleasant place. It took its original name

Looking down Sixty-Third Street in Englewood in the 1880s

of Junction Grove from the three railroad lines that met in the settlement, but in 1868, it was given the new name of Englewood after a forested region in England. It was fitting since, in those days, the community was heavily forested by oak trees.

Englewood stopped being a rural town after the Great Fire of 1871. There was a rush for homes in towns outside the city, and many new arrivals came to Englewood. The town grew tremendously over the next two decades as more families fled the inner city, resettled there, opened businesses, and constructed new homes. While most of these houses were modest frame and brick structures, the land was still cheap enough to induce the wealthy to build a scattering of pretentious mansions, particularly along Harvard, Yale, Ross, and Wentworth Avenues. Waterworks, gasworks, and other utility conveniences were added, and then, in 1889, Englewood was formally annexed to the city of Chicago, along with other towns like Lake View, Hyde Park, and Cicero.

Holmes chose well when he picked Englewood, and his discerning eye brought him to the perfect neighborhood, too. The area around the intersection of Sixty-Third Street and Wallace

Avenue became the town's central business district, largely thanks to its proximity to the Western Indiana Railway station, less than a block away.

If Holmes had been an ordinary businessman, he could have made a small fortune just from the first real estate investment he made. But, of course, he wasn't. If he had not turned out to be a morally bankrupt con man and killer, he would have undoubtedly lived to see electricity introduced to Englewood in 1897 and, three years later, would have seen the face of the future at Chicago's first automobile show. But before any of that happened, Holmes would be dead.

Almost every story written about the murderous career of H.H. Holmes begins with him taking a job at a pharmacy in Englewood after he discovers that Dr. E.S. Holton is dying of cancer and his elderly wife is left running the shop on her own. Soon, Dr. Holton dies, his wife disappears, and Holmes takes over, telling their former customers that Mrs. Holton moved away. It's implied that he killed her, and, in some versions of the story, it's made very clear that he did.

This story has appeared in countless books and articles – including my own – but it turns out it isn't accurate. This story may have been spun from a few details that were available at the time and then fleshed out into a longer imaginative account in the years that followed. Early researchers into Holmes' crimes discovered the story in a few newspaper accounts, accepted them as the truth, and published them, never knowing there were more accurate facts available.

More recent research into the story reveals that newspapers from the 1890s mention only that Holmes purchased the pharmacy from Dr. E.S. Holton, and that there was difficulty with getting him to pay the entire amount that he'd promised.

The longest contemporary version of what really happened was credited to G.A. Bogart, who was a jeweler in the neighborhood. He stated:

From the first day that he was engaged by Mrs. Holton to run the drug store, which he afterward bought from her, he determined to have the business as his own. And to that end, began carrying off the stock piecemeal. Every time he left the store, he carried something away, and very materially reduced the stock before he made a bid for it. After he concluded his deal, he only paid his notes at the muzzle of a gun.

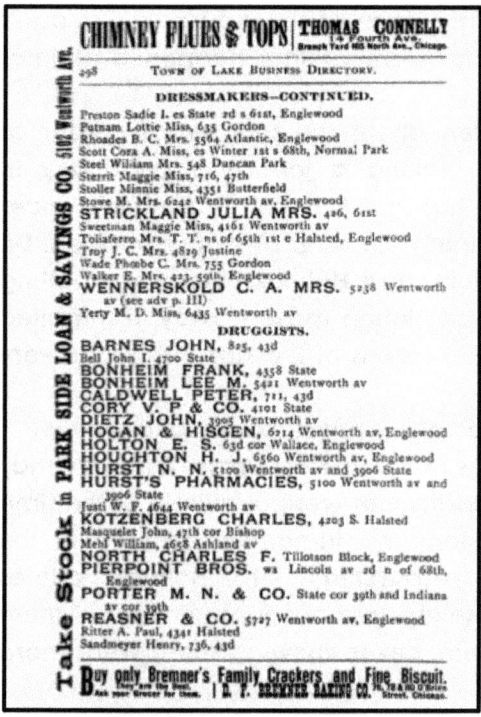

Dr. Holton's listing in the Englewood City Directory before Holmes came to work in her pharmacy

Holmes' version of the story stated that he had started working at the pharmacy in July 1886, when it was owned by a doctor who was in ill health and wanted to sell it.

Even though we can rarely trust anything Holmes said, no one else in Englewood in the 1890s ever claimed that Dr. Holton died or that Mrs. Holton disappeared. And there's a very good reason for that – it turns out that the Holtons were not an elderly doctor and his wife but a young doctor and her husband.

Dr. E.S. Holton was Dr. Elizabeth Sarah Holton, and she was still in her twenties when Holmes bought the pharmacy.

And Holmes didn't come into her pharmacy in 1886 by chance.

She had also attended the University of Michigan, graduating just one year before Holmes. They may not have known each other, but they certainly had acquaintances in common. This was likely why he came to her pharmacy looking for work. It's possible that Dr. Holton decided to sell the pharmacy when she became pregnant with her second child in early 1887, but it's also likely that Holmes began making arrangements to buy the place before that. As the account from the neighborhood jeweler stated, he'd already started stealing from the place before then.

I should also mention that the Holtons were still living in the neighborhood with their two children when Holmes was arrested in 1894. Neither died from cancer, and neither disappeared. They lived in Englewood well into the twentieth century and were both buried at Oakwoods Cemetery, not far from Sixty-Third Street and Wallace.

Before that, however, they had to deal with Holmes. He had been, they had to admit, a model employee. They, of course, had no idea at the time that he was stealing inventory and plotting to take over the place. Holmes knew how to charm people. He charmed the Holtons, and, more importantly, he charmed the customers. When Dr. Holmes compounded even the simplest prescription, he did so with a flourish. His long, pale fingers moved with a surgeon's skill, his handsome face grew intense, and his blue eyes became bright and focused.

He was also a gentleman of fashion and of mild demeanor. His politeness and humorous remarks brought many new customers into the drugstore, especially ladies from the neighborhood. In addition to medicine, he was also adept at dispensing that charm, which he offered freely to the ladies, many of whom invented reasons to frequently patronize the shop.

Dr. Holmes became a familiar figure as he strolled down Sixty-Third Street, tipping his hat to the ladies and exchanging friendly words with the men he passed. After he purchased the pharmacy from the Holtons, he began to be seen as a great asset to the local business community.

After several missed payments, though, Dr. Holton came to a very different opinion about her former employee. Their

Holmes cut a dashing figure in Englewood at the time, charming the ladies and convincing the men that he was a successful businessman. His good looks and fine clothes had all the women talking.

relationship became strained after he continually promised to deliver the money he owed but always failed to do so.

But unlike most of his other creditors, Holmes eventually paid Dr. Holton what he owed her for the pharmacy. She was one of the few people that Holmes dealt with who did not have to file a lawsuit against him.

She was lucky – about that and one other thing: that she lived to tell her story and didn't mysteriously disappear as so many stories have claimed she did.

WHEN HOLMES FIRST CAME TO ENGLEWOOD, THERE WAS frequent discussion among the women in the neighborhood about the fact that the enterprising and handsome young man was still a bachelor. He seemed to be the perfect candidate for marriage – personable, well-educated, good-looking, and wealthy. He had caught the eye of nearly every single woman in town – and some married ones – and yet Holmes didn't seem interested in settling down.

Or so they believed.

In December 1886, Holmes had gone to the office of an attorney named Wharton Plummer. It was the first suit he would ever file, and he did so under his given name, Herman Mudgett. The case asked for a divorce from his wife, Clara Lovering.

In the case, he stated that adultery was the grounds for the divorce – Clara's adultery, not his. Holmes claimed in the documents that he had been a "true, kind, and affectionate husband and had faithfully discharged all his duties." He also claimed that his six-year-old son, Robert, was living in his care. It was truly a delusional document – or it was a clever one. If Holmes had won the case, he would have received a divorce and wouldn't have paid alimony or child support.

But Holmes didn't win the case – it was never even filed. He never followed through with it, although it would turn out to be the last time he ever used his real name in any capacity.

It is interesting in one other way, too. It was a sort-of preview of how Holmes would operate in Chicago – some half-truths, some outright lies, and never finishing what he started. And it was done with a lawyer who was no more honest than Holmes was. Plummer would disappear from Holmes' story for the next five years but would return in 1891 as both an attorney and an accomplice. He wouldn't be the only lawyer in Holmes' life to do the same thing.

The big question about this divorce case, though, is why did he start it at all? Even though Holmes was still married to Clara, those who knew him assumed he was single. I'm sure his behavior gave them that impression.

But Holmes wasn't single – and this wasn't about Clara. Before he had gone to see attorney Wharton Plummer, Holmes had already gotten married – again.

His new wife's name was Myrta Z. Belknap, and he had met her while in Minneapolis, probably before he had started working at the Holtons' drugstore. This news was not revealed to his neighbors and customers until early 1887, and it was received with mixed emotions.

As with much of Holmes' story, his relationship with Myrta comes with a large helping of mystery. It's unknown when they actually met or when they actually married, or even for sure what she looked like. Myrta was described as a "bright, lovable girl," which isn't helpful. There are drawings of her created for the newspapers, but it's impossible to say if they're accurate. There is only one photograph that I have been able to find that claims to be Myrta and her infant daughter, Lucy, but I have found no

(Left) The photo that is alleged to be Myrta Belknap and the daughter that she had with Holmes, their daughter, Lucy. (Right) Lucy as an adult.

records to prove this was her. There are photographs of Lucy as an adult, which might give us an idea of what her mother looked like, but as for Myrta herself, she remains a mystery.

Records say that Myrta was born in October 1862 and, in 1880, was living with her parents, John and Lucy, in Pennsylvania, where she was a music teacher. They moved to Minneapolis in the early 1880s, and in 1885, John was listed as working for the railroad, and Myrta was a clerk in a music store. That may have been where she met Holmes in 1886.

As mentioned, the date of their marriage is unknown, but we do know Clara began using the last name of Holmes in early 1887. That was when it appeared in some Chicago property records. Holmes bought a parcel of land and put it in Myrta's name. But then he had the deed changed so that it looked like her mother, Lucy, was the owner.

It would be on that parcel of land that Holmes would later construct the notorious building that would be dubbed the "Murder Castle."

ANY OF HOLMES' FEMALE CUSTOMERS WHO WERE BOTHERED by the presence of his new wife didn't have to be worried about her for long. He had no interest in having Myrta interfere in the pharmacy's business or curb his flirtatious banter with the ladies.

In late 1888, Myrta announced that she was pregnant. Her daughter was born on July 4, 1889, and was named after both of her grandmothers, leading to her being christened Lucy Theodate Holmes. As far as Myrta knew, Holmes' mother had been dead for many years. She wasn't, and Theodate Mudgett would not learn that she had a granddaughter with her name until the girl was six years old.

After Lucy's birth, Myrta left Chicago and went to live with her parents in Wilmette, Illinois, a community north of the city. Holmes agreed to provide financial support for his wife and daughter and to pay regular visits to Wilmette – and he did, at least for a while.

This is one of the reasons that suggests to me that Holmes may have truly cared for Myrta. Even though he never followed through with the divorce from Clara, Holmes had at least briefly considered doing right by Myrta. It was

The house that Holmes built for Myrta and her family in Wilmette. It was demolished in 1997.

one of the very few times in his life when such an impulse was ever documented.

Holmes also built a home for Myrta in Wilmette. She lived in the duplex with her daughter and her parents. It was located at what was then 38 North John Street – later renamed and renumbered as 726 11th Street – and was a Queen Anne style home with turrets on either side of a wide veranda. It was painted dark red. Later, after Holmes was captured, tried, and executed, his wife, child, and her family were forced to leave the house, which was encumbered by lawsuits, and it was sold at auction.

In 1901, it was referred to as "one of the handsome houses in Wilmette" and in the 1920s, one-half of the house operated as the Wilmette Inn and later, the Wilmette Apartments. The house was later sold to developers and was demolished in 1997.

Myrta remained in Wilmette even after the house was sold. The 1898 city directory shows "Mrs. M. B. Holmes" as a teacher, living with her parents on the northeast corner of Kline Street and Central, but by the fall of 1897 she moved with Lucy to Hinsdale to teach school. Myrta continued her career as a teacher in the Midwest, first becoming a principal and then a school administrator in Duluth, Minnesota. She never remarried and died in 1924.

And it's her death in 1924 that proves Holmes almost definitely felt something like love and affection toward Myrta. Unlike almost all the other women who became involved with Holmes during his years in Chicago, Myrta lived to a ripe old age and died of natural causes.

EVEN BEFORE THE BIRTH OF HIS DAUGHTER AND MYRTA'S MOVE to Wilmette, Holmes had been making plans for the parcel of land he'd purchased in Englewood in early 1887. He wanted to build something that would show everyone just how successful he was. It was a time in American history when cutthroat ambition and ruthlessness were greatly admired – it was a way of doing business. It would have made Holmes just like every other young entrepreneur making a name for himself in those days – although Holmes' brand of ruthlessness would turn out to be much darker than most.

The land that Holmes had purchased using Myrta's name and then transferred to her mother's ownership was across the street from the drugstore he'd bought from the Holtons. It was here that he envisioned an office building that would be the finest in Englewood.

Chicago was in the middle of another building boom, and new structures were being added to the skyline so quickly that the city could barely keep up with inspecting them. And that was something Holmes could use to his advantage.

In March 1887, architects Charles Berger and Edward Gallner began drawing up plans for Holmes' new commercial building. Holmes explained that he wanted it to fit in with the surrounding neighborhood. The lower floor would have columns that matched those on the Newman Block, a building a few streets away at Sixty-Third and Stewart. The building was planned to be a two-story affair, with retail spaces on the first floor and residential apartments, plus Holmes' private office on the second.

A third floor, built to serve as hotel space during the World's Fair, wasn't added for another five years.

Work began on the property in August 1887, with Aetna Iron and Steel initially providing laborers and materials for the project. They were using the plans that had been drawn up by the architects – at first.

That quickly changed. The construction site was directly across the street from Holmes' drugstore, so this allowed him to spend most of every day overseeing the project. He made changes to the building plans, handed out orders, and dismissed the concerns of the experienced men sent by the construction company.

The work attracted the attention of people in the neighborhood. It was not the height of the building that made it so interesting, though. The people of Chicago were starting to get

A later photograph of Holmes' "Castle," taken after he left Chicago and after the third story had been added to the structure. There are no photos in existence that show the original "Castle" with only two floors.

used to the odd buildings known as "skyscrapers" that had started to appear in the downtown business district. Compared to those new ten- and twelve-story buildings, the growing structure in Englewood was relatively small – only two stories when completed. But in square footage, the squat structure was taking up every available inch of its corner lot.

In addition to the way that the building was spreading outward, neighborhood residents were fascinated by the sheer amount of activity that was involved in its creation. Passersby often stopped on the street to watch all the laborers who were hammering away at the frame, floors, and walls. But, strangely, no matter how many men seemed to be working, the actual construction seemed to progress at a remarkably slow pace. Even with its massive dimensions, the building should not have taken a crew of skilled workers more than six months to complete. But for some mysterious reason, more than a year and a half passed between the groundbreaking and the day when the final nail was driven home.

The mystery of the delay was not as difficult to solve as it seemed. However, it would have taken a very careful observer to realize that none of the many men who worked at the site stayed on the job for very long. Most were fired after a week or two, and some lasted only a few days before being replaced. By the time the building was finished, more than 500 craftsmen and common laborers had passed through the site.

People in the neighborhood were interested in watching the work as it progressed, but none of them noticed this oddity about the crew – and none of them knew that it was part of a deliberate plan on the part of the building's owner, who had re-written the architect's plan and was now also the general foreman.

The constant hiring and firing had slowed down the progress of the construction, but it saved him a tremendous amount of money in wages. A workman might put in at least two weeks' work before asking to be paid. As soon as he did, Holmes would accuse him of doing shoddy work and fire him without ever paying him a nickel for the labor he had completed.

More importantly, constantly changing workers ensured that each man worked only on a small part of the building before being replaced. This allowed Holmes to conceal the overall layout of the structure. A carpenter might be fired after putting in a few doorframes, and a bricklayer might be sacked after putting up a single basement wall – never knowing what they would be used for.

Holmes kept his copy of the blueprints away from everyone. Workmen were only given enough information to do their immediate jobs. Only Holmes had a clear picture of the building's entire design. If anyone else had seen them, they might have questioned both his design skills and his sanity.

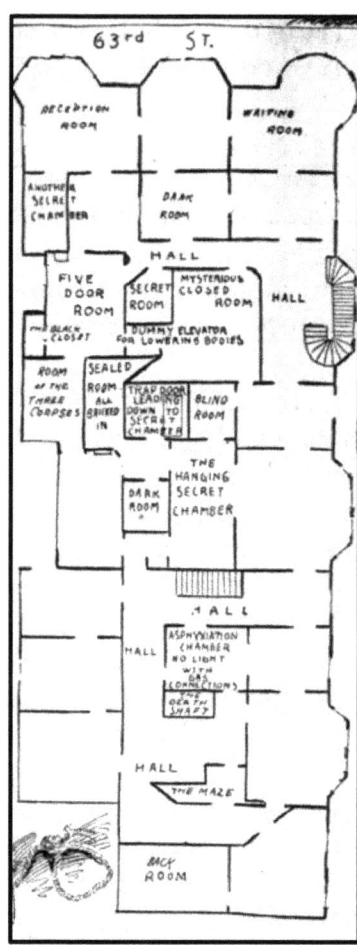

A sketch of the layout of Holmes' "Castle" after his arrest. It was published in newspapers at the time, but its accuracy cannot be guaranteed.

Some of the men Holmes fired later filed lawsuits against Holmes, but he got his attorneys to bog down the suits with endless delays and complicated filings.

There were mysterious blueprints, there was strange construction, and laborers constantly being hired and fired, but this was not what the authorities found most troubling about the project -- it was the fact that Holmes never seemed to pay his bills. When Aetna Iron and Steel tried to recover what he owed them in 1888, Holmes claimed he wasn't liable for the debt because he wasn't the owner of the land – his mother-in-law was. When they later sued, Holmes then alleged one of the steel beams they provided was slightly too short, making the entire contract invalid.

There were plenty of other lawsuits, too. All of them were related to the financing, construction, furnishing, and ownership of the building and would grind their way through the legal system for years. At the time of Holmes' death, the list of people with liens, claims, and mortgages on the property was several pages long.

His methods were basically the same with each of his suppliers. Holmes might have a load of lumber or bricks delivered to the site. Once they were installed, he would claim that the supplies were not up to standard and would refuse to pay for them. When he needed more, he would simply contact a different supplier and do the same thing again.

Some of the items installed in the building were not the kind of construction supplies that could be easily found in other Chicago structures. There was, for instance, an enormous safe that was as large as a walk-in bank vault. When it was delivered, Holmes had it installed in an open area on the upper floor of the building. After it was in place, he had a room built around it and made sure that the doorway was too small for the safe to pass through it. When Holmes then failed to make the payments for the vault, the safe company dispatched a crew to repossess it. Holmes told them they were welcome to remove it but warned them that if they damaged his building in any way, he would file a ruinous lawsuit against the company. They decided to cut their losses and leave the vault where it was.

A newspaper sketch showing the bank vault that Holmes had installed in a second-floor room. It would prove to be used for other things besides storing valuables.

He used the same methods to purchase other items for the building. He claimed they would all be used during his experiments in pharmacology science. These items included a large kiln with a cast-iron door and a grate that slid in and out of it on rollers; a large metal tank; an assortment of containers that were designed to hold corrosive liquids; and enough asbestos-covered metal plates to line the walls of several rooms.

The building was finally completed in May 1890, and for many weeks after, locals continued to marvel at the new addition to the business district. The large building – with its brick façade, turreted roof, bay windows, and mock battlements --- was an impressive sight and one of which its owner had every right to be proud.

Of course, no one admiring the place had any way of knowing what secrets were hidden behind the building's façade.

Shoppers were also thrilled to see the array of fine shops that soon opened on the first floor of the new building. Some were operated by Holmes, and others were leased to merchants, who were eager to do business in what was considered the community's best location. Over the course of the next few years, hundreds of people passed through the doors of the various shops, but the unknowing merchants and their customers never ventured beyond the first floor. They never suspected what the rest of the building might hold.

According to Holmes' plan, the second floor of the building would be rented out as apartments. There was a great demand for such places as more and more people flocked to the outlying communities from the city. Many of the rooms were furnished with beds, bureaus, chairs, rugs, wall decorations, and mirrors -- just as the rooms on the not-yet-built third floor would be when Holmes announced he was opening a hotel for the fair.

Occupants on the second floor, though, must have found it maddeningly difficult to find their apartments at first. They were scattered along a weird network of angled hallways. Dimly lit by gaslights mounted on the walls at uneven intervals, the corridors took unexpected turns, came to dead ends, and led to stairways that abruptly stopped at the ceiling, an indication of a future third floor.

With Holmes' private office on that floor, there were locked doors everywhere. One of the locked rooms was adjacent to the office and contained the walk-in safe he had fraudulently installed in the building. An employee of the building later recalled that safe and a strange incident that occurred with it:

Holmes told me to step inside, and he would close the door. I was to scream, and he would see whether he could hear me or not. I stepped in, the door was closed, and he could faintly hear my voice. When I came out, he said, 'I wish I could put my mother-in-law in there when she has her tantrums.'

It's possible that Mrs. Belknap did throw tantrums, and she would have been justified in doing so. When Holmes was sued for deals related to the building, she was sued, too. Her name was on the title.

The employee who stepped into the safe wouldn't find out why Holmes needed to know if screams could be heard coming from the safe until years later. He, along with the rest of the people who worked in the building, also wouldn't know about the many swindles that Holmes committed there.

He came up with new ideas almost every week. His favorite con was buying goods on credit, selling them for cash, and not paying the original bill. He was particularly fond of swindling bicycle dealers. He often rented a bicycle or two from them and then sold them rather than returning them. He did a similar trick with music boxes. Soon, bicycles and music boxes that had been purchased cheaply from Holmes were all over town.

Some of the people who worked for Holmes didn't know about the swindles, but they did take note of some suspicious activities.

Mrs. Loomis, who worked as a housekeeper in 1890, said:

Holmes would come to me and tell me to pack his things because he intended to go to Toronto that night. I would do so and would suppose he left the house and the city. The next day or the day after, I would accidentally meet him walking through one of the upper hallways on tiptoe. He would be surprised and angry when I saw him but would make some excuse about missing the train or say he just returned. He was always up to some kind of tricks, and I believe he told me those stories of going away so as to establish an alibi.

Robert Latimer, who worked as a janitor in the building around the same time, recalled that Holmes showed him a large collection of fake beards, wigs, and other disguises he owned. He said Holmes would sometimes enter the drugstore, go up a hidden staircase to his office, and be seen later in the hallway looking like a completely different person.

But there were some who worked for him that were aware of his swindles and underhanded dealings. They were less employees than they were partners in crime. The one who was closest to Holmes and took the greatest role in his schemes was a man named Benjamin Pitezel.

Benjamin Pitezel

H.H. HOLMES WAS STILL GROWING UP IN NEW HAMPSHIRE AS Herman Mudgett when Benjamin Pitezel was coming into his own in Kewanee, Illinois. The two men would first meet when Ben showed up at the construction site at Sixty-Third and Wallace, looking for work.

Benjamin Frelan Pitezel was born in 1856. Named for his father, he was the oldest child in a religious family, but Ben would prove to be the prodigal son.

In 1877, he seduced a young woman named Carrie Canning from Galva, Illinois – the daughter of a Methodist minister – and got her pregnant. Thanks to a quickly arranged marriage, a little girl named Jeanette – who always went by Dessie – was born in wedlock, but her birth brought scandal and disgrace to both families.

Two years later, Carrie gave birth to a second daughter, Etta Alice. After her came Nellie, Howard, and Wharton. Ben found himself with the responsibility of a growing family. He was not sure that he was up to the task. He was not a hard-working man. He fancied himself an inventor, and that was partially true. He did register a patent for a new kind of coal bin in 1891, but it never made him any money.

He was good-looking, there was no denying that. He was six feet tall and muscular, with wide shoulders and a broad back. Photographs of Ben in his early twenties show a man with a clean jaw, straight nose, and clear blue eyes. He wore a neatly trimmed mustache and carried himself with confidence. It was easy to see why a young woman, even one raised in a religious household as Carrie had been, would welcome his attention.

Ben's wife, Carrie Canning, who he married in 1877.

But Ben's looks wouldn't last. His bad habits soon left their mark on him. He grew fond of the bottle, and after a few years, the drinking and the hard-living – including bar fights that left him with a broken nose and some missing teeth – coarsened his once-handsome features. Although he never completely lost his good looks, there would be no mistaking him for a gentleman. Rough and often surly, he grew to look like what he was -- a hard-luck case who used his crafty intelligence and his fists to battle his way through life.

Ben's one real redeeming quality was his devotion to his wife and his growing brood of children, whose number eventually reached six, although one child, a boy named Nevit, died of diphtheria just before he turned two. But Ben's loyalty to his family paled in comparison to the grief and suffering he caused by his drinking.

For 10 years, he moved his family from place to place across the Midwest, drifting from job to job in one town after another. He did honest work whenever he could, but his drinking made it hard for him to hold on to a steady job for long. During the 1880s, he worked as a circus roustabout, a hand at a lumber mill, a railroad worker, and a janitor.

Even though he spent short stints in jail for petty larceny and once for stealing a horse, his intentions were mostly good. He wanted to provide for his family, but he was so deep into the bottle that he was unable to break the cycle of alternating drunkenness and sobriety that he found himself in.

An illustration of Ben Pitezel as he looked around the time he met Holmes. His good looks had started to harden after years of drinking.

When the Pitezel family settled in Chicago is unclear, but they likely moved there no later than the fall of 1889. In November of that year, Ben replied to a help-wanted advertisement in a local newspaper. Carpenters were needed for the construction of a new building in Englewood. Applicants were instructed to apply directly to Dr. H.H. Holmes.

There is no record of Ben's first meeting with him, but it's likely that Holmes, who had great skill at picking out someone who was an easy mark, recognized that Ben was both vulnerable and weak-willed. He could be easily manipulated and would turn out to be fiercely loyal to the man who would lead him to his death.

That November day, Ben was hired as a construction worker, but it wasn't long before he was performing many other, far more questionable tasks for Holmes.

The Devil now had his willing accomplice.

IN MAY OF 1890, THE NEW BUILDING CONSTRUCTED BY H.H Holmes and his long string of coming and going workmen was finally completed. Locals in Englewood marveled at the fine façade of this new addition to the business district. It was an impressive sight with its stately columns, bay windows, and mock battlements that suggested a place that might be found overlooking the rolling countryside than a busy street on Chicago's South Side.

But soon, the excitement died down, and folks went back about their business. They soon became used to the extraordinary structure that loomed over the neighborhood and at some point, it was given its nickname. No one knows who first referred to the building that way.

It could have one of the locals, acknowledging its imposing presence. Or it could have been Holmes himself, who had a talent for self-promotion. Whatever the case, soon after it was completed,

Englewood residents began to refer to the new building as the "Castle."

In later years, of course, that name would be slightly altered as the people of Chicago – and the rest of the nation -- finally learned of the horrors that had occurred within its walls. It would no longer be merely the "Castle," when a description like the "Murder Castle" would fit its macabre history so much better.

IN JUNE 1890 – ONE MONTH AFTER THE CASTLE WAS completed -- Holmes decided to sell the drugstore that he had obtained from Dr. Holton across the street. He quickly found a prospective buyer in a young Michigan man named A.L. Jones. He had recently married and had a modest inheritance from his father's estate. Anxious to get started on his own, he planned to move to Chicago and establish himself in business.

After expressing interest in the store, Holmes invited him to come and clerk for the store one day and see how things operated and see how busy it was with his own eyes. Jones took him up on the offer, spent a day in the pharmacy, and was delighted with the steady flow of customers.

Of course, what he didn't know was that Holmes had made sure that trade was especially brisk that day by hiring people to pose as shoppers and add to the customer count. Jones was befuddled as to why Holmes would sell such a profitable business, but Holmes explained that his great success with the drugstore had allowed him to pursue other opportunities. He was so busy that he simply did not have time for the store anymore. His other activities required his complete attention and now, with Holmes stepping out of the drugstore business, Jones would have the entire neighborhood to himself.

A bargain was struck and while the price of the store was hefty, Jones had little doubt that his investment would soon be repaid many times over. Or so he thought.

After Jones returned to Michigan, Holmes sold almost all the stock in the store – or perhaps moved it across the street and stored it away – and left empty shelves to greet the new owner. But Jones took the store anyway and became the new owner in July 1890.

A few weeks later, a delivery wagon arrived at Holmes' Castle, just across the street from Jones' new drugstore. Jones and his wife watched with growing confusion as workmen began unloading all the fixtures for an elegant drugstore – glass-front counters and display cases, polished wood cabinets, marble-topped counters, gleaming soda fountain spigots – and carrying them through the entrance of the vacant corner store of the Castle. Before long, a large wooden sign, carved in the shape of a mortar and pestle, hung above the door. Gold letters in the center announced the location as H.H. HOLMES PHARMACY.

A high-end pharmacy of the day, which offers an idea of how ornate and upscale Holmes' new pharmacy must have been.

The sign was elegant, but the store itself eclipsed its beauty. The people of Englewood had never seen a pharmacy like this one. Beyond the grand entrance with its massive columns was frescoed stucco work that covered the walls and ceiling. The floor was covered with gleaming, black and white diamond tiles. Elixirs and medicines were displayed behind sparkling glass on walnut shelves. A marble-topped soda fountain spanned one side of the room with leather-topped stools and shiny brass spigots for dispensing drinks. It was soon the neighborhood showplace and made the old store across the street look shabby in comparison.

But Jones continued to try and stick it out, even after the soda fountain in his store – which Holmes had bought on credit and never paid for – was repossessed. But he could only last so long and eventually, he gave up and sold the shop to Dr. Edward

H. Robinson. Jones returned to Michigan – ruined by Holmes' scheme.

But the new drugstore wasn't the only retail business that operated in the Castle. Holmes wanted the building to provide him with the kind of income that would allow him to live the sort of life he'd always desired. He saw men like Marshall Field, who'd become a tycoon creating the department store, and robber barons like Potter Palmer, who'd developed most of State Street, and he wanted what they had.

By now, he was already 30 years old, so no longer a particularly young man by the standards of the day. He had been living well, usually beyond his means, and was obsessed with money. He saw the Castle as the first step in providing him with the capital he could use to take his place among the richest men in the city.

On the Castle's ground floor, he leased space to other merchants while continuing to own several of his own. They included a jewelry store, a restaurant, a barbershop, and a company that manufactured glycerin soap. While all were worthy, money-making enterprises, they were still not enough. Dissatisfied with legitimate ventures, he embarked on a new series of brazen schemes.

Holmes began spreading the word that he had invented a machine that manufactured illuminated gas using nothing but ordinary tap water. He claimed that it lit up the entire Castle and was happy to demonstrate it.

In the basement, he began showing off a galvanized iron tank that he called the Chemical-Water-Gas Generator, which one skeptical observer described as "a washing machine on stilts that was full of pipes, pulleys, wires, and taps, and things."

But Holmes demonstrated it by adding water, tossing in a mixture of chemicals, adjusting a few knobs, flipping a switch, and lighting a match. The tank spewed out a strangely colored gas – and a very bad odor – but it also lit up the room.

Of course, the reason for that was simple – the machine was secretly hooked up to the city gas pipes.

As word of the gas-generating contraption spread, the Lake Gas Company came to investigate. After seeing it work, they immediately offered to purchase the machine and the patent for it. The amount they offered varies, but it may have been as much as $2,500 – which would be about $83,000 today.

Unfortunately, for Holmes, this scheme would not work out as he planned. The gas company left a man to study the machine and its process for about a week. At some point he realized the whole thing had been a ruse. A small pipe, concealed at the back of the contraption, was tapped directly into the main line. Holmes was not creating gas from water – he'd just been using the city's supply.

Lake Gas Company didn't prosecute Holmes for fraud, but it did confiscate the machine, leaving a sizable hole in the basement floor.

And that's how Holmes came up with his next scheme – or at least re-worked one that he's already been using.

As early as 1887, Holmes had been peddling what he called Linden Grove Mineral Water. Since college, he'd been trying to develop his own patent medicine, and this was about as close as he came to it. The water was said to be bluish in color – likely from some sort of dye -- and was marketed as being healthy in some way.

But now, Holmes had a new way to market it. He claimed that excavations in the basement had uncovered an artesian well beneath the building and that, by analyzing it, he had determined that it was filled with minerals and had curative powers.

Healing springs were immensely popular at the time and many places, like Eureka Springs and Hot Springs in Arkansas, bottled their water for sale. Why should Chicago be any different? Holmes sold the water for 5-cents a glass and 25-cents a bottle.

The refreshing water proved to be very popular with Holmes' customers, who never guessed that Holmes had simply applied his criminal genius to good old lake water. Discolored from the lead pipes, it was then doctored with a little vanilla extract and a dash of bitters to give it a medicinal taste.

It's hard to know how much money he made from his scheme but one of his lawyers later estimated it was in the thousands.

Another of Holmes' schemes was the Warner Glass-Bending Company. The idea of glass bending was something he'd return to several times over the course of his career, though he never convinced anyone that he knew the first thing about it. He did, however, have an interest in the massive furnaces that were needed to shape sheets of glass into other shapes.

Holmes claimed that he had developed a process for shaping glass using a furnace that was in the basement of the Castle. The idea seems to be that if he put a large sheet of glass over a piece of iron that was bent to the shape he wanted for the glass, he could then heat it up and melt the glass into that shape.

A man named H.L. Warner sold furniture for Holmes and, after the furnace was built, Holmes told Warner that he was going to take out a patent in his name. The patent was never actually filed but Holmes announced the formation of the company and opened an office on Dearborn Street in downtown Chicago. The office, of course, only had one purpose – to solicit money from investors for a product that would never exist.

Homes would invite some of these investors to the Castle, where he made a great show of working in the basement, heating

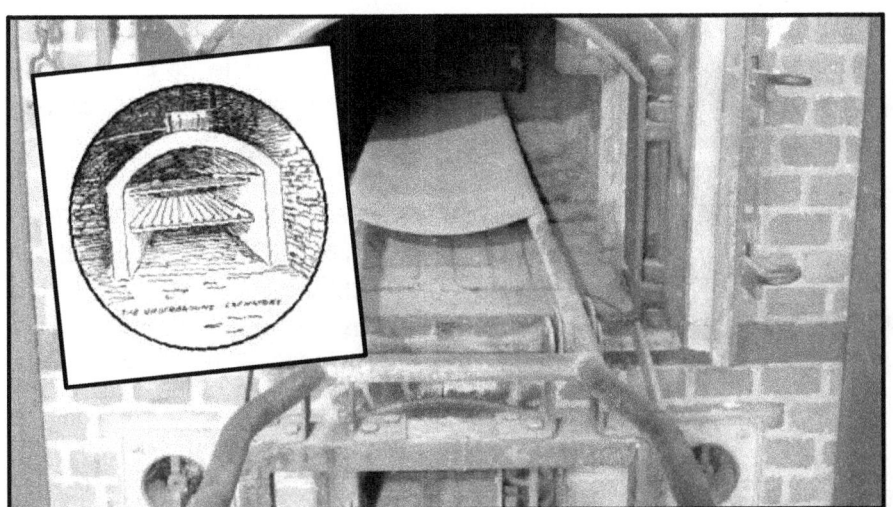

The inset image is a newspaper illustration of the furnace that Holmes had in his basement. The photo is a contemporary furnace that was used for cremations – it's not hard to make the comparison.

up the furnace, and tinkering with plate glass. No one ever saw him bend any glass but occasionally, they were shown small bits of glass that had been bent around boiler irons. They never saw any sign of fire – no coals or anything of the sort – but didn't guess that Holmes was merely using pre-shaped glass as a ruse.

There was one odd story that was told years later that hinted at the *real* use of the basement furnace. A potential investor sent a mechanic to examine Holmes' furnace. The mechanic noted that the stove could produce temperatures that were high enough to bend glass.

What struck the mechanic as odd, though, was the size of the furnace, which, while large, didn't seem to be the correct size for bending glass. Its chamber was constructed of fire brick, and the stove stood eight feet tall and more than three feet in circumference. It was big, the mechanic thought, but was convinced it wasn't even close to being large enough to accommodate a sheet of plate glass.

Later, when the Castle was searched by police officers, a reporter who accompanied them wrote that while he couldn't be sure what the furnace was used for, it was, he wrote, "sufficiently large to admit a human body."

Thomas Bryan

BUT THERE WAS NO SCHEME THAT HOLMES WAS INVOLVED IN during those years in Chicago that was as complicated as the one that he brought back to life in 1892 – the ABC Copier Company.

To make matters worse, a partner that he recruited into the affair was Thomas Bryan, one of the commissioners of the upcoming World's Fair. Bryan was one of Chicago's most prominent citizens, the founder of Graceland Cemetery, and the builder of Bryan Hall, an important political center in the city. After Chicago had been announced as the site of the Fair, Bryan became a commissioner, traveling the world to promote the city and showing off the designs for the new fairgrounds. He even had an audience with the Pope while in Rome.

And in the middle of all that, he was being swindled by Holmes.

Bryan invested in the company with the clear understanding that he was not listed as an officer and that his name was not used to obtain credit. Holmes promised to follow these conditions in writing but then, of course, immediately broke that promise. He used Bryan's name to get credit every chance he had – he also boasted of Bryan's partnership in the company to lure new investors.

Holmes set up an office, hired a secretary named Mary Kelly to work there, and started being busy – doing something. No one really knows what. He wasn't selling copy machines, although a few who did business with the company stated that the machines they were shown worked as advertised. He seemed to be selling territories, where other salesmen would offer the device. For instance, a salesman in Indiana might pay $5,000 for the exclusive rights to sell ABC Copiers in the state and the money went straight to Holmes – who, naturally, double-sold the territories every chance he got.

Business in the office was brisk. According to William Durkee, who was the brother of Kate Durkee, an old friend of Myrta Holmes, the office was a large and prosperous one. At one point, Holmes told him they raised $50,000 for future deliveries within two months.

If that was true – and it was probably an exaggeration since no deliveries were made – it's hard to imagine where the money went. Holmes took out dozens of loans during the time of the ABC Copier Company's revival.

One of them was from Thomas Bryan, who gave him $9,000. Holmes promised to repay it in cash but instead, gave Bryan a promissory note, to be paid within one year. Holmes assured him that the "within one year" part was only a precaution – he was selling some real estate that would allow him to repay the entire loan in a few days. Week after week, he promised the money would arrive any second, but it never did.

Another loan – this one for $3,000 -- was from William Green and Co., a small cement company that Green and his partner, Henry Rogers, ran from a small office in the Rookery Building. The money was supposed to buy glycerin for the copiers but who knows where it really went.

Once it became clear they wouldn't be repaid, Green and Rogers, trying to get their money back any way they could, broke into the apartment of Kate Durkee in Holmes's Englewood Castle. They made off with several pieces of equipment, including the boiler that provided heat and hot water to tenants in the building.

Kate Durkee then sued the men for $10,000 – though this would have been news to Kate. She was the official owner of the Castle at the time, though she didn't live in the city or in the building. Holmes had talked her into putting her name on the deed with the promise that she'd make money from it. He had filed the lawsuit in her name. It was eventually dismissed and if Holmes thought that would keep Green and Rogers from trying to get their money from him, he was wrong.

The two men filed their own lawsuit and in it, they stated that Holmes was the real owner of the Castle and alleged the other names were only on the building's deed to keep Holmes from being liable for the debts. Holmes denied this, but it was true, and Green clearly knew it.

But this was just one of the many lawsuits filed against the copier company before it vanished again. Holmes had a lawyer of dubious reputation working for him – you might remember Wharton Plummer, who was going to represent him in his divorce case a few years before – and it's believed that some of those who sued the company were actually in cahoots with Holmes, using the lawsuits to free up company money.

Making sense of the whole affair was nearly impossible, but that was undoubtedly the way that Holmes wanted it to be.

NO ONE KNOWS FOR SURE WHEN H.H. HOLMES STARTED TO commit murder. There are, of course, the rumors about murders that occurred when he was a boy, and during his college days, but there's no hard evidence to back them up.

The murders that we *know* Holmes committed generally have a clear motive – they were because someone knew too much, had something he wanted, or became an inconvenience in some way. He wasn't a crazed killer looking to satisfy some kind of sexual bloodlust. He killed because of greed or to protect himself.

And it's likely that he did just that around Christmas of 1891.

Two years earlier, in late 1889, Holmes hired Icilius Connor – Better known as "Ned" --- to be a watchmaker and craftsman for the jewelry store on the ground floor of the Castle. He arrived in Englewood in the company of his wife, Julia, and their young daughter, Pearl.

Icilius "Ned" Connor, his wife, Julia, and their daughter, Pearl

Ned had been moving his family around small towns in Iowa and Illinois for a few years. They had landed in Chicago in September 1889, and Ned went to work in a downtown jewelry store where his wages were so low that he could barely take care of his family. But then a new opportunity presented itself.

How Ned learned of the opening in Holmes' store is unclear but regardless of how it happened, he learned that Holmes was seeking a qualified manager for a jewelry store in Englewood.

Dressed in his best suit, he traveled to the Castle to meet Dr. Holmes. He found him in the barbershop, where he was getting a haircut and struck up a conversation. The conversation went well, and Holmes offered him $2 per day, plus room and board in the building. Ned was delighted and even more pleased when Holmes insisted that he stay for supper.

Ned later recalled:

He was then living on the second floor. As you went upstairs, you went up those winding stairs that run in the bay window. Mrs. Loomis was then his housekeeper. Holmes' wife was away; I do not know where. And then there was a young man who was a drug clerk, who was working for Holmes, and he was at the table. There was just three of us at dinner.

The next day, Ned began working for Holmes and said he found him to be a very pleasant fellow. He quickly learned of the hidden rooms and secret passages in the building but thought little of them. They were odd things to be sure, but they were none of his business. Ned Connor knew how to keep his mouth shut, even when he saw and heard things that he probably shouldn't have.

By this time in his life, Ned Connor was a desperate man. He was 30 when he arrived in Chicago and having been born and raised in Muscatine, Iowa, he drifted into Davenport around 1878. Working odd jobs, he found that he had a talent for repairing watches and jewelry and eventually started his own shop. He made very little money. And not because Ned wasn't skilled, he was – but there was a sort of defeated air that seemed to hang around the shop and its proprietor. He was never regarded as a lazy man, just one without much promise. He was friendly enough, well-spoken and polite, but he had a quiet, sort-of beaten dog personality that didn't do much to impress new customers.

And that was why people were so surprised when Ned caught the attention of Julia Smythe.

Full-figured and nearly six feet tall, Julia was considered the feminine idea of her day – a sort of statuesque "Gibson Girl," one of those illustrated women from the pen of Charles Dana Gibson, who were considered the perfectly proportioned women of the era.

At 18, she was the daughter of a well-to-do grocer and had thick chestnut hair and bright green eyes. Many considered her one of the most beautiful girls in Davenport. She was also likely the smartest. She had started keeping the books for

One of the "Gibson Girls" of the era. Julia Connor was compared to these so-called "perfect" women of the era.

her father's store at age 13. From the moment she reached the proper age for courtship, she had more suitors than she could count. Julia enjoyed their attention. She was a bright, healthy, beautiful, and good-natured girl but the man who won her over would have to be something special.

So, people were surprised – and a bit dismayed – when Julia allowed herself to be courted by the seedy and somewhat disreputable Ned Connor.

The two were married in Iowa at Christmas 1882 and their marriage was troubled from the start. With Julia's intelligence, support, and understanding of business, Ned's shop should have turned around – but it didn't. He remained hopelessly inept when it came to making money. Julia was disappointed at first, but her feelings toward him later turned to contempt. But this was not an era when a man could allow his wife to get the better of him and Ned stood up to her, turning their quiet disagreements into full-blown violent – and often public – quarrels.

With divorce in small-town Iowa out of the question, they made the best of the bad situation, and their marriage seemed to improve for a time. After Julia became pregnant, her family hoped that a baby would bring the couple closer together. The child was stillborn, though, adding more stress to the marriage.

Finally, looking for a fresh start, the couple left Davenport. They spent the next seven years in various small towns, where Ned continued to eke out a living. Each time, hope turned to disappointment, followed by failure.

Then on March 15, 1885, Julia gave birth to their daughter, Pearl. She was the only real joy in their life and made them decide to try again and to start over in Chicago, where Ned landed the job with Holmes.

There is little information available about little Pearl Connor – only a few memories committed to writing in the wake of Holmes' arrest. One of them comes from a neighbor, O.M. Knepper, who remembered the little girl playing outside the Castle after the Conners moved in.

Cora Quinlan, a girl about Pearl's age whose father, Patrick, worked for Holmes, remembered that Pearl was nice and that she liked her very much. She had blue eyes, was small for her age, but as a jeweler's daughter, always wore a thin gold ring with a tiny diamond in it.

Pearl seems to have enjoyed her time at the Castle, perhaps more than her parents did. Apparently, they began constantly fighting again. The new trouble between them, Ned would recall later, began because of jealousy.

What happened was perhaps not inevitable, but at the very least, it comes as no surprise. Julia was a pretty, still vivacious young woman who was married to a man she considered a failure. Holmes was the exact opposite. He was a rakish, handsome, and bold businessmen who had achieved tremendous success. To a girl from small-town Iowa, he was an irresistible temptation.

As for Holmes, everyone in Englewood knew he was popular with women. His wife knew it, too. Charles Davis, who ran a shop in the Castle, later said:

Holmes liked to have young women as clerks. They usually worked on one side of the store but always found a reason to cross the store to the pharmacy counter where Holmes was working. When his wife was around, she noticed this and probably said something about it. After that, he rigged an electric bell in connection with a loose board near the top of the stairs from his flat over the store, so that he might be apprised of his spouse coming downstairs. It was noticeable that whenever that bell rang, he seemed to be the busiest man in Englewood.

While Ned worked in the jewelry store, Holmes hired Julia to be a clerk in his store and later, taught her to keep the books. This didn't make things any smoother between Ned and Julia, even if the relationship with Holmes probably started out innocently. It didn't stay that way, however. No one can say for sure when Julia and Holmes became lovers, but it's certain that they were sleeping together by the early part of 1890.

Ned was the only one who seemed not to notice the affair, although it's more likely that he simply turned a blind eye toward his wife's infidelity. For the first time in his life, he had stable employment and a steady income. He didn't want to do anything to jeopardize his position in the store, even if it meant his wife was running around behind his back.

At some point, though, Holmes made sure he knew what was going on. Ned later said that Holmes casually said some things that no one who hadn't slept with Julia could know. He didn't make clear what those things were, but Ned insisted: "He never could have got that information any other way."

Things simmered between the Connors for several weeks before Ned could no longer ignore the situation. A few well-meaning acquaintances had taken him aside and alerted him to his wife's scandalous behavior. Julia was making a fool of him, they said, and he had to do something about it.

Finally, in the spring of 1890, while Holmes was traveling, an ugly confrontation occurred between Ned and Julia. He demanded that she end her affair with Holmes. If she did not, he would leave her. Julia refused and Ned moved out. In late March 1890, he began working as a watchmaker for a store owner downtown named John H. Purdy.

One would think that Holmes would be glad to have a romantic rival out of the way, but instead he took petty revenge. On April 8, Holmes took out promissory notes for $300 payable to the same John H. Purdy, Ned's new employer, and never paid the loans back.

Ned continued to run into Holmes from time to time, and Holmes always tried to get him involved in some sort of business scheme. Sometimes he agreed and Ned would work with him for a short time, and he even briefly got his sister a job at the ABC Copier Company.

Ned had been slow to realize that Holmes had been having an affair with his wife, so who knows how long it took for him to realize that Holmes was trying to seduce his sister, too.

Eva Gertrude Conner had come to Chicago in early 1891, when she was 21, to attend business school. While in the city, she needed a job. For reasons that are baffling to me, Ned sent her to Holmes, and he employed her as a secretary. It wasn't long before office rumors claimed that Holmes' interest in her was not strictly professional.

But Gertie, as everyone called her, had become enamored of a young man she met attending business school. Holmes didn't like this and told Ned so several times. Eventually, Gertie went to her brother and said she could no longer work for Holmes but wouldn't say why. That should have been an obvious sign to Ned that something was wrong, but this is not a man who easily became suspicious apparently.

And perhaps that's because Holmes was in his other ear, telling Ned that Gertie needed to be sent back home to Iowa to protect her from the young man she'd met at school. Bed, not especially bright, probably didn't know what to believe.

But Ned's sister did return to Iowa, but only because she received a letter in April 1891 saying that her mother was very sick and might die. Gertie moved back home to be with her, but it was Gertie herself who died. Ned receiving a telegram about her death on July 18.

A few years later, rumors would spread that Holmes had killed her, but he hadn't. There were, by that time, so many rumors about his time in Chicago that it was hard to figure out what was the truth, but we can safely say that Gertie really did die from heart issues. She had been ailing for years.

By the time of Gertie's death, Ned and Holmes were no longer on good terms – and it's not hard to see why. Holmes had tried to seduce his sister, was still having an affair with his wife, and had failed to pay Ned the money that he owed him for nearly two years. At some point, Ned was brave enough to accuse him of all the wrongs he'd done.

In reply, Holmes told him: "Connor, I have always treated you like a brother. There is nothing I would not do for you."

But Ned snapped back at him, "Holmes, you never intended to treat me fairly. You have never paid me what you owe me, and you have had the money time and time again. And if I ever get a dollar out of you, I will consider it the same as finding it on the street."

Ned and Julia eventually divorced but he stayed in Chicago for a while, hoping she might come to her senses. When she later disappeared, he assumed that she had returned home to her family, and he left Chicago.

He moved first to the small town of Gilman, Illinois, where he opened another unsuccessful jewelry store but married a woman named Vanuel Vaughn. After a year, the couple moved to Assumption, Illinois, an even smaller town, where he again tried to make a living with a jewelry store.

It would be, living in Assumption in 1895, when Ned would finally discover that Julia had never left Chicago at all.

NED CONNOR MAY HAVE STAYED OUT OF HOLMES' TANGLED web of lawsuits and financial scams, but Julia was not so lucky. After she separated from Ned, her name began appearing alongside that of Lucy Belknap and Myrta Holmes on documents that were mired in all kinds of legal issues. She appeared in the paperwork for the ABC Copier Company and, in December 1891, was listed as one of the founders of a new business called the Chicago Intermediate Company. What the company did was as vague as its name, which was perfect since Holmes simply created it to launder money.

It's also notable that this new company was announced less than two weeks before Julia and her daughter disappeared off the face of the earth.

Holmes had grown tired of Julia long before she vanished. Strong-willed and often difficult, she had no intention of being merely Holmes' mistress. She wanted to be his partner and take on an active role in his business affairs. Of course, on paper, she already was – and was deeply in debt thanks to loans in her name – but she didn't know that. Instead, she wanted to be Holmes' full-time bookkeeper, and she wanted him to send her to business college to learn proper accounting.

Holmes agreed to both proposals, although he knew that he couldn't afford to have her learn all his many secrets. He knew he had to get rid of Julia. And so, the Christmas season of 1891 became the last time that Julia and Pearl were seen alive.

A man named John Crowe and his family lived in rooms on the Wallace Street side of the Castle from 1891 until late in 1892. His wife later told reporters that she knew Julia and Pearl well. She added:

She told me one day that her sister in Davenport was about to be married and she was going to the wedding. Christmas Eve 1891, she was in our rooms arranging a Christmas tree for our daughters. Her daughter had been presented with a doll which Mrs. Connor said Pearl could take with her, even though she said she did not intend to take anything with her but the clothes she needed for a hurried trip.

Julia left their apartment that evening talking about the things that she planned to do on Christmas day but saying nothing that led the Crowes to believe that she was leaving for the wedding that night. They assumed the plans were for a day or two in the future. They didn't see her on Christmas because they went to visit friends and arrived home after 11:00 P.M. She told a reporter, "She must have left sometime after midnight on Christmas Eve or in the daytime after we left our house. Nobody seemed to know when she had gone."

They also didn't know *where* She'd gone. If she really left town for her sister's wedding, she never came back. And she never made it there either. Julia's sister really did get married on New Year's Eve, but Julia never showed up for it.

Her apartment remained unoccupied and untouched after she disappeared. Exactly how much time passed is unclear, but later, when Mrs. Crowe heard sounds in the apartment, she assumed Julia and her daughter had returned. She soon learned, though, that a new family named Doyle had moved in.

She never saw Julia or Pearl again.

The Doyle family later reported that when they first looked at the apartment, all of Julia's and Pearl's things were still there. Dishes were in the cabinets and plates had been left on the table as if someone had eaten and then walked out the door. A doll – the one that Pearl had been given as a gift by the Crowes – was on the floor.

Holmes told Mrs. Doyle that Julia had left suddenly after receiving a telegram saying that her sister was dying. She abandoned everything apparently – more clothes were in the dresser, combs, brushes, powder, and other things were on a dressing table, and more of Pearl's clothing was still hanging in a wardrobe.

Mrs. Doyle said that Holmes offered her the discarded clothing, but she refused. There was something about it that unsettled her, she later admitted. Holmes claimed to send them to Julia in Iowa, but he mailed them to Myrta's house in Wilmette instead.

Mrs. Doyle wasn't the only one who told an unsettling story about Julia and Pearl – although the other one was told by someone who likely knew exactly what had happened to the missing woman and her daughter.

Julia was also friends with Patrick Quinlan, who lived in the Castle and was a handyman for Holmes. He also owned a farm in Michigan, where his wife and daughter lived before they later joined him in Chicago. Months before Julia and her daughter disappeared, over Fourth of July week in 1891, Holmes, Julia, Pearl went to stay at the farm and Pearl remained there with Patrick's family for a few extra weeks. When Patrick went home to the farm for Christmas in 1891, his daughter, Cora, asked about Julia and Pearl. Strangely, Patrick told her that Julia had married a man, and they'd moved to California.

During this time, Holmes spoke of Julia and Pearl as if they were alive and even made a show of trying to find them. As late as Halloween 1892, Holmes wrote to Julia's mother, asking where Julia was because she was needed as a witness in a court case. Her parents were astonished. They assumed that Julia and Pearl were still living in Chicago with Holmes.

They were in Chicago, but they were no longer alive. By the time of the letter, Julia and Pearl had most likely been dead since the previous Christmas – and Holmes knew it.

At various times in the future, Holmes would deny killing Julia, and at other times he'd confess to killing her while he performed an abortion on her. Sometimes he claimed that he didn't mean to kill her. He said that she'd just died during the operation. But he told one of his lawyers, D.T. Duncombe, that she became pregnant, and he'd convinced her to have an abortion. Seizing his chance, he killed Julia on the operating table so he could finally rid himself of her.

This may – or may not have, depending on the rumors – been the first murder that Holmes committed. That means it could have just as easily been an accident. Holmes undoubtedly lacked the experience to perform an abortion and for women to die during the operations in those days was far from uncommon.

But even if Julia had been an accidental death, there's no way that Pearl was an accident, too.

Why Holmes murdered Pearl instead of giving her to her father is a mystery. He may have decided that with her mother dead, killing her was the easiest way to deal with her. Perhaps she knew too much about her mother's death – no one knows.

How he killed Pearl is also a mystery. Based on later actions, it's likely that he poisoned her or suffocated her. A few years later, when investigators dug up the basement floor, they found bones that appeared to belong to a little girl between the ages of 6 and 10. Although they weren't in a condition for investigators to be sure, they suspected the body had been dismembered and possibly burned before it was buried.

Pearl, at the time she disappeared, was 6 years old.

But what became of Julia?

In January 1892, not long after Julia had given her notice and abandoned her employment with Holmes – or so he was telling anyone who asked about her – he discovered that a machinist who worked for him named Myron Chappell possessed the specialized skill of articulating, or mounting, human skeletons.

The mechanic with a knack for articulating skeletons – Myron Chappell.

Chappell had acquired this talent several years before while working for a contractor named A.L. Goode, who rented an office at 513 State Street -- the same building where the Bennett Medical College was located.

It was not unusual for the workmen to see bodies brought into the building for dissection and then for them to see the articulated bones on display. Chappell, who was apparently a sort of jack-of-all-trades who was always interested in learning new skills, became fascinated with skeleton articulation, and managed to pick up some firsthand knowledge in the college's anatomy lab.

After replying to a newspaper ad, Chappell had first come to work at the Castle in the fall of 1890. He did several odd jobs for Holmes and at some point, in early 1892, he mentioned

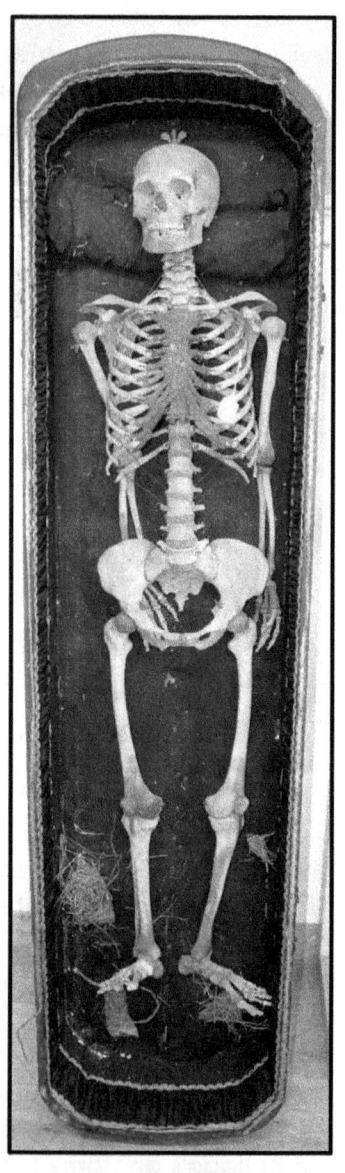

An articulated skeleton like the ones created by Myron Chappell for Holmes to sell to medical schools.

something to his employer about his time at the building that shared space with the medical school. The conversation turned to dissections and skeletons – which Holmes had also been fascinated with since medical school -- and Chappell confessed that he had a knack for articulating human bones. To his surprise, Holmes led him to a dark room on the second floor of the Castle.

They walked into the chamber and, using a lantern, Holmes revealed a partially dissected cadaver stretched out on a table. Chappell could tell that the body was that of a woman, but he later added to police detectives:

It looked more like a jackrabbit that had been skinned by splitting the skin down the face and rolling it back off the entire body. There was considerable flesh on the lower limbs, but on the arms, it was practically gone.

Holmes offered to pay Chappell $36 to finish stripping the corpse of its flesh and to prepare the skeleton as a medical specimen. Chappell, who said he thought Dr. Holmes had been performing a postmortem examination on a deceased patient, readily agreed.

That night, a steamer trunk containing the cadaver was delivered to Chappell's house by Holmes's right-hand man, Benjamin Pitezel. A week later, Chappell returned the cleaned and articulated skeleton to Dr. Holmes, collected his money, and left happy for the extra work.

Luckily for Chappell – but not so much for anyone else – there would be more of the same kind of work for him in the future.

A week after the bones were returned to Holmes, he sold the skeleton to the Hahnemann Medical College for $200. It was on display there for only a few months before it was purchased by a surgeon named Pauley, who hung it up in his office at home.

Pauley was very impressed with the specimen. In all his years in practice, he'd never seen a female skeleton that was almost six feet tall.

 THE SPRING OF 1892 WAS A RELATIVELY QUIET TIME FOR H.H. Holmes. Although lawsuits against him always seemed to be lurking somewhere in the background, his demeanor never seemed to indicate that he was feeling any sort of pressure.

He continued to show up in his drugstore almost every day, he was spotted in the barber's shop getting a shave or seen dining in a local restaurant. There would sometimes be a woman with him. Occasionally, it was his wife, Myrta, visiting from Wilmette, or it might be another in a string of pretty, young women who were there one day and gone the next.

There's no evidence to say that any of these young women became Holmes' victims – but not much to say they didn't either. As mentioned already, Holmes was not a depraved lunatic who was randomly killing people. When he committed murder, it was because his victim had something he wanted – or because he wanted to protect his secrets.

And that may have been what led to the death of a young woman named Emeline Cigrand.

PERHAPS IT WAS THE RELATIVELY QUITE TIME AROUND THE Castle that caused Holmes to focus on how far his sidekick, Ben Pitezel, had fallen into a liquor bottle or maybe he just got tired of seeing Ben show up to work drunk each day – who knows? We do know, though, that Ben's drinking had gotten so bad that Holmes decided to do something about it.

There was no question that Ben had proven himself to be an invaluable accomplice in many of Holmes' schemes. He shared many of his employer's darkest secrets, and what he didn't know for certain, he undoubtedly suspected. And there was no hint that he would ever be disloyal. For that reason, Holmes seemed to have trusted him completely. If it was possible for him to have actual friends, then he certainly considered Ben to be his closest one.

But Ben's drinking was a risk. If his drunkenness got the best of him, who knew what he might accidentally reveal while on a bender?

As it happened, Holmes had recently heard of an Illinois doctor who promised a cure for alcoholism. He was one of the first to consider it an actual disease. Holmes was intrigued by the alleged cure, and when he saw that doctor had opened a hospital that spring in Dwight, Illinois – south of Chicago – he dug into his own pocket, paid the price of the treatment, and checked Ben Pitezel into the place.

The hospital, called the Keeley Institute, was founded by Dr. Leslie Enright Keeley, who owed the great success of his alcoholic cure regimen more to self-promotion than to the proven virtues of the program. No evidence exists that the famous Keeley Cure was based on scientific research, but this didn't stop nearly a half-

The Keeley Institute in Dwight, Illinois

million Americans – including Ben Pitezel -- from subjecting themselves to his questionable methods.

Dr. Keeley was born in Ireland in 1834 and grew up in New York. He later moved west to attend and graduate from Rush Medical School in Chicago. During the Civil War, he served in the Union Army's Medical Corps and then settled in Illinois to start a medical practice.

It was in 1880 that he began widely advertising that he had discovered a cure for alcoholism – a disease that he was convinced was caused by alcoholic poisoning of the nerve cells. His "cure" consisted of a strict dietary regimen accompanied by injections of "bichloride of gold," as well as other secret ingredients, four times each day. It was nothing but a snake oil treatment – there was no gold in the mixture – but it was harmless, even if it did nothing to curb cravings for alcohol.

Shortly after his announcement of the cure, he opened the Keeley Institute in Dwight, and the *Chicago Tribune* ran a series of stories about the gold cure, which is likely where Holmes first heard about it.

After the articles, hundreds of drinkers looking to dry out flocked to Dwight to take the cure. Keeley, of course, capitalized on the publicity, sending "graduates" of the Institute on lecture tours around the country. He also formed the Keeley League, whose dry members met in annual conventions, and he even organized the wives of members into a women's auxiliary group. The Keeley Institute eventually had over 200 branches in the United States and Europe.

After the doctor died in 1900, interest dwindled, and the organization, which had been drawing criticism for years, faded away. It had a good run, though, and made a fortune for Dr. Keeley during its heyday – something H.H. Holmes undoubtedly admired.

The institute was at the height of its popularity in Chicago in 1892, though, and scores of suffering alcoholics were passing through its doors each week. One of them was Ben Pitezel, who came for the full, four-week treatment. That kind of stay at the sanitarium was $100, but Holmes must have believed it was worth it.

When Ben arrived, he was introduced to an open, informal environment, where he was first offered as much alcohol as he wanted to drink. Of course, that soon changed. While living in the sanitarium, he was fed healthy food and given tonics that contained things like morphine, willow bark, ammonia, atropine, and strychnine – yes, poisons. But they weren't meant to kill him, just clean out his system, so the doses were small. He was also, of course, given those four injections of "bichloride of gold" each day.

When he wasn't in treatment, Ben was allowed to stroll around the grounds of the institute, as well as the streets of Dwight, which was then described as a "therapeutic community."

Ben finished his four weeks in this therapeutic community and at the Keeley Institute in early April 1892. He returned home a changed man – a walking testimonial to the truth of Dr. Keeley's many claims. He was sober, healthy, and happier than he'd been in years. He would never touch another drop of alcohol.

Until he did. Within a few weeks, he was drinking again.

But even though he'd wasted $100 to try and get his friend sober, Holmes didn't see his stint at the asylum as a total loss. Ben Pitezel had brought back tales from the sanitarium of a pretty girl who worked there named Emeline Cigrand. Holmes was fascinated with Ben's description of the young, innocent blond, not only because she was beautiful, but she also had the secrets to Dr. Keeley's magical elixir.

Still dreaming of his own patent medicine, Holmes decided to try and get a piece of Keeley's action. He soon started the Silver Ash Institute in Englewood, essentially a copy of the gold cure that substituted gold for silver. He didn't bother to do much advertising, and there is some speculation that it was really nothing more than a cover for one of his swindles, so it disappeared almost as quickly as it arrived on the scene.

But it didn't disappear because Holmes couldn't get the cooperation of Emeline Cigrand. Almost as soon as Ben returned from Dwight with stories about her, Holmes had hired her to work in his office. Her time in Englewood only lasted for a few months – but she left many lingering mysteries behind when she eventually vanished.

Emeline Cigrand was later regarded as the prettiest of the young women who passed through Holmes' life. No original copies of her photograph exist, but newspapers later copied it as a drawing of her looking back over her shoulder in a studio pose that made her look like an actress.

Emeline had grown up in Lafayette, Indiana, and she had worked for one year as a stenographer in the Tippecanoe County Recorder's office before going to work at the Keeley Institute in July 1891. She had been there for less than a year when Ben began his treatment at the facility.

Emeline Cigrand

Attracted by her beauty, he struck up an acquaintance with her and did all he could to try and impress her with his importance. He was a partner, he claimed, of Dr. H.H. Holmes, one of the most prominent businessmen in all of Chicago. Emeline, who had never been to a city larger than Lafayette, was suitably impressed. But to Ben's dismay, it never went beyond friendship between them. Even so, he couldn't stop talking about her when he returned to the Castle.

Holmes – trying to decipher the inner workings of the Keely Institute – wrote to Emeline and, using Ben as his introduction, offered her a secretarial job for $18 a week – more than double what she made at the sanitarium. Excited about the chance to live in the city, she quickly accepted and left Dwight in May 1892.

It's believed that Emeline never lived in the Castle. A second-floor resident, Mrs. Lawrence, never recalled Emeline staying the night in the building except on nights when Holmes wasn't there – or so she said. In a later newspaper interview, she said she considered Emeline to be a fine, upstanding young woman and wise enough to know that Holmes' crony Patrick Quinlan was nothing more than a "dirty little Irishman," as she put it.

Emeline instead roomed first in a boarding house owned by a Mrs. Hunt at the corner of Sixty-Third and Sherman Street, but Mrs. Hunt turned out to be a little too nosy for Holmes' taste. She later recalled that Miss Cigrand was often out in the evenings – usually quite late – and always with Mr. Holmes. She thought this was improper since Holmes was a married man, and she told Emeline she disapproved of her conduct.

A short time later, Emeline moved out and took a room at the home of Mr. and Mrs. Fred Felker on Sixty-Third Court. She was only there for a few weeks and often didn't sleep there. She would go out in the evening, sometimes coming home late to pick up a change of clothing and some essentials. She told Mrs. Felker she was staying with a cousin downtown overnight.

Sometimes, she returned to the Felker house with a man, and Emeline told Mrs. Felker's daughter that his name was Mr. Belknap. Of course, this was Holmes, using the maiden name of his wife. A short time later, Mrs. Felker's son, Curtis, was looking for an apartment in the neighborhood and looked at one in the Castle. There, he met the man he knew as Mr. Belknap, who was now being introduced as Mr. Holmes.

It should come as no surprise that Holmes had started trying to seduce Emeline almost as soon as she arrived in the city. He bought her flowers, took her on sight-seeing excursions around the city, bought her gifts, took her to the theater, and treated her to meals at expensive restaurants. They spent Sunday afternoons bicycling in the park and strolling around the neighborhood. Holmes seemed to be the perfect gentleman, but as Dr. Maurice Lawrence, one of the tenants of the Castle, later said:

It was not long before I became aware that the relations between Holmes and Miss Cigrand were not strictly those of employer and employee. But we felt she was more to be pitied than blamed.

Other tenants noticed, too, and Holmes told some of them that Emeline was his cousin, but no one believed it.

Emeline allowed Holmes to have great influence over her life, letting him tell her where to live and what to do with her money. When she left Dwight, she had $800 that she'd saved from working there, and Holmes borrowed it from her, giving her some real estate – which was worthless if it existed at all -- as security.

She never lived anywhere for long because Holmes didn't want her to. She stayed for just one week with a woman named Mrs. Stanwood at Sixty-Fourth and Yale. She later told a reporter:

She was greatly infatuated with Holmes and never ceased talking about him. I didn't like him. He couldn't look you in the face.

That summer, Emeline visited with a girl she used to work with in Dwight, Ora Gilman. They went to the theater together downtown in the Loop. Ora later recalled:

She told me she was engaged to be married. I don't think she told me the name of the man. She gave me her address, and I called there one Sunday, perhaps two weeks later. It was in the Holmes building, I have since learned. I called at the drugstore and was directed upstairs. She wasn't there. I met a man in the hall who said she worked there but didn't live there, but he gave me the address of a restaurant on Sixty-Third Street where she took her meals. I didn't go to the restaurant. She promised me wedding cards, but she never sent them. I never saw her again.

Emeline was nice in every respect, a very unsuspecting girl, and never much in the company of men.

By the fall of 1892, it's believed that Emeline expected Holmes to marry her, and, in fact, it appears that Holmes allowed her to pass this happy news on to her relatives and friends.

That fall, Emeline wrote several letters to friends and family to tell them about her fiancée, "Robert E. Phelps." She wrote that he was wealthy, generous, and kind and was going to take her to Europe for their honeymoon. In a letter to her younger sister, Philomena, she said that Robert was the son of an English lord, and they planned to visit his ancestral estate while abroad. We also know that Emeline arranged to have a wedding dress made around this time. She told the dressmaker that she was going to be married at the home of her parents.

In early October 1892, Emeline's cousin, Dr. B.J. Cigrand – who was a dentist, a historian, and a writer who lived in Wicker Park on Chicago's North Side and was also the creator of Flag Day – decided to call on Emeline at the Castle after he received the good news about her upcoming wedding.

Her fiancée wasn't there that day, but she seemed happy and spoke often about Mr. Phelps. Showing off his great accomplishments, she took Dr. Cigrand and his wife on a tour of the building, including the third floor, which was then being added to the structure.

Dr. Cigrand later noted how poorly constructed the Castle seemed to be, and he commented about the shoddy workmanship and the poor lumber used to frame up the interior. He wasn't nearly as impressed as Emeline had hoped he would be, but she shrugged off the comments. It seemed that nothing could dampen her spirits with her wedding date so quickly approaching.

In November, Holmes came to Emeline one day with a small stack of white envelopes and asked her to address them to her family and closest friends. He explained that he wanted to have formal marriage announcements printed and would mail them out immediately after their wedding. Emeline gladly did what he asked and wrote out all the addresses that afternoon.

Emeline, of course, had no way of knowing why Holmes really wanted her to write out those addresses. That would not become clear until later – and by then, it was too late for Emeline.

On December 6, Emeline stopped by the apartment of Dr. Lawrence for a visit. She had painted a forest scene on a small tin plate, and she gave it to Mrs. Lawrence as a gift. When asked why she didn't save it to give as a Christmas present, Emeline said she wouldn't be there for the holidays. She would be visiting her parents in Indiana. Dr. Lawrence later remembered that she seemed excited about the visit and was as happy as a child.

When several days passed after the meeting on December 6 and Emeline hadn't been seen around the Castle, Mrs. Lawrence asked Holmes about her. He told her that she had gone away and had gotten married. Mrs. Lawrence was shocked – not only because Emeline had not told her the wedding was happening so soon, but also because she was aware of the intimate relationship between Emeline and Holmes. She said that Holmes seemed uncomfortable by her questions. He didn't look her in the eye and seemed anxious to leave.

The next day, she saw Holmes and Pat Quinlan carrying a heavy trunk to an express wagon. Holmes then climbed aboard and traveled to Wilmette, where his wife lived, and didn't return for two days. When he did, he handed the Lawrences an envelope with an announcement card in it. The card read:

Mr. Robert Phelps
Miss Emeline Cigrand
Married
Wednesday, December 7, 1892
Chicago

When Mrs. Lawrence asked about Robert Phelps, Holmes replied, "Oh, he's a fellow that Miss Cigrand met somewhere. I don't know anything about him except he is a traveling man."

After that, Mrs. Lawrence stated, Holmes refused to speak about Emeline or Robert Phelps again.

Soon after Emeline vanished, her family received notices like the one shown to Mrs. Lawrence. They were baffled. Her sister, Philomena, had spent 10 days with Emeline in Chicago and had never met anyone named Robert Phelps.

They were even more surprised when a wedding announcement appeared in the local Lafayette newspaper that was printed below the headline "MISS CIGRAND WEDS ROBERT E. PHELPS."

Who was this man that Emeline hadn't told her family about? She had spoken about him to others – he was kind, he was wealthy, he'd bought her new clothes and a large traveling trunk.

It is almost certain that Robert Phelps was H.H. Holmes. All evidence points to it. Clinton Sherman, a delivery driver who often picked up packages at the Castle, later said that Emeline had definitely been having an affair with Holmes. He saw them kiss in the office, and she told him that they planned to be married.

Given her story about the "cousin downtown" with whom she stayed overnight, her knowledge of Holmes' wife in Wilmette, and her habit of referring to her fiancée by several different names, Emeline knew their affair was meant to be secret. Though she told several people who didn't know Holmes that she was getting married, she seems not to have told those – like the Lawrences – who knew him.

Holmes killed her, but why did he do it? It's possible that, like Julia Connor, she knew too many of his secrets. She might have seen too much, and perhaps she pressured Holmes into marrying her. Holmes didn't respond well to the threat.

Others suggest that Emeline might have been pregnant or that she *hadn't* known any of his secrets, found one out, and was so shocked by it that she threatened to turn him in to the police. That was something that also would have forced Holmes to silence her.

Whatever the reason, we do know that Holmes did make sure that Emeline never talked to anyone again. He even tried to cover his tracks. In January 1893, Emeline's father, Peter, received a typewritten letter alleged to be from his daughter. In it, she claimed her new husband had turned out to be a drunkard, a gambler, and a bad man and that she was going to Europe.

Cigrand was saddened by the letter, but he knew his daughter would write to him again once she was settled. But she never did. All he had now was the letter and the clipping from the newspaper that had announced her marriage. The notice had read:

The bride, after completing her education, was employed as a stenographer in the County Recorder's office. From there she went to Dwight, and from there to Chicago, where she met her fate. She is a lady of great intelligence and has a charming manner and handsome appearance. She is a lady of refinement and possesses a character that is strong and pure. Her many friends see that she has exercised good judgment in selecting a husband and will heartily congratulate her.

At the Castle in Englewood, Holmes must have chuckled when he wrote out the lines of the notice that he mailed to the Lafayette newspaper, especially the part where he noted that Emeline had gone to Chicago, where she "met her fate."

He was the only one who knew what really happened to her on the afternoon of December 7, 1892 – the same day that Emeline and Robert Phelps had supposedly gotten married.

Holmes was working in his office and asked Emeline to get a document for him that was kept in the large walk-in vault next to his office. While she was looking for the non-existent paper, Holmes silently approached the vault, slammed shut the thick steel door, and carefully locked it.

It's unknown if Holmes could hear her muffled screams – he'd tested out the vault before, remember – but if he did, he must have heard the terror in her shrieks before they started to slowly die away as the air inside of the chamber ran out.

Emeline Cigrand had certainly "met her fate" in Chicago, and she was never seen again – not alive anyway. A few weeks after her disappearance, though, the LaSalle Medical School became the owner of a new articulated female skeleton, which had been acquired from Dr. H.H. Holmes.

There were many hotels that opened in Chicago for the start of the World's Fair, including the famed Congress Plaza, which was then known as the Auditorium Annex

WHEN THE WORLD'S COLUMBIAN EXPOSITION OF 1893 OPENED in Chicago, countless people made the trip to the city to see the fair and they begged, borrowed, stole, and cleaned out their life savings to do it. Chicago offered every type of lodging imaginable to meet the demand. There were high-priced luxury hotels and run-down seedy flophouses downtown. There were boarding houses, both well-kept and rat-infested, on the edge of the fairgrounds and private homes with an extra room or two all over the South Side.

When Emeline Cigrand had shown her cousin, the dentist, around the Castle in the fall of 1892, it was under renovation – a third floor was being added to serve as a hotel during the Fair.

Holmes was a constant presence in the building during this time, although most of his schemes had started to revolve around real estate deals, always with borrowed money and usually with Kate Durkee appearing as the buyer on the necessary documents. Myrta's old friend likely had no idea of the wealth she had – well, wealth on paper but nowhere else.

Meanwhile, the restaurant on the first floor of the Castle became part of one of the most complicated swindles Holmes was involved with around this time.

The restaurant was sold to a young Aurora, Illinois, man named Clarence Phillips. Clarence, like others that Holmes took advantage of, had a problem with liquor. Witness testimonies in the divorce papers that were later filed against him stated that he was almost never sober.

He'd gone into the restaurant business elsewhere, earlier in 1892, and when his partner decided to quit – probably because Clarence was always drunk – Holmes had offered to buy out his stake in the restaurant in exchange for a bicycle.

Yes, a bicycle. It must have been quite the place.

But he told Clarence that he could still make money out of the deal. The product the restaurant had been best known for was baked beans, and Holmes proposed that Clarence sell the beans from a wagon that Holmes would provide.

Clarence thought this was a great deal, and he accepted but the wagon was never built. It would be ready to go soon, Holmes promised him, though, and, in the meantime, he did have some plumbing and handyman jobs that Clarence could make money doing at his building in Englewood.

When it became clear that the bean wagon wasn't going to happen, Holmes eventually offered to sell Clarence the restaurant in the building. The young man took out a loan from a company that Holmes recommended to him, he borrowed $500 from his father to get the business started, and he agreed to pay Holmes $40 a month for rent. His wife told him that if the business wasn't a success, she was going to leave him. Remember those divorce papers that were mentioned?

The restaurant opened, but it was, according to every account, very bad. Even Holmes later compared it to prison food.

While this was happening, Holmes was doing what everyone else in Chicago seemed to be doing in late 1892 – looking for ways to get rich from the World's Fair.

Despite later claims that Holmes built the Castle specifically to be a hotel for the fair, that wasn't the case. It was built long before the fair was even announced. The fact that he was lucky enough to have a building not far from the Sixty-Third Street entrance to the fairgrounds was dumb luck, but he did take advantage of it. Not only would he be able to make money renting out the rooms, but he would also make money simply by announcing that he planned to do so. With such a venture in the works, he could raise money from investors who'd never see a return, buy goods on credit to sell without paying the bills, and then make thousands of dollars in insurance money by setting fire to it.

To Holmes, it seemed like a foolproof plan.

He started right away by creating letterhead for a company official named H.S. Campbell who, using several letters, authorized Holmes to buy goods and materials on account. On September 20, 1892, he made his first stop at Bullard and Gormley, hardware dealers who sent him away with hundreds of dollars in materials for the third floor of the Castle.

He also took out loans from various banks, companies, and individuals. Some of the money was used for construction. The rest went into Holmes' very deep pockets.

W.P. Doyle, who lived in the Castle at the time, helped to construct the third floor and later said that Holmes bought lumber and materials in his name but always paid the bill.

Most of the labor was not obtained so honestly, though. Holmes repeated his schemes from when the Castle was originally built, hiring laborers, keeping them working for a week or two, and then firing everyone to cut back on overhead. After a few days passed, he'd hire new men and repeat the process.

Most of the people who lived and worked in the building had to have known that Holmes was dishonest. There were debt collectors coming and going all the time. Even those who didn't like him, though, were amazed at how daring he was. Charles Davis, a first-floor jeweler, later said:

> *Nearly every particle of this building and its fixtures was got on credit, and very little was ever paid for. If all the writs and liens that have been leveled on this structure were pasted on the walls, the block would look like a mammoth circus billboard. But I never heard of a lien being collected. Holmes used to tell me he had a lawyer paid to keep him out of trouble, but it always seemed to me that it was the courteous, audacious rascality of the man that pushed him through.*
>
> *One day he bought some furniture for his restaurant and moved it in, and that very evening, the dealer came around to collect his bill or remove the goods. Holmes set up the drinks, took him to supper, bought him a cigar, and sent the man off laughing at a joke with a promise to call the next week for his money. In thirty minutes after he took off, Holmes had wagons in front loading up that furniture, and the dealer never got a cent. Holmes didn't go to jail either. He was the only man in the United States who could do what he did.*

The new floor of the Castle looked good, at least on the outside. But there were many oddities in the construction, not the least of which was that many of the closets had two doors, which allowed a person to slip into one and listen to people in the next room without them knowing. There were also sliding panel walls, hidden passages, secret ladders and staircases, and more.

These were not the kind of additions that one was apt to find in any reputable hotel of the day – and yet, Holmes had built them into his. Anyone who might claim that Holmes didn't plan to rob – even murder – guests who stayed at the Castle is sadly mistaken.

But the money he made from guests or from goods he bought on credit and re-sold was nothing compared to what he planned to make from insurance companies when it came time to flee Chicago and burn the Castle down behind him.

A policy was taken out at the time of the third-floor addition with the Queen Insurance Company. A few weeks later, another policy was purchased from Girard Fire and Marine Insurance. A policy from Liverpool, London & Globe followed and by then, a fire at the building would potentially result in a payout of thousands of dollars. A plan was in place if Holmes ever had to act on it.

And he would – but not yet.

As opening day for the World's Fair neared, Holmes paid nothing but the insurance premiums for his hotel. By early 1893, lawsuits were being filed by the companies he'd purchased furniture and materials from, and several were also attempting to repossess what he'd purchased from them.

The problem was that when they got to the Castle, their goods were nowhere to be found. Some had already been sold for cash, but others were so well hidden that Holmes could lead them through the building, opening every visible door, and nothing that was supposed to be installed in the new hotel was anywhere to be found.

Oh, but it was there.

In March, a laborer in the building offered to show the Tobey Furniture Company where their goods were if they gave him $50. After pocketing the money, he led them to a room on the second floor of the Castle and opened a door which had been covered with wallpaper, hiding it completely. When they got inside, they found some of their stock but nowhere near all of it.

They went on the hunt for more hidden rooms in the building and found other pieces of furniture -- along with mattresses that belonged to the Schulz & Hirsh Company – in a secret compartment between the second and third floors.

Immediately, other creditors hurried to the building. They found crockery and furniture hidden in the ceiling, beneath floors, and in compartments between the third floor and the new roof. When they uncovered dark passages between walls, hidden staircases, and unusual dead ends, they dismissed them. They were too small to hide anything in, they thought, and never considered they could be used for anything more devious than theft.

Soon, the search came to an end. Creditors went away frustrated. Some of them found what they had been looking for, but not all of it. Others found nothing at all. The merchandise had either been sold or hidden so well that it couldn't be found. One member of the search party was unfortunate enough to have kicked a hole in a plaster wall, believing there was a door behind it. Holmes was brash enough to send him a $75 bill for the damage he'd caused.

The invasion by his creditors had been a bit of bad luck, but Holmes put it behind him. There was still plenty of furniture to set up the hotel – and more money would soon be coming his way.

IN THE MIDDLE OF ALL THIS, RESTAURANT OWNER CLARENCE Phillips was still struggling to keep the doors of his restaurant open, as well as keep his wife from leaving him.

One day, Ben Pitezel came in and asked Clarence if he'd consider selling the business back to Holmes. He was certainly interested and quickly agreed to a meeting with Holmes and Ben at the Sherman House Hotel to discuss it. Holmes, of course, knew how badly Clarence was struggling and set the price so low that the man would be ruined if he accepted it. Clarence turned him down and ended the meeting.

But Holmes wasn't worried. He wanted Phillips out of the building, so he would just find another way to do it.

Clarence owned the restaurant, but he was still leasing the space. Holmes informed him that, because of the approaching Fair, his rent was being raised from $40 a month to $150 a month.

And that wasn't all. Clarence also discovered that the company that he'd bought the restaurant from wasn't real. He'd been paying his mortgage to someone but had no idea who.

Although I'm sure you can guess who it was.

Clarence was now operating a business he couldn't afford, and he was ruined. He soon went back to Aurora, where his wife filed for divorce.

With Clarence out of the way, the restaurant and the third floor were free to be used to cash in on the World's Fair. Holmes rented out the restaurant, charging an outrageous amount for the rent, and at first, even tried to get someone else to run the hotel for him.

Delos Mateson and Charles Gove had come to Chicago with the intention of starting a hotel for the fair, but when they found Holmes' third floor was for rent, they made him an offer. The two signed a promissory note of $275, which was to cover a mortgage on furniture in lieu of the first month's rent of $300. The two men moved into the building and got to work on April 20, less than two weeks before the scheduled opening of the fair.

But they soon began to have buyer's remorse.

Gove later recalled:

Shortly after we moved in, and before we finished it, things began to look suspicious. Several times in the morning, I found in vacant rooms articles of furniture that were not there the night previous. I wondered at this, and upon looking around, found large quantities of new goods of every description stored between the walls in different parts of the building.

Holmes, feeling safe from his creditors, no longer bothered to hide his ill-gotten goods. And Clarence Phillips, who had not yet vacated the restaurant, got a little bit of revenge. He showed Mateson and Gove a newspaper article about Holmes that told the story of the recent search for stolen items in the Castle. When the two attempted to talk to Holmes about it, he took them to his office and told them to wait, explaining that his secretary would be in to explain in a moment. They waited and waited, then finally gave up and left.

On May 15, less than a month after moving in, they packed up the furniture they'd brought with them and moved out. They never paid off that promissory note, but when Holmes used the note as security on another loan he never paid, Mateson and Gove were dragged into the ever-growing circus of lawsuits that summer.

When they left the Castle, the fair had only been open for two weeks, and the rooms had only been partially furnished. It seems unlikely the hotel hosted even a single guest before they left.

But it would – and the legend of the "Murder Castle" would soon start to grow.

 AS THE GATES TO THE COLUMBIAN EXPOSITION OPENED TO allow the hordes of tourists access to the wonders of the White City, H.H. Holmes was making his brief foray into the hotel business.

There are no greater stories told about Holmes than those about the terrifying inner workings of his World's Fair Hotel. Those stories first began to appear in the wake of Holmes' arrest – which occurred a long time after the Castle had been built.

Based on the wild tales often printed as fact in the scandal sheets that often passed as newspapers in the 1890s, it's hard to say just how much of the stories was fact, how much was fiction, and how much was based on wild speculation created from off-handed comments by police detectives, city officials, and the morbid curious.

But it does seem obvious from putting together an array of all different kinds of accounts that Holmes had something devious in mind when the Castle's third floor was built – and it wasn't just for storing furniture that he'd bought on credit and planned to sell for cash.

We do have to admit, though, that we have no idea how many people actually stayed at the hotel between the time it was vacated by the first hotel operators who were foolish enough to lease the space from Holmes and when it was closed at the end of the summer. There could have been a handful of guests or hundreds – no records were left behind. Based on the guest lists of other such places at the same time, it may have been a lot of people.

The wilder tales about the Castle say that dozens of Holmes' guests never made it back home after the fair, but no one can know that. They just can't. But there were a lot of people who went missing in the wake of the fair, and there were many reasons for that. There were small-town folks, lured by the bright lights of the city, who stayed in Chicago. There were others, having exhausted their savings to get to the fair, who decided to start over somewhere else. And then there were the really unlucky ones who met with foul play while in Chicago, while on their way home, or before they even got to the fair, traveling with their life savings tightly rolled up in a pocket or purse, who didn't keep that cash for long.

People did disappear during the 1893 exposition – this is an established fact – but it was much easier to disappear and start a new life back then than it is today. But what if some of those who disappeared did go to Englewood – and never left? What if they had been guests at the Castle during their trip to the fair and then were never heard from again?

What if?

We can never know for certain that Holmes killed hotel guests during the World's Fair, but if he did, he had the perfect place to do it.

Pipes were later found that pumped gas into the sleeping rooms on the third floor – and they were not for the lights. There were control valves in Holmes' office below. The gas could have been used for the purpose of robbery and to incapacitate the sleeping guests, just in the same way that chloroform could have been used to knock them out.

There were chutes between the walls that led to the basement – and they weren't for laundry. Holmes kept a medical table down there, as well as all the tools for autopsies. He had attended medical school, so this might be considered a hobby – a weird one, but still a hobby – but we also know that he frequently sold articulated skeletons to doctors and medical schools, and they didn't come from corpses he'd obtained by legitimate methods.

Those not turned into medical specimens could have been dissolved in quicklime or burned in the very large furnace that Holmes had obtained for his glass-bending scheme – you'll recall the one the technician described as just the right size for a human body.

But if Holmes did claim dozens of victims at his hotel, why would he do it?

One word: Greed.

He had no morals and no conscience. He also murdered for convenience, when someone became a threat to him, or they'd outlived their usefulness. He never thought twice about it because he had no feelings of guilt. His need for money was insatiable, and it was impossible for him to legally – or illegally-- get enough money to satisfy his needs.

Guests who brought valuables to his "hotel" – cash, jewelry, watches, etc. – were nothing more than a source of income to him. They had something he wanted, and it never crossed his mind that he shouldn't have it. He had no problem with committing murder to satisfy his greed, which is the reason why the number of victims he claimed – during the World's Fair and otherwise -- will never truly be known.

And that's one of the reasons that H.H. Holmes remains one of the most frightening serial killers in American history.

THERE IS ONE OTHER THING ABOUT H.H. HOLMES THAT WE CAN say without doubt and never argue about – that he was a pathological liar. He was simply incapable of telling the truth about anything. He lied about even the simplest things, largely because lies were the tools of his trade, as they are for every swindler and con artist. There was nothing he said that could be trusted or accepted at face value.

For this reason, there is no chronicle of Holmes' life and crimes that can be accepted as completely accurate. Each of us who dares to try and present a *true* picture of his life simply does the best that he or she can.

Personally, I have written likely half a dozen accounts of Holmes' life. Every one of them is different because I learn new things. I've also found out some things I once thought were true are impossible, far-fetched, or lies. I wrote it again, and then I wrote it once more, twice, three times. Each time, though, I believe I've gotten closer to the truth – in fact, I think I'm finally there.

I haven't done it alone, of course. I've ferreted out stories from newspapers, dozens of accounts, family members of the characters in our story, and by trying to rule out what accounts given by Holmes were truth and which ones were fiction. To be honest, though, I think pretty much everything that came out of his mouth was fiction or at least partially so.

And it's because of all the lies he told over the years that we can never be sure just when he met a young woman named Minnie Williams, whose murder, he stated in his later "confession" – well, one of his confessions -- was his only regret.

If we believe Holmes' version of the story, he was introduced to her in New York City in 1888 while engaged in underhanded business dealings using the name Edward Hatch. This wasn't true.

Or it may have been in Boston one year later, when he was traveling under the alias of Harry Gordon. This wasn't true either.

On some occasions, he claimed to have met her even earlier, on a trip to Mississippi in 1886. He didn't.

And once, he told the truth and admitted that he hadn't met her until the day when a local employment agency sent her to his office in response to an advertisement that he placed in search of a stenographer.

We can accept this as the truth because we know for certain that Minnie Williams was in Chicago in early 1893, and we know she took Emeline Cigrand's former job as Holmes' private secretary. And, like Emeline, she became his mistress a short later.

As with Emeline, there are several misconceptions about Minnie Williams. Some accounts have suggested that she was a prostitute, which was not the case. Others say – based on the speed at which she started an affair with Holmes – that she was "worldly" or "morally impaired" – phrases used to "slut shame" women at the time. But according to everyone who knew her, she was quite the opposite.

Minnie had never had any serious suitors as a young woman and spent little time around men. Most assumed she had no interest in romantic love. Friends and acquaintances described her as being extremely naïve and guileless. When you combine those things, you end up describing the perfect target for the suave and slippery H.H. Holmes.

Minnie Williams

But Minnie might have fooled everyone, perhaps even Holmes himself, for a time.

Minnie was a pretty girl, although she did not possess the widely acclaimed beauty of Emeline Cigrand. She was short and slightly plump, with light-brown hair and a smooth, chubby face. She had an air of simple sweetness about herself, which many called her most appealing feature.

Minnie may not have been as stunning as some of Holmes' other conquests, but she had one thing about her that more than made up for that fact – she was the heiress to a considerable fortune. It was fortune that she had gained through tragedy.

Minnie was born in Mississippi in 1865, not long after her father, H.B. Williams, saw the Confederacy that he served crumble in defeat. A younger sister, Anna, who everyone called Nannie, was born in 1871.

The sisters were very young when their father was killed in a railroad accident in 1872. Worse, their heartbroken mother died a short time later, leaving the Williams sisters as orphans. Soon, though, Minnie was taken to Dallas, Texas, and into the home of a kindly uncle, Dr. J.N.B. Williams. He raised her as his own child.

(Above) Minnie was enrolled at the Mansfield Male and Female College in Louisiana.

(Right) The Boston Conservatory, where Minnie studied music after she had graduated from college.

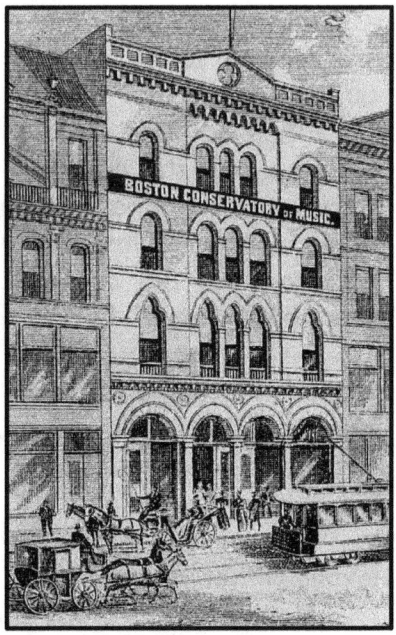

Her younger sister, Nannie, remained in Mississippi. She was adopted by another uncle, Methodist minister C.W. Black, and his wife. They'd never been able to have children of their own and gladly took the little girl into their home in Jackson.

Minnie wouldn't see her baby sister again for more than 15 years.

When Dr. Williams died in the late 1870s, Minnie –who was only 10 years old – inherited property in Fort Worth that was worth around $40,000. It was a large inheritance at the time, but unable to do anything with it at her age, she went to live with a kind family friend, John Massie, who would also care for her like a daughter for many years. He later enrolled her at the Mansfield Male and Female College, and when she finished there, she went to Massachusetts to study at the Boston Conservatory in 1886.

While at school, she received a letter from her uncle, Reverend Black, who filled her in on some of her family history, including the fact that she had a sister she didn't remember. When she finished at the conservatory in 1889, she traveled to Mississippi to see Nannie for the first time since they were small children.

Nannie, of course, had no memory of her older sister at all, but the two of them quickly made up for lost time. They became very close and spent the rest of the year together.

Minnie stayed in touch with her sister after she returned to Boston for postgraduate work at the New England Conservatory in 1890. It was around this time, John Massie wrote, that Minnie began writing to him for money. She had left her studies to start performing in the theater and needed the cash to start her own theatrical company.

Minnie's younger sister, Anna "Nannie" Williams

It quickly failed.

A friend of Minnie's from Texas noted that Minnie could be very willful and that no one could change her mind once she decided to do something. She added:

> *When she announced that she was going onstage, all her friends tried to dissuade her. I did not hear of it until after it had failed. The venture only lasted a few weeks and was the plan of a schoolgirl fresh from singing exercises at a conservatory who thought she could act. She found she could not.*

Even after the failure of her ambitions to run a theater company, though, she refused to quit acting. She traveled next to Denver and took the stage there, but her career only lasted a few weeks. According to John Massie, her next stop was Chicago in early 1893. And it was there, while looking for a legitimate job, that she met H.H. Holmes.

Minnie sent several letters to friends in Colorado that were dated early 1893, and each had return addresses on Chicago's North Side. The apartment she lived in the longest was on Roslyn Avenue, a small street near Lincoln Park.

A short time later, she wrote to John Massie and told him that she'd secured a job as a stenographer for the Campbell-Yates Company – which you might remember was one of Holmes' phony business fronts. Her signature first appears on company paperwork in February, when Holmes was being sued by Henry Yarrow, who owned a cigar stop at the Castle. Holmes was trying to push him out of it so that he could rent the building to the men who opened the first hotel there.

Like Emeline Cigrand, Minnie never lived in the Castle. Holmes kept her in the Roslyn Avenue apartment on the North Side. This kept her conveniently far away from the dubious business that Holmes was conducting in Englewood, much of which was being done in her name.

It's likely that to Minnie, Holmes at first seemed to be a dedicated, hard-working man who, on the surface, seemed to be highly successful. Of course, he made his money from swindling and cheating. His Castle seemed impressive – again, on the surface – but underneath the glossy exterior was poor and shoddy construction. It hadn't been built by determination and skill but by Holmes' frenzied, never-ending schemes.

Ironically, if the hard work and ingenuity that Holmes put into his various questionable dealings had been channeled into honest labor, he might legitimately have achieved the financial success that he so desperately wanted.

But Holmes was simply not wired that way. He was unable to do something honestly when cheating, lying, and stealing was so much easier. When his energies were not devoted to carrying out his many frauds, scams, and more sinister pursuits, he spent all his time trying to outwit his creditors.

Even when Holmes could afford to pay his debts, he simply refused to, but by late 1893 -- when the country was mired in the depression that followed a financial panic -- Holmes likely didn't have the funds to satisfy his debts, even if he had wanted to pay them, which, of course, he didn't.

But his many creditors became more insistent, and the lawsuits against him multiplied, causing him to become more desperate to stay one step ahead of them.

LATER THAT SPRING, NANNIE WILLIAMS BEGAN RECEIVING letters from her sister Minnie in Chicago. By then, Nannie was living in Texas, staying at the house John Massie had arranged for her sister. Minnie had visited her there a few times during her restless travels, and the sisters remained in close touch through letters.

Thanks to that constant flow of correspondence between the two young women, Nannie soon learned all about Minnie's fiancée, a dashing doctor named Harry Gordon. She wrote about how handsome and intelligent he was and added that he was quite wealthy.

Oddly, since Minnie worked as Holmes' secretary and dealt with company business every day, she had to know that his name wasn't Harry Gordon. This seems to imply – at least to me – that Minnie was complicit in at least some of Holmes' schemes. At the very least, she knew about them. At worst, she was taking part in them. So maybe, he wasn't hiding as much dubious business from her as we originally thought.

And maybe, Minnie wasn't the naïve pushover that her friends and family assumed she was either.

It's possible that Minnie expected to make a lot of money from her association with Holmes. Between her involvement in many of his plans and her continued requests to John Massie for money, it's possible that she saw Holmes not only as a co-conspirator but as her meal ticket. Perhaps she thought she could use him to relaunch her theatrical career, free of the past financial restraints. If true, then it's likely she knew the deals she was getting involved in weren't entirely legal.

As for her and Harry being engaged, it's possible that she was telling people they were so she could excuse her intimate relationship with Holmes. Or maybe Holmes had promised her that he'd marry her, as he did Emeline Cigrand. But if he did, I doubt she believed it. I think Minnie was aware of the fraudulent engagement and pretended they were getting married for financial reasons.

I think it's even possible that Minnie thought she was conning Holmes, not the other way around. If she did believe that, though, then she was almost as naïve as everyone thought she was. She was certainly no match for H.H. Holmes when it came to swindles. He was able to get her to put her signature on just about anything.

When describing Minnie, he later said that she was generous, loving, and kind and that he was touched by her "innocent and child-like nature." But I have doubts about the truth of this.

Some less-than-flattering stories later emerged about Minnie, including one told by Cora Quinlan, the daughter of Holmes' crony, Patrick Quinlan. Cora made it clear that Minnie openly flaunted her sexual relationship with Holmes, which made the claims of her "innocent, child-like nature" difficult to believe.

Cora said that she and her mother had moved to the Castle to be with her father in May 1893, and on the first night there, Holmes allowed them to use his office to sleep since their apartment wasn't ready for them yet. Cora thought it was very strange that there was a bed in his office – until she met Minnie Williams. It was clear, even to a child, that while she was told Minnie worked for Holmes, she certainly didn't act like she was employed by him.

Cora allowed her interviewer to use his imagination about what she meant when she referred to Holmes, Minnie, and the bed, but he got the point.

Clinton Sherman, a delivery driver who worked for Holmes, often saw Minnie around the Castle, and while others seemed to like her, he couldn't stand to be around her. Privately, she ordered him around, swore at him, and called him names, he said. Minnie once told him that he was as much of an animal as his horse. Clinton Sherman, I should mention, was African American, and Minnie grew up in Mississippi – the daughter of an officer in the Confederate army during the Civil War.

Minnie was apparently uninhibited, racist, and rude, but she was also involved, willingly or unwillingly, in Holmes' schemes. On paper, she became the owner of a property in Wilmette on which Holmes built a new house for his wife, Myrta, and daughter, Lucy, who was now 4 years old. Her signature appears on the deed, but it's impossible to know if she knew the house was for Holmes' family – or that he was cheating the construction companies involved.

In March – likely at Holmes' urging – Minnie wrote to John Massie and requested $3,000. Massie later said that he thought she'd put her theatrical dreams behind her and didn't understand why she'd need the money, but he gave it to her. He sold a small portion of the land she owned in Fort Worth and sent her the check, which was cashed, and then the full amount of it was loaned to Horace A. Williams – another alias of H.H. Holmes.

Meanwhile, Minnie had written again to her sister, who was now working as a teacher in Midlothian, Texas, and invited her to come to Chicago to see the World's Fair and then accompany her and Dr. Gordon on their honeymoon to Europe.

The invitation had been Holmes' idea.

Holmes controlled Minnie, just as he now controlled her property in Texas. But having a title to some real estate was not the same as having the cash it was worth in hand. The land needed to be turned into liquid income, but the 800 miles between Chicago and Fort Worth were a problem.

And the distance wasn't his only problem. There was something else between Holmes and Minnie's inheritance – her younger sister, Nannie.

From reading the letters that Minnie received from Nannie, Holmes had a feeling that Nannie had a much shrewder sense of the world than her older sister did. Despite being raised as the ward of a Methodist minister, she seemed suspicious of Holmes and his intentions. She knew that Minnie could make an easy target for a swindler, and Nannie seemed determined to make sure that didn't happen.

And while Nannie may have been worried about Holmes' intentions toward her sister, Holmes himself was aware of the threat that Nannie posed when it came to him getting his hands on Minnie's money.

If Minnie suddenly had an accident or disappeared, her sister would immediately raise the alarm with the authorities. He couldn't take that chance. The only way for his plan to move forward was to make sure that both Williams sisters were out of the way.

He took the first step in his plan by convincing Minnie to invite her sister to come and visit the fair with them in Chicago.

WHILE NANNIE WAS ON HER WAY TO CHICAGO, THE FIRST lawsuit was filed over the new house in Wilmette. The Weber and La Bahn brick company sued Minnie for nonpayment for the bricks used to construct the house. The suit stalled on June 7, though, because the company's attorneys were unable to find her so that she could be served with the paperwork.

Without telling anyone, Holmes had moved Minnie to a rented apartment in a house on Wrightwood Avenue. Holmes often stayed there, too, and they'd rented the place using the names "Mr. and Mrs. Harry Gordon."

Soon after, Nannie Williams arrived from Texas. She was greeted at the train by her sister and by Holmes, whose immediate brotherly warmth, as she called it, both surprised and disarmed her. Her concerns may not have vanished immediately, but they soon would.

Nannie was very excited to see the city, and Holmes insisted on taking her sightseeing right away. They spent several hours in downtown Chicago. Nannie was shocked by the huge number of carriages, carts, and wagons on the streets, the bustling crowd on the sidewalks, and the new skyscrapers that looked down at them

from high above. They drove along Lake Michigan and through Lincoln Park before turning onto Wrightwood Avenue.

Holmes took the sisters to the apartment he'd recently rented so Nannie could get settled. Holmes had temporarily vacated the place so that Minnie could share the apartment with her sister for the duration of Nannie's stay in the city. It was another indication to Nannie that her sister was in safe hands.

In fact, Nannie was soon so charmed by Holmes that any doubts she had about him disappeared. Within days of her arrival, she was referring to him as "Brother Harry."

On July 3, 1893, "Brother Harry" took "his girls" to the fair. Although Minnie had already attended the Exposition with Holmes a short time before, she was thrilled to see the fairgrounds again with her sister. Nannie, like all first-time visitors to the White City, was overwhelmed by the size and sheer spectacle of the place. They spent an entire day, seeing as many things as time would allow, and ended the evening watching a spectacular fireworks display from the roof of the Manufacturers and Liberal Arts Building.

The following day, Holmes prompted Nannie to write a letter to her Aunt Lucy in Mississippi, the wife of the uncle who had raised her. Most of the letter talked about the honeymoon trip that she was going to take with her sister and brother-in-law. Holmes had filled her in on the itinerary, which would be taking them to Old Orchard Beach, the popular resort area in Maine, and to London, Paris, and Berlin. Brother Harry would take care of all the expenses, she wrote, so her aunt and uncle wouldn't need to worry about anything.

Holmes wanted it to be clear to her family that they would be traveling for quite some time, and so, if Nannie was out of touch, there was no need to worry because she'd be safe and sound with Minnie and dear Brother Harry.

On July 4, the day the letter was written, Minnie left town for a short trip to Milwaukee on company business. Holmes and Nannie decided to visit the fair again in her absence. That evening, Nannie told the landlord's daughter that they'd taken a ride on the massive Ferris Wheel that was the centerpiece of the Midway.

The next morning, after Minnie had returned, she and her sister were spotted taking a walk near the house. Nannie was

excited because she was finally going to see Brother Harry's fabulous office building in Englewood. He'd promised to give her a guided tour of the place.

It's assumed that Holmes took both women to the Castle on July 5. If that's true, the building must've looked very drab to Nannie when compared to the amazing pavilions she'd seen at the fair. As far as we know, he led the two women inside and perhaps even offered them a tour of the unusual hallways, the dreary basement – and perhaps even the airtight vault near his office.

We can only assume he did these things because after they were spotted taking that walk on the morning of July 5, Minnie and Nannie Williams were never seen alive again.

ON JULY 6, SEVERAL TRANSACTIONS REGARDING THE ownership of the property in Wilmette were made in Minnie's name. She also signed a promissory note that was payable for more than $6,000 to Horace A. Williams – the man who didn't exist. The transactions had all been arranged by Minnie's fiancée, Dr. Gordon.

On July 7, attorneys for Weber and Le Bahn showed up at the Castle, still looking for Minnie. E.H. Robinson, who ran the drugstore on the first floor, said he hadn't seen her in a while and suggested asking Holmes for her whereabouts. He would know where to find her.

That same day, the landlord on Wrightwood Avenue discovered that the Gordons' apartment was empty. A note had been left behind by Brother Harry, explaining they'd had to move out.

Soon after, a trunk that belonged to Nannie arrived at the train depot, and a notice of its arrival was sent to Wrightwood Avenue. No one claimed it, though, and the bag sat in the Chicago express office for more than a year.

This same week Kate Durkee – the Holmes accomplice in name only – came to town to visit the World's Fair. She called at the Castle to see Myrta. Of course, she wasn't there, but she did see Holmes. A few days later, she made plans to meet Myrta and go to Wilmette with her. That afternoon, though, she received a telegram saying that her sister-in-law in Omaha was very sick, and she left that evening. Holmes took her to the train and helped her to get her luggage on board. That was the last time she ever saw him.

By then, Myrta had already moved into her house in Wilmette with her daughter and her mother, having no idea that it was owned by a woman who had been passing herself off as her husband's wife. Of course, Myrta also had no idea she wasn't legally married to Holmes either.

As for Holmes, he was making other plans – plans that didn't involve Chicago. His audacious swindles and elaborate schemes to dodge process servers were finally catching up to him. The curtain was closing on the Castle, but Holmes had one more fraud up his sleeve.

In July 1893, Holmes hired a man named Joe Owens to do odd jobs around the Castle – jobs for which, of course, he was never paid. After nailing boards over doorways, removing broken copying machines from the basement, and helping Holmes move his office to a room on the third floor that had been lined with asbestos, Joe was given Minnie's old job as secretary of the Campbell-Yates company.

He said that Holmes freely admitted to him that the company was a dummy corporation organized so that insurance on the Castle wouldn't be in his own name. He instructed Joe to tell the insurance companies that he had met Minnie Williams – even though he hadn't – and to say that H.S. Campbell was a real person, even though he knew perfectly well that Campbell was Holmes himself. Joe later said:

Holmes had a hypnotizing way about him. He had a certain influence over me that I cannot explain, but through which I did just about anything he asked me to.

I have a simpler explanation about why Holmes told Joe Owens all these secrets, and it has nothing to do with his supernatural powers of hypnotism – he probably didn't think Joe would survive the fire that occurred on August 13, 1893.

Joe was one of the only people in the building when it happened. That's the first clue. The few others were long-time residents and employees of the businesses in the building. If anyone had been in the hotel rooms on the third floor, they were gone when the fire occurred.

Mrs. Lawrence, the tenant in the building who'd been close with Emeline Cigrand, later said that a guest who was sick had been staying there but, fortunately, had left the day before the fire.

Mrs. Lawrence believed that Holmes had arranged for the blaze and named Patrick Quinlan

Patrick Quinlan – the "dirty little Irishman" – who served as the janitor at the Castle.

– the dirty little Irishman, as she called him – as the one who likely lit the match. She claimed that in the days before the fire, Holmes had removed furniture, books, papers, and valuables from the third floor. He even made Patrick remove the knobs and locks from the doors and fixtures, and a marble sink and a porcelain tub from the bathroom.

Holmes would claim that an arsonist had set fire to the building, but he didn't know who the culprit was, but Mrs. Lawrence didn't believe that for a second.

By the time the fire department had arrived and put out the blaze, the third floor of the Castle had been mostly gutted. But it wasn't a total loss. The second floor was only slightly scorched, and the ground-floor shops were unharmed.

This was not the result that Holmes had in mind. He had thousands of dollars of fire insurance on the Castle with four different companies. He'd wanted the Castle to burn to the ground.

When it didn't, there was little or no money in the policies for him. If he made any money at all, it was a small sum. Some of the claims spent years being dragged through the courts, and by the

The temporary roofline that was added to the building after the August 1893 fire. It was never removed and appears in every photo of the Castle.

time any rulings could be made, the insurance companies had learned that H.S. Campbell wasn't a real person, so any policies in his name were void.

Work soon began to try and clean up the mess from the fire. An unsightly temporary roof was added to the building to protect the interior. If you're wondering what that looked like, you've probably seen it. It was never removed. There are no drawings or photographs that were taken of the Castle before the fire in August 1893, when the Castle was in its heyday. Every photograph of it you have ever seen comes from later – after Holmes' was known across the country. It was then that it was documented in drawings and in photos. They are the only images that survive of the Castle today.

While the cleanup was happening, Holmes discovered that trying to defraud several insurance companies at once was a terrible idea. By the time the World's Fair ended in October, two of those companies were investigating him carefully and were beginning to unravel his fraud.

In addition, his effort to burn down the Castle -- as most suspected he'd done – had spurred his many creditors into action. More than two dozen of them joined forces and contacted the Lafayette Mercantile Company, a collection agency, and general manager George Chamberlain began looking into Holmes' activities.

Holmes was starting to feel the heat and, for once, it seemed the stress from juggling so many schemes at the same time was starting to get to him.

In the wake of the fire, workmen had tossed charred pieces of debris down from the roof and next to a small home where a man named John Nichols lived with his family. Dust from the falling debris covered everything in the Nichols house.

Nichols began asking around for Patrick Quinlan so he could complain. Quinlan couldn't be found, but Nichols' complaints made it back to Holmes, who exploded into a rage.

Holmes waited in an alley between the Castle and the house, watching for Nichols. When he finally saw him, Holmes charged up to him and grabbed hold of his shirt in a clenched fist. He shouted into the man's face, "Nichols! You're the fellow that has been giving me a lot of trouble and cost me $50 by having to get a chute made!"

Nichols insisted he'd done nothing wrong and tried to explain, but Holmes drew a revolver and jammed it up against the other man's stomach.

Would he have killed him? We'll never know. A police officer who was walking past saw the confrontation and took the gun away from Holmes. Nichols refused to press charges. Before this, he'd always had a good relationship with Holmes, and even two years later, when others in the neighborhood were saying terrible things about Holmes in the press, Nichols refused to say a word. He knew the incident was completely out of character for the man he knew. Holmes was reaching a breaking point.

But it was only going to get worse.

Soon after, druggist E.H. Robinson happened to run into Holmes on Van Buren Street in downtown Chicago. Holmes was in one of his disguises, but Robinson recognized him. Holmes asked him for a favor – he needed money, and if Robinson would pay him up front for two months' rent on the drugstore, he'd count it as three months paid.

And there was more. One of the insurance companies that Holmes attempted to defraud hired an investigator named F.G. Cowie to find out more about him. During the fall of 1893, Cowie and his deputies shadowed Holmes throughout the city and dug into the inner workings of the Campbell-Yates Company. Cowie later said:

I was continually running across evidence that Holmes was leading a double life. In fact, at times, it might be said he was leading a quadruple life.

The Plaza Hotel on the South Side, where Carrie Pitezel posed as Minnie Williams

Cowie searched in vain for the men who were listed as the company's board of directors. None of them seemed to exist, although Cowie believed that he'd found the company's secretary, Minnie Williams. He claimed she was living at the Plaza Hotel on Lake Avenue, near 38th Street, with Holmes and a man named Benjamin Pitezel. It was a strange story, not because of that, but because Minnie had, by all accounts, disappeared months earlier.

It was, of course, not Minnie. It was Ben's wife, Carrie, who'd found herself being dragged along unwittingly into several of Holmes' schemes. Holmes even gave Carrie some of Minnie's old dresses and hats, claiming that his "Cousin Minnie" had gone back East.

And Carrie wasn't the only one who played this role. Patrick Quinlan's wife, Ella, was also pressed into service to pose as Minnie on several occasions.

Holmes wanted to create as much confusion as possible. He was stalling for time, gathering as much money as he could before he left town.

In November, Holmes was hauled into George Chamberlain's office at the Lafayette Mercantile Company with 25 of his creditors. But Holmes had a deal to offer them – to make things right, he would sign over some very valuable real estate to settle his debts. The deeds were to property owned by Minnie Williams and Kate Durkee.

By then, no one trusted Holmes. The creditors assumed the name on the deeds were fake, so Holmes spent more time obtaining documents for them that showed the women were real. The property was accepted as payment against nearly $50,000 of Holmes' debt. However, there was a clerical error on one of the deeds, making it necessary to send the paperwork back to Holmes for correction. It had not been an accident. Holmes had purposely included the mistake so he could buy himself a little more time.

Another meeting was called, and Holmes was reminded by Chamberlain that the plan had been made to settle his debt so that he could avoid arrest. He needed to return to the office with either the corrected deeds or the matching funds. If he didn't, he was going to be turned over to the police.

Holmes didn't bring the deeds or the cash, and he wasn't arrested – he simply didn't show up for the meeting.

He left town instead.

Holmes returned to the Chicago area several times over the course of the next year, usually to visit his wife, Myrta, and their daughter, Lucy, or to take care of some small bit of business, but as he told jeweler Charles Davis, "Chicago has become just a little too hot."

But Davis never assumed anything would happen to the man who seemed to have nine lives. He readily admitted that Holmes was a man the police certainly ought to get – but Davis always assumed he was much too smart to get caught.

And for a while, he was right.

AS WE RETURN TO THE SUBJECT OF HOLMES' CASTLE, THIS brings us full circle in this chapter. For the most part, it doesn't play a role in our story for at least the next two years. After the fire, Holmes had little use for it and rarely ever set foot in the place again. It may never have been the busy hotel that legends have made it out to be, but there is still plenty of reason to think there was more going on there than most people knew.

At this point in time, Holmes hadn't yet been accused of a single murder, yet we know that he had committed several. Things were happening with the Castle, but they were still a secret.

Well, a secret to most people anyway.

Stories were later spread, usually by delivery drivers, about mysterious trunks that were carried out of the building – trunks that smelled oddly or whose contents made unsettling sounds when they were jostled back and forth. Most of them were likely just trunks filled with things Holmes had bought on credit and never paid for, but there were others that may have been filled with something else.

When Joe Owens had been questioned about the fire that occurred in the Castle, he told investigators that he believed it had been set partially for the insurance money – but he also thought an attempt had been made to burn it because there were secrets in that building that Holmes didn't want anyone to know.

He refused to say any more on that subject, but like the delivery drivers who told their tales, he did hint at times when he helped Holmes or Ben Pitezel carry suspicious trunks out to wagons – trunks from which there came a smell so foul that it unsettled his stomach.

He was certain that smell had been the stench of death.

IT'S THE EARLY MORNING HOURS OF AUGUST 31, 1888, AND A thick fog rolls along the streets and into the alleyways of London's East End. A woman walks down a dark street alone.

The sound of music from one of the nearby dance halls can be heard in the distance. There's the sound of a man calling out and a woman laughing, but those sounds are far away from this lonely street. The only sound here is the tapping of the woman's worn-down shoes as she walks along the cobblestones. A few coins are clenched in her hand, with which she hopes to pay for her lodging for the night.

But then, there's another sound, the light footsteps of someone else – a man. The woman turns to face him, but before she can get a look at his face, his hands close around her neck, and they begin to squeeze. She gasps for air as the man's gloved hands tighten their grip. Her vision flickers, then fades, and everything goes black as she slumps to the pavement.

The man roughly lets her fall, and then bends down over her, pulling away her clothes. A hand reaches into his coat and emerges with something long, silvery, and sharp. The blade of the knife reflects the dim gaslight from a nearby lamp – and he begins his bloody work.

That man will soon be known as "Jack the Ripper."

The murders that have been attributed to him have become known throughout the world and remain some of the most infamous unsolved murders in history. Before he vanished without a trace, at least five women met their end by the blade of this unknown man – and some believe the true number of his victims may be even higher.

His first, though, was Mary Ann Nichols, who was killed at 3:40 A.M. on August 31 in the Whitechapel district of London's East End.

AT THE TIME OF THE MURDER, WHITECHAPEL WAS OVERFLOWING with immigrants and refugees from Ireland, Russia, and other areas of Eastern Europe. By 1888, more than 80,000 people were living in this small, crowded neighborhood, and with work and housing conditions worsening, most were plunged into poverty. More than half the children born in the East End died before they were five years old, and robbery, violence, and alcoholism were commonplace. These conditions drove many women to prostitution to survive.

It was estimated that there were at least 62 brothels and 1,200 women working as prostitutes in Whitechapel. There were also about 8,500 people sleeping in common lodging houses in Whitechapel each night, making them essentially homeless. The cost of a bed for one night was roughly four pence. Working as a prostitute was often the only way that a woman could come up with the coins to snag one of these "first come/ first served" beds for the night.

Mary Ann Nichols was one of those women. She was a native of London who spent a good deal of the 1880s driftless and alone. Her marriage to a man named William Nichols had fallen apart after the birth of their sixth child, when William began sleeping with a neighbor woman. Mary Ann began drinking and was unable to stop. She left home and began a dismal journey through London's workhouses and hospitals, sleeping rough in Trafalgar Square with countless other homeless people, and ended up as a prostitute in the East End when she reached the end of the line.

Mary Ann Nichols

By August 31, 1888, she was stumbling toward a lodging house – having earned and then drunk away the four pence she needed several times that day – and ran into an acquaintance at 2:30 A.M. at the corner of Junction Street and Whitechapel Road. It was the last time she was seen alive by anyone but her killer.

Just over an hour later, two men walking west along Buck's Row, saw what they thought was an abandoned canvas cover lying on the street. Closer inspection, though, revealed it to be the body of a woman. Her throat was cut, and she was lying in a pool of blood.

But it was only when her clothing was removed at the local mortuary were the horrible incisions on Mary Ann's body revealed. Her abdomen had been sliced so deeply that her intestines threatened to burst out of her. The police were stunned by the unusual degree of brutality – it was unlike what they were used to seeing in this part of the city – but they had no idea then how common it would turn out to be.

One of the common misconceptions about "The Five" – as the Ripper's historically accepted victims have been dubbed – is that

Annie Chapman

they were all prostitutes. They weren't. The tragically homeless of Whitechapel far outnumbered the sex workers who lived out their terrible lives there.

Annie Chapman – the Ripper's second victim – had once lived a better life. Far from the slums of Whitechapel, she had spent her youth, and later, part of her married life, in Windsor, not far from the royal castle. She had never been wealthy, but she'd had a decent life. But somewhere along the way, Annie's future veered off course, and she became estranged from her family and addicted to drink. By 1888, she was isolated, starving, and suffering from chronic illnesses. On September 5, 1888, she got into a physical brawl with another woman, Eliza Cooper, over a disputed bit of soap. She was badly beaten, and her corpse would later show signs of it.

Her body was discovered on September 8, just after sunrise, in an unsecured yard behind 29 Hanbury Street. It is believed she went there looking for a place to sleep.

Like Mary Ann Nichols, her throat had been cut. Annie's abdomen had been sliced open, and a section of the flesh from her stomach was pulled away from her body and placed over her left shoulder. Another section of skin and flesh had been placed over her right shoulder. An autopsy also revealed that her uterus and sections of her bladder and vagina had been removed.

Just like before, her killer left no clues behind.

The Ripper's next two victims – Elizabeth Stride and Catherine Eddowes – were both killed on the same night, or rather during the early morning hours of September 30, 1888.

Elizabeth had ended up on the uncertain streets of Whitechapel after an unfortunate early life and the death of her

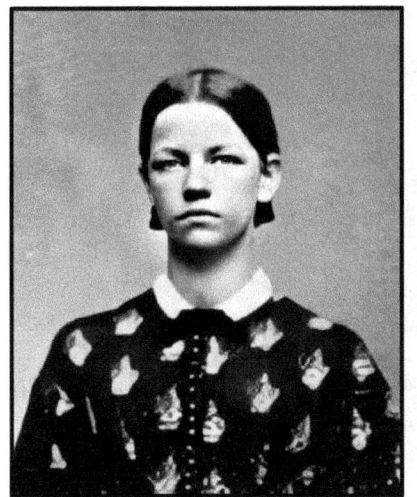 

(Left) Elizabeth Stride and (Right) Catherine Eddowes. Their bodies were found on the same early morning hours of September 30, 1888.

husband. The couple had attempted to prosper in the hostile environment of the East End with a coffee shop, but it closed after she became a widow, leaving her homeless.

She was last seen on Berner Street on the night before her murder, dodging an evening rain. The next sighting of her had been by a grocery man whose horse shied away from something in the street outside of Dutfield's Yard. He got down from his wagon, lit a match, and peered closely, finding a woman with a sliced throat. No other damage had been done to her body, which led detectives to surmise that she hadn't been a victim of the same killer – or that he'd been interrupted in his work.

It was the latter that was likely the case. The Ripper soon struck again, and this time, he took his time.

On September 29, Catherine Eddowes had been arrested for public drunkenness after a police officer found her passed out in the street. After a few hours at Bishopsgate police station, Catherine was slightly recovered from her binge and was ready to be released. If only she had stayed behind bars, her life might have been saved.

Mitre Square, where the body of Catherine Eddowes was discovered.

Instead, though, she walked out of the station at just after 1:00 A.M. and started walking in the direction of Mitre Square, where her body would be discovered less than an hour later.

The state of her corpse was much worse than that of Elizabeth Stride. Her throat had been cut from ear to ear, and her abdomen sliced apart by one long incision. Her intestines had been pulled out and placed over her right shoulder. One section of intestine had been completely detached and placed between her body and left arm.

Her left kidney and most of her uterus were also removed. Her face was disfigured with her nose cut off, her cheek slashed and two cuts carefully removing her eyelids. Two triangular incisions— which pointed towards Catherine's eyes—had also been carved on each of her cheeks. A severed piece of one ear lobe was found inside of her clothing. The police surgeon who conducted the autopsy stated that in his opinion, the mutilations would have taken at least five full minutes to complete by a man with surgical knowledge and medical skill.

A team of detectives fanned out from Mitre Square, working their way backward into Whitechapel. They discovered two clues in their search.

One of them was a bloody piece of apron that might have belonged to Catherine – but no one knows for sure. For this reason, whenever you see it announced that someone has revealed the identity of Jack the Ripper based on DNA from the apron, take it with a very large grain of salt. The apron may not have been

Catherine's, and even if it was, it was badly handled by the police at the time, who had no concept of dealing with forensic evidence.

In the alleyway where the apron was found, graffiti was written on the wall with chalk. At first glance, it appeared to be antisemitic and read:

> *THE JUWES ARE THE MEN THAT WILL NOT BE BLAMED FOR NOTHING*

You might have noticed that spelling of the word J-U-W-E-S. Was it a misspelling or something else? Because there is a word that's spelled that way. But I'll come back to it.

Initially, some believed the message implied that a Jew or Jews, in general, were responsible for the murders. This kind of graffiti was common in Whitechapel. The influx of immigrant Jews had led to a lot of prejudice against them. So, was it written by the killer when he dropped the apron – or did the two so-called clues have nothing to do with the murders and just happened to be there?

Police Commissioner Charles Warren ordered the writing to be washed off the wall before dawn. It was assumed that he did this to prevent an antisemitic riot in the East End, but he might have recognized the word "JUWES" for what it could have been – spelled correctly and not a mistaken spelling for Jews.

It's been suggested that the word referred to the three killers of Hiram Abiff, a legendary figure in the world of Freemasonry. This particular phrase would only have significance to a high-level Freemason, like Charles Warren, and it was a clue that a fellow Mason like himself committed the murders. It's been suggested that Warren – based on the rules of the secret society – would have had to protect this man until he could be stopped in a non-public way.

But we're getting way off track here. The point is that the apron and the graffiti may be important – or just as easily mean nothing at all. So, keep that in mind.

By the night of the double murder, nearly everyone in London knew the killer's name was "Jack the Ripper." That was a name that came from the newspapers. Reporters who wrote about the murders knew the killer needed a name. This was the first major murder story that had international appeal, so journalists tried everything to keep the story on the front pages – including giving him a moniker that sounded shocking.

As the murders were being reported, the police, newspapers, and others received hundreds of letters about the case. Some letters were well-intentioned offers of advice as to how to catch the killer, but the vast majority were either hoaxes or generally useless.

Dozens of those letters claimed to have been written by the killer himself, but only three of them have been taken seriously – the "Dear Boss" letter, the "Saucy Jacky" postcard, and the "From Hell" letter.

The "Dear Boss" letter was sent to the Central News Agency on September 25 and was forwarded to Scotland Yard. At first, the police assumed it was a hoax, but when Catherine Eddowes was found three days after the letter's postmark with a section of one ear cut from her body, the promise of the letter writer to "clip the lady's ears off" got their attention. But the letter writer – who signed his name as

The "Dear Boss" letter, believed to be one of the three letters that might be authentic and written by the notorious killer.

"Jack the Ripper" for the first time – promised to send some ears to the police, but he never did.

The "Saucy Jacky" postcard was mailed on October 1 and was also sent to the Central News Agency. It arrived that same day and made mention of the "double event" – the two murders of Elizabeth Stride and Catherine Eddowes – but no one knows for sure if this was written in advance of the murders or after, taking advantage of the publicity to claim "Saucy Jack" had killed the two women.

The "Saucy Jack" postcard

The "From Hell" letter was the most disgusting of the three. It was sent to George Lusk, the leader of a Whitechapel Vigilance Committee that was also hunting the killer, on October 16. The handwriting and the style of this letter is unlike the other two, and it arrived with a small box, which George opened and discovered contained half of a human kidney. The

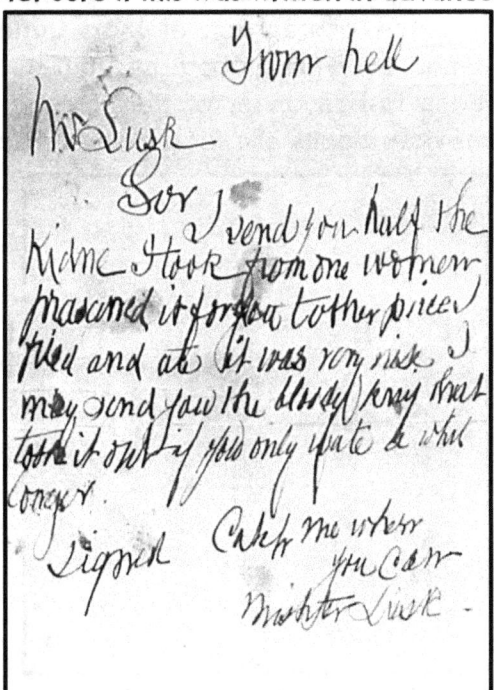

The infamous "From Hell" letter that was sent to George Lusk

writer claimed he'd "fried and ate" the other half.

Some say the kidney belonged to Catherine Eddowes, while others dismiss it as a practical joke. The kidney was examined by Dr. Thomas Openshaw of the London Hospital, who determined that it was human and from the left side of the body – but nothing else.

Years later, the police suspected that the first two letters were written by a journalist, coining the killer's name, and keeping the story alive. But no one could ever debunk the ominous "From Hell" letter, and it remains a mystery to this day.

Just like the identity of the killer himself.

OF ALL THE RIPPER'S VICTIMS, HIS FIFTH AND LIKELY LAST, MARY Jane Kelly, remains the most mysterious. Her death made her famous, but her backstory is mostly unknown.

The photograph of Mary Jane's corpse on her bed, with almost everything about her that made her human entirely gone, is the last reminder of the Ripper's killings. In a break from his previous habits, the Ripper went inside to kill, and he apparently took the time to satisfy his murderous lusts because he knew he wouldn't be interrupted.

Mary had been living in a squalid room at 13 Millers Court with Joseph Barnett, a fishmonger whom she had a relationship with. But Joseph had moved out a few weeks earlier after learning that Mary had returned to prostitution to make money.

Living upstairs from Mary's flat, Elizabeth Prater heard a cry of murder at about 4:00 A.M. on November

The house where Mary Jane Kelly had been living – and where her body was found – at 13 Millers Court.

(Above) An illustration of Mary Jane Kelly, implying she was a prostitute with the phrase "Lost Woman."

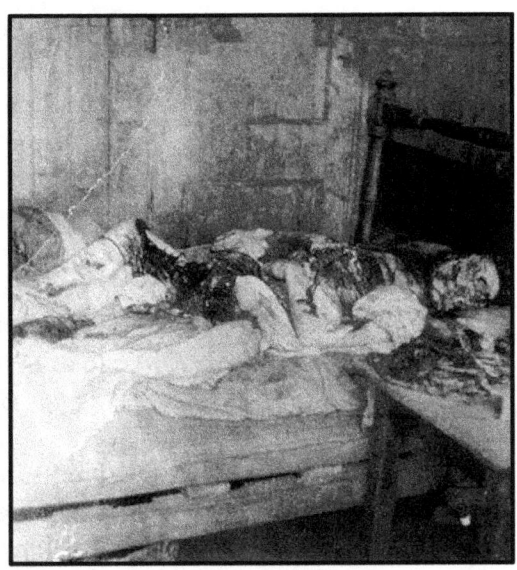

(Right) The savaged body of Mary Jane Kelly. The killer had mutilated her so badly she no longer looked human.

9, but she did nothing about it. Mary's lifeless, mutilated body was discovered seven hours later.

Mary's face had been hacked beyond all recognition. Her throat had been severed down to the spine, and her abdomen was emptied of all its organs. Her uterus, kidneys, and one breast had been placed beneath her head, and the other viscera from her body had been placed at her feet. Sections of her abdomen and thighs were on a table next to the bed. The killer had removed her heart and had taken it with him when he left the scene.

One police inspector who later reviewed the case concluded that the gore-soaked scene at Miller Court had finally broken the mind of the killer. Perhaps it did. It is certainly true to say that no other murder that occurred could be compared to it.

This meant that the identity of Jack the Ripper died with Mary Kelly, but that hasn't stopped anyone from trying to figure out who he was.

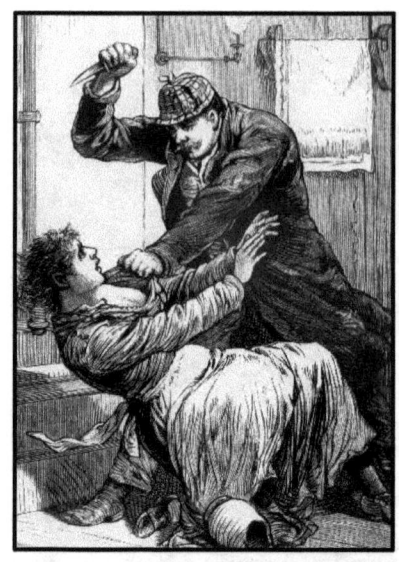

MOST RESEARCHERS BELIEVE THAT ALL FIVE MURDERS WERE THE work of a single killer. There were other murders – as many as six more – that occurred in Whitechapel at this time, but most don't feel they can be strongly connected to "The Five."

Others argue that the idea of five victims is a myth and that only three of the murders – Nichols, Chapman, and Eddowes – were committed by the same man. And still others say there was no "Jack the Ripper" at all, but a group of unrelated murders that were all blamed on one man – a shadowy figure that was never caught and might not have existed at all.

Even so, the search for Jack the Ripper as a lone, crazed killer has become a cottage industry in the century and a third since the murders occurred. There have been a lot of theories about his identity over the years.

Some claim it was a Whitechapel undertaker named Robert Mann, who examined the bodies after they had been found.

Sir Melville Macnaghten, the Assistant Commissioner of the London Metropolitan Police, claimed to know the identity of the Ripper. He named Montague John Druitt, a country doctor's son and young barrister who inexplicably drowned himself in the River Thames in early December 1888.

Another leading suspect was an artist named Walter Sickert. He took a keen interest in the crimes and told friends he believed he'd lodged in a room used by the killer because his landlady suspected a previous lodger of the killings. Even though his name has come up repeatedly evidence shows that he spent most of the fall of 1888 outside of Great Britain.

Some have also accused Prince Albert Victor, the Duke of Clarence and the grandson of Queen Victoria, of being the Ripper. He was alleged to have had a child with a woman who lived in Whitechapel. The belief is that the Royal family and the government tried to remove any evidence of the child by killing the baby and anyone who knew about it.

And there were butchers, doctors, and madmen also accused of the crimes. The theories just seem to have gotten wilder as the years have passed. There's even one outlandish claim that novelist Lewis Carroll – who wrote *Alice in Wonderland* – was the killer because he made anagrams of Jack the Ripper in his books.

There were also stories that blamed the murders on an American. Many in London believed that only an American could be saved enough to have committed such brutal crimes. The police even questioned members of Buffalo Bill Cody's Wild West Show, who were performing in the city around the time of the murders, believing that since the cowboys and Native Americans in the troupe carried knives, they might have used them on the five women.

Another man who was accused was Thomas Neill Cream – who lived in America but was a Canadian – but his method of serial murder was poison. Cream killed as many as 10 people in three countries, targeting mostly lower-class women, sex workers and pregnant women seeking abortions. He was convicted, sentenced to death, and was hanged in November 1892. Cream was named as the Ripper thanks to a rumor started by hangman

James Billington, who claimed that Cream's last words were "I am Jack the...", seemingly a confession to being Jack the Ripper. However, Billington is the only source for this alleged statement, and official records show that Cream was incarcerated in Illinois during the Ripper murders.

A less far-fetched suspect was a St. Louis man named Francis Tumblety. He was an American medical quack who earned a small fortune posing as an "Indian Herb" doctor throughout the United States and Canada. He was an eccentric self-promoter and was often in trouble with the law, was known to have a hatred of prostitutes, and had a collection of women's sex organs. Records state that he was in London during the time of the murders, which makes him one of the more intriguing suspects, even if he is rarely mentioned by historians.

Unfortunately, we can't say the same thing about another American who has, in recent years, also been accused of being Jack the Ripper.

The man's name is, of course, H.H. Holmes.

THERE ARE MANY REASONS WHY HOLMES WAS NOT JACK THE Ripper, not the least of which is the fact that Holmes didn't kill because of some sexual compulsion. He was not a madman or a psychopath. He was a sociopath, or perhaps even pure evil. He thought only of himself. He had no conscience, but he committed murder when he believed it was necessary – when someone was no longer useful, was a threat to him in some way, or simply because they had something he wanted.

The Ripper murders were maniacal slaughters, and the bodies of "The Five" were left on display for the public and the police to see. They were not even remotely similar to the murders committed by Holmes. His murders were secret homicides that he took great care to conceal. He didn't want the bodies of his victims to be discovered. He took great care to dispose of them – burning them, hiding them, and even turning them into medical specimens to hide any evidence that could point his way. After he was eventually captured, he told countless lies about his crimes and the number of people he killed. We will never know the extent of Holmes' crimes because the last thing he wanted to do was to put his victims on display and show them off to the public, the police, and the press.

Holmes may have been a monster, but he was *not* the same monster who committed the murders in Whitechapel.

At the time of his arrest, the police never suspected him of being Jack the Ripper. He was linked – mostly by rumor – to a lot of murders that he didn't commit, but not those committed in Whitechapel.

One of them was the murder of a woman named Kron who was killed in November 1893 in Wilmette and not far from where his wife, Myrta, lived. A police inspector named Fitzpatrick scoffed at the suggestion that Holmes had committed the crime. He told reporters, also mentioning a famous Chicago crime of the era, the murder of Dr. Cronin:

That theory is ridiculous. The murder of Mrs. Kron was done in too crude a manner for Holmes to have anything to do with it. He was a scientific criminal and would never think of engaging in a burglary or shooting a person in cold blood. You might as well connect him to the Cronin murder, or even with the Jack the Ripper horrors in London, England. No, Holmes had nothing to do with the case.

But you may be thinking these are just opinions. The police never connected Holmes to Jack the Ripper in the 1890s and, as you can see from what I have said about Holmes' motives, I don't think we can compare the Ripper murders to what Holmes did. The methods seem to be very different from one another – but that's my opinion.

I can dismiss the idea as much as I want, but is there any hard evidence that proves Holmes wasn't Jack the Ripper?

Yes, it turns out there is, but you might be wondering how the idea that H.H. Holmes was Jack the Ripper got started in the first place. It wasn't by police detectives, historical scholars, true crime buffs, or really anyone investigating the case. It came from a novel -- a work of fiction.

However, I think perhaps the identity of the book's author helped give the theory more substance than it should have had. The book was called *Bloodstains,* and it was written by Jeff Mudgett, a great-great-grandson of Holmes via Robert, the son he had with his first wife, Clara. In the novel, Jeff learns about his ancestor and discovers Holmes' diaries, from which he learns that Holmes escaped execution and lived to be nearly 100 using drugs he developed to maintain his youth.

It's while his character is reading the fictional diaries that he also notices that Holmes' handwriting matches the writing in the Ripper letters that were sent to the press and George Lusk in 1888.

The book had a small run but in the wake of books like The *Devil in the White City*, which had helped to make Holmes widely popular again, people mistook the novel for non-fiction. I'm not sure how they did it, but that's what happened.

At first, Mudgett freely admitted the theory wasn't real, and the diaries were just a plot device, but then he started pushing the theory that Holmes was the Ripper, which confused things even more. It wasn't long before he ended up in a limited documentary series called *American Ripper*, which made things even worse.

One thing you learn when dealing with television and documentaries is that the creator of the program can skew the story to turn into anything he wants it to be. In the end, the show never proved Holmes was the Ripper, but it never put much effort into telling the truth either.

And that truth is that Holmes never made it any closer to London than New Hampshire in 1888, when he made a trip there to visit members of his family. But, as we often find with Holmes himself, it's hard for many people to let truth get in the way of a good story.

But what about the evidence?

As we know, the Ripper murders occurred in the Whitechapel District of London's East End. All of them took place between the end of August and early November 1888.

So, where was Holmes during this time?

First, while there is no record of him ever leaving the country, that's still kind of vague, so we must go with what we do know and with what we can prove.

Holmes' daughter, Lucy, the child he had with second wife, Myrta, was born in Englewood on July 4, 1889. While there is, of course, no record of exactly when she was conceived, we do know that he was there for her conception nine months before she was born, which would have been August 1888.

On October 9, 1888 – right in the middle of the murders – Holmes registered to vote in Englewood. The court clerk wrote in the names in the voter rolls, so it's not his signature, but, by law, he had to be there, in person, to register. So, we know exactly where Holmes was on that day.

In the summer and fall of 1888, Holmes was also dealing with three lawsuits in Chicago. He was being sued by Simon Waixel (a

Chicago voter roll detail, dated October 8, 1888.

drug store supplier), George Kimball (a glass dealer), and Aetna Iron and Steel, who had provided construction and materials for the Castle the year before.

And there was one meeting with his attorney that we know occurred in late September or early October. We know this because, on September 24, Aetna Iron and Steel filed a lengthy affidavit about their business with Holmes, to which Holmes had to reply within 20 days. His attorney tried to object to this, but the court denied it. So, in accordance with the ruling, Holmes' answers were filed with the court on October 12, 1888. This means that Holmes had to have been in Chicago between September 24 and October 12.

Two of the Ripper's victims -- Elizabeth Stride and Catherine Eddowes – were both killed on September 30, so there's no way that Holmes could have been the killer. You didn't just hop on a plane back then and jet home. A trip from London to Chicago would have been by boat and train and would have taken at least a couple of weeks – if not longer.

I'm the first to admit that we'll never know the entire truth about H.H. Holmes, the Castle, or the murders he committed, but we can say for certain that he was *not* Jack the Ripper.

H.H. HOLMES WAS A MAN IN LOVE – OR SO HE SAID.

It's hard to believe that he could have found the time for another woman with everything he had going on in 1893. Not only had he taken over a World's Fair hotel that summer, but he was also building a home for his wife – well, one of his wives – Myrta, in Wilmette, pretending to be married to Minnie Williams – and then dispatching her and her sister, Nannie -- disposing of what may have been bodies from the back door of his building in Englewood, dealing with lawsuits and search warrants, and continuing a number of schemes and swindles that kept money flowing in and out of his many bank accounts.

And yet, somehow, Holmes squeezed in enough time to court an Indiana schoolteacher that he'd later marry in 1894.

Holmes was also, by this time, a man on the move. Chicago had, as he mentioned to one of his tenants in the Castle, become too hot for him, and he needed to get out of town and let things cool off. On his way out the door, he'd attempted to burn down the Castle and collect the insurance money, but that plan had failed miserably. He even ran into trouble trying to cash in on the damage, managing only to make the insurance companies that held his policies suspicious.

So, H.H. Holmes packed up and went west. It's tempting to think that maybe Holmes had gotten tired of being in trouble and had decided to marry again, forget about his old life, and get a fresh start on the right side of the law – only to fall back to his old ways. If that had been the case, we could have some sympathy for him, but that clearly was never his plan.

Holmes was just getting started on the next chapter in his criminal career.

HOLMES FINALLY SKIPPED OUT OF CHICAGO IN EARLY JANUARY 1894, leaving Myrta and Lucy in their new home in Wilmette. His first order of business was to head for Denver. During his time with Minnie Williams, he had learned the reason she had tried to continue her stage career in that Colorado city – she'd had an older brother there named Baldwin. He had recently died in a mining accident, and Minnie was the beneficiary of a payout from the company.

Of course, Minnie Williams wouldn't ever collect anything again, so Holmes decided that it was his duty to pick up the money on her behalf.

It was in Denver where Holmes married a young woman named Georgiana Yoke. He was using the name Henry Howard when the ceremony took place, but that wouldn't be the thing that made the marriage null and void – that would be the fact that she was the third woman he was married to at the same time.

But, as we know about Holmes, he never let anything like the law get in the way of what he wanted.

Holmes had met Georgiana back in early 1893, when she arrived in Chicago from Indiana. He'd had his hands full with

Minnie Williams – and a lot of other things – at the time and never had as much time for Georgiana as he would've liked. But, of course, all that changed when he decided to burn his bridges in Chicago and flee the city.

Georgiana Yoke had been born on October 17, 1869. She was a petite 23-year-old when Holmes met her, but she could never be called conventionally pretty. She had a sharp nose, slightly pointed chin, and blue eyes that were so large they were distracting. But she was a vibrant, intelligent woman who was so charming that people overlooked her physical imperfections.

Holmes' third wife – three at the same time, by the way – Georgianna Yoke

Well, not everyone. One reporter described her as a blond who, "would have passed as an unusually handsome woman except for her large eyes, which were almost considered a defect."

The newspapers also later spoke of her "adventurous" reputation, which in those days implied that she slept around. The reporter added, "She had a reputation in Seymour and Columbus, south of franklin, which is not altogether enviable."

This reputation was later disputed by everyone who knew her, saying that it was the product of small minds. It turns out that it's more likely that Georgiana was a headstrong woman who wasn't afraid to speak her mind, which was frowned on by most men in the 1890s.

An Indiana judge, who was also Georgiana's landlord at one time, praised the young women, saying that:

She was just one of those women who can make you like them. She was the most winning person and everybody who came into contact with her acknowledged the spell of her presence. She would make friends rapidly. She was not a woman of expensive tastes or distinguished manner. It was because she was so simple and elegant that people felt drawn to her.

The Siegal, Cooper & Co. Department Store, where Georgianna worked when she arrived in Chicago.

Raised in Central Indiana, Georgiana spent two years teaching school in Franklin, once saving all her children from a school fire, but then she abruptly quit that job and moved to Chicago in 1893. She lived with an uncle when she arrived and got a job at the Siegal, Cooper & Co. department store. She stayed there for a time and then took a better position at the Fair, a store farther north on State Street.

At some point that spring, she met H.H. Holmes, and they began a relationship, but it's hard to say when that was. We do know that she attended the World's Fair with another man – a Mr. Chapman, who also worked at the Siegal & Cooper store – but they may have been only friends. Some rumors say that she met Holmes first at the Fair, though no one is sure of that either.

Mrs. Mary Yoke, Georgiana's mother, said that the two were acquainted for over a year before the wedding, which means that Holmes met her in January 1893, or even earlier. This seems unlikely, but it's certainly possible.

While we know more about Georgiana than we do most of Holmes' other women, details about her time in Chicago and her relationship with Holmes remain mysterious. She spent very little time around the Castle or around people who served as the best witnesses to Holmes' movements before he left the city.

We can assume, though, based on his previous relationships, that Holmes' seduction of Georgiana went at a rapid pace. Holmes was likely fervent in his pursuit of her, and she was likely as easily won over by his smoothness and charm as the women who had come before.

Or was she? There are many historians who don't believe that Georgiana was as naïve as Holmes' other conquests. It's been suggested that she may have known more about Holmes' crimes than any other person, except perhaps Ben Pitezel. And she may have not only known about his crimes but may have been a willing participant in some of them.

The other women may or may not have known that Holmes operated under several aliases, but Georgiana certainly did. She knew the name she called him was not his original name or the only one he was using.

Holmes had an explanation for all this for Georgiana and her mother. Both his parents, he claimed, were dead – his mother from some disease and his father from a foot injury that turned into lockjaw – which is creative, you must admit.

His siblings had also passed away at an early age leaving him alone in the world, except for an aunt in Africa and an uncle in Texas. His uncle was his late mother's brother, a childless bachelor named Henry Mansfield Howard, who had a special fondness for his nephew. He had promised to leave him all his property – which was actually Minnie's property in Fort Worth -- but only on the strange condition that he start using his uncle's name as his own. This was what he was now calling himself.

Georgiana knew that Henry had previously gone by H.H. Holmes but apparently accepted his bizarre explanation.

And she also knew he'd used another name, too. When they went to Texas, he did business under the name O.C. Pratt. He told Georgiana that, through business associates in Fort Worth, he had learned that a group of squatters had moved onto his uncle's vacant ranch and Holmes was faced with the dangerous task of having to evict them. He was sure that his efforts to reclaim his rightful property would be successful, but precautions were necessary. He was dealing with desperate men, and in Texas, a bullet was the traditional means for settling disputes, he said. As a result, Holmes thought it best to proceed using an alias. She accepted this explanation also – or so she later said.

It's possible that Georgiana simply chose to believe the stories that Holmes told her. She may have been as gullible as she seemed, or maybe she knew more about Holmes' crimes than she would ever admit. We'll never know for sure, but it seems hard to believe that she could be as blind as she would've had to have been in the months that followed their January wedding.

Before Holmes and Georgiana left Chicago, Georgiana's grandmother, Isabella Yoke, died and left a portion of her sizable estate to her granddaughter. It was only about $2,000 after it had been divvied up among all the family members, but even so, that was the kind of woman that Holmes liked – one that had recently come into money.

But it may be a mistake to think of Georgiana as just a payday to Holmes. He appears to have been genuinely fond of her. He kept her with him as he traveled throughout 1894, even when it would have been much easier to leave her behind.

Mary Yoke later spoke of Holmes' affection for her daughter, and she seemed to be taken with her daughter's fiancée. Not only had his lawyer, Wharton Plummer, said that he was the perfect gentleman when she wrote to check up on his character, but Holmes represented himself to her as a wealthy man, telling her all about the building he owned on Sixty-Third Street. When their marriage occurred on January 17, 1894, she said that it was with her approval and encouragement.

Although Holmes had stated that his only living relative was his aunt in Africa, Mary Yoke was under the impression that Holmes had a cousin in Chicago who traveled with them to Denver to serve as a witness at the wedding.

The cousin, she said, was named Minnie Williams.

Minnie had, of course, been dead for about six months when Holmes married Georgiana, but Minnie passing herself off as a cousin and witnessing the wedding has been part of Holmes' folklore for decades. She didn't – but it's easy to find sources that say she did.

This misconception likely got started because of Mrs. Yoke's faulty recollection. Holmes probably told her that he had a cousin named Minnie Williams who was accompanying them to Denver – which was a lie that served two purposes.

For one, he was still telling people that Minnie was alive. You might recall that he had the wives of both Ben Pitezel and Patrick Quinlan wearing Minnie's old clothes and impersonating her around town. Having one more person – like Mary Yoke – to confirm she was alive and kicking couldn't hurt.

Also, since Holmes and Georgiana would be traveling together to Denver, it probably eased Mary's mind to know they'd be accompanied by a chaperone. It wasn't proper then for an unmarried man and woman to travel alone together.

Before Holmes had chosen the date to leave Chicago, he'd started laying the groundwork for what would happen in Denver once he got there. In October and November, he sent letters to J.H. Waddle, the manager of the Arkansas Valley Smelter, where Baldwin Williams had been killed. He was following up on a letter that Minnie herself had sent to Waddle stating that her financial advisor – and you can guess who that was – said that sufficient time had passed for the accidental death

The Arkansas Valley Smelter in Colorado, where Baldwin Williams had been killed in an accident

Leadville, Colorado, in 1894 when Holmes and Georgiana were in town, fraudulently collecting the settlement for the death of Minnie's brother

payment on her brother to be paid. After insisting that the matter needed to be resolved at once, the problem was put into the hands of the mine's insurance company. They bargained a little but eventually agreed to pay Minnie $1,050.

Holmes' next letter to Waddle explained that Minnie and Nannie Williams had assigned their rights in their brother's estate to a party in Chicago because they were going on an extended trip. Holmes would be traveling to Colorado to collect the money which would be paid to the Chicago party through him.

On January 8, 1894, Holmes – accompanied by Georgiana – arrived in Leadville, Colorado, and went to the office of J.H. Waddle. He was handed over a letter from Minnie Williams that said that Holmes should collect the money that was due. Holmes was taken to the administrator's office where, as far as Waddle knew, Holmes was given a portion of the money. The manager refused to pay the full balance because Minnie and her sister had not provided sufficient proof that they were the sole heirs to their brother's estate.

Since there wasn't going to be any further correspondence from the Williams sister, Holmes had to settle for only part of the money. Waddle later reported that Holmes stayed in Leadville for two or three days, hoping to change the administrator's mind, but had no luck.

After the wedding in Denver, the newlyweds traveled to Fort Worth, Texas, where Holmes went to work laying claim to the rest of Minnie's inheritance. Luckily, when he got to town, a familiar face was waiting for him – Benjamin Pitezel. He was there to help Holmes with his latest scheme, but unknown to Ben, there was another, bigger scheme taking place behind his back.

Ben knew part of what was happening – but not all of it. If he had, he likely would have left Fort Worth and never looked back.

BEN PITEZEL WAS FRESH OUT OF TROUBLE HIMSELF WHEN HE headed for Texas. Back in September, shortly after the fire at the Castle, Ben left Chicago for Terre Haute, Indiana, without telling his wife where he was going. Carrie didn't hear anything from him until late October when lawyers contacted her and told her that her husband was in jail for passing bad checks.

Using the name Robert Jones, Ben went to clothing stores, picked out suits, and told the proprietors that he'd be back with money to pick them up later. Then he would return after the banks closed for the day with a phony check. The stores handed over the suits and took the checks but then a quick confirmation with the issuing banks the next day showed that the checks looked nothing like the ones the banks actually used. Ben then sold the suits and pocketed the cash racking up between $6,000 and $7,000 with his scheme before he was arrested.

Ben told the authorities that he believed the checks were genuine when he wrote them, but no one believed it.

He was locked up and was stuck in jail waiting for his trial, until finally, in November, Holmes paid his bond, and he was able to return home.

Most likely, the scheme had been Holmes' idea in the first place and it's also likely that Ben was unhappy that he'd left him sitting in jail for so long. It's possible that angry words were exchanged and it's also possible that Ben told him that he was finished with him. That seems drastic, based on how loyal Ben had been in the past, but something must have happened for Holmes to do what he did next.

On December 19, Holmes sent a letter to Ben's Indiana attorney, H.H. Wallace, and asked him to tell Ben that he was in danger of being arrested and brought back to Indiana. Holmes claimed that he had helped Ben's family financially while he was in prison and couldn't get Ben to pay him back. This wasn't true, which makes me think that Ben wanted to get out of business with Holmes and Holmes didn't want that to happen. If he could get the lawyer to tell Ben he was in trouble, Holmes could step in and make Ben grateful for his help.

But Wallace refused. And not only that, but he also made a deal with the prosecutor in Terre Haute to get Ben cleared of the crime.

Whether he was unhappy with him or not, Ben didn't stay away from Holmes for long. By the end of the year, he was deeply involved in a new scheme. Holmes had taken out a large insurance policy on Ben's life, which he'd started making payments on in the Fall of 1893, so he couldn't afford to let Ben start living the straight and narrow.

After the policy had some time to grow in value, Holmes and Ben would stage what appeared to be a deadly accident. Ben would go into hiding and a badly disfigured and unrecognizable corpse would be substituted in his place. Holmes would then identify the remains as those of his friend.

The insurance company would pay on the policy, and the two men would split the proceeds. It was a simple concept and only tricky in that Holmes would have to come up with a suitable corpse to pass off as Ben. But he'd done things like this in the past, he assured Ben, and it wouldn't be a problem.

Ben was sold on the idea and was soon back in the clutches of H.H. Holmes. But, of course, unknown to Ben, Holmes had no plan

Fort Worth, Texas, in 1894, around the time Holmes, Georgiana, and Ben were in the city, plotting to get their hands on Minnie Williams' inheritance.

to steal a medical cadaver to use as a replacement for his accomplice. He knew exactly where to get the perfect corpse for his purposes, but he had no intention of telling Ben.

Ben Pitezel's life was now insured for $10,000 by the Fidelity Mutual Life Association of Philadelphia.

Both men firmly believed that nothing would go wrong. In fact, Ben was so sure of Holmes' intentions that when he left for Texas to meet him, he brought along his young son, Howard, with him. He had taken the boy out of Wentworth Elementary School so he could travel with his father but there's no record of whether he attended school in Texas while Ben was there.

Before Holmes arrived from Colorado with a new wife, a new name, and wild story about murderous squatters living on his uncle's land, Ben had walked into the Tarrant County clerk's office and – using the name Benton F. Lyman – transferred some property on the corner of Second and Rusk Streets in Fort Worth from Minnie Williams to Alexander E. Bond. The deed had been written in April 1893 and had been notarized by Harry H. Holmes.

Minnie had been paid $1 for the land.

Though Holmes was not a notary public, the county clerk didn't see anything wrong with the deed. Regardless, Benton Lyman also produced a letter that was signed by Cook County clerk Henry Wulff stating that Harry Holmes was a real person and the seal on the deed was legitimate.

Henry Wulff was a real person – and his seal and signature were all over paperwork for many lawsuits against Holmes – but his signature on this letter was a forgery. And Alexander E. Bond was, of course, another of Holmes' aliases.

Another deed transferred Minnie's Rusk Street property from Bond to Benton Lyman for the sum of $7,800. That deed was entered into Texas record on January 16.

So, Benton Lyman – a.k.a. Ben Pitezel – got to work making plans for a building to be erected on the property. Around the time the foundation was completed, a man named O.C. Pratt was appointed as the superintendent for the construction. He had just arrived in town with his new wife.

After staying briefly at the Arlington Inn, Pratt – who, of course, was Holmes – and his bride spent six weeks at a rooming house before moving into an apartment above a downtown hat shop. The landlord at the rooming house liked Georgiana very much but he had little good to say about Holmes. In a later interview, he recalled:

Pratt was a well-dressed man of about 5 feet 7 and but for a habitual scowl his face was not unattractive. That scowl, however, ruined him with me. It was a sneer at all the world.

At the construction site, C.T. Scott, who worked as an agent for Benton Lyman, said he distrusted Holmes right away but wasn't exactly impressed by Ben Pitezel either. He later said:

I saw both men frequently, Lyman having business with me and Pratt generally coming with him. Lyman seemed duller than

Pratt, and did not present as an attractive appearance, seemingly having no higher aspirations than superintendent of a lot of workmen.

On paper, the new building belonged to Ben, but Holmes chose and purchased all the materials and made all the decisions about how the place would be built. He bought any materials that caught his eye as well as any materials the builders said they needed – all on credit. When a fire broke out near the building while he was away, Holmes sent the fire department a box of cigars to thank them for their hard work in keeping the Lyman building safe.

But being grateful to the firefighters didn't mean that he wanted them around. A fireman named Oberhoff later recalled stopping by to check out the building in progress one day and Pratt giving him such a horrible look that he knew he wasn't welcome and didn't go back anymore.

He was right. Holmes and Ben didn't want anyone to look too closely at what they were doing. Once there was enough of a building constructed, a sign that read NO ADMITTANCE was put up in front. Although several local workers were hired, they took steps to keep everything about the place secret, even bringing Pat Quinlan down from Chicago to spend several months working on the building with them.

By then, they had to bring in outside help. After they started firing and hiring workers, no one wanted to work for them anymore.

It will come as no surprise that Holmes used the exact same swindles in Fort Worth that he'd used in Englewood to get his new building completed. A photograph of the building that was taken after it was later sold by the bank and turned into a hotel, shows a structure almost identical to the Castle except for the fact that it was twice its size.

There is no clear record as to what Holmes planned to do with the building. He didn't stay around the city after it was built

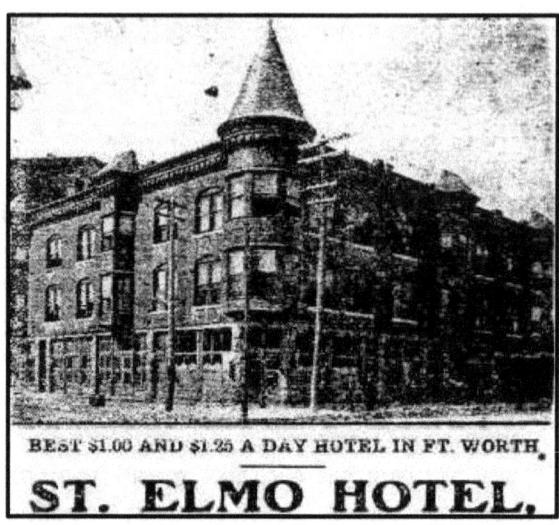

The "Castle" that Holmes built in Fort Worth later became a hotel. It looked almost identical to the building that Holmes had constructed in Chicago.

and seems to have made no effort to start any kind of business there. It appears that it was constructed for the sole purpose of giving Holmes more opportunities to swindle people. If he had learned one thing from the Castle in Englewood, it was easy to take out loans and buy things on credit when you had a shiny new property as collateral.

And that's exactly what he and Ben did. They bought everything for the building on credit, failed to pay the workers, and used the place to take out a string of substantial loans.

On April 23, 1894, with the building nearly complete, he and Ben placed a trust deed for $22,500 on the new property and assigned it to James R. Mitchell of Colorado. They took out another loan on the property for $10,000 with a local bank, followed by more loans from other banks and companies.

This amounted to tens of thousands of dollars in money that Holmes would never pay back, but that still wasn't enough for him. He got up to his old tricks of buying furniture and other items on credit and selling them for cash. He then revived his old bicycle dealer swindling trick and updated it to try it with something new – horses.

But this was Texas. And here, people took horses a lot more seriously than people in Chicago took bicycles.

Holmes met with a man named E.B. Edwards, who ran the Exchange Stable in Fort Worth. He had seen Edwards driving a handsome team of black horses and for some reason, Holmes decided that he wanted them. He offered to buy them from Edwards for a $400 promissory note, secured by property in his warehouse. Edwards agreed to the price and offered to accept the note, if he could convert it into cash right away. Holmes agreed but said the note would take a little time because it would require the signature of Benton Lyman on it.

Three days later, Edwards had the signed note in hand, but when he tried to cash it, found that the bank wouldn't honor it. He returned the note to Holmes – who apologized for the inconvenience – and handed over $375 in cash for the horses. He drove them away with a buggy and harnesses he'd bought from another merchant on credit.

What became of those black horses is unknown, but what we do know is that this was the only honest horse deal that Holmes made in Fort Worth.

Holmes had made a fortune in Texas, and any other swindler, after that kind of windfall, would've taken the money and left town, but not H.H. Holmes. He always seemed to have a craving for risk and a brazen disregard for danger. He managed to get away with his crimes by sheer audacity, not because his schemes and murders were so brilliant.

Holmes was a sociopath who simply didn't believe he'd ever be caught. But he'd soon find that he couldn't charm his way out of all his trouble, especially when it came to horses in Texas.

That spring, Holmes and Ben Pitezel began buying horses around the state, paying for them with worthless deeds and promissory notes, then reselling them for cash.

But this soon started to draw attention from the authorities. A grand jury investigated, and O.C. Pratt was indicted. After that indictment, more investigations were launched. A businessman who had written to a county clerk in Chicago learned there was no notary in Cook County named Harry Holmes. The banks started looking for payments on the loans they'd made, and, worse, friends of Minnie Williams – who knew the property where the new building was constructed had belonged to her – realized they hadn't heard from her in a long time. They started talking to detectives, and officials started looking much closer at Benton Lyman and O.C. Pratt.

It was time to flee, and likely only a few steps ahead of the law, Holmes and Pitezel – with Georgiana in tow – fled Fort Worth in the middle of the night.

Holmes and Georgiana, with a very large bankroll, made a quick trip back to Denver, then moved to St. Louis for what looked to be an extended stay.

But the law in Texas wasn't quite finished with Holmes.

In July, a deputy sheriff from Fort Worth named Rea managed to track Holmes to Englewood and the Castle. He started asking questions and spoke to someone he described as "a man of high standing who knew Holmes and conversed with him often." It was almost undoubtedly Charles Davis, the jeweler, who never missed an opportunity to talk about Holmes. From him, Deputy Rea learned that "Mrs. Pratt" was not the only woman in Holmes' life. Davis – or whoever he talked to – believed that Minnie Williams was still alive and was Holmes' mistress.

Deputy Rea told Davis that Minnie had secured $2,500 in cash in Fort Worth in the spring of 1893. I'm not clear where this information came from or what the deputy was talking about, but I do know that when Rea said this, Davis had a quick reply. He told the lawman that if Minnie got $2,500, she was not alive today.

When Patrick Quinlan heard the deputy sheriff was in town, he tried to send a warning to Holmes that people were looking for him, but he couldn't reach him.

Deputy Rea was also unsuccessful in his search. Holmes was very hard to find at that moment. He was in St. Louis, as we already know, but in July 1894, he was someplace that he had never been before.

MR. A.P. GEST WANTED NOTHING MORE THAN TO OPERATE HIS own drugstore. He'd been a clerk, working for other druggists for most of his life, and he wanted the chance to go into business for himself. He scrimped,  and he saved, squeezing every penny until it squeaked, and finally had enough to purchase a drugstore at Fourteenth and North Market Street in St. Louis.

But after a couple of months, he realized that being responsible for a business was not all it was cracked up to be. He still owed the Merrell Drug Company that he'd purchased the place from and still owed his suppliers for his products and fixtures. He simply didn't have enough money to make it work. His longtime dream in ashes, he spoke with a broker named Doran and offered him $25 if he could find someone to take the store off his hands and assume the debt.

In June, a stranger walked into the store one morning with a letter from Doran in his hands. He introduced himself as H.M. Howard and announced that he wanted to take over Gest's failing drugstore.

Mr. Howard told Gest that he'd been traveling around for some time, but he was tired of it and wanted to settle down in St. Louis with his new wife. He was aware that Gest wasn't making much profit from the store but claimed not to be bothered by it. As he told Gest:

I want a business to occupy my attention. If it brings me enough to pay my living expenses for a while, it will satisfy me. I

was married in Franklin, Indiana, back in February and my wife will soon receive a large share of her father's estate.

Gest didn't care that his store was about to become this man's hobby, he just wanted out. He originally asked for $1,000 for the business but agreed to take $850, if Howard paid the finder's fee to Doran, too.

The two men met with representatives from the Merrell Drug Company and worked out terms – Howard would pay $50 in cash toward the balance owed by Gest and the rest would be paid in promissory notes and shares of stock in the Campbell-Yates Company. Howard assured them that the stock was valued at $100 per share.

It wasn't, though. Why? Because it wasn't a real company.

Howard was obviously H.H. Holmes, and even if he had cash on hand for the drugstore, he would never have gotten involved in something that he couldn't do dishonestly. After paying off Gest with worthless paper, Holmes asked the broker, Doran, not to record the mortgage right away. Having the debt recorded might hurt his credit standing and prevent him from stocking the store. Doran, to his later regret, went along with the request and put the paperwork in a drawer.

With a new store and spotless credit, Holmes started buying goods from drug suppliers, Stickney cigars, Hennessey whiskey, and other St. Louis merchants with promises to pay later.

He and Georgiana ate their meals together in the store and stayed at a nearby apartment that had been rented to them by M.A. Shinnick. The landlord later said:

All the time they were at my house, I never got a square look at Howard. He wouldn't look anyone square in the face.

Meanwhile, Ben Pitezel had also landed in St. Louis, and he brought his entire family with him. They took up residence above a grocery store owned by the McClintock family.

Early in July, Ben told Carrie that he was going into the lumber business and left on a trip down south to purchase wood. While he was gone, Holmes dropped by the Pitezel apartment to see Carrie. He wanted to tell her about the plan he and Ben had been working on, which would result in a huge payout for both of them from Fidelity Mutual Insurance.

Holmes asked her, "Did Ben tell you about the insurance?"

Carrie replied, "Yes, and I don't think much of it. I don't want anything to do with it."

But Holmes reassured her that everything would be fine. If there seemed to be anything wrong with the plan, they wouldn't go through with it.

When Ben came home – without lumber, so there's no telling where he really was – she told him about Holmes' visit and again expressed her unhappiness about the scheme he was cooking up with Holmes. Ben told her the same thing that Holmes did, telling her everything would be fine.

After Ben's return to St. Louis, he helped Holmes with his drugstore swindle. In mid-July, posing as a man named Brown, he went to Doughtery-Crouch, a drugstore supplier, and told them that he was interested in buying the drugstore at Fourteenth and Market, which the owner, H.M. Howard, had offered to sell him for $325. He explained that he didn't have that much himself but promised the company that if they loaned it to him, he'd pay it back quickly and would make them his only supplier, guaranteeing them years of business. They agreed, and Mr. Brown soon had the cash for his new drugstore.

So, with the Merrell Company's mortgage still not reported, the Doughtery-Crouch Company took out a mortgage on the same store but filed the record on July 18, 1894.

Right away, Mr. Howard and Mr. Brown started packing up all the stock from the store, ready to sell it, and split the money they'd make from the scheme.

But they had a bit of bad luck the next day when a Merrell salesman stopped by the store and found the place closed and empty. The salesman got suspicious and told the broker, Mr. Doran, and Doran called the police.

Holmes was arrested in East St. Louis but tried to talk his way out of trouble. He coolly explained that the store no longer belonged to him and recommended the authorities get in touch with the new owner, Mr. Brown.

But the police weren't buying the story, especially after they seized $400 worth of goods that he'd bought and billed to H.H. Holmes, H.A. Pease, and other aliases. He was taken to the courthouse, where he was charged with fraud and selling mortgaged goods. He wasn't going to be able to talk his way out of this one.

Holmes was taken to a cell at Four Corners, the notorious St. Louis jail, and the metal door slammed closed behind him. He was now in a place where he had never been before.

For the very first time in his criminal career, H.H. Holmes was behind bars.

The Four Corners, the notorious St. Louis courthouse, jail, and morgue, where Holmes was locked up in 1894.

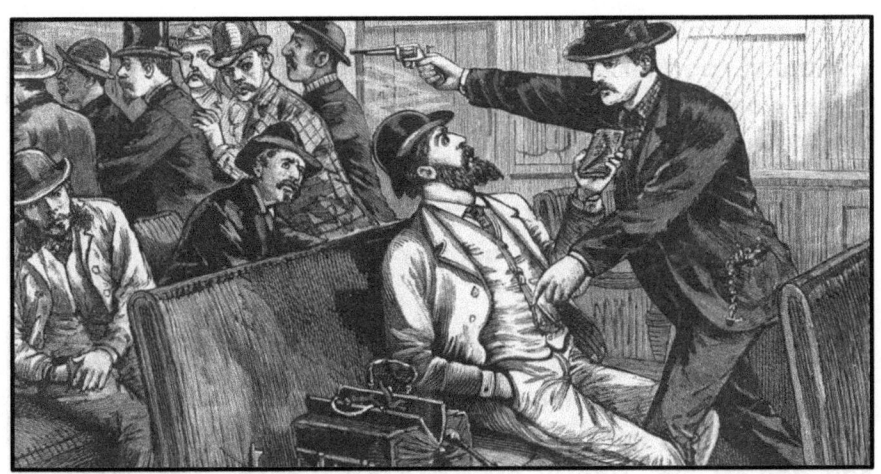

TEN DAYS AFTER H.H. HOLMES WAS ARRESTED, HE WAS BAILED out of jail by his most recent wife, Georgiana. When he walked out of St. Louis's Four Corners jail that day, he had a smile on his face. He seemed happy, which was a bit odd for a man who had just spent a week and a half behind bars for the first time in his life. Holmes had been getting away with just about every kind of crime imaginable for  years, but after finally getting caught, he leaves jail looking like the cat who caught the canary. Why?

Things certainly hadn't gone well for him in St. Louis. He'd embarked on one of his usual schemes but this time, Holmes made a serious miscalculation. He believed that he could escape the city while his creditors blustered and threatened like the ones he owed money to in Chicago had done for years. But the Merrell Drug Company charged him with fraud and Holmes was arrested and locked up.

Georgiana immediately called on the law firm of MacDonald and Howe to try and get her husband released. An attorney and younger brother of the firm's managing partner named Jeptha Howe, went to see Holmes in jail. At first, he said he'd take the case but then backed out, stating that Holmes didn't have the money to pay him. He passed the case off to another lawyer, Thomas Harvey.

Harvey was assured by Mr. Howard that if he were released from jail, he could get the money to settle the claims the drug company had against him. Harvey arranged for a bail bondsman who managed to get Holmes released -- but then the bondsman got nervous about the $500 risk he was taking and changed his mind. Word went out to the authorities to arrest Holmes again – they could find him.

Attorney Jeptha P. Howe. The St. Louis lawyer initially passed Holmes off to another member of his firm but would soon be involved in the man's many dangerous schemes.

Holmes was no fool. As soon as he had been freed, he and Georgiana were on their way to the Union depot to get tickets on the first train out of town. They had already boarded a train when a Sgt. O'Malley casually walked up to them and told them that their trip was going to have to be postponed – Mr. Howard was under arrest again. Georgiana went into a frenzy, weeping and striking the policeman. She was hysterical as Holmes was taken away, shouting to all the other passengers that her husband was being persecuted.

With Holmes back behind bars, the furious Georgiana rushed home to Indiana and then returned to St. Louis with a stack of real estate paperwork. On July 29, a deed of transfer for a lot in Oak Cliff, Texas, was transferred to Thomas Harvey for $10 as security for his fee and for the now $800 bail needed to free Holmes before his trial.

Of course, the lot really wasn't worth much of anything. It had been transferred from Minnie Williams to Henry Howard more than a year earlier – long after Minnie had been able to sign anything over to anyone.

But, of course, Thomas Harvey didn't know that. With the real estate collateral, he put up $800 in bail money and Holmes was released again. Now, all he needed to do was wait for Holmes to settle matters with the Merrell Drug Company so the whole mess could be behind them.

But Holmes had no plans to settle anything. He climbed aboard the first train leaving St. Louis for New York. From there, he'd go on to Philadelphia where he planned to stage the greatest insurance swindle in his career.

So, why had Holmes been smiling when he walked out of jail? Because his arrest and jail time had turned into a happy twist of fate for him – or so he believed at the time.

That belief would eventually lead to his undoing.

BY THE 1890S, THE DAYS OF THE WILD WEST OUTLAWS WERE A thing of the past. The real-life exploits of outlaws like Jesse James were, by then, the stuff of dime novels and adventure books for young boys. The bandits of yesterday would soon swell the ranks of organized crime in the twentieth century, but there were a few holdouts that were still around – like the Hedgepeth Four, a gang of train robbers, who were every bit as dangerous as the James brothers and Butch Cassidy. The gang was led by Marion Hedgepeth, an outlaw said to be so handsome and colorful that WANTED posters often made mention of his good looks and always-polished shoes.

While Holmes had been committing swindle after swindle, usually only making a few hundred dollars here and there, Hedgepeth had been stealing tens of thousands of dollars with every robbery.

And perhaps that's the reason that H.H. Holmes was so excited to meet him when he made his acquaintance at the Four Corners prison. For Hedgepeth, this must have been a new experience because no one had ever felt lucky to have met him before.

William A. Pinkerton, the son of the famous detective agency's legendary founder, once described Marion Hedgepeth by saying he was:

One of the really bad men of the Old West. He was one of the worst characters I ever heard of. He was a bad man clear through.

And that summer, he crossed paths with H.H. Holmes.

Train robber and bandit, Marion Hedgepeth

Marion Hedgepeth, although he is no longer remembered today for anything other than for his meeting with Holmes, was truly an old-school badman. If he had lived a generation earlier, his name would undoubtedly be more widely remembered and he would have been named along with men like Billy the Kid, Clay Allison, and John Wesley Hardin, as one of the deadliest gunmen of the era.

Hedgepeth was born on a small farm in Prairie Home in Cooper County, Missouri, but aside from that, nothing was known about his childhood, not even his year of birth. He left home in his teens and drifted west, where he fell into a life of a crime and earned a reputation as a killer so deadly that he once pulled his pistol and shot down a man who already had him covered with a rifle. By the time he was 20, he was wanted by the law in Wyoming, Colorado, and Montana for crimes that ranged from cattle rustling to bank robbery.

Hedgepeth always dressed like a dandy. He was usually seen in a well-cut black suit, a shirt with a large wing collar, a cravat decorated with a diamond stickpin, and a derby hat, which covered his black hair and shaded his piercing dark eyes. The newspapers of the day dubbed him the "Handsome Bandit," a moniker that didn't make him seem as ruthless as he was.

In 1882, he joined up with a pair of burglars named Cody and Officer. Later that year, the three of them robbed a store in Tuscumbia, Missouri, and walked away with $1,400 in cash. A posse trailed them as far as Bonner Springs, 20 miles west of Kansas City, but Hedgepeth and the others easily escaped.

Several months later, Hedgepeth and Cody were cornered while attempting to blow open a safe in a small Kansas town. After a terrible gun battle, Cody was killed, but Hedgepeth escaped.

The law caught up to him for the first time in November 1883. Tried back in Cooper County, Missouri, he was convicted of highway robbery and sentenced to seven years in the state penitentiary. While awaiting transfer to prison, he overpowered a deputy, severely wounding him, and escaped from the jail. A chase ensued, but it was a short-lived one. He was quickly recaptured and hurried off to prison before a lynch mob of local citizens could be formed.

Shortly after arriving at the penitentiary in Jefferson City, Hedgepeth met and befriended a train robber named Adelbert "Bertie" Sly. When they got out of prison in 1891, they recruited another pair of hardcases – James

The Missouri State Penitentiary in Jefferson City, where Hedgepeth first spent time behind bars

Hedgepeth after his release from the penitentiary in 1891

"Illinois Jimmy" Francis and Lucius "Dink" Wilson. The foursome then began a series of bold, brutal, and usually bloody robberies.

Within a year, the Hedgepeth Four gained a national reputation, even earning a write-up in the *New York Times* as "the most desperate gang of train robbers that has operated in this country for many years."

The gang's first major crime was the robbery of the office of a Kansas City streetcar company. A few weeks later, they pulled an almost identical job in Omaha. They also robbed post offices in St. Louis and several smaller towns, always timing the heists to match the arrival of payday funds for mines and factories in the surrounding area.

On November 4, 1891, the gang struck again, this time robbing the Chicago, Milwaukee & St. Paul Express at Western Union Junction, three miles outside of Milwaukee, Wisconsin.

Hedgepeth dynamited the express car, critically injuring one of the messengers inside. After cleaning out the safes, the bandits moved through the coaches with sacks in hand, collecting watches, jewelry, and cash from the passengers. They rode away with more than $5,000 – which is the equivalent of about $165,000 today.

Two weeks later, on November 30, the Hedgepeth Four committed their greatest – and their last – holdup at Glendale, Missouri, a small town outside of St. Louis.

Around 9:15 that evening, as the Frisco Express was pulling out of the station, Hedgepeth jumped aboard the train and broke into the cab. With gun in hand, he ordered the engineer to "pull her up straight ahead."

On January 15, 1892, the Adams Express Company released a "Wanted" broadside seeking Marion C. Hedgespeth shown on front page, and Lucius Wilson, shown on second page, for the November 1891 train robbery

As the train came to a halt, Bertie, Jimmy, and Dink, rode up hard on horses, firing pistols into the passenger coaches for terrifying effect.

Hedgepeth ordered the engineer out of the cab and marched him back to the express car. Placing a gun to his head, he told him that he needed to convince the messenger to open the door – and to do it fast. The engineer, fearing for his life, did as he was told, but the messenger replied by firing a rifle through the window.

Hedgepeth shoved the engineer out of the way and climbed down to the tracks. He walked around the side of the express car and wired a large bundle of dynamite to the side of it. He lit the fuse and ducked out of the way.

The massive blast tore off the entire side of the express car. The messenger wasn't dead, but he was hurt and deafened by the explosion. As he stumbled out of the ruins of the rail car, Hedgepeth gunned him down. Then, he blew open the safe with a smaller charge and scooped out envelopes and bundles of money. He dumped at least $25,000 in cash into a burlap bag.

Meanwhile, Bertie took the opportunity to remove the gold watch and chain from the dead messenger's pocket. Then, after firing a dozen or more additional rounds into the passenger coaches, the four bandits disappeared into the woods.

The brazenness and violence of the robbery stunned the local law enforcement community. Within a week, a special train from Chicago arrived in St. Louis carrying William A. Pinkerton and a team of the agency's best operatives. Along with the St. Louis police, they began searching the city for the robbers. Plainclothes officers in teams of four roamed the streets day and night, with orders to "kill Hedgepeth on sight." By then, though, the gang had gone its separate ways.

"Illinois Jimmy" Francis had taken his share of the loot and returned to his eighteen-year-old wife and infant son in Kansas City. The Pinkertons tracked him to his home, but before they could arrest him, he and his brother-in-law were shot and killed by a posse that had been hunting him down because of a botched train robbery outside Damar, Kansas.

Hedgepeth, Bertie, and Dink, meanwhile, had headed out to California. In December 1891, Robert Pinkerton, aided by the chief of police and a detective named Whitaker, managed to track down Bertie in Los Angeles, where he was arrested on the day after Christmas. At the time of his arrest, he was carrying the gold pocket watch that he had taken off the body of the slain messenger from the Glendale robbery.

"Dink" Wilson was never seen again.

Hedgepeth also continued to elude his pursuers – for a while anyway. When he was accidentally captured, it happened because of a little girl.

On Christmas morning, a man and his wife appeared at the St. Louis police headquarters to report to an understandably unimpressed Chief of Detectives William Desmond that their daughter had discovered a dime in a neighborhood shed.

Probably seeing the look on the detective's face, the man hurriedly added that he followed his daughter back to the shed to see if any more money could be found. He struck a match and discovered a hastily covered hole in the corner of the building. He'd found something inside of it.

He reached into his pocket and placed two objects on the desk. Detective Desmond could barely suppress his excitement as he looked at a Colt revolver and a torn money envelope of the type removed from the express company safe during the Glendale train robbery.

The cops hurried to the shed, where they found a supply of bullets and several more express company money envelopes. They were all empty. They soon learned that the house where the shed was located had been rented by a man who called himself H.B. Swenson. He had packed up and left in a hurry just a few days after the train robbery. He'd bought a ticket to San Francisco.

On February 10, 1892, Swenson was surrounded at a San Francisco post office that had been staked out by the police for days, waiting for him to return. Swenson was immediately identified as Marion Hedgepeth. He was wearing two Colt revolvers when he walked into the post office that morning but never had the chance to draw them. He was returned to St. Louis under heavy guard.

His trial became a nationwide sensation with hundreds of women crowding into the courthouse every morning to get a glimpse of the "Handsome Bandit." He became the toast of the city. He received visits from reporters and even from the public. Flowers from his female admirers were delivered to his cell every afternoon.

The jury, however, turned out to be resistant to his good looks and charm. In the spring of 1892, Hedgepeth was found guilty and sentenced to serve 25 years hard labor in the Missouri State Penitentiary.

But Hedgepeth seemed unconcerned by the verdict. He had no intention of going to state prison. He spent the next two years at Four Corners jail while his attorneys appealed his case. During that time, he made headlines for his escape attempts. In June 1894, a piece of iron was found hidden in his cell that he was trying to file into a key. He was locked up in solitary confinement for a short time and then returned to his regular cell to plot his next attempt.

As it turned out, though, he wouldn't need homemade keys or sheets tied into ropes to dangle from windows with – fate gave him another shot at freedom when he ended up sharing a cell with a swindler who had been locked up after trying to defraud a local drug company.

And that was how Marion Hedgepeth – the notorious bank robber of the day – met H.H. Holmes, who would go on to become known as one of the most infamous criminals of all time.

THERE'S NO QUESTION ABOUT WHETHER HOLMES RECOGNIZED his cellmate. He read the newspapers, and for the last two years, Hedgepeth had been making headlines. Holmes couldn't have missed the stories about the crimes of the Hedgepeth Four. He admitted as much to the bank robber.

But why then, did Holmes do what he did next?

For some inexplicable reason, he decided to spill his guts about the entire insurance scheme that he had planned with Ben Pitezel – all of it: the big policy, the staged accident, the substitute corpse, and the pay-off.

Why would he tell his secrets to a man he barely knew?

Was he awed by Hedgepeth's celebrity and chose to confide in him for his approval?

Or did Holmes believe that his crime was sensational enough to match the daring of Hedgepeth's robberies? Was he trying to "one up" the bank robber?

Or was it simpler than that? Did Holmes just need information, as he would claim, that only a man like Marion Hedgepeth could provide?

Holmes had apparently been thinking about the scheme while in jail. He felt there was a crucial missing ingredient in his plan – a lawyer. He needed the services of an attorney who didn't mind getting his hands a little dirty in exchange for a lump sum of cash in return. He hadn't been able to think of anyone, even among his questionable Chicago attorneys, who was suitable. But perhaps Hedgepeth might know someone. And Holmes offered him $500 for the name of a lawyer who could help with the scheme.

According to Hedgepeth's later version of events, he suggested Holmes speak with Jeptha Howe, the attorney who had earlier declined to take his case. Holmes explained to Hedgepeth that, as a druggist, he would use his training to make the substitute body look as though it had been killed in an accident – no one would actually be hurt.

But Hedgepeth later said that he sensed Holmes was up to something much more sinister. Holmes had not only offered him a $500 finder's fee but had suggested that Hedgepeth flee the country with Holmes and Georgiana if he could escape from jail. But as Hedgepeth later wrote:

I am now convinced that he would have sooner or later murdered me had I been able to have accompanied him on his intended trip abroad.

We'll never know if Hedgepeth really "sensed" anything about Holmes. It's possible that he just thought he was a two-bit swindler who was talking a big game but even so, he did tell Holmes about Jeptha Howe.

The firm of McDonald and Howe had represented Hedgepeth at trial and had done a fairly remarkable job. They hadn't gotten him off the hook – he was still sentenced to 25 years – but two years later, he still hadn't seen the inside of the penitentiary, and they managed to get him 12 appeals so far.

As to the honesty of Jeptha Howe, Hedgepeth was happy to call him a criminal. He knew that Howe had underworld connections in St. Louis and was acquainted with him enough to know he'd be willing to help with a swindle. He told Holmes that he should use Hedgepeth's name when he approached the man. In return, Holmes promised to send Hedgepeth his money just as soon as he collected the insurance payout.

On July 31, Holmes was bailed out of jail. He was smiling when he walked out because he believed that being locked up with Marion Hedgepeth had been an unexpected stroke of good luck. He'd found the attorney that he needed, and he was now convinced that his plan couldn't fail.

As for Hedgepeth, he was feeling lucky, too. He had some leverage to use over his attorney if he took Holmes' deal, plus there was also the promise of the $500 reward.

There was also something worth much more than that. He didn't plan to need it because he took Holmes at his word that his $500 commission would arrive as promised – but if it didn't, he had some valuable information about Holmes that might be worth a great deal to the authorities.

There truly is no honor among thieves.

SOMEHOW, BEN PITEZEL HAD MANAGED TO STAY OUT OF THE mess that had landed Holmes in jail. While he was working to get bailed out, Ben was still with his family in the furnished, three-room apartment above the grocery store on Carondelet Street. The place was seedy, with peeling wallpaper and grimy, worn-out furniture, and it was crowded, thanks to the fact that Carrie Pitezel had brought her brood of five children with her from Chicago.

She was living there with Dessie, Alice, Nellie, Howard, baby Wharton, and Ben, whenever he was around, but she was confused about the poor conditions of their new, albeit temporary, home. Ben had been faithful about writing her letters while he traveled, and she knew that he and Dr. Holmes had made a lot of money while in Texas.

What she didn't know, however, was that her husband had ended up with only a pittance from those swindles. Most of the money had remained with Holmes, who had convinced Ben to let him hold onto it. Holmes explained that he had a real estate venture on the horizon that would double both men's investments in a matter of months.

Ben just kept going along with whatever Holmes told him. He was a faithful and loyal friend and was constantly amazed by Holmes' criminal cunning. He knew that with his share of the money from the real estate swindle in Texas, the drugstore scheme in St. Louis, and pending insurance scam they had planned, he and his family would be set for life.

During that summer in St. Louis, Ben was still trying to sell Carrie on the insurance swindle that would happen as soon as Holmes was out of jail. He had laid out the details for her already and explained how easy it would be. Carrie knew about the $10,000 life insurance policy that named her as the sole beneficiary. Ben had shown her the documents the previous November, soon after it had been issued. In their cramped and dirty apartment, he told her how he and Holmes intended to cash in on the policy and how the money that he made would allow the family to find a nice house and finally settle down and live a happy life. She had always wanted him to go straight and now he'd finally be able to do so.

Holmes had decided to stage Ben's phony death in Philadelphia, where the Fidelity Mutual Life Association had its main office. Holmes believed that this would make it faster for him to settle the matter of his friend's alleged demise.

Ben had explained to Carrie that he was going to travel to Philadelphia using the name of Perry. He had no idea how long he would be away, but he told Carrie that the next time she saw him, he would be a wealthy man.

He'd been telling Carrie this all summer but to his dismay, she still wasn't excited about the swindle, even as the date for his departure got closer. Carrie didn't know Holmes well. In fact, even though her husband had been working for him for nearly five years, she rarely spent time in the same room with the man. When she did, it was because he was asking her to do things she didn't approve of, like dress up in Minnie Williams' old clothes, or approve of Ben helping to swindle an insurance company.

During the summer they'd spent in St. Louis, Holmes had dropped by the apartment on two or three occasions, bringing treats for the children and handing out a little cash to help the family with groceries.

Despite these small bits of generosity and the kind way he acted toward her, though, she didn't much care for the man. There was something about him that made her skin crawl. She didn't trust him, and she couldn't understand Ben's complete loyalty to him. She had feared for years that Holmes would get Ben into some kind of terrible trouble and she feared that this insurance scheme would be the very thing that would land Ben in prison.

Carrie hated that their lives had come to this, but she also hated the fact that she and Ben were unable to buy their children clothing, or toys, or books, and that they often had barely enough to eat.

Eventually, Carrie gave in. She'd go along with the scheme, but she made Ben promise that when it was over – and they had the money that had been promised to them – Ben would be finished with Dr. Holmes once and for all.

Ben agreed. This was the last thing that he'd ever do with Holmes, he told her, and he also promised her that the swindle in Philadelphia would be the last dishonest thing that he would ever do. Crime – any sort of crime – would be forever in his past.

Unlike his earlier promise to quit drinking, this was a promise that Ben Pitezel was able to keep.

CARRIE WASN'T THE ONLY MEMBER OF THE PITEZEL FAMILY THAT was troubled by the relationship between Ben and Dr. Holmes. Her 17-year-old daughter, Dessie, knew much more about what was going on than her parents believed she did. Dessie was old enough to be on her own, and if not married, at least with a job or working as a domestic for some well-to-do Chicago family.

But Dessie refused to abandon her mother. She knew she needed her to care for the younger children at times when Carrie wasn't well, or when her father had abandoned the family for one of his so-called business trips with Dr. Holmes. When Ben was away, Carrie barely functioned, consumed with worry about what might happen to Ben or what might happen to all of them if Ben was injured, arrested, or even killed.

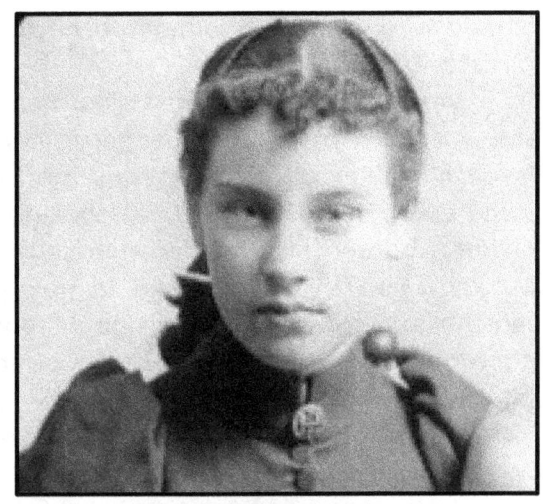

Ben and Carrie's oldest daughter, Dessie

And, of course, there was her father's drinking. Ben's "cure" at the Keeley Institute was now in the distant past. He'd stuck with sobriety for a little while, but while in St. Louis, he went back to frequenting the taverns and saloons again. When Ben was out of house at night, Carrie locked herself in the bedroom and cried, leaving Dessie to make sure that her siblings were fed, washed, and put to bed.

One night, not long before he was supposed to leave for Philadelphia, Ben staggered home after a night in a local tavern and found Dessie doing some sewing at the table. Ben sat down with her and after blearily gazing at the young woman for a few moments, he spoke up and slurred that he was afraid that she might read about something in the newspaper. Dessie asked him what it might be about and was shocked by his answer. She later recalled that he replied, "About my being dead."

Ben refused to tell her anything more. He just assured her that if she saw anything in the newspaper about his death that's he shouldn't believe it – it was all a trick. After that, he pulled himself to his feet and wandered off to bed, leaving the stunned girl sitting at the table.

Dessie didn't understand what Ben was trying to tell her, but she was upset by it. She knew her father had many faults, but she loved him. They all did. He drank too much and was involved in some shady things, but he was a kind, loving man, and all his children adored him. Dessie often prayed that he'd stop drinking but knew he likely never would. So, now she just decided to believe that his late-night ramblings about death and newspapers were caused by the liquor. By the next morning, she'd mostly forgotten about the incident.

It wouldn't be long, though, before it would come back to haunt her.

A few days later, Ben had breakfast with his wife and children and told each of them goodbye. Each child received a hug and a kiss on the cheek and Ben gave Carrie a long embrace. He wiped away the tears that streamed down her cheeks, and he gave her a sad smile. He promised he would return soon. He told them, "Be good, children. Take care of your mother and I will see all of you very soon. And when I do, I promise to bring you surprises."

Ben closed the door behind him and walked down the street to catch the trolley that would take him to the Union Depot. He left St. Louis that day on the noon train for Philadelphia.

And he would never see his family again.

WHEN HOLMES WAS RELEASED FROM JAIL, HE WAS FINALLY reunited with Georgiana. She had been a wreck while he was locked up, publicly proclaiming that her husband was the victim of unscrupulous competitors. It had all been a misunderstanding – he'd done nothing wrong.

She gave every indication that she was a confused, anxious young wife, but privately, she likely wondered if Holmes had finally failed to outrun the law.

But now he was free – at least until his trial. But that was a trial that Holmes didn't plan to stick around for. As soon as he and

Georgiana arrived at their apartment, they started packing. They were on their way to Philadelphia, where they'd soon meet up with Ben Pitezel.

Holmes told his wife that they had to travel separately. He was skipping bail, which meant the authorities would be looking for him. But if the cops were hunting him, they'd also be hunting Georgiana, who'd helped arrange his bail. So, he directed her to go to Lake Bluff, Illinois. Once there, she'd spend a few days with a friend, who'd been urging her to visit for a few years.

Meanwhile, Holmes would go on to Philadelphia and find a place for them to stay. They agreed to rendezvous there in one week.

By the time they left St. Louis, Ben Pitezel was already in Philadelphia. While eating at a small neighborhood restaurant owned by Josiah Richman at the corner of Ninth and Cherry, he asked Richman where he could find a place to stay. He said he was a stranger in the city and was looking for a place to board temporarily until he found a house to rent for his wife and children, who would be joining him in several weeks.

As it turned out, Richman's sister owned a boarding house, and he provided Ben with the address. He proceeded directly to Susan Harley's lodging house at 1002 Race Street and rented a room for himself. He settled in and waited for Holmes to arrive.

There's no record of when Holmes arrived in Philadelphia, but we do know that by Sunday, August 5 – the day Georgiana's train pulled into the station from Illinois – he was staying at a rooming house at 1905 North Eleventh Street, which was owned by a retired doctor named Jane Alcorn.

He fetched Georgiana from the station and brought her back to the rooming house, where he'd earlier registered them as Mr. and Mrs. H.M. Howard. At tea with Dr. Alcorn's family, Holmes talked about his plans for his time in the city. He told them that he represented a firm marketing a device for copying business documents and had come to Philadelphia to see about leasing several of the machines to the Pennsylvania Railroad Company.

Dr. Alcorn later confessed to liking the couple very much. She considered the handsome, self-assured businessman and his pretty, soft-spoken wife some of the finest tenants she'd ever had.

She'd be just one of the many people who were utterly shocked when it was later revealed she'd had tea with a multiple murderer and swindler and a young woman who was just one of several of his wives.

Downtown Philadelphia in 1894

Over the next few days, Georgiana mostly stayed at the rooming house while Holmes and Ben Pitezel worked out the final details of the plan. Ben had started to establish himself using the name B.F. Perry and created an identity as a dealer in patents.

This worked well since Ben already knew the business. Several years earlier, he had tinkered together a cleverly constructed coal bin, which had been designed with a door that kept coal from being stolen and prevented coal dust from escaping and polluting the air. He patented his invention in 1891 and attempted to market the device in Chicago. Nothing had ever come of the venture, but Ben had acquired enough firsthand experience that he could pass himself off as someone who bought and sold patents for other people's inventions.

There were only two hurdles left to clear. They needed to find a suitable place for Pitezel to set up shop and Holmes had to come up with a corpse to pass off as Ben. But then, the whole scheme was nearly derailed before it could even get started.

Holmes and Ben were having lunch in a downtown restaurant when Ben suddenly remembered something. Perhaps it was because of his drinking or perhaps because he was just careless, but he had forgotten to mail the most recent premium on his life insurance policy.

As he stammered out an apology. Holmes merely stared at him for a moment. Then, he slammed his hand down so hard on the table that the cutlery flew into the air and a cup of coffee was spilled. Without a word, he rose from his chair, tossed a handful of coins on the table, and walked out of the restaurant.

Ben followed him down the street, apologizing as he struggled to keep up, but Holmes said nothing.

That same afternoon, a clerk at Fidelity's branch in Chicago received a telegraphic money order for $157.50, the semiannual payment on life insurance policy #044145, registered under the name B.F. Pitezel.

The clerk entered the payment in the books, noting that it had arrived just in time. The payment was past due, but that day was the final day of the grace period before cancellation. If it had arrived one day later, the policy would have lapsed, and B.F. Pitezel's life would have no longer been insured.

A FEW DAYS LATER, HOLMES AND BEN FOUND THE PERFECT location for the patent office front. The building, located at 1316 Callowhill Street, was a dingy, run-down, three-story structure of faded brick that occupied a space next to others just like it on one side of a dirty block.

Directly across the brick street was an abandoned station of the Philadelphia and Reading Railroad, now crumbling, dark and desolate. Ben was supposed to draw as little attention to himself as possible so the building was chosen because it was in a neighborhood where he could open for business without attracting too many customers to his door.

The place had been vacant for some time, largely because of its terrible location. The ground floor had been converted into

The patent office storefront on Callowhill Street. The office was the narrow building in the center and a banner that read "patents" can be seen hanging in front below the window.

a small shop, with a display window facing the street and a metal awning out front that hung crookedly over the sidewalk. The second floor of the building contained two small bedrooms, which were more than suitable for Ben's needs.

The landlord must have been thrilled to have a new tenant. It had been empty for so long that he'd reduced the rent to just $10 a week.

But the price wasn't what made it so appealing to Holmes. There was another feature about the building that made it the perfect location for what they planned to do there. Oddly, it was probably the main reason why so many other potential tenants had turned it down.

The building in which Ben would open his patent shop was located directly behind the Philadelphia city morgue.

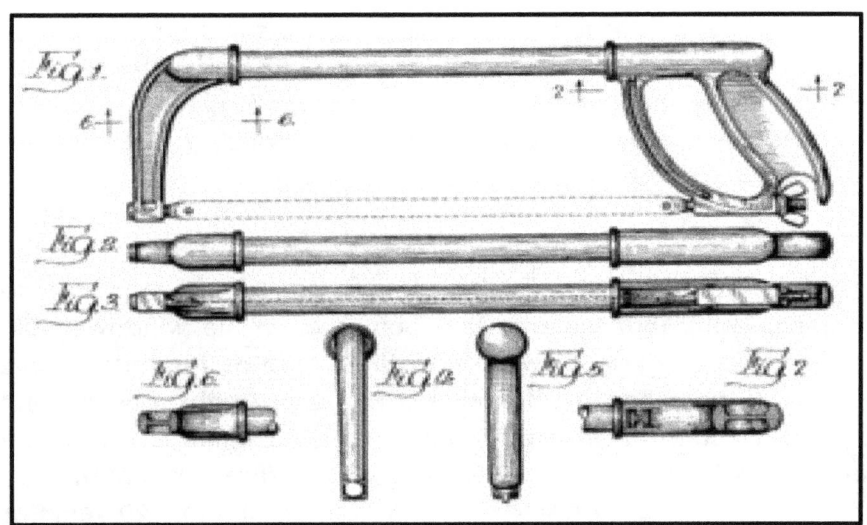

IT WAS AUGUST 17, 1894, AND BEN PITEZEL RAN THE WET TOWEL over the dusty window of 1316 Callowhill Street in Philadelphia. The dirt and grime of an unknown number of years smeared into a muddy mess on the glass and so Ben tossed the contents of his bucket onto it and tried again. After some elbow grease, he finally managed to get a clear view through the front window. There wasn't much to see, but he didn't want to put any more effort into it than he needed to. Ben didn't plan to stay here long.

Once the window was clean, he went back into the shop. He picked up a sign and placed it in the freshly polished window so that it could be clearly seen from the street. The sign read: B.F. PERRY – PATENTS BOUGHT AND SOLD

Ben never expected to buy or sell any patents during his stay in Philadelphia. He was just killing time, establishing a presence on the street, and interacting with the neighbors a bit, so when the time came for him to disappear – and leave a corpse in his place – everyone would assume the dead man was Ben.

But Ben didn't yet know just how convincing the so-called "illusion" would turn out to be.

AS FAR AS WE KNOW, THE FIRST – AND PERHAPS ONLY – customer to enter B.F. Perry's patent office was a man named Eugene Smith. That the sign that Ben stuck in the window could ever attract any kind of walk-in traffic almost defies imagination, but a neighbor had mentioned the place to Smith after walking by and spotting it. On Wednesday, August 22, Smith left his home on Rhodes Street and went over to see the office for himself.

Smith was a carpenter by trade but for the last 20 years or so, he had been dabbling in inventions. Starting with the E. Smith Saw Tooth in 1875, he'd patented four different devices, all of which had to do with saws. Most recently, in January 1893, he'd been granted a patent on a device for setting saw teeth into handsaws and he was eager to figure out a way to make money from it. He thought that perhaps Mr. Perry could be the man to help him.

He later described the interior of the office, which was a place that a more sophisticated man would have described as very shabby. It had been furnished with cheap, secondhand chairs,  a beat-up desk and rickety wooden filing cabinet. The walls were mostly bare but there was a crude wooden shelf that held an assortment of chemicals – benzene, ammonia, and chloroform among them – all in brown bottles with stoppers.

Smith put out a hand and introduced himself to Mr. Perry, explaining why he had dropped by. Perry listened attentively and asked him to bring the device into the shop so that he could examine it.

Ben was likely truly interested in the man's device. It may have even crossed his mind that he really could make a living buying and selling patents if he put some effort into it. If he did, he could forget about the wild scheme to fake his death and make a new start on the right side of the law.

Or perhaps he was just bored being stuck in the office every day while he waited for Holmes to finish the last details of the plan. Smith may have been nothing more than a distraction – who knows?

Newspaper illustration of Ben Pitezel printed several months after the death of "B.F. Perry"

Smith returned to Perry's shop several times and the next time he came in, he brought the working model for his sawtooth device with him. Perry took it over to a table and examined it. While he waited, Smith asked several questions about the shop, his plans, and how long he had been in business, but Perry's answers seemed vague. He explained that he had moved to Philadelphia from St. Louis and had only been in the city for a short time.

A few minutes later, Perry complimented Smith on the cleverness of his device and assured him that he could do something for him. But when Perry explained that he would need to keep the model in his shop, Smith was dismayed. There seemed to be no safe place to store the device, and he hated to think of his model just shoved into a corner. Perry assured him that it would be safe. He said he intended to install a counter, but his tools were still in St. Louis.

Smith saw his chance for work and offered to build Perry a nice counter. Perry mulled it over for a moment and then agreed. After agreeing on a day to do the job, Smith picked up his hat and started to leave but just then, the door opened, and he turned to look as a man walked into the shop.

Smith would later identify him as H.H. Holmes.

By the time, Holmes realized there was someone in the shop with Ben, it was too late. To his dismay, the man turned and looked at him. Holmes didn't want any witnesses who could connect him to Ben. He hesitated, thinking he would turn and leave, but then he didn't. He stiffly walked past the two other men, nodding to them and went up the stairs to the second floor.

Mr. Perry excused himself for a moment and with no explanation for Smith, turned and followed the other man upstairs.

Smith watched him and sat down in one of the straight-backed chairs in front of the desk. He gazed idly around the office, waiting for Perry's return. He fidgeted in his seat, stood up, sat down again, and finally gave up waiting. He was waiting for Perry to give him a receipt for the device he was leaving with him. Finally, he wrote a note for the man that said he'd return soon to build the counter, and Smith left the store.

Once Smith was gone, Holmes told Ben he had important news. He'd just received word from a doctor he knew in New York who had a cadaver they could use as a substitute for Ben's body. Holmes just had to go to New York, secure the corpse, and return to Philadelphia. If all went smoothly, they would have the insurance money in their hands in a matter of weeks.

On August 30, Eugene Smith returned to the patent office with his toolbox. He and Mr. Perry went to the lumberyard to buy some boards for the counter. On the way back, Perry suggested that they stop in for a drink at Fritz Richard's saloon, located just a few doors away from the patent office.

Smith ordered a beer, Perry drank whiskey, and then they went back to the patent office where Smith put together an unfinished wood counter. Perry paid him 50-cents for the job – which would be about $30 today – and he assured Smith that

things were progressing nicely with his sawtooth invention. He had already contacted several investors and suggested that Smith stop by in a few days and perhaps he'd have good news for him.

Shortly after 6:00 P.M. on September 1, Holmes was summoned from his room at Dr. Alcorn's boarding house to speak to a man who had come to see him. He later told the landlady that the caller was a man from the Pennsylvania Railroad Company, and they would be meeting again in the morning to close out contracts for the copier.

It wasn't – it was Ben Pitezel. What they spoke about will never be known for sure, but according to a statement that Holmes later gave to the police, Ben came to say that the deal would have to be delayed. He had received a telegram from St. Louis saying that baby Wharton was seriously ill and he had to go home.

It does seem as though Ben was planning to leave town, but since Wharton wasn't actually sick, he had likely changed his mind about the scheme and decided to retrieve his family from St. Louis and perhaps go into hiding.

Ben's next stop was Pierce's tobacco shop for a couple of cigars for his journey and then he went to Pritchard's saloon for a drink. He got change for two $10 bills and returned to the patent shop, where he likely packed up his things.

Ben was done with the scheme -- at least for now.

H.H. HOLMES WASN'T HAPPY ABOUT HIS PARTNER'S announcement. He believed he was on the verge of the largest reward of his career so far. But to make his plan work, he needed Ben Pitezel. And he needed him dead.

We'll never know sure why Holmes decided to kill his partner, a man who had always been loyal to him and never questioned his schemes, but maybe Ben's decision to return to St. Louis was the reason. Perhaps Holmes decided that he couldn't let Ben go and still trust him with his secrets.

Or maybe Holmes felt disappointed by Ben's willingness to stick to the plan they'd made and to Holmes, murder was a reasonable reaction to that.

Or more likely, Holmes had been planning to murder his friend all along. If he had ever really planned to use a substitute corpse, he changed his mind while in Philadelphia.

Very early the next morning, Holmes left the boarding house. He told Georgiana that as soon as his business was concluded, they'd be leaving Philadelphia. She was feeling sick and wasn't eager to travel, but Holmes insisted that she be packed and ready to leave for the train station when he returned.

Holmes walked quickly to Callowhill Street. The neighborhood was mostly silent as he walked to the patent office, unlocked the door, and quietly went inside. He stood in the center of the floor and listened for a sound he'd hoped he would hear – the snores of a man who'd had too much to drink. Holmes was familiar with Ben's habits. He'd given him money the previous night and he knew that some of it would be spent on liquor.

Holmes crept up the stairs and found Ben asleep. From his pocket, Holmes withdrew a handkerchief and a small chemist's bottle. He uncorked the bottle and then, holding it away from his own face, he saturated the cloth with the liquid from the bottle. It was chloroform, a substance used by doctors to keep a patient unconscious by carefully administering small doses.

Knocking someone out using chloroform is not as easy as it looks on television, when a cloth is pressed to a person's face, and they instantly pass out. Chloroform must be given to someone carefully. It's more dangerous than ether and too much can kill someone very easily. A person who wasn't skilled in using it would have a difficult time causing an uncooperative person to pass out. But if a person was drunk, or at least unconscious already, killing someone with chloroform would be easy for a trained physician or chemist -- especially one who'd had plenty of practice already.

That morning, Holmes committed a murder during which he left behind enough evidence that details of the killing can be pieced together reasonably well. From all evidence, Holmes' old friend died without putting up a fight.

But there was one last thing that still needed to be done. Once Ben was dead, Holmes arranged the body to look as though Ben had been killed by accident.

He broke a bottle of benzine and placed a pipe next to Ben's body. He wanted to create the impression that he'd try to light his

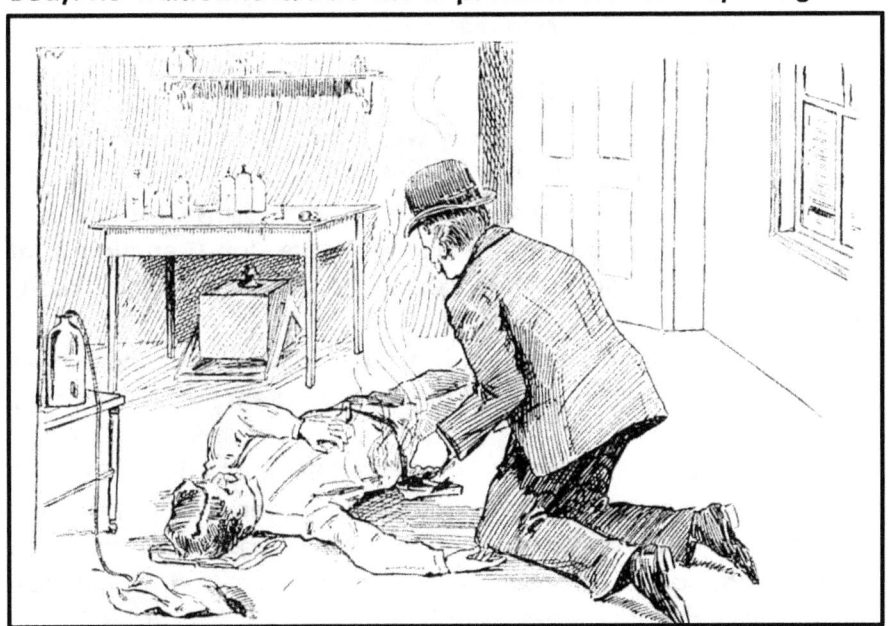

A newspaper illustration of Holmes burning Ben's face and clothing after he murdered him at the Callowhill Street office.

pipe too close to a bottle of flammable chemicals. Then, using the fumes from the chemicals that had been spilled, he lit a match.

A ball of fire whooshed into the air, forcing Holmes to duck backwards. The flames scorched Ben's skin causing reddened blisters to appear. The hair on his face burned away and his head was scorched by the fire. If anyone looked at him the man, they'd know right away, Holmes believed, that he'd been killed by the explosion.

Holmes now raced back to Dr. Alcorn's boarding house and told Georgiana that they were leaving right away and going to Indianapolis. Still sick, she didn't want to go but didn't argue with him.

He also gave her some instructions:

Tell Dr. Alcorn that we're going to Harrisburg. The St. Louis matters aren't fully settled and if too many people know where I am, I'm likely to be arrested again.

Georgiana understood. She didn't want her husband in jail again. By 10:25 that morning, they were on a train to Indianapolis.

Meanwhile, back at the patent office, Ben's body was left lying on the floor. The corpse was on its back, arms over its chest. Holmes probably expected it to lie there long enough that decomposition would further cover the traces of what really happened.

But he hadn't counted on just how determined a carpenter named Eugene Smith was about selling the patent for his invention.

ON MONDAY AFTERNOON, SEPTEMBER 3, AS HOLMES AND Georgiana were arriving in Indianapolis, Eugene Smith returned to the patent office on Callowhill Street. There was no answer when he knocked, so he opened the unlocked door and called out, "Hello? Mr. Perry? It's Eugene Smith!"

Greeted by nothing but silence, Smith walked in. The front room was dark and seemed vacant. There was no sound at all.

Smith called out again, but once more, there was no answer. He left the office and closed the door behind him.

Smith looked around the neighborhood, trying the saloon where they'd shared a drink, of course, but there was no sign of the man. He couldn't find anyone who'd seen Perry since Saturday night. With a sigh, Eugene went home and decided that he'd try again tomorrow.

The next day, Smith returned to Perry's office. There was still no answer to his knock, but the door was still unlocked, so he decided to investigate.

He entered the shop and walked behind the counter, where Smith's desk was located. Beyond the desk were the stairs. As Smith placed his foot on the first step, he listened intently for any sound on the upper level but still heard nothing.

But then he noticed the smell coming from upstairs. Ben had told him that he kept a laboratory on the second floor where he used benzine and an assortment of acids to manufacture washing powder, but this certainly wasn't the smell of cleaning products.

Smith slowly climbed the narrow staircase. As he neared the second-floor landing, he could see a bedroom straight ahead of him. He peered into the dimly lit room. A gloom hung in the air, casting long shadows over an empty bed with some tangled sheets and a thin blanket on it. He could see nothing else in the room, but that horrible smell was much thicker on the second floor.

Looking away from the bedroom, he turned to see what was behind him – and he froze.

On the floor of the other bedroom was what appeared to be a human body, its feet angled toward the open window and its head closer to the door. The face was blackened and swollen, and while Smith couldn't tell who the man was – he feared the worst. He was afraid it was B.F. Perry.

He decided not to look any closer. Instead, he fled the building and ran down the street toward the Buttonwood police station.

DR. WILLIAM SCOTT, WHO OPERATED A SMALL PHARMACY ON the ground floor of his home at Thirteenth and Vine, had just opened his store when Police Officer William Sauer came into the shop. He explained that a dead man had been discovered that morning at 1316 Callowhill, and from the evidence, it looked as though he had been killed in an explosion. He asked Dr. Scott if he would mind coming over and examining the remains.

Wondering what grisly sight awaited him, Dr. Scott followed the policeman a few blocks to a faded little building, through a dusty office, and up some narrow stairs to a bedroom. Two men were bending over the corpse – a second police officer and a man in workman's clothing who looked very pale and was clutching a handkerchief over his face. Dr. Scott took out his own handkerchief and clamped it over his mouth and nose. Even so, he nearly gagged at the smell in the room. He leaned down to take a closer look at the corpse and was immediately puzzled by some of the oddities about it.

Smith later told a jury:

The face was much mortified, indicating putrefaction. There was considerable stench in the room, and we found around the room a broken bottle and some uncorked bottles on the mantel.

We found the face discolored and distorted, or full of pools, the inner skin and the outer skin, separated and watery-like. The odor was terrible. The tongue was swollen and stuck out of his mouth and red fluid issued from his mouth.

The doctor added that he'd expected to find a man burned to death, or blown to death in an explosion, but instead of shattered bones and mangled flesh, he found a body that was not only intact but stretched out almost neatly on the floor. Stiff and straight, legs carefully together, the dead man was on his back, his left arm extended at his side. His right arm, bent at the elbow, was resting on his chest and his hand cupped over his heart. It looked like he'd died in his sleep, except for the fact that he'd clearly charred by fire.

The doctor and the police officers on the scene also found everything that had been left behind – the burned match, the pipe, the broken bottle of benzine, and the row of chemical bottles with their corks removed.

As Dr. Scott was examining the body, a police officer proposed a theory. He suggested to the doctor that, while lighting his pipe, the deceased had struck a match too close to the bottles, whose contents contained a volatile mix of chemicals, and the flame ignited the chemical fumes and caused the fatal explosion.

It was exactly what Holmes wanted them to think.

But Dr. Scott had his doubts. If there had been an explosion, surely the dead man's pipe would have been damaged by the blast. Almost certainly, it would have gone flying across the room. But the pipe was sitting unscathed and upright a few inches from the corpse's head, as though it had been neatly placed there. In addition, the broken chemical bottle near the corpse looked as though it had been dropped, not shattered by an explosion. But Dr. Scott didn't have a better explanation than the one offered by the policeman, so he focused his attention on the corpse.

The dead man's face had been burned, but their only witness, Eugene Smith, said the corpse appeared to be a man named B.F. Perry, with whom Smith had done business. He confirmed that the clothing, hair color, and general size of the body matched that of the patent dealer.

As Dr. Scott studied the blackened face and scorched facial hair, he recalled that he had met Perry on an earlier occasion. About a month earlier, a stranger who introduced himself as a new arrival in the neighborhood had come into Scott's pharmacy to make a small purchase. The man's face had stuck in Dr. Scott's mind.

But now, he had reached the limit of what he could do for the investigation. A formal autopsy needed to be conducted, and the corpse would need to go to the county morgue – which was

The city's second morgue was a short distance from the patent office. It had opened earlier that same year after gruesome accounts of the conditions at the original morgue.

clearly visible from the window of the room where the body had been found.

To Dr. Scott and the police officers, this seemed to be nothing more than a grim coincidence – but was it?

If the body had not been found so quickly by Eugene Smith, it would have decomposed, and the proximity of the morgue would have hidden the smell of Perry's corpse from the neighbors.

If not for Eugene Smith, there's no way of knowing how long the corpse might have been left in that room. And no way of knowing if B.F. Perry would ever have been identified at all.

The corpse was transported to the morgue, and a postmortem exam was conducted by Dr. William Mattern, the coroner's physician, that same day. Morgue Superintendent Thomas Robinson and Deputy Superintendent Benjamin Robinson assisted him. Dr. Scott, who by now was quite interested in the case, was allowed to attend as a witness and he jotted down notes in a book that he had brought along with him.

They found the heart empty, indicating a very quick death. The lungs were very congested and, like the liver and spleen, were filled with blood. A glance at the state of the kidneys revealed that Perry was a man who, Dr. Scott wrote, "never refused a drink when he had the chance to take it."

The stomach was empty of food, but it contained a significant quantity – as much as an ounce or two – of a fluid that proved to be chloroform.

Mattern took note of one additional detail. While flames had clearly burned Perry's right arm – the one that was resting across his chest – there were no burn marks on the underside of the arm, the part lying against his body. Mattern  believed this could only mean one thing – that the burning had been done *after* the arm had been placed on the dead man's chest.

Dismissing the theory of an explosion, the doctors concluded that the man had died suddenly from chloroform poisoning. There was no way, in their opinion, that the man could have killed himself in such a way and then placed his body in the position in which it was found. A second person had very clearly arranged it that way.

This meant that Holmes' attempt to make it look as though Ben had died by accidental explosion had been a failure. The coroner had seen through his ruse and passed on a report to the police.

Detectives, though, weren't interested in their findings. They had decided that Perry had died in an explosion. And the next day, a coroner's jury ruled the same way. It turned out to be a stroke of almost unbelievable luck for H.H. Holmes.

The body of B.F. Perry remained in the morgue for five days before being buried in an unmarked grave in a potter's field at Mechanic's Cemetery. But, of course, the story of that mysterious corpse was far from over.

AT THE SAME TIME THAT THE CORONER'S EXAMINATION WAS happening, Holmes was traveling by train to St. Louis.

When Holmes and an ailing Georgiana had arrived in Indianapolis, he'd taken her to Stubbin's European Hotel, a small place just one block from the Union depot. Georgiana rested there for the next two days. Holmes remained with her during this time, occasionally going out for an hour or two to attend to messages and unspecified business.

Then, on the afternoon of September 5, he returned to the hotel room and told her that he needed take care of some business out of town. He'd be back in a few days and would ask the hotel owner's wife to check in on her while he was away and ensure that she received the proper care.

Holmes left straightway for St. Louis. He was going to see Carrie Pitezel, the widow of the man he'd murdered just a few days before. He intended to get there before the family could learn of Ben's death, but he hadn't counted on Eugene Smith finding the body as quickly as he did – or for B.F. Perry's strange death to make national news.

While Ben, Holmes, and Georgiana had been in Philadelphia, Carrie had been waiting patiently in the dirty flat in St. Louis, waiting on news from Ben. She had been hoping since the day he'd left that he might change his mind about the swindle and come home, but as the days passed without news, she came to realize he intended to go through with it.

But even so, she must have been startled when she saw a tiny item in the September 6 issue of the *St. Louis Globe-Dispatch* newspaper. It was a single column, and it reported the strange circumstances surrounding the death of a Philadelphia patent dealer named B.F. Perry.

Carrie had been told by Ben not to believe the story but even so, her stress, embarrassment, and shame got the better of her. When Holmes arrived at the Pitezel home, he found the household in a terrible state. A doctor had been called to administer a sedative to Carrie, who was in shock.

It wasn't so much that Carrie believed the story of Ben's death; it was more that this was the thing that sent her temporarily over the edge. It had been a difficult time in St. Louis for the family. Carrie's stress had given her blinding headaches for which there seemed to be no relief. The children had been sick, they rarely had enough food, and the apartment they lived in was suffocating in

B. F. PERRY'S TRAGIC DEATH.

Speculation as to the Causes of a Former St. Louisan's End at Philadelphia.

Special Dispatch to the Globe-Democrat.

PHILADELPHIA, PA., September 4.— With a blackened face and charred arm, B. F. Perry, aged about 40 years, who recently came from St. Louis, was found dead this morning in a second-story back room at 1316 Callow Hill street. A broken benzine bottle, a pipe filled with tobacco and a match which had been ignited lay on the floor, silent witnesses to his death.

The man died under the most peculiar circumstances, and three theories are advanced as to the cause of his death. The first is that it was the result of an accident; the second, that he might have ended his own life, and, finally, that death might have been caused by foul play. Circumstances surrounding the case seem to bear out the idea of accident, the direct cause of death seeming to be an explosion of benzine or chemical substance.

Perry was a sort of patent broker or merchant. He moved into the house 1316 Callow Hill street about three weeks ago. The structure is a two and a half story building, with a store in front. When Perry went into the house he improvised a counter and posted two or three signs on the walls. Across the front window he hung a muslin sign stating that patents were bought and sold inside. The last time he was seen alive was Saturday night. Between the hours of 7 and 8 o'clock on that evening he entered a saloon in the vicinity of his residence and purchased a pint of whisky. After leaving the saloon he went directly to his house. Yesterday morning Eugene Smith, of Rhodes street, who had business with Perry, entered the store, but could not find the proprietor. The door being unlocked, he concluded that Perry was out, and left, intending to return again. This morning as Mr. Smith was passing the place he decided to go in and see Perry. Upon entering the place he found it deserted. Growing suspicious, he went upstairs, and in the middle room of the second floor was startled by seeing Perry lying in the center of the floor. Upon examination he found the man was dead.

The newspaper story that Carrie Pitezel saw in the St. Louis newspaper about the tragic death of "B.F. Perry," which she knew was her husband, Ben.

the summer heat. Ben had given her with money when he left but it was already gone, forcing Carrie to try to feed her family by taking in laundry and sewing.

When Carrie had read the small article about B.F. Perry's death at the kitchen table that morning, she had started to cry. Her weeping brought the children to her side. It was Alice who looked down and saw the name of B.F. Perry in the newspaper and recognized it from the letters that her mother had mailed to Philadelphia each week. She cried that Papa was dead and then she started to weep, too.

The other children were stunned into silence and then they, too, began to cry. Even Dessie began crying, despite her father's warnings not to believe any reports of his death.

And that was how a doctor had been summoned to the apartment and why Holmes had found the family in a state of despair when he arrived.

Even though Carrie had never been fond of Holmes, her misery, loneliness, and then happiness at seeing a familiar face overwhelmed her when he arrived, and she threw herself against his chest and began to sob again.

Holmes patted her back and tried to console her. He led her to a chair and pressed a clean, white handkerchief into her hands. As she continued to cry, he assured her that Ben was perfectly fine. The dead body described in the newspaper was the substitute corpse he'd told her about. Ben was well. He was hiding out and would join the family soon.

But the distraught woman refused to be comforted. Holmes asked her impatiently why she was so upset, and Carrie launched into a litany of complaints about her illnesses, the children being sick and hungry, and their lack of money. Holmes asked her what the children believed of Ben's fate and Carrie replied with a heavy sigh that they believed him to be dead. Holmes nodded in approval and told her, "Good. Do not relieve them of that notion. It will make matters easier."

Before Carrie could object to doing something so cruel, Holmes took Dessie aside and spoke with her. He assured her that everything would be fine, gave her some money, and sent her out to buy some groceries for the family.

When Dessie was gone, Holmes turned his attention back to Carrie. She had to get control of herself – she had an important role to play over the next few days. The success of the plan, which would lead to Ben coming home to her, depended on her assistance.

He took a business card from his coat pocket and put it in her hand. Tomorrow morning, he said, she must go to the address printed on the card and bring with her the life insurance policy that Ben had left in her care.

Carrie looked at the card. The name printed on it was Jeptha D. Howe, Esq. and the address was at the Wainwright Building in downtown St. Louis.

Before Holmes left the apartment, he asked Carrie about the letters that Ben had sent her from Philadelphia. She showed them to him, and he picked out a few to keep, then told her to destroy the rest. He didn't want them to be seized as evidence at some point. He warned her that if she didn't help with the plan and stay quiet about what she knew, she'd not only get Ben in trouble, but herself and the children, too.

Carrie agreed to do what Holmes told her. She knew she had no other choice.

Jeptha Howe was not surprised when Carrie Pitezel showed up at his office the next day. He had also seen the death notice in the St. Louis newspaper the previous day. He knew that Holmes'

The Wainwright Building, one of the early skyscrapers in St. Louis, where Jeptha Howe's offices were located.

plan was finally happening, and he was ready to move forward with his end of the deal.

And Howe wasn't the only one reading the papers.

At the Four Corners prison, Marion Hedgepeth had also been requesting the daily newspapers from his jailers. He searched each day for any indication that the scheme hatched by the swindler named Howard was truly happening. When he saw the story about the death of B.F. Perry he was likely filled with a grim sense of satisfaction.

That $500 finder's fee that he'd been promised was certainly going to come in handy someday.

TWO DAYS AFTER HOLMES VISITED THE PIETZEL APARTMENT, George B. Stadden, the manager of the St. Louis branch of the Fidelity Mutual Life Insurance Association, received a brief letter and a newspaper clipping about the death of a Philadelphia man named B.F. Perry. The letter, which was written in a neat, feminine hand, though filled with misspellings, was from Mrs. Carrie Pitezel, who wished to inform the company that the individual who was the subject of the article was her husband, Benjamin F. Pitezel, holder of the life insurance policy #044145. Stadden read the article again and then left his office to send a telegram to Philadelphia.

The telegram was received by Fidelity Mutual's president Levi G. Fouse. He was also in his office that Saturday morning to receive the telegram from his St. Louis manager. The message read:

> B.F. Perry, found dead in Philadelphia, is claimed to be B.F. Pitezel, who is insured 044145. Investigate before remains leave there.

Fouse then contacted his claims manager, Ophir LaForrest Perry, who looked up the file. He discovered that Benjamin Pitezel's policy had been issued on November 9, 1893, by the company's Chicago branch and that Pitezel was indeed insured for $10,000 – an impressive sum in 1894, that's worth around $355,000 today.

This makes it clear why Holmes was so intent on making this scheme work.

But there were a few things that seemed peculiar to the experienced claims manager. The policy had been issued less than a year before the man's sudden death, a circumstance that automatically provoked a bit of concern. In addition, the most recent payment had arrived by telegraphic money order on the very last day of the grace period. And then there was the matter of the man's alias. Why had B.F Pitezel been using the name Perry instead of his own?

The home of the Fidelity Mutual Life Insurance Association in Philadelphia

Red flags were wildly waving at the Fidelity Mutual company.

Fouse contacted another trusted man in the company, the treasurer, Colonel O.C. Bobyshell. He was dispatched to the city morgue to see if the corpse in question matched the physical description of Ben Pitezel, as it was recorded in the policy application. When he returned, he told Fouse that even though the dead man's face was badly disfigured, the general appearance of the body did match that of Ben Pitezel. He also informed Fouse and LaForrest Perry of what the coroner thought of the case, which was, as we know, different from the official version of events.

1316 Callowhill Street after Ben's patent office signs had been removed. Insurance investigators were not as willing to believe the man died in an accident as the police were.

This sent LaForrest Perry to 1316 Callowhill Street, where, accompanied by a police officer, he spent more than an hour examining the scene. Except for the removal of the corpse, the room had been left untouched. The pipe, burned match, and broken bottle were still on the floor, exactly where they had been found. To Perry, the evidence looked more like a set-up than an accidental explosion, as the police continued to claim. After returning to the office, he reported his theories to Fouse, who immediately wired a message to Edwin H. Cass, manager of the Chicago branch, and told him to learn everything that he could about Benjamin F. Pitezel, especially the names of his acquaintances.

Levi Fouse spent the rest of his weekend at home, giving little thought to the Pitezel matter. On Monday morning, though, he arrived at his office to find a message waiting for him from a St. Louis lawyer named Jeptha D. Howe, the attorney for Mrs. Carrie Pitezel. Howe informed Fouse that he, along with a member of the Pitezel family, would soon be traveling to Philadelphia to identify the body and collect the $10,000 life insurance policy.

BACK IN ST. LOUIS, HOLMES WAS DEALING WITH THE MANY moving parts of his scheme. He'd had some experience with swindling insurance companies and knew that a family member would be required to identify Ben's remains.

His original plan was to have Carrie go to Philadelphia for the identification, but he'd changed his mind. He didn't think she could be trusted to carry off the deception. She was already in an overwrought state and the sight of the corpse, or even tough questions from insurance investigators, would likely cause her to break down completely and blurt out the truth.

Worse yet, she might recognize the body in the morgue as that of her husband, and not a substitute corpse. Holmes had done what he could to obliterate Ben's features, but he preferred Carrie not to see the body at all. He would have likely done anything necessary – from heartfelt pleas to outright threats – to keep her in St. Louis.

As it turned out, there was no need for Holmes to bother. Carrie was sick and her infant son, Wharton, was even sicker. She told Holmes that she couldn't possibly travel such a distance. Her oldest daughter, Dessie, was also needed at home.

That left the next-oldest child, Alice, to be given the job. Holmes quickly acted as though Alice coming to Philadelphia had been his plan all along and even claimed he'd talked to Ben about it. He hadn't, of course, but Alice was a perfect choice for what he needed. Alice was smart enough to follow directions, but not so clever that she might figure things out and jeopardize the scheme.

Although Carrie was concerned about sending the girl off with Jeptha Howe, who would also be making the trip, Holmes assured her that Alice would be in good hands. He'd already arranged for his cousin to take care of Alice when they arrived in Philadelphia. Holmes assured her that his cousin was a lovely and highly responsible young woman that he trusted completely. Carrie recognized the cousin's name – in fact, she had pretended to be Holmes' cousin on one occasion. Her name, he told Carrie, was Minnie Williams.

That evening, September 9, Holmes and Jeptha Howe met to make their final preparations. Howe had been drafting paperwork granting Holmes the power of attorney over Carrie Pitezel. He'd never need to worry about what happened to the insurance money.

The following morning, Holmes left St. Louis, headed once again for Indianapolis.

ON THE SAME MORNING HOLMES LEFT ST. LOUIS, EDWIN CASS, the manager of Fidelity Mutual's Chicago office, was looking over the records for policy #044145 and identifying the agent who had sold it to Ben Pitezel. He telephoned the agent, Leon Fay, and asked him if he remembered setting up the policy and anything he might know about Pitezel. Did he know where he worked, or any of his friends?

As it happened, Fay did know something about Ben. Several years earlier, before he had started in the insurance business, Fay had been involved in various enterprises, one of which had put him into contact with a wealthy businessman in Englewood.

And then, the previous Fall, that same businessman had walked into Fay's office and asked about the price of a $10,000 insurance policy for himself. Fay had provided the information but never heard anything else from the man. Several weeks later, though, Benjamin Pitezel -- who said that he had been referred to Fay by the first fellow -- showed up in his office and applied for his own policy in precisely that amount. When asked, Fay explained that the gentleman in question was the owner of a large

Holmes' "office building" in Englewood

office building at Sixty-Third and Wallace named H.H. Holmes.

The following day, Cass took the train to Englewood. He had no trouble finding the building. It stood out among the others nearby. When he approached the building, his trained investigator's eye immediately spotted the scorching of fire damage near the roofline. The top two stories of the structure looked vacant, the windows dark and empty. The ground floor, however, was lined with shops, most of them open for business.

By asking around, it didn't take Cass long to discover that Dr. Holmes had not been seen in Englewood for nearly a year. However, C.E. Davis – the talkative jeweler – did provide Cass with a promising lead. Even though Holmes had quite a reputation with the ladies, Davis knew that he was married and had a wife and daughter living somewhere on the North Shore, perhaps in Wilmette.

Cass investigated and discovered Holmes' suburban address. He traveled to Wilmette and found the place, a neat, two-storied house on a quiet street. His knock was answered by a servant girl, who led Cass into the parlor, and then went to fetch her mistress.

Myrta was very polite to Cass, but he could tell she was uneasy about his presence. She explained that her husband was rarely at home because his business affairs required him to travel all over the country. The two of them kept up a regular correspondence, though, and she was happy to pass along any messages that Mr. Cass might have for him. Since Holmes frequently moved, she sent letters to Frank E. Blackman, a financial agent on

Myrta's house in Wilmette

Dearborn Street, and Blackman passed information to her husband. He always had a forwarding address and had been acting as a sort of post office for Holmes.

Cass wrote out a list of questions for Myrta to convey to her husband and then, on September 17, Cass received a reply from Holmes, postmarked from Cincinnati. In it, Holmes pretended to think that Ben's body was in Chicago – probably to stall things a little – and he offered to travel there if his expenses were covered. He also noted that Ben owed him $180, which he wanted deducted from the insurance payout.

The next day, a follow-up letter arrived from Holmes that said he discovered his friend's body was in Philadelphia. Holmes wrote:

I shall be in Baltimore in a day or two and take an afternoon train to Philadelphia and call on your office there, and if they wish me to do so, will go with some representative of theirs to the coroner, and I think I can tell if the man there is Pitezel. From what I read here I cannot see anything to lead me to think the person killed was other than a man by the name of Perry.

Yours Respectfully,
H.H. Holmes

HOLMES ARRIVED BACK IN INDIANAPOLIS ON SEPTEMBER 11, completely unaware of what was happening with the insurance company. He found Georgiana to be feeling much better, although she was unhappy with the dinginess of the hotel where he'd left her. She was cheered up, though, when she received the present that Holmes had brought for her – a heart-shaped locket on a gold chain -- and was even happier when he packed up her belongings and moved her to the more luxurious surroundings of the Grand Hotel.

For the next few days, Holmes treated Georgiana to a shopping spree, took her to the fanciest restaurants in the city, and accompanied her on an overnight trip to her parents' home in Franklin.

When the couple returned to Indianapolis on September 15, they checked into the Circle Park Hotel. Later that day, while Georgiana napped, Holmes left their suite to check his messages. It was then that he'd received the letter from Myrta, through Frank Blackman, that contained the questions from Edwin Cass.

The Grand Hotel and (below) an ad for the Circle Park Hotel, both in Indianapolis. Holmes was always wary of staying in the same place for too long.

Making excuses to Georgiana, he left Indianapolis that night and took a late train to Cincinnati, where he composed and mailed a reply to Cass. He didn't want anyone to know where he was, so mailing a letter from Indianapolis was out of the question.

In his letter, he answered questions from the insurance investigator about Ben's dental work, health, and description. He also pretended that he thought the body was in Chicago.

He then followed the first letter with a second, mailed the next day, offering to meet representatives from the company in Philadelphia and claiming that Ben owed him $180. That part was classic Holmes. Only he would have the nerve to ask for a cut of money that he planned to steal.

After Holmes gave the second letter to the hotel's desk clerk to mail, he asked to be awakened early so he could catch the first train out of Cincinnati in the morning.

On the same evening that Holmes mailed the second letter to Edwin Cass, attorney Jeptha Howe arrived at the Pitezel family's apartment to collect Alice for the trip. It was Alice who opened the door for him, wearing a faded calico dress. A leather satchel, packed with a handful of other dresses that made up her entire wardrobe, was waiting by the door.

Alice Pitezel

Carrie, still suffering from whatever ailment had struck her down, rose from her sickbed to kiss her daughter goodbye. She urged the attorney to take good care of her. Howe assured her that he would and, noticing that Alice's shoes were so worn out that her toes stuck out of the holes at the end, promised to buy her a new pair when they reached their destination.

Alice hugged each of her siblings and then followed Howe out the door. With her bag in one hand and Alice's hand in his other, Howe led her to the nearest streetcar stop. After they boarded, Howe asked the girl if she'd brought any spending money with her. Alice replied that her mother had given her a 5-cent piece. Digging in his pocket, Howe took out a silver dollar and pressed it into the girl's hand with a smile.

It was undoubtedly the most money she'd ever seen in her life. Alice thanked him politely and tucked the coin into her satchel.

A short time later, they arrived at Union Station and boarded a train going east. That first train was nearly empty. Alice was allowed her own seat across the aisle from Howe, where she curled up and went to sleep. She awoke hours later, just as the train was arriving at the Cincinnati station, where they changed trains.

The second train was more crowded, and she shared a pair of seats with Howe. Alice took the seat by the window and watched the dark landscape as they rolled by, catching glimpses of lighted windows and eventually, saw people starting to stir in the small towns they passed through as the sun started to rise.

It was just after dawn when Alice realized that Howe was talking to someone across the aisle from him. Then she heard the other man say her name – she was startled to see it was her father's friend, Mr. Holmes. He exchanged seats with Howe so he could sit next to her.

Holmes told her how brave she was and explained that she had a difficult job ahead of her, but he and Mr. Howe would help her through it. He had instructions for her about how she needed to act around the insurance people. They were cruel people who wanted to make sure that her family didn't get the money they were supposed to get. But Holmes could make sure that didn't happen if Alice did exactly what he told her to do.

First, she must never say that she saw or spoke to Holmes on the train. Secondly, she must pretend that Holmes and her father were only casually acquainted and not the good friends that they were. Finally, she had to say with absolute certainty that the body in the morgue was her father. Other than that, she just needed to act in a natural manner. Holmes and Mr. Howe would take care of the rest.

He asked Alice to repeat his instructions and when he was satisfied that she'd do what he told her, he disappeared down the aisle of the train. She wouldn't see him again until a few days later.

When the train reached Washington, D.C., Alice left the train with Mr. Howe. Holmes continued to Philadelphia. He believed that

Washington, D.C. in the 1890s

it would be better if they traveled on separate trains for the last leg of the trip.

When Holmes reached the city, he returned to Dr. Alcorn's rooming house, registering again as Mr. Howard. The doctor was happy to see him, and he told her that he was back in the city to conclude his deal with the Pennsylvania Railroad Company. Negotiations were taking longer than he had expected and he was unsure when they would finally conclude.

Holmes wanted to rent his old room for himself and his wife, but he also needed a room for his little sister, Alice, who was spending the winter in his care. He said that Georgiana and Alice were enjoying a holiday in Atlantic City, but he planned to travel there in a few days and bring Alice back with him. Georgiana would likely stay in Atlantic City for a few more weeks before joining them in Philadelphia. Dr. Alcorn had two large bedrooms vacant on the third floor, so Holmes agreed to take all of them.

While Holmes was registering at the boarding house, Alice and Mr. Howe were taking in the sights of Washington. Alice, who had seen nothing of the world beyond the small towns of the Midwest and the rundown neighborhoods of Chicago and St. Louis, was overwhelmed by the grandeur of the nation's capital.

But for now, their visit had to end. Late that night, they left by train for Philadelphia, checking into two rooms at the Imperial Hotel during the early morning hours of Thursday, September 20.

Alice, although exhausted, tossed and turned that night. Now that they were in Philadelphia, she was scared. She knew that soon she would have to lie to the men from the insurance company and try to convince them that the dead man she'd been brought to look at was her father.

She knew the dead man wasn't really him – Mr. Holmes had told her – but she wasn't sure that anyone would believe her story. If she messed up, she knew her family would get into trouble, and so would she.

The Imperial Hotel in Philadelphia, where Alice and Jeptha Howe stayed on their first night in the city

But Alice didn't need to worry. She wouldn't have any trouble identifying the body of Ben Pitezel as her father.

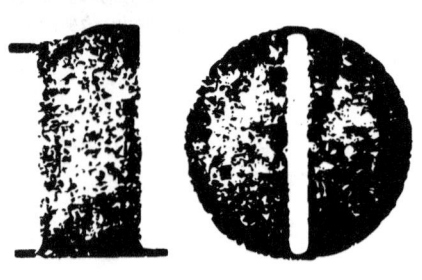 ALICE PITEZEL SAT ALONE IN A HOTEL ROOM IN PHILADELPHIA. In front of her on a small desk was a sheet of paper and an inkwell. She clutched a fountain pen in her delicate hand as she wrote a letter to her family in St. Louis.

Dear Momma and the Rest:

Just arrived in Philadelphia this morning... Mr. Howe and I have each a room at the above address. I am going to the Morgue after a while. We stopped off in Washington and Maryland. Yesterday, we got on the C. and O. Pullman, and it was crowded so I had to sit with Mr. Howe. We sit there quite a while, and pretty soon one came and shook hands with me. I looked up, and here it was Mr. H. He said he thought it was his girl's face, so he went to see, and it was me. I don't like him to call me babe and child and dear and all such trash.

How I wish I could see you all and hug the baby. I hope you are better. Mr. H. says I will have a ride on the ocean. I wish you could see what I have seen. I have seen more scenery than I have seen since I was born. This is all the paper I have so I will have to close and write again. You had better not write to me here for Mr. H. says that I may be off tomorrow. If you are worse, wire me.

Good-bye kisses to you all and two big ones for you and babe. Love to all.

Alice

Alice had promised to write to her family while on her trip, and she proved to be a faithful correspondent. In the weeks that followed her departure from St. Louis, she composed a series of letters that are heartbreaking today, thanks to the events in her life that followed. Sadly, though, most of the letters failed to reach her family, although Alice never knew that.

Nor did she know what a critical role her simple letters would play in the climax of the tragedy that was still to come.

ON SEPTEMBER 21, ALICE AND ATTORNEY JEPTHA HOWE WENT to the Fidelity Mutual Assurance Building in downtown Philadelphia, where they met with company president L.G. Fouse and his assistant, La Forrest Perry.

Howe had brought with him various documents and credentials, including a letter from Carrie Pitezel, giving him permission to act on her behalf. Carrie had also supplied him with some letters that Ben had sent her over the summer, proving that he had been using the name B.F. Perry. The return address on each envelope included the Perry name and the address of the office where the body had been found.

Fouse asked why Ben had been using a false name, and Howe replied that because of some "embarrassing financial transactions," Pitezel thought it "advisable to change his name and location" for a while.

Fouse looked over the letters, which left no doubt that Pitezel had been passing himself off as B.F. Perry. But, even so, this did not prove that the dead man was Ben Pitezel. In response, Howe offered a detailed description of Ben's appearance, which, of course, matched the appearance of the dead man.

Fouse then turned his attention to Alice, who had been sitting quietly during the discussion. Smiling down at the slender girl in her worn and faded clothing, Fouse asked her what her father had looked like, and Alice naturally agreed with everything Howe had said. After thinking for a moment, she added that he had a permanently bruised thumbnail and "twisted" lower front teeth.

Fouse was kind to the girl when questioning her, but he later said that he unkindly found Alice to be "reticent, embarrassed, and stupid."

Fouse told the two of them that a friend of Ben's named H.H. Holmes would be joining them soon, and when he arrived, he and Howe pretended to be strangers. The two shook hands in a polite exchange, and then Holmes seemed to notice Alice for the first time. He leaned down, smiled at her, and said, "You are Alice, are you not? Don't you remember me, my dear? I knew your family in Chicago."

Alice shrugged and then apologized with a whisper that she was sorry she didn't remember him.

Holmes and Fouse then got down to business, with Holmes replying to the same question Fouse had asked Jeptha Howe about Ben using a false name. Holmes also said that Ben had run into some "financial difficulties" a few months earlier and suggested he likely thought it wise to conceal his identity from his creditors.

Holmes then described what he expected would be found on the dead man's body if he was, in fact, Ben Pitezel. He mentioned a scar on the lower leg and a blemish on the back of his neck that was so bothersome that Ben rarely wore collars.

President Fouse, completely taken in by the farce acted out by Holmes and Howe, made final arrangements for the group to travel to the cemetery for the exhumation of Ben Pitezel's body. They would meet the next day back at the insurance company's office and proceed from there to the potter's field.

When Holmes arrived at the Fidelity Building on Saturday, Howe and Alice were already there. They were upstairs in President Fouse's office, along with LaForrest Perry and another man, the carpenter Eugene Smith, who had been asked to come along to help identify the remains. There is no doubt that Holmes recognized him as the man that he had seen in Ben's patent office several weeks earlier. He was likely hoping that the man did not recognize him in turn. At first, Smith seemed not to know who Holmes was – but that would change.

They left the office around noon and traveled to the city morgue, where Dr. William Mattern, the coroner who had performed the autopsy, and Deputy Coroner Dugan joined them. The group would have to change streetcars twice to get to the potter's field at the edge of the city, where Ben had been buried on September 15 after remaining at the morgue for 11 days. The body had not been embalmed, so there was no question that the exhumation was going to be a horror show.

It was on the second streetcar that Eugene Smith finally recognized Holmes as the man he had seen in the patent office. He asked him how he came to be present for the identification, and Holmes hesitated for a moment before answering. He then said that Ben – who Smith knew as Perry -- worked for him in Chicago. When contacted by the insurance company, he had offered to come to Philadelphia to offer whatever assistance he could.

Smith asked him, "What line of business do you follow?"

Holmes replied that he was a patent agent, obviously planning to end the discussion, but Smith was undeterred. Smith was nearly obsessed with getting his invention sold, so he asked Holmes if perhaps he could help him find some investors for the device that he'd brought to Ben at his shop.

Holmes was non-committal, but Smith just kept talking. It's likely he was just chatting to distract everyone from the grim task ahead of them with a little conversation, but my impression is that this man was extremely irritating. He asked Holmes how the insurance company was able to get in touch with him about Pitezel's death.

Holmes sighed, "I travel a good deal throughout the United States. The company telegraphed Mrs. Pitezel, who relayed the message to me."

Smith, whose interest was now piqued, asked, "If you travel so much, how did she know where to reach you?"

This time, Holmes' only reply was an icy glare. The conversation was over, and from that point on, the two men rode in silence.

As the streetcar reached its destination, Smith was unsure about what he should do. He suspected that Holmes was the man he had seen at the patent office several weeks earlier, but there was no way he could be absolutely sure. If he was, then his story about how he knew Perry didn't add up. If he wasn't the same man, though, Smith would look like a fool. He didn't want to make a mistake. The insurance company's president, L.G. Fouse himself, had asked for his assistance. After mulling things over in his head, he decided the safest course would be to say nothing.

Months would pass before Eugene Smith fully understood what a terrible mistake that he'd made that day by not announcing his suspicions about Holmes.

By then, of course, it was far too late.

When they arrived at the City Burial Ground, the group was met by Dr. Lemuel Taylor, the official in charge of the cemetery. He had been notified just that morning about the impending postmortem, and he had quickly ordered his crew to exhume the plain wooden coffin and take it to a storage shed on the edge of the graveyard.

The entire group crowded into the small shed, where the coffin had been placed on a table. Dr. Taylor, using a spade, pried up the lid of the coffin. Immediately, the foul stench of the unpreserved corpse filled the room. Coughing and gagging, the men pressed handkerchiefs to their faces while Howe drew Alice away from the coffin and led her outside of the shed into the fresh air. Tears were streaming down her face.

Ben's body had already started to decompose before it was discovered. Now, three end-of-the-summer weeks later, it was in such repulsive condition that even Dr. Mattern stepped back from the open coffin. The skin was now black and rotting and could be easily scraped away from the body.

But he began his examination by lifting the corpse's hands and looking closely at the fingernails. It was difficult to detect bruises since all the nails were discolored by decomposition. Cutting open the seam of the right pants leg, he searched for a scar on the rotting flesh of the shin but could see nothing. He was unable to find the wart on the neck either. Finally, he stepped back and spoke, "I cannot find the marks," he said.

The sight and stench of the body had left him pale and shaken. Peeling off his gloves, he stepped over to a bucket of water in the corner, splashed some on his face, and began scrubbing his hands.

But Holmes couldn't allow the identification not to be made. He was the only one in the group who didn't seem affected by the black and bloated corpse. He stripped off his jacket, rolled up his sleeves, and picked up Dr. Mattern's discarded gloves from the table.

Holmes pried the darkened nail from the end of the corpse's right thumb and passed it over to Dr. Mattern. He told him to clean it with alcohol and see what he could find.

He then took the body in hand and showed Dr. Mattern where the scar would be on the wrinkled flesh. Mattern rubbed the skin away from the leg with his thumb, and there was the scar, just where Holmes said it would be.

Holmes then announced that the body needed to be turned over. Dr. Taylor, who was reluctant to have any contact with the body, stuck a spade into the coffin and used it to turn the body over. Holmes and Mattern assisted him by tugging on the clothing. When the corpse was facedown, Holmes directed their attention to a growth on the back of the neck. He used a scalpel that he'd removed from his inside coat pocket to etch a circle around the spot. He sliced off the growth and, after wrapping it, as well as a bit of Ben's mustache in paper, handed them to Dr. Mattern.

Holmes then announced with certainty that the body in the pine box was his friend, Benjamin Pitezel. But that was not enough for a legal identification. Alice still had to identify the remains.

The body was restored to its original position in the coffin. Dr. Mattern found a sheet of newspaper, which he draped over the dead man's face, tearing away a hole so that only the mouth was exposed. Then, the lid was arranged so that the body was concealed from the neck down. Stepping out of the shed, Holmes returned a few moments later with Alice. He led her gently by the hand and walked her over the coffin.

She was sobbing and shaking violently, but Holmes made her look inside the box. He spoke to her quietly. "Alice, look at those teeth. Are they not your father's?" he asked her.

Still sobbing, Alice forced herself to look at the horror in the box, then quickly nodded yes – they were her father's teeth, she announced.

Dr. Mattern was still not completely satisfied that the body belonged to Ben Pitezel, but the identification was good enough for the insurance company.

As Dr. Taylor and his assistant replaced the coffin lid, Holmes stated that he would pay whatever it cost to have the body cremated. Howe said that he'd have to get permission from the widow for that, though he agreed that cremation seemed like the best choice.

What was left unsaid was that it was also the best way to get rid of any evidence that might remain.

AFTER HOLMES RECEIVED A CHECK PAYABLE TO CARRIE PITEZEL from the Fidelity Mutual Insurance Company the following day, he started making plans to return to St. Louis with it. He told Jeptha Howe that he would be taking over the care of Alice and would return her to her family. Howe shook the young woman's hand and thanked her for her help and her courage. He undoubtedly believed that she would soon be safely back at home with her family.

It's likely that Alice believed the same thing when she and Holmes boarded a westbound train that evening at the station – but both were wrong.

Alice wasn't safe, and she would never see her family again.

AFTER LEAVING PHILADELPHIA, THE PASSENGER TRAIN STEAMED west towards Indiana. But during the trip, around the time that the train crossed into Ohio, Holmes explained to Alice that she would not be going back to St. Louis right away.

Holmes had been corresponding with Alice's mother, who was feeling much better and was back on her feet. For reasons too complicated to explain, Holmes told the girl, they had decided that Alice's family should move away from St. Louis, perhaps to Indianapolis, Detroit, or somewhere farther east.

Before moving, though, Carrie wanted to visit her family in Galva, Illinois. Since it didn't make sense for Alice to travel all the way to St. Louis and then back again, Holmes had suggested a new plan – he would place Alice in a hotel in Indianapolis, then continue to St. Louis to retrieve two of her siblings, Nellie and Howard. He would bring them back to Indianapolis to stay with Alice, while her mother, Dessie, and baby Wharton would make the trip to Galva. Soon, the entire family, including Ben, would all be reunited and live happily ever after.

That's the way that all good fairy tales end, of course, and this was one that was designed for the benefit of Alice Pitezel. And naively, the innocent young woman believed the tale. She was naturally disappointed that it would be a little longer before she could see her mother, but it was comforting to her that she would soon have Nellie and Howard keeping her company.

When the train arrived in Indianapolis, Holmes took her to Stebbins House Hotel and rented a room for her. At 15 years old, Alice was reasonably capable of taking care of herself, although the hotel keeper's wife agreed to check on her and make sure she had plenty to eat while her "uncle" – as Holmes claimed to be – was away on business. During her time alone in the city, Alice wrote more letters to her family, but there was little in them of importance since her main topics of conversation seemed to be laundry and fruit.

When Holmes left Alice at the hotel, he had one more stop to make before he left Indianapolis – he went to the Circle Park Hotel, where he enjoyed a brief reunion with Georgiana.

She had stayed in Indianapolis while Holmes was in Philadelphia. She filled her days with needlework, reading, window-shopping, sightseeing, and with another short trip to visit her parents in Franklin. She had also developed a friendship with Mrs. Rodius, the wife of the hotel's owner, who later noted that her many conversations with Georgiana often mentioned her absent but wealthy husband, who owned property in Texas, Chicago, and Germany. In fact, they would soon be traveling to Europe and might move there permanently once her husband had settled his affairs in the States.

These stories about Holmes – who Georgiana called "Mr. Howard – intrigued the hotel owner's wife, and she looked forward to being properly introduced to him when he returned to Indianapolis. But as it turned out, she never had the chance.

Late in the afternoon of Monday, September 24, Holmes suddenly appeared at Georgiana's hotel. He brought her several small gifts – and bad news. He had to leave again right away, but he promised to return in a week. He was off to St. Louis, he said, to deal with the matters that had landed him in jail several months earlier.

Holmes left Indianapolis for St. Louis on September 25, but before he did, he typed out a long letter to his brother in New Hampshire and told him that when he'd left for New York from Gilmanton in October 1888, he had been traveling to Minneapolis but had been injured in a train wreck that caused him to have amnesia. Only now, six years later, did he remember who he was and was now planning to return home, set up a business, and take care of his wife and child. The letter was forwarded to Clara Mudgett, and it included an address in Chicago where letters to him could be sent.

Holmes then left for St. Louis, not to deal with his past legal affairs but to see Carrie Pitezel and Jeptha Howe and snag his share of the insurance payout. Howe had taken $2,500 as his share of the payout and, after expenses, that left $7,200 for Carrie – most of which she would never see. Holmes kept all but $500 of it, explaining that Ben still owed $5,000 on a note for the property in Fort Worth. Carrie was startled by this but didn't object. She simply wanted to get her family out of Holmes' dirty business, and if it cost them all the money that Ben had helped the man earn, then so be it.

When Holmes arrived at the Pitezel apartment, the first thing that Carrie asked about were the locations of Ben and Alice. Carrie was no longer sick or stuck in bed, but she looked exhausted and thin.

The years of unhappiness and worry had prematurely aged Carrie Pitezel – the months ahead were going to be even worse for her physical and mental health.

Holmes assured her that Alice was fine. She was staying in the finest hotel in Indianapolis. Ben was still in hiding. The scheme had worked perfectly, but there were still precautions that had to be taken. Even though the insurance people had fallen for the swindle, they still might continue to investigate the case for a while. Ben was currently lying low in Cincinnati, waiting for his wife and children to arrive.

And that created a problem, Holmes told her. It wasn't safe for Carrie to travel with all the children. That's why he'd left Alice in Indianapolis. If the insurance company did have detectives on the case, they would be on the lookout for a lone woman traveling with five children. Because of this, Ben and Holmes devised a plan in which Holmes would take Nellie and Howard to Indianapolis, where they would pick up Alice and head for Cincinnati. Holmes had already rented a house there for the winter. He would leave the three children in the care of his cousin, Minnie Williams, who had agreed to care for them until Carrie arrived.

In the meantime, Carrie would go to Galva with Dessie and Wharton and visit her parents. After a few weeks, the three of them would travel to Cincinnati to join the others. When they arrived, Ben would be reunited with his family.

Carrie's head was spinning after Holmes explained his plan to her, but worried and nervous, she felt she had no choice but to keep going along with whatever Holmes told her to do. She didn't have much money, her husband was hiding from the authorities, and one of her children was hidden in an Indiana hotel. She was desperate to see Ben and would do whatever she was told to make that happen. She didn't like the scheme that Ben had gotten himself into and was terrified he would be arrested, but she needed to see him, and, in the end, she told Holmes that she'd do whatever he asked.

On Friday evening, September 28, Carrie brought Nellie and Howard to the train depot and turned them over to the care of H.H. Holmes. She thanked Holmes for helping them and then knelt to hug her two children. The embrace lasted so long that Holmes became impatient and went to send a telegram before boarding the train.

The telegram was received by a clerk at the Stebbins House in Indianapolis named Robert Sweeney. It asked the staff to make sure that Alice was ready to leave and be taken to the train station the next morning to meet her two siblings and himself when they arrived.

After loading the children's trunk on the train, Holmes took Nellie and Howard by the hand and led them to seats in the Pullman car.

Carrie watched as they sat down, waving once more as the children smiled at her. She remained on the platform long after the train was out of sight. She walked out of the station with a heavy heart, thinking of nothing but her children – three of whom were now in the care of H.H. Holmes.

Carrie's mind swirled with dozens of worries and concerns, but the one thought that didn't cross her mind was that Holmes was even more evil than she'd ever dreamed – and that he'd

Nellie and Howard Pitezel

already decided that the entire Pitezel family had outlived its usefulness.

WHEN HOLMES STEPPED ONTO THE TRAIN THAT MORNING, HE began a journey like no other he had ever taken before. Except for the brief times when he settled in Fort Worth and in St. Louis, he had traveled almost ceaselessly since leaving Chicago. But his previous wanderings would pale in comparison to the seemingly mad journey that began on September 28 – the day that he took Howard and Nellie away to join their older sister.

The journey that Holmes began only seemed mad, however. In truth, there was a frightening, devious design to it. By moving from city to city, dragging his young victims along with him, he attempted to create a path that was so complex that no one would ever be able to follow it.

He moved the Pitzel children, Georgiana, and eventually, Carrie Pitezel and her other two children, all over North America. He always arranged for them to be in different train cars and different hotels so no one in any group had any idea he was moving other groups around at the same time. Georgiana probably had no idea that he was in charge of the Pitezel children or that he was checking on Carrie and her other two children. Carrie would often be in the same city as her children, believing they were somewhere else, while the children always thought their mother was at their grandparents' home in Illinois.

Holmes had, of course, by this time, decided that all the Pitezels needed to die. His exact motivation for killing the children has never really been explained. The most popular explanation has been that the murders satisfied the bloodlust that drove him to kill throughout his career, but this is based on the kind of speculation that created the Holmes legend – not on fact.

Again, there is nothing on record that says Holmes killed for enjoyment or because of madness. He didn't murder for sport – he killed for profit and to protect himself.

His most obvious motive for killing the Pitezels was that they all knew too much. Alice had seen the body, and she now knew her father was dead, even though Holmes was claiming he was still alive. Holmes couldn't trust her not to tell her mother and siblings the truth.

Carrie and Dessie still believed that Ben was alive, though I'm sure he felt they knew far too much about his scheme to remain alive. Something had to be done about that, and as Holmes began his strange journey around the country, he started making plans for the destruction of the entire family.

And he would begin with the children.

WHEN HE ARRIVED IN INDIANAPOLIS, HOLMES FOUND HOTEL clerk Robert Sweeney and Alice Pitezel waiting on the platform. Alice was thrilled to see her brother and sister, and the three of them talked excitedly as their train continued to Cincinnati.

When they arrived, Holmes checked them into a cheap hotel close to the depot called the Atlantic House. He signed the register as "Alexander E. Cook and three children."

The Bristol Hotel in Cincinnati

The next morning, Saturday, September 29, he moved them to different lodgings, the Bristol Hotel, located at Sixth and Walnut streets. Still using the name Cook, he rented a single room with two beds for himself and the children. As soon as they were settled, Holmes announced that he was going out on an errand and was taking Howard with him. Nellie and Alice were ordered to stay in the room. He took the young boy out with him to look for a vacant house to rent.

The first stop that Holmes made was a real estate agency owned by J.C. Thomas. George Rumsey, a clerk with the company, greeted Holmes and Howard from behind his desk. He later stated that he assumed that the two of them were father and son but thought it odd that the boy was so shabbily dressed while his father was wearing what looked to be an expensive suit. When Holmes told Rumsey that he was looking for a house to rent, the clerk ushered him into the office of the owner.

Holmes introduced himself to J.C. Thomas as A.C. Hayes. He was looking for a small house to rent in a quiet neighborhood for himself and his family. Thomas found just the thing for him – a tidy place at 305 Poplar Street. Holmes, who apologized for being in a hurry, rented the house sight unseen. He paid $15 in advance, received the keys from Thomas, then took Howard by the hand and headed for the door, pausing only for a moment at George Rumsey's desk to ask for directions to the nearest used furniture dealer.

Holmes' next movements were later gleaned from a woman named Henrietta Hill, who lived at 303 Poplar Street. A few hours after Holmes had obtained the keys to the house next door, she saw a horse-drawn furniture wagon pulling up in front of it. As she watched with great interest to see what her new neighbors were like, she saw a man unlock the front door for two workmen who were in the process of hauling a large stove out of the wagon and into the house. She saw a young boy, his hands in his pockets, standing in the front yard, watching what was happening in silence.

Miss Hill would eventually admit to finding two things about the scene to be quite curious. The first was the enormous size of the stove. It was a huge cylindrical thing, more suitable for a large building than a modest-sized house. The second thing was that there was nothing else in the wagon – no fixtures, no other furniture, nothing but that huge stove. She knew that the house next door was vacant. If a family was moving in, surely, they would need some furniture.

She shook her head and went back inside. But this was not the last curious event that she would experience connected to her new neighbor.

Early on Sunday morning, Miss Hill's doorbell rang, and she opened the door to find her new neighbor standing on her porch. He apologized for bothering her, he said, but because of a change in his business affairs, he would not be renting the house next door after all. He had already purchased a perfectly good stove, however, and he wondered if Miss Hill would like to have it. She was welcome to it, free of charge, of course.

After he tipped his hat to her, he turned and walked off down the street, never to be seen in the neighborhood again.

It would later be learned from Holmes himself that the house turned out not to be suitable for his needs. It wasn't nearly as isolated and quiet as he'd been led to believe. He'd also seen the neighbor woman watching him from her porch, and he knew her type – a neighborhood gossip who would soon be sticking her nose into his business. Before long, everyone for blocks around would know about the new tenant who had rented the empty house and brought nothing with him but a big stove and a little boy. He was forced to change his plans.

Next time, Holmes thought, he would be more careful.

The English Hotel and Opera House

THAT SUNDAY AFTERNOON, HOLMES PACKED UP THE CHILDREN'S belongings, and they moved again, this time back to Indianapolis. When they reached the city, Holmes checked them into the English Hotel where he registered them as "A.C. Cook and Three Canning Children," using Carrie's maiden name. The hotel overlooked the Soldiers' and Sailors' Monument downtown. On the other side of the square was the Circle Park Hotel where Georgiana was still waiting for her husband to return.

Holmes told the owner of the English Hotel, Herman Ackelow, that he was the children's uncle and that his sister, their widowed mother, would be joining them in a few days. He made arrangements with Ackelow and his staff to have meals delivered to their children in their room whenever he was away and asked that Mrs. Ackelow occasionally check in on them.

Holmes provided the three children with letter-writing materials so they could contact their mother, who was now – they believed – with their grandparents in Illinois. But, of course, none of the letters reached Carrie. Holmes took them away to mail but kept them instead.

The 10 days that the children spent at the hotel were not happy ones. Months later, Herman Ackelow told detectives that he would send his oldest son up to the children's rooms with meals, and he would find them crying, heartbroken and homesick. They wanted to see their mother or at least hear from her. There is no doubt they were bored, irritated with their mother for not writing to them, and getting on each other's nerves.

Meanwhile, Holmes was celebrating the success of his scheme with Georgiana at her hotel. He took her shopping, took her to the finest restaurants in the city, and bought her gifts of dresses and jewelry. Unfortunately, though, he had to go away again, so he suggested that Georginia go and visit her parents until his return. As soon as he was back in the city, he'd wire her and let her know.

Georgiana reluctantly agreed, and he put her on a train to Franklin later that same day. Once the train was out of sight, Holmes returned to the Pitezel children at the English Hotel. With Georgiana out of the city, he could safely take them on an excursion to alleviate some of their boredom. The children were complaining and unhappy about not seeing their mother, but Holmes asked them to be patient. It wouldn't be much longer.

The most difficult of the three children was Howard. Alice and Nellie had been disappointed when told they had to wait a little longer to see Carrie, but Howard was inconsolable. Being stuck in the hotel room for the active boy was bad enough, but to learn that he had to wait even longer to see his mother sparked a crying fit that went on for nearly a half-hour.

Finally, Holmes took them out and bought them books,

Washington Street in Indianapolis in 1894

crayons, and pens so that all three of them could write to their mother and tell her how much fun they were having with "Uncle Howard," as Holmes insisted that they call him. He took them to a restaurant and treated them to fried chicken, potatoes, milk, and lemon pie. After eating, they walked along Washington Street, pausing to watch an artist who painted small landscape pictures for every customer who bought a pair of shoes.

Holmes assumed that the outing would keep the children satisfied for a while, but no sooner had they returned to the hotel than Howard started throwing a tantrum – kicking, crying, and shouting that he did not want to be locked up in the room again. Holmes had to bodily drag the boy across the lobby.

Back in their room, Alice and Nellie did their best to comfort their brother. It wasn't until Holmes threatened to give him a beating that the boy finally stopped crying and settled down.

Holmes stormed downstairs, and on his way out, he ran into Herman Ackelow, who had witnessed Howard's tantrum from behind the front desk. Ackelow asked about the boy, who he believed was Holmes' nephew. He worried about the children. He knew they missed their mother terribly, and he couldn't imagine why she hadn't arrived in Indianapolis or at least hadn't written to them.

Holmes' face turned somber at the hotel owner's questions, and he sadly shook his head. The boy was a bad one, he told Herman, bad since the day he was born. He felt terribly sorry for his sickly sister, a widow who had been left with nothing when her husband died. Holmes was not sure what to do with the troublemaking boy. He thought about perhaps hiring him out to a farmer or even placing him in an institution.

Something had to be done about him, Holmes said with a sigh, and it needed to happen very soon.

ACCORDING TO LATER TESTIMONY FROM A MAN NAMED Albert Schiffling, the owner of Schiffling's Repair Shop in Indianapolis, a well-dressed gentleman came into his store on the afternoon of

October 4, 1894. The man had two slim black cases under his arm. Introducing himself as a doctor, the gentleman placed the cases on the store counter and opened them up. He pushed the cases toward Schiffling and stated that he would like to have the items inside sharpened. How long would that take?

Schiffling saw that the cases were filled with an assortment of shiny medical instruments – scalpels, knives, blades, and saws. He considered for a moment and said that he could have them ready by Monday. The man agreed and so Schiffling wrote out a receipt and handed it to the doctor.

Holmes thanked him and left the shop. Outside, he consulted his pocket watch in the fading light. It was too late to look for another house today. He would start the search tomorrow.

ON FRIDAY, OCTOBER 5, HOLMES WALKED INTO A REAL ESTATE agency owned by Samuel Brown in the small town of Irvington, about six miles from downtown Indianapolis. Brown greeted the man warmly – he had a reputation as a jovial, warm-hearted man – but was immediately taken aback by the rudeness of his visitor. Holmes, without so much as a "good afternoon," stated that he had rented a house from J.C. Wands and had been told that Mr. Brown had possession of the key. He would like to have it – right away.

Brown was happy to get it for him, if for no other reason than to get the unfriendly man out of his office and handed it over at once. Without a word, Holmes plucked it from his hand, turned and walked out of the office.

Brown watched after the man as he left, glad to have settled whatever business he might have with him. But he would remember him -- that was certain. He was not accustomed to being treated with such discourtesy and later, when asked about H.H. Holmes, he would immediately recall their encounter.

Later that day, Holmes returned to the children's room at the English Hotel and announced that he had decided to take Howard away with him. He hated to have the poor boy all cooped up the way in a hotel room like this, so he'd made arrangements for

Howard to stay with his cousin, Minnie Williams, until Carrie could arrive. Minnie was a wealthy lady with no children of her own and she would take good care of him. She owned a farm in Terre Haute and Howard would get all the fresh air and exercise that he needed.

The girls, of course, would remain in Indianapolis for Carrie to arrive, so Holmes asked Alice to make sure that all of Howard's belongings were packed in his trunk and ready to go the following day.

But when Holmes returned on Saturday morning, Howard wasn't there. When he demanded to know where the boy was, Alice sheepishly admitted that he'd slipped out. She and Nellie had been packing his things and when they turned around, he was gone. Even Alice was exasperated by Howard by this time.

Holmes was furious. He had pressing matters to attend to and no time to be running all over the hotel searching for the boy. He told Alice that he would return in a day or so. When he came back, he warned her, Howard had better be waiting and ready to go.

When Holmes returned to the hotel on Monday, Howard was sitting on the floor with his coat on, playing with a wooden top. He had heeded the warnings of his sisters and didn't dare make Holmes angry again. Holmes told Nellie and Alice to tell their brother goodbye. The girls burst into tears as they covered his cheeks with kisses.

They would never see Howard again.

THE COTTAGE IN IRVINGTON THAT HOLMES HAD RENTED FROM J.C. Wands was much more secluded than the one he had been forced to abandon in Cincinnati. The small, one-and-a-half story house with an attached barn stood a short distance from Union Avenue on the outskirts of town. There were no other houses in the immediate neighborhood – only the Methodist Church, which was directly across the street. The west side of the house was shaded by trees and to the east was a large, grassy field. The tracks of the Pennsylvania Railroad were about two hundred yards to the south.

The occasional wail of a passing train was all that broke the isolated stillness of the area.

Even so, on Tuesday, October 9, an unexpected visitor named Elvet Moorman arrived at the cottage. He was a lanky, 16-year-old who worked for the owner, doing odd jobs

The cottage in Irvington rented by Holmes

and milking the cow that was in the barn out back. When he strolled up that morning, he saw two men unloading some furniture from a wagon and carrying it into the house. Standing nearby was a mustached man in shirtsleeves and a young boy in a gray coat.

Elvet went out back to milk the cow and had been there for a while when the man with the mustache came into the barn and asked Elvet to help him assemble a large coal stove that he'd bought.

Elvet agreed and as they started working on it, he asked the man why he did not make a connection for gas and use a gas stove instead of an old coal-burner.

Elvet never forgot his reply. The man said to him, "Because I do not think gas is healthy for children."

Moorman nodded and helped the man finish up. He left as soon as the job was completed. As he carried the milk can past the house, he said hello to the little boy in the gray coat, who stood by himself on the front porch. The boy

Elvet Moorman

never smiled or spoke – he simply offered Moorman a sad little wave.

Elvet Moorman didn't know it at the time, of course, but aside from the man with the mustache – he was the last person to ever see Howard Pitezel alive.

AS THE DAYS PASSED, THE PERRY-PITEZEL CASE BECAME A fading, albeit disturbing, memory for President Fouse and the officers of the Fidelity Mutual Company. The policy had been settled, and the case was closed. Only one man in the company was still thinking about the details of the case and he was suspicious about many parts of it. Of course, it was his job to be suspicious – his name was William Gary, and he was Fidelity's chief investigator.

From the very start, Gary had questioned the theory that Pitezel had been killed in an accidental explosion. He was a former Philadelphia police detective and had pulled some strings to get a look at the crime scene evidence. He didn't agree with the officers who'd examined the body. Gary had a more practiced eye. He saw the burned match, the broken bottle, and the pipe and like the doctor who'd been at the scene, he believed it was a setup. He was willing to bet that the evidence had been arranged by the dead man's killer.

But insurance company officials had settled the policy against Gary's advice and had moved on to other things. Only Gary was still stewing about the situation.

In early October, Gary happened to be in St. Louis on a completely unrelated matter and found himself thinking about the Pitezel case. He decided to do a little poking around on his own and when he finished his other business, he paid a visit to attorney Jeptha D. Howe.

While sitting in Howe's office, Gary chatted with him about the Pitezel case, inquiring about the sum that Howe had received for his work. He was startled by the impressive figure and intrigued when Howe grumbled about how he had earned every penny and added, "It should have been a third."

Gary left the lawyer's office more convinced than ever that the case had been settled too quickly. There was something wrong about Ben Pitezel's death. He had no hard proof -- and couldn't quite put his finger on what had happened -- but he knew that there were questions that still needed to be answered.

On the morning of Tuesday, October 9, fate literally put the answers to his questions right in his hands.

Gary was in the office of Fidelity's St. Louis branch manager, George Stadden, when a message arrived from police chief Lawrence Harrigan, requesting that an agent of the company call on him at once. Harrigan had just received a letter that involved a case that was handled by Fidelity Mutual.

Gary went to police headquarters and Harrigan handed him a lengthy letter that he had received earlier in the day. The letter was from a prisoner in the city jail who had shared a cell a few months earlier with an accused swindler named H.M. Howard.

The prisoner's name was Marion Hedgepeth.

While celebrating his great success with the swindle of Fidelity Mutual, paying off Jeptha Howe, and showering gifts on Georgiana, Holmes had forgotten that there had been one other person that he was supposed to pay when insurance money landed in his hands.

And as Hedgepeth promised himself he'd do if Holmes failed to provide him with the promised finder's fee of $500 in the aftermath of the swindle, Hedgepeth turned over everything he knew to the police.

In the lengthy letter, Hedgepeth described the entire plan that Howard had laid out for him from the phony storefront to the substitute body, the role of an attorney, and everything else. And then he threw in a twist:

Howe tells me now that Howard would not let Mrs. Pitezel go back and identify the supposed body of her husband, and that he feels positive and certain that Howard deceived Pitezel and that

Pitezel in following out Howard's instructions was killed and that it was really the body of Pitezel.

Hedgepeth had already tried several tricks to get out of prison, so the authorities weren't putting much stock in the letter. William Gary, though, believed it at once. There were things in the letter that Hedgepeth couldn't have known unless Holmes or Howe told him some of the details of the plan personally.

He knew that something had been amiss with the case, and this proved it. He took a sworn statement from Marion Hedgepeth – which essentially just confirmed the details in the letter – and with a rogue's gallery photograph of swindler H.M. Howard in hand, Gary returned to Philadelphia that evening.

The next morning, he met with officers of Fidelity Mutual in President Fouse's office and reported his discoveries. Refusing to admit that they had been fooled, Fouse and his colleagues scoffed at Hedgepeth's accusations. They argued that the bandit was simply trying to pass off phony information to get his prison sentence reduced.

President Fouse was stunned when he saw the photograph that Gary showed him of the man known as H.M. Howard. It was, of course, H.H. Holmes, whom he'd recently met.

Gary acknowledged that Hedgepeth was undoubtedly trying to curry favor with the authorities, in addition to getting back at Howard for not paying him his promised fee. But Gary insisted the story was true. The letter contained information that Hedgepeth could only have learned from one of the conspirators, including the mention about the almost-late insurance payment, for example.

Fouse found this argument hard to refute, but his many years of experience in the business simply made it impossible for him to believe that he could have been so easily fooled. He knew how to clear up the questions. Could he see the photograph of this H.M. Howard that Gary had brought back from St. Louis?

As soon as Gary handed it across the desk to him, all the color drained out of his face. It was a photograph of H.H. Holmes, the man who had so generously come to Philadelphia to help identify the remains of his dear friend, Ben Pitezel.

For President Fouse, that photograph was all he needed to be convinced by Hedgepeth's story and the next morning, Gary left Philadelphia with instructions from the officers of the Fidelity Mutual Insurance Company to use every means at his disposal – including hiring the famed Pinkerton Detective Agency -- to track down and apprehend Dr. H.H. Holmes.

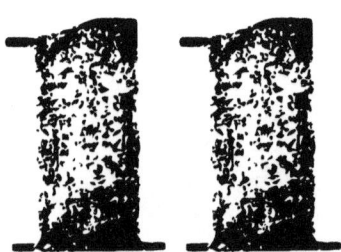 BY THE TIME THAT FIDELITY MUTUAL INSURANCE INVESTIGATOR, William Gary, began the manhunt for H.H. Holmes, his quarry had already left Indiana. He had returned to the hotel for the two Pitezel girls on the evening of Wednesday, October 10.

Alice and Nellie had tried to fill the long days in his absence in the usual way – drawing pictures, reading, and playing simple card games. But sometimes, they did nothing more than stare out the window at the busy street outside. At other times, the hotel owner's family later recalled they were found weeping in each other's arms, missing their mother, father, siblings, and even their little brother, Howard, who Mr. Holmes had taken away to live on a farm until the family could be reunited.

When Holmes packed up the girls and checked them out of the hotel that night, Alice and Nellie must have been excited, believing they were that much closer to their family and home. And they walked to the train station, Holmes, of course, assured them that they'd all be together again soon.

They had no way of knowing there was more sorrow ahead.

ON OCTOBER 11, GEORGIANA RECEIVED A LONG-AWAITED telegram from her husband, asking her to meet him right away in Detroit.

On Friday morning, she left her parents' home in Franklin, took a train to Indianapolis, and then boarded another train, which steamed toward Detroit. The ride lasted all day and into the evening, and Georgiana was dozing in her seat, suffering from a migraine, when a man sat down beside her.

She was startled to discover that it was her husband.

Evidently, he had been riding in a separate car all day. He told her that he would not have even known she was on the train if he had not gotten up to stretch his legs.

Or so he told her. The fact that Holmes went to great lengths to hide the Pitezel girls from Georgiana lends credence to her later claims that she knew nothing about this part of his scheme. I don't see any possible way that she was completely unaware of his frauds and swindles, but I'm not sure her knowledge of his crimes extended to murder.

When they arrived in Detroit an hour later, Holmes obtained a suite at the Hotel Normandie, registering under the name "G. Howell and wife, Adrian." Georgiana, still suffering from her headache, went immediately to bed, which offered Holmes the perfect opportunity to slip out of the room.

Holmes had ridden with Alice and Nellie on the train until it was about an hour outside of Detroit. Then, after inventing a story about how he didn't think it would be a good idea to be seen

Hotel Normandie in Detroit

arriving in the city with them, he had taken his bag and moved to another car. The girls were told to get off the train at Detroit and wait on the platform until he came to get them.

Alice and Nellie followed his instructions, just as they had all along. They sat, slumped on a bench outside the station with their satchels, for hours. He finally came to get them around midnight, after Georgiana was settled at her hotel.

Holmes took them by cab to the New Western Hotel, where he rented a room for them under the names "Etta and Nellie Canning." Then, he hurried back to the Hotel Normandie, changed into his nightshirt, and climbed into bed next to his sleeping wife.

Georgiana felt better in the morning, and Holmes told her that business might keep them in Detroit for a while, so he moved them to a boarding house on Park Place. When he checked in, he told the proprietor that he was an actor.

Holmes took their luggage to their room and helped Georgiana get settled in. While she was resting, he went off in search of yet another secluded house – like the one he'd found in Indiana.

ON THE SAME DAY THAT HOLMES WAS DRAGGING ALICE AND Nellie to Detroit, Carrie Pitezel was packing a trunk for herself, Dessie, and baby Wharton for their own journey to Detroit.

Following orders given to her by Holmes, Carrie had traveled to her parents' home on Friday, October 5. For six days, she had anxiously waited for some word of her husband's whereabouts. A letter from Holmes had finally arrived in Galva on October 11. It said that Ben was in Detroit and that she should plan on traveling there in the middle of the following week. But desperately lonely for her husband and her three absent children, Carrie decided to defy Holmes. She wired him to expect her arrival on Sunday, October 14. She did follow one of his instructions, though – she destroyed the letter she'd received from him as soon as she read it.

This was Carrie's first act of defiance against Holmes. It wouldn't be her last. Eventually, her willingness to stand up to him would save her life.

When Carrie's train arrived in Detroit on Sunday afternoon, Holmes was on the platform waiting for her. Dessie, carrying Wharton in her arms, followed her mother off the train. Carrie had never really recovered from her recent illness, and the strain of the preceding months had left her feeling weak and feeble. She left it to Dessie to carry Wharton to a waiting carriage as Holmes gathered their luggage and rode with them to their hotel.

On the way across town, Carrie questioned him about her other children. How were they doing? And why had she not received any letters from them?

Holmes assured her that all three of them were fine. They were in Indianapolis, he said, in the care of a very nice widow lady. They had been enrolled in school and were very busy, but he was sure that she would receive letters from them soon.

But when she asked the name of the woman to whom the children had been entrusted, he claimed that he could not remember. It was a peculiar name, and he had been referred to her by a real estate agent that had helped his wife's parents move from Franklin, Indiana, to Indianapolis. As soon as he remembered the name, he'd be sure to let her know.

But he urged her not to worry. She would be seeing her children very soon. In fact, once Carrie's visit with Ben in Detroit was over, he'd take her, Dessie, and the baby to Indianapolis to see the others. He even had a place for them to live. His wife's

The Brunswick Hotel in Detroit

parents would not be moving into the city for several months and Carrie and the children could stay in their new house rent-free.

You might wonder why Carrie continued to swallow the stories that Holmes seemingly concocted out of thin air – but why not? He was a smooth talker, and a born liar and Carrie couldn't comprehend the lengths that he was capable of when it came to deceiving her.

The rest of the trip to the Brunswick Hotel was made in silence. When Holmes registered them as "Mrs. C.A. Adams and daughter," Carrie was shocked. She pulled Holmes aside and whispered to him furiously, asking him why he'd used a false name. Holmes soothingly explained that it was safer that way and Carrie went along with it.

After leaving the three Pitezels in the care of the hotel housekeeper, Minnie Mulholland, Holmes left for the evening. Minnie took the new guests to their room, settled them in, and left them to rest. She quietly closed the door behind her when she left. She later recalled that she had never seen a woman who looked more worn down by the cares and troubles of the world.

When Holmes left the hotel, he went straight to the New Western, where Alice and Nellie were staying. He checked them out of the hotel and moved them to a boarding house at 91 Congress Street, which was owned by a woman named Lucinda Burns.

On that same day, Alice sat down and wrote a letter to her grandparents in Galva, Illinois. It would be the last letter that she ever wrote.

Dear Grandma and Grandpa, it read:

Hope you all are well. Nell and I have both got colds and chapped hands but that is all. We have not had any nice weather at all. Tell mama that I need a coat. I nearly freeze in that thin jacket. We have to stay in all the time. Howard is not with us now.

I wish I could see you all. I am getting so homesick that I don't know what to do. I suppose Wharton walks by this time, don't he? I would like to have him here, he would pass away the time a good deal.

There is little about this letter that isn't heartbreaking, but the line *"Howard is not with us now,"* is especially ominous in a way that Alice couldn't possibly know.

The rest of the letter is filled with loneliness and boredom – the only complaints that ever appear in her letters – and manage to sadly convey the misery of her confinement in anonymous hotel rooms and of her long separation from her family.

Of course, what she did not know at the time she penned the letter, was that her mother, her sister, and her baby brother were lodged in a hotel only a few blocks away.

But that wouldn't matter – she'd never see any of them again.

AS HE'D DONE IN INDIANAPOLIS, HOLMES HAD BEEN LOOKING for a rental house since he'd arrived in Detroit. He found one on Monday, October 15. It was a small, secluded place at 241 E. Forest Avenue, on the outskirts of the city. In the cellar, he dug a hole. It was four feet long, three and a half feet wide and three and a half feet deep. It was just big enough to hide two bodies – as long as neither of them were very large.

On the morning of Wednesday, October 17, Holmes began making plans for an outing for Alice and Nellie. He was going to tell them that he was taking them for a boat ride on the Detroit River. He'd promised this earlier, but it had been too cold. It didn't matter what the weather was like, though, he had no plans to let the two girls see the river.

But before he could leave the boarding house where he was staying with Georgiana on Park Place, a telegram arrived for him. It was from Frank Blackman, Holmes agent on Dearborn Street in Chicago. It wasn't good news.

Forced to abandon his plans for the rental house on Forest Avenue, Holmes began planning to leave Detroit instead.

When he returned to the boarding house that evening, he surprised Georgiana by telling her that – because he loved her so much – he was going to take her on a sightseeing trip to Niagara Falls. At the time, it was the premier tourist destination in North America and Georgiana must have been delighted by this news.

Holmes explained that they'd have to travel there by way of Toronto, where he had some business matters he needed to attend to, but she barely heard what he said about business. All she knew was that her husband was finally taking her someplace that didn't mean more nights in dreary hotels in dreary cities. She couldn't wait to leave.

Early on the morning of October 18, while Georgiana packed, Holmes told her that he needed to run an errand. He headed straight for Carrie's hotel. She had hoped that he was bringing her good news about her husband, but those hopes were soon dashed. It hurt him to tell her, he said, but she would have to wait a little longer to see Ben. He had searched all over Detroit for a vacant house where the two of them could meet, but he was unable to find a suitable place. Ben just couldn't take the chance that someone might recognize him. He was supposed to be dead, wasn't he?

Carrie's heart was broken once again, but Holmes assured her that he had a new plan, one that he and Ben had worked out the previous evening. Carrie and Ben would have their rendezvous outside of the country, in Canada. Ben was already on his way to Toronto. Carrie, Dessie, and Wharton would follow him on the 8:30 A.M. train to Toronto, for which Holmes already had their tickets.

When they arrived in the evening, they would wait on the platform for Holmes to come and get them. He was leaving Detroit, too, and would be right behind him.

Carrie sighed in resignation and took the tickets from Holmes. She would do what he asked – anything to see Ben again and then finally get to Indianapolis to collect the other children.

Before he left, he asked Carrie, "Won't you let me have your big trunk? I want to take some things to Toronto. I'll put your things in a locker; they'll be perfectly safe, and when you go down to Indianapolis, where the children are, you can get them, and it will save the custom officers overhauling them."

Carrie agreed and Holmes gave her some strict instructions – do not let the express companies touch her luggage. She was to hire a man on the street. Holmes didn't tell her the reason for this but he knew express companies keep records of luggage – independent operators did not.

Holmes was doing all he could to keep their travels secret.

Holmes' next stop that morning was the boarding house where Alice and Nellie were staying. The girls listened with little enthusiasm when Holmes gave them their traveling instructions and train tickets. Then, he left them rushed back to the other boarding house, where Georgiana was waiting.

Holmes and Georgiana arrived in Toronto later that same evening. He took her to the Walker House Hotel and registered them under the name "Howell."

A few hours later, he left Georgiana in their room and returned to the Grand Trunk Railway Depot, where he

Grand Trunk Railway Depot in Toronto

Grand Union Hotel in Toronto

found Carrie sitting on a bench, next to Dessie, who cradled the sleeping Wharton in her arms. The two women looked drained, exhausted, and furious. They had been kept waiting for nearly two hours. Holmes apologized, explaining that his train had been late.

When Carrie asked where Ben was, Holmes broke the news that they'd just missed him. He'd ducked out of town to stay ahead of detectives and was now in Montreal. Holmes had promised that he'd find a house there, furnish it, then send word to Ben so he could return. Carrie, who'd expected to find Ben waiting for her in Toronto, had reached her limit. She burst into tears.

Holmes moved their luggage to a carriage and took them to the Grand Union Hotel, not far from the place where he and Georgiana were staying. He checked them in as "Mrs. C. Adams and daughter" and promised to call on them the next day with more news of Ben.

But Holmes did not return the following day. Instead, he spent the day shopping and sightseeing with Georgiana. After dinner that night, Holmes took his wife back to their room and announced that he had decided to take a walk around town to relax. He promised to be back soon.

When he left, he headed straight for the railroad depot, arriving there just in time to meet the train from Detroit. After collecting Alice and Nellie, he turned them over to the porter at the Albion Hotel, slipping the man a hefty tip and enough money to cover overnight lodging for the two girls.

At this point, you can't help but be impressed by how Holmes was managing things. He was moving three sets of people from city to city and usually lodging them within blocks of each other, while keeping all of them completely unaware of the deception.

The Albion Hotel, where Holmes placed Alice and Nellie into a room.

But what's even more impressive than just the constant motion was that he was getting them all to continue to go along with what he told them to do.

With Georgiana, this was simple. She loved him and, in my opinion, was aware of some of his crimes. She had to know that the constant moving and traveling was the result of something illegal.

With Carrie, he led her along with promises that she'd soon be reunited with her husband and children. He knew this was what she wanted more than anything else and he manipulated her by dangling the reunion in front of her.

But how he did this with Alice and Nellie, that's another story. Alice, in particular, didn't like him, as she'd made clear in one of her letters. And yet, she still stayed alone in hotels, traveled on trains to unknown places, and did what he told her to do, dragging her younger sister along with her.

Why did she do it? Better yet, when she was alone in a hotel or on a train, why didn't she tell someone what was going on? Surely, this young woman – as backward and uneducated as she might have been – must have realized that Holmes was up to something underhanded.

Was she concerned about her father? No, because she thought he was dead – something else she never told anyone about. It might have been concern for the rest of her family. She knew her father had been involved in something criminal before he died. Maybe she feared calling attention to it could mean trouble for the family.

Or maybe it was just that Alice, coming from a poverty-stricken background, feared creating a problem for Holmes – a man she didn't like but who was a doctor, a businessman, and her father's employer. He was in a different social class than the Pitezel family. For that reason, she was *supposed* to respect him. And because her mother had placed her in his care, she knew she was supposed to obey him.

Or perhaps it's just because Holmes was Holmes – he had tricked Alice into going along with his plans, just as he had swindled and conned many who were older, wiser, and more experienced than Alice over the years.

Alice Pitezel was just no match for a man who would later brag that the Devil had been at his side on the day he was born.

ON SATURDAY MORNING, HOLMES ARRIVED AT THE ALBION Hotel and took Alice and Nellie for a walk. After they returned to their lodgings, he paid for their room for one more night, explaining to hotel clerk, Herbert Jones, that the girls were his nieces and they were waiting for the arrival of their mother, who was due in from Detroit later in the week.

Then, he hurried off in search of a real estate office. He had promised to take Georgiana to Niagara Falls that afternoon and he still had work to do.

On the morning of Wednesday, October 24, someone knocked on the front door of the home of Thomas Ryves, an elderly man who lived on St. Vincent Street in Toronto. Thomas shuffled to the door and opened it to a well-dressed gentleman who explained that he had just rented the house next door for his sister. The man explained that she would be arriving in a few days, and he wondered if he could borrow a shovel to dig a place in the cellar where she could keep potatoes.

Thomas gladly offered the loan of a shovel, which he kept in a shed out back. After thanking him, the stranger walked past the rear of the house. A few moments later, he passed by with a spade in his hands. He gave Thomas a friendly wave and returned to the house next door.

The house that Holmes rented in Toronto – No. 16 St. Vincent Street. It was there where the corpses of Alice and Nellie were found months later

Later that day, Thomas saw a wagon pull up in front of number 16. On the front seat of the wagon was the driver – a short fellow in a slouch hat – and the same gentleman who had borrowed the spade. As he watched, they unloaded an old bed, a mattress, and a large trunk from the wagon and carried them into the house. He wondered why the man had no more furniture with him and he watched throughout the day for the wagon to return with more belongings – but it never did.

The next day, October 25, Herbert Jones was behind the front desk of the Albion Hotel and noticed the arrival of the uncle of the two little girls who were staying alone in a room upstairs. Moments later, after settling the daily bill, he went upstairs to get his nieces from their room. They left the hotel together again, as they had on many mornings. They'd apparently been spending part of each day sightseeing. Sometimes, they stayed out until supper time, but usually they returned in a few hours.

But this day was different. This time, the girls never came back at all.

That same afternoon, Carrie took Dessie shopping at Eaton's department store on Young Street. They stayed for several hours,

Eaton's Department Store on Young Street in downtown Toronto

looking about in wonder at the vast array of goods that the store had to offer. When the baby finally became fussy later in the afternoon, they decided that it was time to go back to the hotel.

They were almost at the exit when Carrie suddenly found herself face to face with H.H. Holmes. For a moment, both froze in their tracks and then, to Carrie's surprise, Holmes' face turned white. Then, recovering himself, he whispered to her that he had been looking for her everywhere. He told her, "I have a bit of news. I rented a house, but there have been two men watching it. You cannot see your husband here. You will have to go to Ogdensburg."

Carrie worriedly asked what she should do, and Holmes told her that, if she had made any purchases, she should send them directly to her hotel. He wanted her to leave Toronto that night. Holmes cautioned her to wait for him while he looked around the department store to see if she was being followed.

Nervous and frightened, Carrie and Dessie waited for more than 10 minutes before Carrie finally sent her daughter to look for Holmes. When he could not be found, they fled the store and hurried back to the hotel, where they began packing their things.

Holmes showed up around 5:00 P.M. He said nothing about his disappearance in the department store and Carrie was too upset to ask about it. He handed her some train tickets and told her to leave immediately for Prescott, Ontario, then cross the border to Ogdensburg, New York. He would meet them in Ogdensburg the next day.

After making sure that Carrie was clear about his directions, Holmes hurried off.

He needed to make a stop at the rental house at No 16 St. Vincent Street before he left Toronto. There was one last task that needed completing there.

A few hours later, Holmes was back at the hotel where he shared a room with Georgiana. He dashed up to the room and told her that they needed to leave Toronto at once. He had decided that it was time to finally make their long-delayed trip to Germany. They would leave on a steamship from Boston, although on the way there, he had several business stops that he needed to make.

Georgiana was thrilled by the news but puzzled by her husband's almost frantic behavior. For the first time since she had known him – always aware of some of his swindles and schemes – he was acting as though someone was chasing him.

And unknown to Georgiana, someone finally was.

INSURANCE INVESTIGATOR WILLIAM GARY HAD THOUGHT ST. Louis was the best place to begin his search for H.H. Holmes. On October 12, he had arrived in the city with LaForrest Perry, and they went looking for Carrie Pitezel. When they arrived at the apartment where she had been living, they were informed by a neighbor that she had abruptly left town the week before, along with her infant son and oldest daughter. From the rogues-gallery photograph that Gary showed him, the neighbor was able to identify Holmes as a man who had called on the Pitezels several times during the late summer and fall.

Gary had recently received a report from Edwin Cass, Fidelity's Chicago branch manager, so he knew that Holmes had a house in Wilmette, Illinois. The two men made that their next destination and boarded a train for Chicago.

The following day, they called at the house where Myrta and her daughter lived. But she was no more helpful to them than she had been with Edwin Cass when he had questioned her a few weeks before. But once again, a neighbor offered some useful

Chicago Police detectives John Norton and John Fitrzpatrick, who Gary and Perry conferred with during their hunt for Holmes

information. Dr. Holmes, the neighbor said, was rarely seen in the neighborhood. According to rumors, though, he was well known in Englewood, a community on the city's South Side, where he had run into some trouble with the law.

That same afternoon, they traveled to Englewood. They spent the rest of the day – and most of the next day – questioning Holmes' neighbors and acquaintances in Englewood and Chicago, including his agent, Frank Blackman, who took the first opportunity he had to wire Holmes and let him know that insurance investigators were on his trail. This was the telegram with the bad news in it that caused Holmes to flee Detroit ahead of schedule.

Gary and Perry then went to confer with the Chicago police and interviewed two detectives, John Norton and John Fitzpatrick. As they told the insurance men what they knew about Holmes, his business dealings, and the many lawsuits filed against him, they confirmed the suspicions about the man that Gary already had. He soon had a much clearer picture of the man, his many financial misdeeds, debts, frauds and swindles, and about his earlier insurance scheme that involved burning his Englewood building. He also discovered that Holmes and the late Ben Pitezel were wanted in Texas for fraud and horse theft.

It was now obvious to Gary that he was chasing a bold and clever criminal whose trail extended from Philadelphia to Fort Worth, to St. Louis, Chicago and who knew where else.

At this point, Holmes might be anywhere in the country. Two men working on their own – even ones as experienced as the two fraud investigators – were in way over the heads. What they needed was the ability to conduct a nationwide manhunt. So, the next morning, Gary wired his recommendations to the company's president. It was time, he said, to call in the Pinkertons.

Founded in 1850, the Pinkerton Detective Agency quickly became one of the most important crime solving and law enforcement groups in the United States. While there were scores of other private police agencies in the country, none of them had the notoriety or success rates than the agency founded by Scottish Immigrant Allan Pinkerton did. In a time when small town – and even large city – police departments lacked the manpower and resources to carry out difficult investigations, the Pinkertons, with their famous "We Never Sleep" motto, became the best hope for bringing many criminals to justice.

By the 1870s, the Pinkertons had the world's largest collection of mugshots and library of criminal files. At one time, there were more Pinkerton agents than there were in the standing army of the United States, a fact that led to the state of Ohio outlawing the agency within their borders in case they were ever hired out to overthrow the government.

They achieved notoriety chasing famous outlaws and preventing looting in Chicago after the Great Fire in 1871, but not everything about the agency was admired. During the days of labor unrest that came in the late nineteenth century, the Pinkertons were often hired by large companies to keep out labor unionizers or striking workers. They were often accused of intimidating union workers, inciting riots, and attacking strikers. The most notorious example of this was the Homestead Strike of 1892, when Pinkerton agents killed 11 people while enforcing strikebreaking measures set by the company. Two brigades of state militia troops had to be called out to restore order.

But despite this, Pinkerton detectives were known for their ruthless pursuit of criminals, and they were the perfect agency to call by Fidelity Mutual in their nationwide search for H.H. Holmes. If the Pinkertons couldn't find him, no one could.

But somehow, Holmes stayed one step ahead of them.

He had left Toronto just before detectives arrived, but they were closing in, and Holmes must have known it. Staying in Canada might have been the best thing to do since the Pinkertons didn't have the authority to extradite him, but instead, Holmes fled with Georgiana.

They spent one last night in Canada. in the town of Prescott, and then moved on to Burlington, Vermont. This was close enough to Ogdensburg, New York, that Holmes could travel back and forth to see Carrie and her two children without arousing suspicion from his wife. At this point, Holmes had one less group to worry about secretly moving around New England. Alice and Nellie would no longer be a bother.

Carrie, Dessie, and Wharton arrived in Ogdensburg on October 26. After arranging a room at the National Hotel, she waited for further instructions from Holmes. He showed up that evening and laid out his latest plan. He would soon be leaving town – she assumed he was also in Ogdensburg – but Carrie and the children were to remain there until November 1. Then, they would come to Burlington on the early express train and Holmes would meet them at the depot. In the meantime, he would arrange for Ben to travel to Burlington, where he and Carrie would finally have their reunion.

Once again, Carrie accepted Holmes' plan without question or debate.

In Burlington, Holmes and Georgiana had moved into Ahern's boarding house, where Holmes registered them as "Mr. Hall and wife." Later that same day, using the name "J.A. Hudson," Holmes rented a furnished house at 26 Winooski Avenue. He told the agent that he was renting it for his widowed sister, Mrs. Cook.

The next morning, Holmes went to the train station to meet Carrie and her children. He waited for them to appear, but they weren't on board. When they finally arrived on the afternoon train, Holmes was furious. "Why didn't you come on the train I told you to?" he demanded to know.

Carrie replied that she was told the

South on Winooski Avenue, along No. 26, in Burlington. It was here where Holmes moved Carrie and her remaining children where they waited for the alleged arrival of Ben Pitezel.

morning train was an express train and she had been told it was bad traveling with a baby on a fast train.

Holmes snapped at her, "Whenever I tell you to do anything, I want you to do it. When I tell you to take a train, I want you to take the train that I tell you to take."

Upset by his browbeating, Carrie maintained an icy silence as he took them by carriage to the rented house on Winooski Avenue. As he was leaving, he told her that Ben was still in Montreal but would be arriving soon.

The next morning, Holmes returned to the house and asked Dessie if she would like to go out and see a little bit of the city. With Carrie's permission, Dessie agreed. As Holmes climbed aboard the streetcar with the young woman, he casually asked her if her father had ever mentioned anything to her about a plan involving life insurance.

Dessie said that he had, but she did not agree with it. She knew from his behavior that night when he'd come home drunk, talking about his death, that her father had been worried about the plan, too.

Holmes told her, "Your papa is all right. He's over in Montreal. You won't even know him. He has a new set of teeth and he's all fixed up so nice you won't know him at all. He's very anxious to see you. But be perfectly quiet and don't tell your mother you know about the scheme."

But Holmes surely must have known that he couldn't trust Dessie to remain quiet if things continued much longer. He was undoubtedly thinking of ways to dispose of her, Carrie, and Wharton – just as he had the rest of her family.

A few hours later, he returned Dessie to the furnished house and assured Carrie that there was a possibility of Ben showing up at any time. Privately, though, he told Dessie that Ben would never come to the house while she was there. He offered to take her to the home of one of his friends while her father was visiting. It goes without saying that if Dessie had gone anywhere with Holmes after revealing that she knew about the insurance scheme, she would not have survived. But Holmes made no firm arrangements with her. Instead, he left again, after giving Carrie some money to use for food.

Holmes left the house but didn't go far. He watched and he waited from down the street and soon after Carrie and the children left to purchase groceries, Holmes returned to the empty rental house.

He went down to the basement and, crouching next to the coal bin, he took out a brown bottle that he'd been keeping carefully wrapped in cloth and arranged it at a spot where it would be easily found – although only by the person that Holmes wanted to find it. He made one last adjustment and then he left.

Carrie did not see or hear from Holmes for nearly a week after her arrival in Burlington. She assumed that he had gone to fetch Ben, so when he showed up at the house alone on the night of November 7, she flew into a rage and accused him of lying to her all along.

Holmes insisted this wasn't the case but when Carrie threatened to pack up and go to Indianapolis to see her children,

Holmes confessed that they were not there anymore. He had moved them to Toronto, and they were staying in a house that he had rented from a spinster woman. They had been there for the past week and were doing fine. He had bought them warm coats so that they wouldn't be cold and Alice had grown into a fine young woman. Why, just a few evenings ago, she had fixed him a wonderful dinner.

As for Ben, Holmes produced a telegram from his coat. Ben had just been in touch with him. He'd been very sick – that was why he wasn't in Burlington. Carrie burst into tears and Holmes suggested – not meaning it, of course – that perhaps Carrie should go to Montreal and see him. But then what would Carrie do with Dessie and the baby?

Carrie wept and said she didn't know.

Then Holmes played down Ben's illness, suggesting it was the same old problem he'd always had, "It's probably his drinking again. Supposing he would die, what would you do? He has got one grave marked for him already."

Carrie was somewhat mollified. She even chose to believe Holmes when he promised her that he would bring Ben down from Montreal as soon as he either recovered from his illness or sobered up.

There seemed to be no limit as to how many lies Carrie would swallow. She so desperately wanted to believe that everything would be all right that she held tightly to even the slightest hint of good news that Holmes offered.

That evening, Holmes told Georgiana that he was leaving the next day on business, and he wanted her to meet him in Lowell, Massachusetts, in one week. From there, they would travel to Boston and board a steamship for Europe.

As usual, he didn't tell Georgiana where his business was taking him before he met her in Lowell. He did plan to take her to Berlin, but first he was determined to keep the promise he'd made in a letter he'd written back in September.

Herman Webster Mudgett was going home to Gilmanton, New Hampshire.

MEANWHILE, PINKERTON DETECTIVES WERE HOT ON HOLMES' trail. Holmes was operating under the assumption that he was running from a couple of insurance investigators, not the most famous detective agency in the country. Within a week of the Pinkertons being asked to join in the case, an agent had spotted the elusive Mr. Holmes.

A team of detectives had picked up his train in Prescott and followed him to Ogdensburg and from there to Vermont. It would have been simple for them to arrest him in Burlington, but they hoped that he might lead them to other conspirators in the insurance swindle, so they placed him under surveillance instead.

The Pinkertons even shadowed him as he drove through an early New England snowstorm to arrive at his parents' home on November 8.

Later, when Holmes wrote of the reunion with his parents with all the melancholy of a romance novel, he used the biblical analogy of Lazarus rising from the grave. But at the sight of their child, whom they had not seen in seven years, Levi and Theodate Mudgett – church-going people who were well-versed in the scriptures – were more likely reminded of the story of the Prodigal Son.

Holmes stayed five days in his hometown, revisiting his childhood haunts and dishing out extravagant lies to his parents and relatives about his life. At some point during this period, he also made a

Before leaving America, Holmes made one last visit to his hometown of Gilmanton – for reasons that remain unknown.

trip to Tilton to see his abandoned wife and his now 15-year-old son, Robert.

By all accounts, they were overjoyed to see him and Holmes' reunion with Clara – who had remained faithful to her husband, always believing that he would return to her one day – was an emotional one for Holmes, if we believe his story.

He claimed to be touched by her devotion and perhaps, for only a moment, he felt a twinge of regret. If he did, though, it didn't last for long. He lied outrageously to her and told her that, even though he had to leave again on an urgent business trip, he would return to her for good in April. There was, however, one small matter that he felt compelled to admit to her. He was embarrassed to admit it, but a little less than a year ago, he had accidentally married another woman.

The story that he spun for Clara was ridiculous, even by Holmes' standards. A year earlier, as he had already explained in a letter, he had been injured in a train wreck out west and had been taken, unconscious, to the nearest hospital. When he awakened, he was unable to remember who he was.

But what he hadn't yet told her was that, while suffering from amnesia, he was visited by a patron of the hospital, a beautiful, wealthy young woman who brought flowers to the sick and read to us from books, and with her gentle voice sought to bring cheer to the dull hospital wards. He and this angel of mercy, whose name was Georgiana Yoke, had fallen in love. After he recovered from the accident, they were married.

Deeply moved by her husband's constant suffering as he vainly tried to recall his past, Georgiana had secured the services of a great surgeon who performed a "wonderful operation" on his brain. When he awoke from the ether, he discovered that his memory had come back to him, and he told Clara, "To my unspeakable horror I realized what a wrong I had committed in marrying this sweet woman who had administered to me as I lay helpless and sick in the hospital. For it was only then that I remembered that I was a married man, and that my real wife was you, dear Clara."

Amazingly, Clara believed every word of this incredibly silly story. Holmes either had a knack for great storytelling or one for finding the most gullible people imaginable. I'm not sure which it was.

Although whether Clara believed him or not didn't really matter. He had no intention of ever seeing her – or any other member of his family – again. After a week spent living in his past, he was ready to move on and leave it behind him forever.

Why he made this trip home remains a mystery. It is one of the most puzzling and surprising twists in a story that's already filled with them. There was nothing about this family reunion that did anything to serve Holmes' plan for getting safely out of the country. But for some reason, he did it.

Holmes registered them at the Adams House Hotel in Lowell before moving to a boarding house.

FINALLY, ON NOVEMBER 13, HOLMES TRAVELED TO LOWELL, where he met Georgiana and, together, they went to Boston. From there, they would board a ship and leave America once and for all.

He registered them at the Adams House as H.M. Howell. The next day, he went to a boarding house and rented a room. He planned to be there for a little while before they departed for Germany.

Before he went anywhere, though, he needed to address the small problem that he had with the last three remaining Pitezels.

Holmes composed a letter to Carrie, stringing her along a little more, and instructing her to meet him in Lowell in one week, where Ben would finally be waiting for her. Before she left Burlington, though, he had one small task he needed her to perform.

For reasons too complicated to explain in a letter, he had stashed a bottle of expensive chemicals behind the coal bin in her house. He had since become worried that the bottle might be damaged if left there, so as soon as Carrie finished reading his letter – and destroying it – he needed her to move the bottle and hide it somewhere better in the basement. That way, it would be safe until Holmes could come and retrieve it.

Then, undoubtedly regretting that he would not be present to witness what happened when Carrie caused what was actually a 10-ounce bottle of nitroglycerin to explode, he hurriedly mailed the letter.

According to a detective who later visited the Burlington house, Holmes had not just hidden the bottle in the basement. He had also rigged a springboard that, when stepped on, would violently break the bottle of nitroglycerin and it would explode.

If this trap really existed, though, is unknown. There is no letter to prove it – Carrie destroyed it – we have only her word that it existed at all. In addition, this would have been kind of a convoluted, risky method of murder anyway and one that wasn't guaranteed to succeed. Nitroglycerin is dangerous, and the springboard might have shattered the bottle. If it did, it would have exploded. Carrie would have been killed certainly, but it might have left Dessie and Wharton alive. Holmes could have gotten rid of all of them in ways that were much more effective and less likely to attract attention.

Many have dismissed this as one of many unverifiable "near miss" stories that people later told about their interactions with Holmes. By the time he was brought to trial, it seemed that half the people who knew him had some story about a narrow escape, many wilder than a bottle of nitroglycerin.

On the other hand, the detective said the bottle was there and so was the springboard trap. If Holmes hadn't been trying to blow the family up, it's hard to imagine what else he would be doing with a bottle of explosive liquid.

WHEN HOLMES AND GEORGIANA ARRIVED IN THE BOSTON area, they weren't alone. They still had Pinkertons on their trail. And in Boston, the Pinkertons found a police department that was happy to cooperate with them.

Officers from the Boston Police Department cooperated with the Pinkertons to arrest Holmes.

Holmes was effectively cornered and when agents discovered he was inquiring about travel rates and ship departures, they decided it was time to strike.

In preparation for Holmes' arrest, Coroner Ashbridge in Philadelphia, issued a warrant for Holmes' arrest by the Pinkertons on the grounds that the identification of Ben's body might have been incorrect.

But Boston Deputy Police Superintendent Orin Hanscom feared this warrant wouldn't be enough. He met with John Cornish, head of the Pinkertons' Boston office, on Friday, November 16, and learned that Holmes had been traced to Texas and was suspected of illegal dealings there.

He wired the sheriff of Fort Worth and asked him if Holmes was wanted for anything there. He received a three-word reply: "LARCENY. ONE HORSE."

That was good enough for Hanscom. Holmes would be arrested as a horse thief. Again, Texans take that kind of thing very seriously.

On the afternoon of November 17, Holmes had just stepped out of the boarding house at 40 Hancock Street and suddenly found himself surrounded by four Boston police detectives.

Soon, there were also uniformed officers on the scene. Holmes smiled, put up his hands, and surrendered without a struggle. It wasn't his first arrest, and he was sure that he could find his way out of this one, too.

But he'd soon discover that he couldn't. He still believed that he was wanted for nothing more than an insurance swindle. He had no idea that the men who had been chasing him were Pinkerton agents.

A recent photo of 40 Hancock Street, the former boarding house where Holmes and Georgiana were staying.

For the Pinkertons, Holmes was just another criminal. They had no way of knowing at the time of his arrest just how important the arrest would turn out to be.

At the time, they regarded Holmes as the mastermind behind an insurance scheme. It was unique, but he was still just a swindler. Later, when the enormity of his crimes became known, though, the Pinkertons would achieve greater fame than ever before.

They would be hailed as the agency that captured a man who would gain national infamy and gain the reputation as what the newspaper called "THE MOST DASTARDLY CRIMINAL OF THE AGE."

NOVEMBER 19, 1894.

NABBED A NEAT SWINDLER

Man with Many Aliases and a Long Record Captured at Boston.

LIFE INSURANCE COMPANY A VICTIM

Paid the Policy on the Identification of a Bogus Corpse and Only by Accident Discovered They Had Been Swindled— One Conspirator at Large.

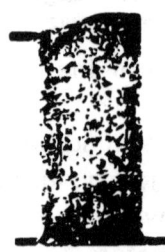 HOLMES' ARREST MADE NEWS – FIRST IN BOSTON, THEN ACROSS the country, and eventually around the world. The first stories appeared in Boston newspapers, then Philadelphia, then Chicago, then all over New England, the South, the West, and beyond.

The papers used headings and headlines like:

USED A BOGUS CORPSE – SWINDLING CHICAGOAN ARRESTED.

CORPSE HAD A PART – THE CONSPIRACY OF HH HOLMES

TURN A $10,000 TRICK – HOLMES AND PITEZEL WORK A GRAVEYARD INSURANCE SCHEME

The arrest wasn't generating banner headlines yet, but it soon would be. And no one was using the word murder yet, but it wouldn't be long before the authorities began to realize the true extent of Holmes' crimes.

The late nineteenth century was an era when people were fascinated by swindlers, con artists, and hucksters. That fascination would turn Holmes into a media sensation. Reporters initially called him an "adventurer whose deeds make him a most formidable rival to the most villainous characters ever depicted in fiction."

Soon, the entire country was gripped by a powerful fascination with Dr. Holmes and -- before the real horrors were revealed and it was discovered just how much blood was on his hands - reporters and the public alike seemed to have an admiration for the man and for the sheer audacity of his crimes.

At first, the public was enthralled by Holmes' audacity and daring - and then they began to realize the monster that he truly was.

They didn't understand that Holmes was a monster, a sociopath with no conscience and no belief that he'd ever be caught and punished. He'd been literally getting away with murder for years and no one had ever done anything about it. He was a man who was as dangerous as he was bold.

And that boldness was apparent on the day of his arrest.

When Holmes walked out of the boarding house that day and found himself surrounded by police officers, he did what Holmes did best - he lied.

First, he said they had the wrong man, then admitted who he was, but claimed he wasn't guilty of anything, then admitted that he'd gotten word that detectives were looking for him because of a murder in Chicago that he most certainly did not commit. Finally, he agreed to accompany the officers to the police station, where he was sure he could clear up this misunderstanding.

But when he arrived at Boston police headquarters, he was taken to the office of Deputy Superintendent Hanscom, where he was informed that he had been arrested on a warrant from Texas for the theft of some horses.

At that moment, Holmes must have been filled with both dread and relief. He was terrified of the idea of serving time in a Texas prison but was pleased that none of his more serious crimes had been discovered -- or so he thought. Whatever emotions coursed through Holmes' body at that moment, he quickly recovered his customary coolness.

And then LaForrest Perry walked into the room.

Even after calling in the Pinkertons, the main investigators for Fidelity Insurance, including Perry, continued their own investigation. Assisted by Major James E. Stuart of the U.S. Postal Inspector's Department, they had traced several of Holmes' letters to Burlington, Vermont.

With that information, Perry immediately went to Vermont. Along the way, he received word that a man and a woman resembling Holmes and Carrie Pitezel had been spotted in New York City, where they had checked into a fashionable midtown hotel.

Perry quickly changed his plans and headed for New York. He arrived at the hotel that evening and learned from the desk clerk that the couple had gone to the theater. Perry waited for them in the lobby for several hours before discovering he'd been chasing a false lead. It wasn't Holmes or Carrie – it was a case of mistaken identity.

Disheartened, he returned to Philadelphia for some badly needed rest. As soon as he arrived there, however, he received a telegram from the Pinkerton Boston office, informing him that Holmes had been followed there. Reinvigorated by the news, he hurriedly boarded a train for Boston and arrived soon after Holmes was arrested and hauled into police headquarters.

When Perry walked through the door of Deputy Hanscom's office, Holmes half-rose from his chair and, extending his right hand, he greeted the investigator in a friendly tone. There was a note of surrender in his voice when he spoke to him. "I guess I know what I'm really wanted for," he said.

In truth, Holmes was relieved. He'd rather spend five years in a Pennsylvania penitentiary than a single year in a Texas jail. He decided right then and there to confess to the insurance fraud, believing that by doing so, he could direct suspicion away from the scores of other crimes that he had committed. With Perry looking on, and Hanscom and Pinkerton John Cornish asking questions, Holmes proceeded to offer his first complete – and of course, mostly fabricated – confession.

Always the con man, Holmes assumed a guise of heartfelt sincerity and cooperation. While looking his interrogators in the eyes, he began to speak in a way that seemed to be completely truthful. When the story required it, he even managed to conjure up an expression of sorrow, pity, or remorse. He had spent his life perfecting the skill of getting people to believe what he was telling them, and he used that skill once again on the police officers and investigators.

Holmes readily admitted that he and Ben Pitezel had conspired to defraud Fidelity Mutual of the $10,000 from the life insurance policy. The body found at 1316 Callowhill had been obtained from an old medical school friend who was now a doctor in New York. The two of them had worked together on insurance scams in the past.

Holmes packed the cadaver in a trunk, had it shipped to Callowhill Street, and then hurried back to Philadelphia. After he gave the claim ticket for it to Pitezel, Holmes had left the city again, leaving his partner with directions on how to fake an accidental explosion after the corpse was delivered.

Ben had botched the job a bit, Holmes chuckled, but he'd fled Philadelphia and was alive and well. Holmes said he'd seen him on several occasions since that time in Cincinnati and Detroit. He wasn't sure of the exact dates, but Pitezel was just fine.

The investigators were eager to know the name of the physician who had supplied Holmes with the body, but Holmes staunchly refused to betray his accomplice. He apologized to the officers, saying that he didn't wish to make them angry, but for the time being, he didn't want to reveal that information. He assured them that his motives were selfless. His friend had a good reputation, and such a scandal might ruin his career.

Realizing that Holmes would not give up the name – and suspecting that the true reason for his reluctance was that the individual didn't actually exist – Hanscom and Cornish turned to another, even more pressing matter -- the whereabouts of Alice, Nellie and Howard Pitezel.

To account for the missing children, Holmes concocted a tale that was almost as confusing as the route that he had taken during the weeks that he had the children in his custody. According to his story, Ben Pitezel, after faking his death, fled to Cincinnati and hid out there in a hotel. Holmes, meanwhile, traveled to St. Louis and had taken Nellie and Howard from their mother. He had picked up Alice in Indianapolis and brought all three children to Cincinnati, where he had put them up in another hotel. Carrie and her remaining children were to follow a few days later. In the meantime, Holmes was to rent a house where she and her husband could have a private reunion before Ben went down South to hide out for the winter.

Although Carrie went along with all his plans, she was adamant that her children must continue to believe that their father was dead. She was terrified that if they discovered the truth, they might let the secret slip out and everything would be ruined. Carrie insisted on this – if the children found out Ben was alive, she would call the whole plan off. Holmes respected Carrie's wishes and agreed that the children could not be trusted with the secret.

Unfortunately, Holmes told the investigators, an unexpected incident occurred soon after his arrival in Cincinnati. Ben's terrible loneliness got the better of him and, as he had throughout his life, he decided to drown his sorrows in whiskey. As soon as Holmes had registered Alice and the other children at their hotel, he paid a visit to Ben, who was very drunk. Under Ben's persistent questioning, Holmes foolishly revealed the whereabouts of the three children.

The next day, while Holmes was visiting the children, the hotel room door suddenly flew open, and Ben barged in. The children gaped in wonder as their father – apparently returned from the grave – stumbled into the room and began to weep over how much he had missed them. He had completely ruined the plan.

After Ben sobered up, Holmes explained their predicament. Carrie's rule that the children remain clueless about Ben's fake death had been violated, and Holmes was as much to blame as his drunken partner was. The only solution, as far as the two men could see, was to keep Carrie away from the children so that she would not find out what had happened.

That same day, Ben departed for Detroit with little Howard. Holmes followed shortly after with Alice and Nellie. To fool anyone who might be following them, he disguised the younger girl as a boy.

Soon after he arrived in Detroit, Holmes received a disturbing message from Chicago. An associate wired to tell him that a pair of police officers from Fort Worth had been nosing around town, asking questions about Holmes and Pitezel. It was clear that the law was on their trail and might trace them to Detroit at any time. Believing that he had no time to lose, Holmes turned the two girls over to their father, who immediately left for New York with plans to board a steamship that was bound for South America. If he could not book passage right away, he planned to take the children by train to Key West, Florida.

Holmes had every reason to believe that Ben and the children were well. He could not say precisely where they were – either

South America or Florida – but he knew for a fact that all of them were, at that very moment, residing in the sunshine of some tropical locale.

The investigators gathered in the police superintendent's office exchanged a look of skepticism between them. As convincing as Holmes was – and he'd had a lot of years to practice – they were not prepared to swallow his story. Cornish warned him that if Ben Pitezel was not produced alive, that they must consider him dead.

Holmes said that he understood. He clarified a few points for them about the extent of Carrie Pitezel's part in the scheme, but he didn't wish to betray Ben's trust in him if he didn't have to. Holmes added, "I have almost got to do it to protect myself. It is not that I wish to go back on him by any means."

Deputy Superintendent Hanscom asked, "You expect in any event that there will be imprisonment to go with it?"

Holmes replied, "I certainly do. I told my wife – I begged her – to go away and drop it because I expected a term in the penitentiary."

Hanscom spoke up, this time with a smirk on his face. "Of course, it is desirable for you not to be held for the greater offense," he said.

Holmes shook his head and told him, "I certainly don't want to be held for murder. While I am bad enough on smaller things, I am not guilty of that."

Perhaps the strangest aspect of Holmes' "confession" was the reaction that it received from the investigators. Despite how forthcoming Holmes seemed to be, his explanation for where the children had ended up clearly seemed to be desperately contrived.

Nevertheless, his interrogators seemed less concerned with what had happened to Alice, Nellie, and Howard than what became of Ben Pitezel. They continued to believe, no matter what he said, that Holmes had murdered his partner. But the idea that terrible harm had befallen the children apparently never crossed their minds.

Perhaps this was because the notion of anyone murdering three young children was simply too outrageous to consider. Only a bloodthirsty madman would slaughter helpless children and Holmes, even though he was a confessed criminal, was clearly not a murderer.

Or at least that's what they believed at the time.

WITH THE INSURANCE SCHEME CONTINUING TO UNRAVEL, investigators began seeking other players in the game. While Holmes' interrogation was taking place, a Pinkerton agent posing as a messenger sent by Holmes was in Burlington, delivering a letter for Carrie Pitezel. The letter, penned by Holmes as Hanscom dictated it, directed Carrie to bring Dessie and Wharton to Boston right away.

If Holmes' plot against the remaining Pitezel family members had gone according to plan, the Pinkerton agent would have found nothing at 26 Winooski Avenue but smoldering ruins. But Carrie's suspicions had been aroused by the fluid-filled jar that had been hidden in the basement. She had managed to avoid the trap that had been left for her and instead of hiding the jar somewhere else in the cellar, she carefully took it outside and buried it in the yard.

Accompanied by the Pinkerton agent, Carrie and the children traveled to Boston, where they were met at the station by another man they assumed worked for Holmes. He was, in truth, Inspector

---

HUNTING FOR PITZEL.

Chase Difficult Because He May Be Living or Dead.

THE BURIED BODY TO BE EXHUMED.

The Chicago Police Have Struck a New Clew and Trailed Him to St. Louis. Holmes Declares the Williams Girls Are Alive and In New York City.

PHILADELPHIA, Nov. 24.—It was definitely ascertained that the body buried for that of B. F. Perry, or Pitzel, which was found in a house on Callowhill street early in September, will again be exhumed and another effort made to identify it. Dr. Mattern, one of the coroner's physicians, visited Superintendent of Police Linden and was closeted for a short time with the superintendent and President Fouse of the insurance company. The outcome of the consultation is that the body will be disinterred for the purpose of having Mrs. Pitzel endeavor to identify it.

It will be remembered that Mrs. Pitzel was too ill to come on from St. Louis at

When Carrie Pitezel realized she was on her way to police headquarters, she fainted in shock.

Whitman of the Boston police. The two men loaded Carrie and her children into a cab bound for police headquarters.

When she realized their destination, she fainted in shock. She revived a few moments later, only to be overwhelmed by hysterical weeping. She seemed to be on the verge of a nervous collapse. Arrest, imprisonment, and the shame that went with them, were her greatest fears. At that time, she had no idea that even worse things were still in store for her.

Under questioning, Carrie nervously lied to detectives several times – and her interrogators knew it. But they also knew she was lying out of fear and panic, not because she was innately dishonest, like Holmes was.

When she was asked about her participation in the insurance scheme, she immediately denied knowing about the fraud ahead of time. As far as she knew, she told them, her husband had gone off to Philadelphia to start a legitimate business under the name of Perry. When she read that Perry's corpse had been discovered at the building on Callowhill Street, she naturally assumed that Ben was dead.

Hanscom asked her if she had known anything about the scheme before she read about the death in the newspaper and Carrie lied again and said that she hadn't. She was asked several more times and each time, she insisted that she had no knowledge about what Holmes and her husband had planned.

She explained that Ben's death was tragic, and she was still in grief when Holmes showed in St. Louis a week later with amazing news – that Ben wasn't actually dead. But Carrie said she was completely in the dark about the insurance scheme until Holmes took her to Jeptha Howe's office to collect the payment on her husband's life insurance policy. That was when she became suspicious. Even then, however, she was only following Holmes' orders and – she believed – the wishes of her husband. At no point, she continued to insist, was she an active conspirator in the plan.

Even though Carrie's desperate denials seemed false to Hanscom and the other investigators, her bewilderment about her husband's present whereabouts was undoubtedly real. Even the most jaded among them, convinced that she was lying, were moved to pity by the cruel way that Holmes had manipulated her.

Hanscom leaned down and spoke to her in a soft, sympathetic tone, "He has kept you moving, hasn't he?"

Tears were streaming down Carrie's face when she nodded that he had.

Hanscom asked her directly, "Do you believe now that your husband is alive?"

Carrie replied but her voice was filled more with hope than conviction, "Well, there must be something to it. I am sure I could not swear to it, for I don't know for a fact that he is alive. All I know is what you have been telling me and what he has been telling me, and that is all I know."

But Hanscom asked her again about Holmes moving her And her children from place to place across the Midwest and Northeast and as Carrie answered, she let out a long sigh, "Well, I have been moving from one point to another. I have been just heartbroken, that is all there is about it."

Hanscom nodded in sympathy before he spoke again, "Yes, I know. We are sorry for you."

Then, speaking gently, he asked Carrie to explain to them where she had moved from, and in what order the cities had in as Holmes moved her around the country.

Carrie did the best she could. She left her parent's home, went to Chicago, then Detroit, Toronto, Ogdensburg and then

Burlington. She stated that she had great confidence in Holmes at first, but over time, her confidence was shaken. She told them simply, "I thought maybe he was fooling me or something."

But Carrie's greatest concern was the current location of her three children. She hadn't set eyes on Alice since September, when the girl had gone off to Philadelphia in the company of Jeptha Howe. When asked who Howe was, Carrie said that he was an attorney from St. Louis, with an office in the Wainwright Building. Hanscom shot a look at John Cornish, who scribbled down the information as Hanscom turned the subject back to Carrie's missing children.

He asked her: "What was his reason for taking them? What reason did he give?"

Carrie said that, at first, Holmes had taken them so that she could go home and visit her parents and not be bothered by them. Since her parents were getting old, he took the children to allow her some peace.

Hanscom tried to clarify the story. He asked if Holmes took the younger children to meet Alice, who was staying with a widow lady whose name Carrie never learned. He also asked her if Holmes ever told her that the children were with their father, as he had told the investigators.

Carrie replied: "No sir, he told me he took them to Toronto, that is all I know about it."

Hanscom asked her several times if the children were supposed to be with Holmes' friends and she repeatedly said that she didn't know.

Hanscom stared at her, not sure what to think. Her answers were so strange and evasive that he felt sure she must be withholding information. He couldn't believe that a mother would send three of her children off with anyone – especially a man like Holmes – without knowing such basic facts as where they were going, how long they would be there, and who would be taking care of them.

Hanscom finally spoke, his tone grim, "We believe this man to be a very bad man, and we want to get at the truth."

Carrie cried out, "Well, that is as far as I know! I can't tell you anymore because I don't know!"

"You did not understand then that these children were going to join their father?"

"No, sir."

"There is a boy and two girls?"

Carrie started to cry again, "Whoever told you that?"

Hanscom quietly replied, "We have been talking with him. We are not doing anything to undertake to make you feel bad. We are trying to get at the matter and sift it. He kept you moving about the country from point to point, and you look as though you have been through a great deal. We want to get all the light we can. We don't believe this man very much. That is why we are asking you these questions."

Hanscom had leaned in close as he spoke to her and suddenly Carrie grabbed the lapels of his coat, "Do you know where the children are?" she demanded.

Hanscom sadly shook his head. He told her, "That is one of the things we want to find out. We want to find them as much for your sake as for any other reason in the world. In fact, we may say that all these questions that are being asked now regarding the children are on your behalf."

But Carrie seemed to fall into some kind of stupor. She was now staring blankly at the floor. Her eyes were filled with tears and when she whispered her next words, her voice was hollow and hopeless: "I thought I would see my children here," she said.

The interview came to an end. Carrie was informed that she was being held on a charge of conspiracy after the fact. Terrified and knowing no one in Boston, she begged that Dessie and Wharton be allowed to remain in a cell with her overnight. Since the police had made no provisions for them, they agreed.

When Carrie got up from her chair, she found that she could barely stand, let alone walk. Hanscom beckoned to one of his officers and supported by the burly policeman, and followed by her teenage daughter and infant son, the stricken woman was led off to a cell for the night.

EVEN THOUGH IT WOULD BE MONTHS BEFORE THE DEPTHS OF Holmes' depravity were revealed, his arrest was already considered a triumph of modern law enforcement. In the days that followed his capture, the press lavished praise on all the agencies involved, from the Pinkertons to the insurance investigators to the Boston Police Department.

But there were other parties anxious to share in the credit and among those trying to put themselves in the spotlight was Fidelity Mutual president L.G. Fouse, who lost no time in revising his role in the drama from a bumbling man who was easily fooled to a sharp executive who suspected fraud from the start. While being interviewed by reporters on November 18, he declared that he knew something was wrong almost immediately and had done everything he could to stop the police from being settled.

According to Fouse's new and improved story, he had seen through Holmes as soon as the man set foot in his office. It was Jeptha Howe who had tricked him by playing on Fouse's good nature.

Fouse told the newspapers:

If there was anybody in the world calculated to throw a man off his guard, it was Howe. He was an innocent, boyish-looking fellow, with a frank and honest face. When I began to question him, he appealed to my soft side. He told me I was a man of experience in these things, and he was only a novice at the bar, and he begged me not to hinder him in his efforts to win success.

He may have liked the St. Louis attorney, Fouse confessed, but his keen nose for deception convinced him that he needed to order some of his men to investigate Howe and Holmes and, before long, his suspicions about them were confirmed. After that, it was only a matter of time before the conspirators were brought to justice – all thanks to the efforts of President L.G. Fouse.

But despite having master detective and insurance company president L.G. Fouse on the case, Jeptha Howe was still at large at the time of that interview.

On Monday morning, November 19, though, a group of St. Louis police officers, who were acting on an urgent telegram from Philadelphia police superintendent Robert Linden, showed up at Howe's office and placed him under arrest on conspiracy charges. He was taken down to headquarters and interrogated by St. Louis police chief Harrigan and investigator William E. Gary for several hours before he was released on a $3,000 bond.

When he left the police station, Howe was accosted by reporters on the street. They pressed him for a statement and Howe gave them one:

I will say the same to you that I have said to Mr. Gary and the chief. I do not, in the first place, believe that a fraud has been committed. I believe that the body identified by Pitezel's fifteen-year-old daughter was that of her father. The marks of identification were perfect. As to how Pitezel met his death, I cannot say. But as I said to Mr. Gary, if a fraud has been committed, I am as anxious to have it investigated as anyone and will do all in my power to bring the guilty to punishment.

I took the case in good faith and acted as any attorney would have done. Mr. Gary asked me if I would be willing to return to the company my fee if this was proved a fraud. I told him that I would not only be willing but would not under any circumstances keep any part of it.

Howe added that he was outraged at the injustice of the accusations against him and the injury that it had caused to his good name. He intended to leave for Philadelphia at once to prove his innocence and repair his reputation.

But it didn't take long for Howe's righteous indignation to appear to be nothing more than hot air once Chief Harrigan gave his own statement to the press.

Soon after the attorney's release, he revealed the contents of the letter that Marion Hedgepeth had sent to the police. The letter, which had cracked open the case in the first place, blatantly named Howe as one of the conspirators. Harrigan also revealed that, according to Hedgepeth, Howe had attempted to smuggle keys to him in his cell and aid him on various occasions to attempt escape. The charge was confirmed by jail guard J.C. Armstrong, who, in a sworn statement, declared that he was approached by Howe for the purpose of getting his assistance in Hedgepeth's escape.

This was not good news for the attorney.

IN PHILADELPHIA THAT SAME AFTERNOON, A GRAND JURY convened to hear the testimony of President Fouse and Coroner Ashbridge. The jury indicted Herman Mudgett, a.k.a. H.H. Holmes, Mrs. Carrie Pitezel, and Jeptha D. Howe. They were charged with conspiracy to defraud and cheat the Fidelity Mutual Life Association Company of $10,000.

But there was one very significant name missing from the indictment -- Benjamin Pitezel. The authorities were now starting to believe that – no matter what Holmes claimed – Ben couldn't be indicted because he was dead. The lack of an indictment began a heated debate within law enforcement circles and became a topic of intense fascination for the press.

Everyone seemed to have an opinion about whether Holmes murdered his partner or not. The newspapers played up the melodrama for all it was worth, treating the Holmes-Pitezel case more like a sensational suspense novel than an unfolding news story. The story was now solidly front-page news, and dozens of theories began to emerge.

One of those theories came from the irrepressible L.G. Fouse, who was no longer a stranger to reporters. He insisted that the remains found at the Callowhill Street building had belonged to Ben. He had a theory about the case that he advanced to reporters, which was eerily close to what actually happened. He said that Holmes had set Ben up for murder, disfigured his body, and staged the explosion. A corpse was supposed to be substituted for Ben, he said, but Holmes double-crossed him and said that the body buried in the potter's field was Ben Pitezel – not a substitute corpse.

Fouse firmly believed that Holmes was eager to make a confession to fraud as a ploy to ward off a more serious charge of murder.

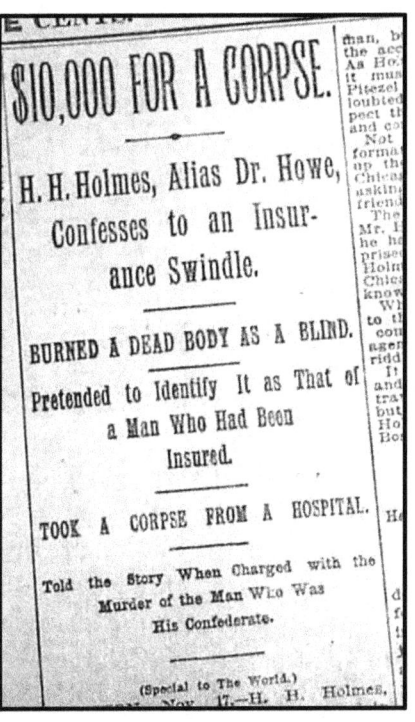

Coroner Ashbridge agreed. He didn't believe the body that was found in the patent shop had been a corpse that Holmes obtained in New York. There were no marks on the body that indicated that it had been folded into a trunk after rigor mortis set in. It simply couldn't be done. The body, he also believed, was Ben Pitezel. He couldn't say if his death had been deliberate – it was possible he'd died from an accidental overdose of chloroform – but he was convinced Holmes killed his partner so he wouldn't have to share the insurance money.

The Boston police inmitially had their own ideas. They theorized that perhaps the dead man was not Ben Pitezel at all but another man who had been lured to the patent office under some pretext and was then murdered there by the two conspirators. Ben, said one officer to a group of reporters, was a drinking man, and it would have been an easy matter for him to secure a victim from some of his barroom acquaintances.

On Monday afternoon, this theory suddenly seemed more credible when L.G. Fouse received a telegram from William Gary, informing him that Ben had been known in Fort Worth as Benton T. Lyman and might be still at large and using that alias.

But this was all merely speculation. There was only one person who really knew what had happened at the Callowhill Street building on the morning of September 2 – and he wasn't talking.

Well, he was talking, but he wasn't telling the truth.

PHILADELPHIA BUREAU OF POLICE DETECTIVE THOMAS Crawford arrived in Boston on Monday morning. He brought with him arrest warrants for Holmes and Carrie Pitezel. Both had agreed to waive their rights to formal extradition hearings.

Around 7:30 that evening, the prisoners boarded a train to Philadelphia in the company of Crawford, LaForrest Perry, and a pair of Pinkerton agents. Dessie and Wharton Pitezel also traveled with them, as did Georgiana, who continued to be loyal to her husband. She did her best to keep up appearances, but her tightly drawn lips and anguished eyes betrayed her fear and shame.

After 10 months of marriage, Georgiana was now faced with confronting the truth -- that her entire life with Holmes had been a lie, or so the police officers were telling her.

I'm still not convinced about that. I continue to believe that Georgiana knew that Holmes had many dealings outside the law. But I don't think she knew everything. The police believed she was another of Holmes' victims, not an accomplice. I think, more accurately, she was somewhere in the middle. She knew about some of his crimes, but she would be shocked when she found out about the others.

Georgiana was a stressed, nervous wreck, but Holmes was just the opposite. Although handcuffed to Detective Crawford, he seemed relaxed and unconcerned about his predicament.

Impeccably dressed in a handsome wool coat, matching vest, black tie, and stylish gray trousers, he spent the better part of the trip entertaining Crawford with a version of the history of his criminal career.

It wasn't an accurate version of events but who could expect it to be, coming from Holmes?

In the story he spun on the way to Philadelphia, he claimed that he'd been born, raised, and educated in Burlington, Vermont. After graduating from the local university, he taught school for a while in Burlington, then went off to study at the University of Michigan. It was there that he first made the acquaintance of an individual – then a fellow medical student and later a doctor in New York – who supplied him with the body that he used in the recent insurance swindle.

But Fidelity Mutual was not the first insurance company that he had cheated – far from it, in fact. He and his physician friend (whose identity he still refused to reveal) had first worked out the scheme 12 years before. Short of funds, they had taken out a $12,500 policy on the friend's life. They obtained a bogus body in Chicago, brought it east, and successfully "palmed it off" on the insurance company.

Since that time, Holmes claimed that he had repeated the fraud on several occasions. He offered details about one of them to Crawford. After insuring his life for $20,000, Holmes illegally purchased a cadaver from a Chicago medical school and then traveled to Rhode Island, where he checked into a seaside hotel. At the time, he was sporting a full beard, which he had been growing for nearly six months. Around sunset, Holmes left the hotel, announcing to the desk clerk that he was going for an evening swim. Once out of sight, he hurried to an isolated spot several miles from the resort, where, in the underbrush near the beach, he had stashed the cadaver. After dragging the body down to the shore, he cut off its head and arranged the mutilated corpse so that it looked as though it had been washed up by the waves.

Then, after shaving off his beard, Holmes returned to the hotel the following afternoon. Unrecognizable, he registered under a different name. At the front desk, he inquired if the desk clerk knew of a guest that was staying there named Holmes. The clerk told him that Mr. Holmes had checked in the day before but had gone out for a swim that evening and had not been seen since. After he failed to return at nightfall, a search was made and the mutilated body – presumed to be Mr. Holmes, who had evidently drowned and had been partially eaten by fish – was found on the beach.

It seemed like a success, but Holmes told Crawford that it had not worked out. The scheme unfortunately "fell through," he sighed, and he was unable to collect on the policy.

While the story – along with the rest of Holmes' tall tales – was fascinating to Crawford, he and his fellow law enforcement officials already knew that everything Holmes said had to be regarded with skepticism. The story of the headless corpse seemed wildly improbable, but it was no more unbelievable than the next story he told.

Clearly anticipating that he would soon be suspected of even greater crimes, Holmes told the police officer another extraordinary tale.

While living in Chicago with his second wife, he said, he'd fallen in love with a pretty young woman who worked for him as a "typewriter girl." Before long, the two became intimate and were sharing a furnished apartment on the outskirts of town. A few weeks later, the older sister of Holmes' mistress arrived for a visit. Insanely jealous, the mistress soon began accusing her sister of flirting with Holmes.

One day while he was away, the two women had a violent argument in his office. During the quarrel, his mistress grabbed a wooden chair and smashed her sister's skull with it. The young woman fell to the floor, dead. When Holmes returned, he was stunned to discover that his lover had murdered her sister, but he wanted to do all he could to protect her. So, he took the corpse, put it in a trunk, weighed it down with rocks, and sank it into Lake Michigan in the middle of the night.

Holmes told the detective:

> *This was a year and a half ago. The younger sister, in danger of arrest for murder, was anxious to escape. She owned some property in Fort Worth, amounting to $40,000. Pitezel and I took this property off her hands and gave her the money to flee the country. We then bought horses, getting credit on the strength of the Fort Worth property. But the deeds were not straight, and we needed money to keep things going. So, the two of us agreed to work the insurance scheme, and that's how this trouble began.*

So, in other words, the whole mess was someone else's fault.

If Holmes' jealous mistress hadn't killed her sister, then he would not have ended up in financial trouble and been forced to try and defraud the insurance company.

But Crawford was smarter than most of the other people that Holmes usually dealt with, even though Holmes would later claim that he seemed so gullible that he'd told Crawford the story of the two sisters just for fun. He'd made the whole thing up. Sometimes he claimed that both women were alive, or they were both dead, but mostly he maintained that one of them had killed her sister and was in hiding – just like he told Detective Crawford.

On the train that day, though, Crawford considered the story that Holmes told him for a moment and then he asked Holmes if he had been involved in any other crimes.

Holmes casually waved his hand, and he laughed, "Oh, I have done enough things in my life to be hung a dozen times."

The railway carriage was silent for a time as the train steamed through Providence. Then, Holmes leaned over toward the detective and whispered to him, "See here, Crawford – I think my wife can raise $500. I'm a hypnotizer – learned to do it from a fellow doctor. I can hypnotize people very easily. If you let me hypnotize you so that I can escape, I'll give you the $500."

But Holmes chose poorly if he thought he could fool Crawford so easily. The detective laughed at him. "Sorry, hypnotism always spoils my appetite. I'm afraid $500 is no inducement when weighed against possible dyspepsia," he quipped.

This episode was later widely reported in the press and was taken as another example of how brazen and self-assured Holmes truly was.

Of course, his claims about being a hypnotist were dismissed as sheer nonsense – at that point anyway. Later, when he was seen as a demon of almost supernatural evil, people would begin to believe that he was capable of almost anything.

THE TRAIN ARRIVED IN PHILADELPHIA ON TUESDAY EVENING, November 20. Still handcuffed to Crawford, Holmes was led directly to the City Hall police station. Carrie's nervous condition was such that she was still unable to walk without the support of one of the Pinkerton men.

At the station, Holmes was led directly into a darkened cell on the second tier, where he was grilled for several hours by Superintendent Linden, President Fouse, and O. LaForrest Perry. After that, he was taken down to the identification department, where he was photographed and measured for the rogue's gallery. Fingerprinting wasn't yet in common use in the United States.

While Holmes was being processed into the jail, Carrie was being locked into her own cell. A chair had been placed in the

Philadelphia City Hall in the mid-1890s

corridor outside her cell for Dessie and the baby and they were seated there under the sympathetic watch of a police matron.

The sight of her two children just beyond the bars of her cell offered little comfort to their mother, who wept continuously from the moment the door clanged shut behind her.

The pitiful condition of Mrs. Pitezel was becoming a matter of increasing concern to both the authorities and the public at large. Even the officials at the insurance company, who regarded her, at the very least, as an accessory after the fact, were moved by Carrie's situation. Naïve and, as the newspapers put it, of "no more than ordinary intelligence," she had clearly been cruelly manipulated by Holmes, who had – as Coroner Ashbridge and many others believed – made her into a widow as part of his devious plan.

A newspaper illustration of Carrie Pitezel after her arrest

Even more worrisome was the unresolved mystery of her three missing children. For the first time, a few people began to entertain the horrific possibility that Holmes might have not only murdered Ben Pitezel but his children – Alice, Nellie, and Howard – too.

A front-page story in the *Philadelphia Ledger* put the fears of many into print on Wednesday, November 21:

The question of the disposition of Pitezel's three children, who were taken by Holmes to be placed in the care of their father, is agitating the authorities. An effort is being made to find them, but as of yet, it has been unsuccessful. The police think that if the charge of Pitezel's murder can be substantiated against Holmes, there will be little doubt that he has added the killing of the children to his long list of crimes, for which he himself admits he should be hanged.

WHILE HOLMES WAS LOCKED UP IN THAT DARK CELL IN Philadelphia, news about his crimes was finally making their way to Chicago.

Within 24 hours of his arrest, nearly 50 victims of his various frauds had lined up at the Englewood police station to put in claims against his property and hopefully recover some of the funds that he had illegally taken from them.

Every day, a fresh batch of stories sprang up in the Chicago papers about his seemingly endless swindles – the worthless patent medicines, the magical spring water, the phony gas-generating machine, and the dozens and dozens of underhanded dealings with building contractors and furniture suppliers.

Dozens of acquaintances and associates stepped forward to recount tales of his deceptions – often with an appreciative chuckle at the sheer daring and nerve of the man. As one newspaper put it, Holmes "swindled with a dash and vim that won the admiration even of those he tricked."

Chicago had seen so many men of Holmes' type over the years that the residents could not help but appreciate a man who stole with such flair.

The *Chicago Times-Herald* printed an interview with, of course, C.E. Davis, the owner of the jewelry shop on the ground floor of Holmes' Castle. He told a reporter numerous stories of Holmes' swindles and frauds, explaining that it wasn't a lawyer who kept Holmes out of trouble but the sheer rascality of the man that pulled him through. "He was the only man in the United States that could do what he did," Davis added.

Holmes' notoriety continued to grow and soon, a legend was taking shape – Holmes was "the arch-conspirator," the "boss crook of the century," and the "swindler of men and betrayer of women, who has left behind a wake of ruin and tears that not all the courts of America can wash away."

The *Chicago Tribune* referred to his crooked work and proclaimed that he was "about the smoothest and best all-around swindler that ever struck this town." Holmes' astonishing versatility, many said, raised him above ordinary criminals – as well as his remarkable power over women. The *Tribune* claimed that Holmes had ruined at least 200 "pretty young girls" and had six wives and 25 children scattered all over the country.

But these flattering stories of the debonair master swindler were soon to be overshadowed by those that hinted at a darker side to his criminal career. There were rumors that Holmes had done much worse than swindling and seduction – or even the murder of a faithful accomplice.

By Wednesday, November 21, two names had finally been publicly linked to the bizarre tale of sibling rivalry and bloodshed that Holmes had told to Detective Crawford on the train to Philadelphia – Minnie and Nannie Williams.

With assistance from the authorities in Fort Worth, Chicago detectives had already started to uncover a great deal of information about Minnie Williams, including her background, her upbringing, her relationship with Holmes and, of course, her considerable inheritance. The *Tribune* reported that "people in Englewood who knew Holmes and the Williams girl can tell enough stories to fill a book."

Among those with intriguing stories to tell was the former caretaker of the Castle, Pat Quinlan, who soon fell under official scrutiny, suspected of assisting Holmes in his bloodiest crimes. But on the evening of Tuesday, November 20, he was interviewed by detectives about what he recalled concerning Minnie Williams. Quinlan confirmed many elements of Holmes' version of events, including the fact that a wooden chair had been in his office – just like the one that Minnie allegedly used to fracture the skull of her sister.

Most people, however, believed that Holmes' account about the two women having a deadly quarrel was a complete fabrication. But others – who hadn't cared for Minnie much -- maintained that, from the first, Minnie had been an active accomplice of Holmes and had stuck with him "through all his peculiar career."

Still others – including the girls' uncle, Reverend C.W. Black of Jackson, Mississippi, who had not heard from either of his nieces since July 1893 – remained convinced that Holmes, perhaps assisted by Ben Pitezel, had killed the young women so he could get his hands on the property in Fort Worth.

And the Williams sisters were not the only young women that people were starting to believe had come to a bad end at the hands of H.H. Holmes. On November 21, a front-page story in the *New York Times* stated:

"H.H. Holmes, the life-insurance swindler now under arrest in Philadelphia, is charged with being the cause of the mysterious disappearance of a third woman during his operations in Chicago. That person is Miss Kate Durkee, and she is said to have had considerable property."

The article went on to say that creditors of Holmes' had made a desperate effort to find out who and where Kate Durkee was, but it was believed that she was some accomplice of his since some of the property that he had illegally obtained had been placed in her name. But "Miss Durkee dropped from sight and, like the Williams sisters, has left no trace behind."

George B. Chamberlain, the owner of a Chicago mercantile company and one of Holmes' many creditors, had no doubts about the woman's fate. Interviewed by reporters on November 22, he stated that, "Miss Durkee was murdered."

But Kate Durkee was alive and well and living in Omaha. In interviews after reporters tracked her down, she spoke of signing papers when Holmes asked her to because, as she put it, she had no head for business. But she was smart enough to notice that no little girl was mentioned in reports from Boston about Holmes and his wife. This Mrs. Holmes, Kate realized, was not her friend, Myrta.

When a few of Holmes' other possible victims also turned up alive, it began to look as if all the missing people were probably fine, including Ben Pitezel and the Williams sisters. Even the Fidelity Mutual branch in Chicago thought Ben was alive, saying, "We know he was in a South Side saloon drinking whiskey less than two weeks ago."

He wasn't – but it seemed possible at the time.

Oddly, in all these questions raised about possible victims of Holmes, the names of Emeline Cigrand and Julia Connor didn't come up.

> **NOT A GO-BETWEEN**
>
> Lawyer Howe of St. Louis Claims to Be Guiltless.
>
> His Connection With the Holmes-Pitzel Case an Honest One.
>
> **THE MATTER MOVES TO OMAHA**
>
> Kate Durkee, Supposed Victim of the Conspirator, Alive and Well in Nebraska's Metropolis—What She Knows.
>
> PHILADELPHIA, Nov. 22.—Lawyer J. P. Howe of St. Louis, indicted for complicity in the conspiracy against the Fidelity Mutual Life association, arrived here today and surrendered to the police. To a number of reporters Howe told of his connection with the case, which briefly stated was that he had been engaged by Mrs. Pitzel to prosecute her claim, and he had done so in the usual manner, receiving $2,500. According to Howe's story there were no underhanded methods on his part and he had simply given his advice to the woman on matters of identification and legal technicalities.
>
> Lawyer McDonald had an interview with Police Superintendent Linden. Mr. McDonald went into an explanation of the manner in which he gave Howe the letter of introduction to Captain Linden

With rumors of Holmes' true villainy starting to pile up, reporters began digging into every aspect of his life, from his boyhood in New Hampshire to his medical school years in Michigan to his busy years of swindling, building, and manipulating people in Englewood.

The press tracked down Clara in New Hampshire and revealed to her that her husband was the H.H. Holmes that was currently in the news. After learning the truth about what Herman Mudgett had become, she took a carriage to his parents' home and gave them the news. They refused to believe her at first, insisting that Herman had always been so innocent and would never have dared do anything like what was being reported in the papers. They would continue to insist that their son was innocent for months, finally conceding that he wasn't a criminal, merely insane, toward the end.

But Clara accepted the truth. As far as is known, she never saw Holmes again and never met any of his other wives.

HOLMES' NEW NOTORIETY MADE HIM A GOLD MINE FOR THE tabloids, especially in Chicago. Thanks to the zeal with which the press was digging into Holmes' life, what happened next was inevitable.

On November 25, a small notation appeared in the corner of page one of that day's *Chicago Tribune*. It was the first printed description of Holmes' property at Wallace and Sixty-Third Streets in Englewood. According to the writer, who apparently broke into the building and took a look around:

In America's whole domain, there is not a house like that one, and there probably never will be. Its chimneys stick out where chimneys never stuck out before, its staircases do not end anywhere in particular, it has winding passages that bring the rash intruder back to where he started with a jerk and altogether it is a very mysterious sort of building.

The *Chicago Herald* offered its own story on the building in Englewood. By now, it was in sad shape – a partially dismantled place with a fire-damaged third floor and an unsightly temporary roof. Businesses on the first floor were still in operation but the flats on the second floor were largely abandoned. Only Patrick Quinlan and his family still lived there.

And as the newspaper noted:

The history of that house and the doings within its walls would fill a very large book with some exceedingly grotesque chapters.

For the first time, the newspapers, the public, and the police were beginning to take notice of the bizarre and mysterious building that would soon be known across the country as the "Murder Castle of Dr. H.H. Holmes."

13

H.H. HOLMES WAS A MASTER MANIPULATOR AND CON ARTIST.

Anyone who spent any time around him quickly realized he was a man who was used to getting what he wanted. This wasn't because he was delusional in some way, but because he could talk just about anyone into anything. He also had a rare gift for being able to smoothly adapt his story according to whatever situation he found himself in.

During the early days of his captivity, he put up a stoic front, posing as a repentant sinner – a man who knew that he had done wrong and was prepared to accept the punishment that awaited him. In Pennsylvania, the maximum sentence for conspiracy was two years. He had no interest in going to prison, but he could certainly handle such a short time if that's what he ended up with. He was confident in the fact that he could talk his way into the shortest sentence possible.

Carrie Pitezel, on the other hand, continued to be overwhelmed with grief and shame. During her first long night in the Philadelphia jail cell, she wept and moaned for so long and so loudly that Police Surgeon Thomas Andrews was called to examine her first thing in the morning. He gave her a sedative, but even so, she remained curled up on her cot most of the day, weeping and groaning. Once or twice, she got unsteadily to her feet, shuffled to the door of the cell, and looked forlornly out at her toddler son, who wobbled up and down the corridor with Dessie, grasping a tin cup that had been provided by a police matron.

The third member of the conspiracy, Jeptha D. Howe, was due to arrive in Philadelphia on the evening of Wednesday, November 21, but failed to appear. Instead, his employer, Marshal McDonald – the former district attorney of St. Louis and law partner of Howe's brother, Alphonso – arrived quietly in the city in Howe's place. After checking into the Lafayette Hotel, McDonald sought out an old friend -- Police Superintendent Linden.

After the two men conferred for several hours, the two of them met with reporters, where Linden declared that Jeptha D. Howe was innocent of the conspiracy claims brought against him. The young man had simply been fooled by the experienced criminal, Dr. Holmes.

While it was true that many innocent people had been unknowingly led astray by Holmes, the statements from the attorney and the police superintendent didn't explain why Marion Hedgepeth was so quick to name Howe when Holmes asked him if he knew of any crooked attorneys in the city. Or excuse his attempts to break Hedgepeth out of jail or that he obviously knew that he was breaking the law when he took Alice Pitezel across the country to collect on a life insurance scam. Those things were conveniently ignored.

When asked where Howe was at the present time, the superintendent told reporters that he was on his way to Philadelphia at that very moment but had stopped in Washington D.C. on the way to seek the advice of Senator Cockrell of Missouri, an old family friend. Howe was expected to arrive in Philadelphia the following morning and would turn himself over to the authorities at that time.

Howe arrived in Philadelphia, as promised, the following morning at 10:00 A.M. He was met by Marshal McDonald, who escorted him to City Hall and Superintendent Linden's office, where he formally surrendered to the authorities.

McDonald agreed to let his client answer some questions and at about halfway through his interrogation, L.G. Fouse of the Fidelity Mutual Insurance Company entered the office. Howe rose from his seat, shook hands with him, and said, "Mr. Fouse, you treated me with such kindness and courtesy, I am sorry that you think I am a criminal."

Fouse looked at him coldly before he replied, "So am I. And it will take a good deal to convince me of your innocence."

When Howe protested that Fouse was only prejudiced against him because of the false accusations leveled by Holmes, Fouse responded with a sharp laugh. He had a reply for Howe that must have stung. "You knew Holmes," he snapped, "and, in fact, you met him on your way to this city. In the office of our company, you both met as strangers. You exclaimed when told that he was in this city, 'Who is this man? What does he mean? What is he here for?' And when you were introduced, you acted in a way that led us to believe you had seen him for the first time. If you can explain to me why you did this, I will believe you innocent."

But McDonald brought the questions to a halt and took his client to the office of District Attorney George S. Graham, who set his bail at $2,500. The money was paid later that day by William McGonegal, a friend of McDonald's. After his release, Howe told reporters that he would remain in Philadelphia for a day or so to consult with his local attorney, A.S.L. Shields, before returning to St. Louis to await his trial.

That night, Howe and McDonald went to the South Broad Street Theatre, where they watched a performance by St. Louis actress Della Fox. Afterward, reporters said, Howe seemed relaxed and carefree, chatting, and laughing with McDonald as they walked up Broad Street to the Lafayette Hotel.

While Jeptha Howe was dining in fine restaurants and enjoying a night at the theater, Carrie Pitezel was still sitting in jail. By Friday, November 23, arrangements were made to transfer her – and Holmes – to the county prison, commonly known as Moyamensing.

The Broad Street Theatre that Howe attended while the other members of the conspiracy were locked up in jail.

Early that morning, while the prisoners were being escorted from the cells, Assistant District Attorney William Kinsey, Police Surgeon Andrews, and Benjamin Crew, secretary of the Society to Protect Children from Cruelty, consulted about whether it was wise to allow Dessie and the baby to remain with their mother. Crew urged that the children be placed in the care of his organization.

When Carrie overheard this, she burst into hysterics and wailed, "You will not take my baby from me, will you?"

Immediately, Dr. Andrews placed his arm around the overwrought woman, assuring her that they would not separate her from the baby. He told Kinsey to send Dessie and the baby to the jail, too, stating that Carrie was in no condition to take care of the child by herself. Unbelievably, Carrie, Dessie, and Wharton were taken by wagon to the county prison – a group incarceration that was undoubtedly breaking some kind of law.

Holmes, meanwhile, was also being transferred to the same prison. He was loaded into a stinking van filled with drunks – which he later called a "crowded conveyance with the filthy lot of humanity" – and was locked into a 9x14 stone cell.

And the Devil found himself behind another set of bars – for now.

WHILE PRISONERS WERE BEING TRANSFERRED AND THE LAWYERS WERE TRYING TO shift the blame for everything that had happened onto Holmes, speculation about the fate of Ben Pitezel continued with the public and the press. Speculation was rampant, and rumors ran wild. Many believed he was dead, but others were willing to consider other ideas. L.G. Fouse, for one, had been receiving tips from his investigators that Ben had been spotted in Chicago as recently as early November, in Detroit a few weeks before that, and was currently said to be in New York City.

Moyamensing Prison, where Holmes and Carrie – along with Dessie and Wharton – were sent to wait for their trials.

To make things even more confusing, a man named E.A. Curtis – who owned a furniture warehouse in Englewood where Ben had allegedly stored some of his belongings before leaving Chicago – claimed that he knew Ben's precise whereabouts and could locate him within 36 hours, for a suitable reward, of course. But even if the reward had been offered, Ben, of course, would not have been found.

From his prison cell, Holmes did his best to keep things confusing by retracting some portions of his earlier statements and denying others. His only outright lie? he claimed. That was his story about the Williams sisters and the rivalry between them that led to Nannie's death. That was a hoax – he'd made the whole thing up. Why would he do that? He said that Detective Crawford seemed like such a gullible fellow that he wanted to have some fun with him.

Minnie and her sister were both alive and well. In fact, Ben Pitezel had even met up with Nannie in New York and had given her $1,000 so that she and her sister could hide out down south. The point of all that was that Ben Pitezel was just fine. Like the Williams sisters, he was also alive and well.

You can trust me, Holmes was essentially saying. Why would I lie?

The authorities could think of many reasons why Holmes might lie, and this time, they were at least a half step ahead of him. They were already considering exhuming the body that had been buried in the potter's field and, this time, having Carrie identify the body. As speculation about Ben's fate continued to heat up, this possibility began to be more seriously considered.

Ben Pitezel made frequent appearances in the newspapers after Holmes' arrest, as speculation ran rampant about whether he was dead or alive.

And that was something that Holmes – knowing what they'd find during a second exhumation – started to worry about it. He received the local newspapers in his cell each day and read all about the plan to dig Ben up again.

Then, on Friday, December 7, he learned something else. Carrie had broken down and revealed all that she knew about the insurance scheme. By that point, Dessie and Wharton had finally been removed from her cell and placed in the care of the Society to Protect Children from Cruelty. That had likely been the breaking point for Carrie, and every secret that she'd tried to keep came spilling out.

Holmes knew that time had run out. He needed a new plan. When Ben's body was identified, he knew he'd been charged with murder, so he came up with a daring ruse.

Just before Christmas, Holmes summoned Superintendent Linden to his cell and, with a great show of remorse, announced that he had decided to make a full confession. He had been lying all along, he said. The dead man that was buried in the potter's field really was Ben Pitezel – but Holmes hadn't killed him.

Ben Pitezel, Holmes declared, had committed suicide.

Claiming to be overwhelmed by the holiness of the holiday season, Holmes had decided to unburden his soul to Superintendent Linden, a stenographer, and a few assistant prosecutors. Not all of them could fit comfortably in Holmes' cramped cell, so the prosecutors were forced to sit in chairs in the corridor.

To the sound of only the stenographer's pen on paper, Holmes began his latest confession.

According to his new version of events, he had visited the building on Callowhill Street perhaps four or five times after Ben set up his phony patent dealer's business. In late August, Holmes dropped by and found Ben in a very despondent mood. He had clearly been drinking. When Holmes criticized him for it, Ben replied, "He guessed he had better drink enough to kill himself and have done with it."

After loaning Pitezel $15, Holmes left. Then, a few days later, on Saturday, September 1, Ben came to see him at the boarding house where he was staying and said he'd gotten a telegram that his baby was sick, and he needed to go home. Holmes told the assembled men:

I raised no objection to his going. When we got the arrangements all made, he said, 'You will have to let me have some money to go with.'

Holmes asked him what had happened to the $15 that he had given him a day or two before, and Ben told him that he didn't have it. Holmes refused to give him any more money, and Ben left. Holmes continued:

The next morning, about 10:30, I went to his house. I had been provided with a key to go in. I found no one there either on the first or second floor, where his sleeping apartment was. He had a cot up there, which I do not think he ever made up.

Holmes then went to the Mercantile Library for an hour or so and then strolled over to Broad Street, where he kept a private mailbox. After checking for letters, he bought a newspaper and walked back to Ben's shop. It was still empty. Holmes went upstairs and read the paper, and by the time he finished, it was noon.

Holmes went downstairs, intending to write some letters at Ben's desk, and that was when he spotted something lying on the desktop. It was a scrap of paper with a cipher on it that Holmes claimed the two men used for secret messages. He quickly decoded it and discovered that the message read: "Get letter out of bottle in cupboard."

Puzzled, Holmes quickly followed the directions and discovered a suicide note. He said, "It told me that he was going to get out of it, and that I should find him upstairs, if he managed to kill himself."

Holmes ran up the steps to the third floor and saw Ben lying on the floor. He checked his pulse and felt his skin, finding it cold. He knew Ben was dead. He was lying on his back with a towel on his face. On a chair next to him was a gallon bottle of chloroform, rigged up with a length of rubber tubing that drained the deadly liquid into his mouth. The fumes were so overpowering that Holmes was forced to flee from the room.

At this point, Linden asked him what had become of the suicide note.

Holmes answered, "I did not keep the letter which was in the bottle but destroyed it with the other papers the next day on the train going from Philadelphia to St. Louis."

Holmes continued his tale. As he gazed down at his lifeless partner, he quickly realized that – regrettable though it was – Ben's suicide provided him the perfect opportunity to continue his scheme. He now had no need for a substitute corpse. He quickly began making the arrangements to make Ben's death look like an accident.

Holmes concluded this statement by describing his hurried departure from Philadelphia that evening and his trip to St. Louis late the following Wednesday. He arrived on Thursday morning and purchased a newspaper and saw a report that the body had been found. He told Linden:

I went to Mrs. Pitezel's and found that they had also seen the report. The children were greatly worried, but Mrs. Pitezel was not, as she believed the scheme had been carried out. We talked the matter over for a couple of hours and I came back that night and saw Howe and explained what had been done, not telling him that it was Pitezel but leaving him to believe that the plan of placing a substitute corpse had been carried out. I then retained him on behalf of Mrs. Pitezel to procure money from the company.

When Holmes reached the end of the confession, Linden looked at him skeptically. Perhaps the story was true, he said, or perhaps Holmes had found Ben in a drunken state and then forced him to swallow the chloroform.

Even though the police superintendent's suggestion was far too close for comfort, Holmes angrily denied that he had done any such thing. He insisted that his partner had already been dead when he discovered him. He wouldn't kill his good friend and resented Linden's claim that he might have done so.

But Linden was dismissive of Holmes' bluster. He demanded to know that if Ben was dead, then where were his three children?

Holmes replied without hesitation. He had obviously known he would be asked this question and had concocted a solution to go along with his account of Ben's suicide.

"They're in safe hands," he replied. He explained that he had brought them to Detroit and had placed them in the care of a former mistress.

The woman who had Alice, Nellie, and Howard, he told Superintendent Linden, was Minnie Williams.

WHILE HOLMES WAS WORKING ON CONFESSION NO. 2, AS police officials began calling it, things were heating up halfway across the country in Chicago.

The *Chicago Herald* loved Charles E. Davis, who ran the jewelry shop in the Castle and spoke about Holmes anytime he got the chance. They had first discovered him and knew they could always return to him for a good quote when they needed one. As Davis told reporters:

Holmes was lavish with money when he could get it. He must have made $200,000 when he was here, but I believe it's all gone. In fact, from what I know about the man, I'm inclined to believe that he would have never attempted this alleged insurance fraud if he had not been very hard up. But I don't believe it was a fraud in the sense of the dispatches. I should not be surprised if that was Pitezel's body that was burned and if Holmes knew all about his death.

Some neighbors in Englewood suggested digging up the basement of the building and Davis encouraged it. He told reporters:

There is a mud floor in the basement, and no one will ever know all its secrets until it is dug up from end to end and to a depth that would baffle the ordinary midnight knave who sought to hide the victims and the evidence of his crime.

I don't know anything, but I believe the mystery of the disappearance of Minnie Williams and her sister might be solved by digging in the cellar. Such a search has already been talked of by neighbors who have no possible grudge against Holmes, but want this mystery cleared up. Holmes had a vault in his room whose closed door would stifle any cries.

As a reminder, Holmes had once managed to convince Davis to get into the vault and try it out. There were scores of people who claimed to have had near misses with Holmes, but Davis actually had one.

Davis continued:

He also had an elevator from his floor to the cellar which he could operate alone, and this made it easy for him to convey the evidence of his crime to the dark security of mother earth.

The *Herald* also spoke with Dr. Robinson, who still ran the drugstore that he had taken over from Holmes. He said that he was surprised that Holmes had confessed to insurance fraud. He gave his own interview, saying:

I knew Holmes to be a remarkable man and he could have made money easily in a legitimate manner had he chosen. At first, he was careful not to jeopardize his liberty, but he brought upon him such enormous expenses, owing to the companionship he kept, that it became necessary for him to go further and further. Still, I had my doubts about his murdering the girl. I had a talk with a deputy sheriff of Fort Worth. He wanted me to assist in tracking Holmes, but I declined. I do not think he owns this building – it has changed hands five times in a couple of years.

And the papers kept digging, hoping to engage the interest of the authorities to dig deeper into what was going on in the wake of Holmes' arrest. A few reporters sought out his Chicago attorney, Wharton Plummer, who said that he was totally ignorant of the way Holmes did business. He told a reporter:

H.H. Holmes is an honest man and why do I know it? Why, I know the man. I own the property at 701 and 703 63RD Street. I did not get it from Holmes, but through other sources. The title is all right. As to Holmes defrauding people – I never heard of it.

Of course, Plummer's statements were ridiculous. He'd been involved enough in lawsuits over the title for the building to know very well that it was not "all right." If Plummer really believed Holmes was an honest man, then he was one of the dumbest attorneys to ever practice law.

Reporting in Chicago began reaching its peak on November 25 when the *Chicago Tribune* devoted one entire page – with more columns on additional pages – to the story of Holmes' infamous career. The story detailed everything from his early career through such dealings as the ABC Copier Company, his basement artesian well, and even the electric buzzer that warned him when his wife came downstairs to the drugstore. It detailed his purchase of the drugstore from Dr. Holden and his attempts to get out of paying for it.

The huge article was a mixture of fact, misconception, and outright exaggeration but it galvanized the people of Chicago – and it certainly got the attention of the authorities.

Reporters also found Myrta in Wilmette, where she was still living with her five-year-old daughter, Lucy, in the house that Holmes had built and deeded to Minnie Williams. As usual, she had no interest in being interviewed about Holmes of his business. She told reporters:

Naturally I know a great deal of Mr. Holmes' business. I do not intend to be interviewed about it, for it is his business and no one else's. I have no doubt he will clear himself of all accusations if given a fair opportunity. Every businessman has his enemies, and Mr. Holmes has some who would like to overwhelm him.

Our domestic relations have been.... pleasant.

Mr. Holmes left on 1 of January and he has been here twice since then on brief visits, and I was with him on during the winter on one of his business trips to the south. We have one child, a little daughter, and have been married about nine years. I hear from my husband two or three times a week and he continually sends me money for my needs and wants. That does not look like trouble between us, does it?

If what Myrta told the press was true, then it certainly puts the relationship between them in a different light. But was it the truth? It's important to remember that newspaper quotes from this era aren't always completely reliable. We can check the facts with other accounts at the time but even the most honest newspapers weren't above punching up their quotes now and then.

For instance, the line that Davis allegedly gave to the *Herald* about Holmes's evidence being hidden beneath "the dark security of mother earth" doesn't really sound like something a 24-year-old jeweler would say without laughing.

I wanted to mention this before I revealed that Myrta later denied giving that reporter an interview at all. When another reporter knocked on her door after the story ran, she refused to speak to him. He was frustrated when she closed the door in his face and called out that it wasn't fair – she'd just given another interview the previous evening.

Myrta snapped at him:

I was not interviewed last night, and I did not see a reporter last night. One came here about midnight and alarmed the whole neighborhood. It seemed he was not going to leave at all. If I'd had a kettle of hot water, lady or no lady, I would have thrown it on him. My mother got up to see who it was, but he did not see me at all. It seems the newspapers have no feelings. I have not seen the interview supposed to have been had with me and I do not want to see it. I will not see it. I do not read the papers and I will not allow one to come into my house. Whatever was in that interview is a lie, and you can say that for me if you want to. You will do me a favor if you will, for some of my friends might think I was interviewed.

But as it turned out, though, Myrta was the one lying – not the original reporter from the *Herald*. The information in that article turned out to be generally accurate. Myrta started denying it to keep the newspapers – and her neighbors – off her back.

But it was too late for that. Stories about Holmes rapidly spread and soon Myrta's ne'er-do-well husband was being blamed for every unsolved crime in the north suburbs. And, by association, Myrta was being blamed in a way, too. Neighborhood gossip about her grew continuously worse.

She'd been playing the organ and singing for the Wilmette Episcopal Church but now things for her there were precarious. While many members of the congregation had avoided her, most considered her a pillar of the church and saw her as nothing more than the wronged wife of a shrewd villain.

Or at least that was how it had been. At this point, the women of the church had started to discuss expelling her from the congregation.

HOLMES' SECOND CONFESSION WAS MET WITH MORE skepticism from the authorities than his first attempt to explain away his crimes.

Officials scoffed at his claim that Ben had committed suicide, particularly by the ridiculous method that Holmes described. The notion that a man would lie flat on his back on the floor with a towel on his face, like a man in a barber's chair, and suck chloroform through a long rubber tube was completely preposterous. The whole story seemed like exactly what it was -- a silly fabrication to explain away the incontrovertible evidence of a dead man lying on a bedroom floor with a stomach full of chloroform.

Still, the identity of that dead man remained a matter of debate. Dismissing Holmes' latest story, Inspector Gary and his colleagues from the insurance company continued to search for Ben and the missing children in various parts of the country.

Coroner Ashbridge would not be swayed from his belief that Ben Pitezel had been murdered. He maintained that anyone looking for Holmes' partner need look no further than the potter's field and urged once again that the body be exhumed. But throughout the winter, officials continued to go back and forth about the issue.

Meanwhile, Holmes kept busy in his cell. He monitored the news reports about his case, schemed with his lawyers, and did everything that he could to impede the investigation. Georgiana, still standing by her husband, paid him occasional visits. Having a pretty young wife at his side was obviously beneficial for Holmes' public image and so he did everything he could to remain in her good graces.

Newspaper illustration of Holmes in his cell at Moyamensing Prison.

Holmes' insistence that the dead man found at the patent office was Ben Pitezel created a legal complication since the conspirators had been charged with using a substitute corpse to pull off their swindle. Shortly after Holmes offered the second confession, the officers at Fidelity Mutual retained a respected local attorney named Thomas Barlow to represent the company in the case.

By early May, a new indictment had been filed,

charging Holmes and Howe, along with Marion Hedgepeth, with "having conspired to cheat the Fidelity Mutual Life Insurance Company by alleging that one B.F. Pitezel... had died as the result of an accident." Designed to cover every possibility, this indictment was valid whether Ben was dead or alive – a suicide, a murder victim, or fugitive.

On May 27, 1895, Holmes was brought to trial under this second indictment in Philadelphia's Quarter Sessions Court with Judge John Hare presiding. He was led into the courtroom shortly before 11:00 AM, exchanged a few words with his counsel – R.O. Moon and Samuel P. Rotan – and then gazed around the courtroom, casually twisting one of the waxed tips of his handlebar mustache.

We'll never know if he noticed one of the observers in the courtroom that day, but it's possible he did. That man – a detective from the Philadelphia police department – was there at the request of District Attorney George Graham and would soon play a very important role in the events that surrounded H.H. Holmes.

As for Holmes, he was dressed that day in a handsome black suit, with a black tie and a heavy gold watch chain strung across his vest. He had put on weight while behind bars, despite his plans to exercise daily and watch his diet. It was later commented that he looked more like a bank manager than a man on his way to becoming America's most famous criminal.

The proceedings began with the empaneling of the jury. Graham offered no objection to the first 12 men who were seated, but Holmes' attorney Moon was less easily satisfied. Noting the extraordinary publicity surrounding the case, he asked permission to question the jurors if they had formed any opinions about the guilt or innocence of his client. In the end, several jurors were excused after Moon's challenges. Another, who suffered from heart disease, asked to be excused because he feared that a lengthy trial would endanger his health.

But he shouldn't have worried – the trial only lasted one day.

Graham began by clarifying the nature of the conspiracy charge, recapping the facts in the case, and reviewing the contents of Holmes' two confessions for the jury. He told the jurors:

No matter which statement of the prisoner you choose to believe, it makes no difference to the Commonwealth's case, since both of them show the intent to cheat and defraud the insurance company.

Graham pointed out that the dead man could not possibly have been killed by an accidental explosion, nothing that his flesh showed no signs of blisters on the body, only burns that had to have been made after the men was dead.

Without ever raising the charge of homicide, Graham made it clear that, in his opinion, Ben Pitezel had been murdered. He referred repeatedly to Carrie – whom he placed in a prominent seat in the courtroom – as "the widow" and stated clearly that he did not believe "the suicide story."

He ended his opening statement on an ominous note, referring to "Pitezel's three little children," who had been "under Holmes' care." He lowered his voice as he spoke, "Whatever has become of them, only God and the prisoner knows."

Graham was already setting the stage for further charges against Holmes, although only he and the detective that he'd asked to come to court that day were aware of it at that time.

L.G. FOUSE WAS THE FIRST WITNESS CALLED TO THE STAND. HE offered a detailed account of his dealings with Holmes and spent quite a lot of time describing the man's cool, if not cold-blooded, behavior during the postmortem inspection of the exhumed corpse. The jurors looked grim – and slightly queasy – as he spoke about the easy manner with which Holmes wielded the surgical scalpel and breezily sliced the identifying marks from the body of his former friend and partner.

Two more witnesses – Police Superintendent Linden and Colonel O.C. Bobyshell, former president and current treasurer of Fidelity Mutual – testified briefly before Judge Hare adjourned for the day.

After conferring with Moon and Rotan at the end of the day, Holmes realized that his position was hopeless. The district attorney had managed to box him in, using his own confessions and the new indictment to force him into submission on the conspiracy charge. He instructed his lawyers to try and cut a deal with Graham. In exchange for a reduced sentence, Holmes would change his plea to guilty. The following morning, going along with the client's wishes, the two attorneys entered a guilty plea on Holmes' behalf, and the trial came to an abrupt end. The judge announced that he would defer sentencing until after the trial of Jeptha Howe.

Holmes and his lawyers were removed to the "cell room" in City Hall to wait for the wagon that would take him back to the county prison. Strangely, Holmes was in a celebratory mood. He was confident that Judge Hare would sentence him to only half the maximum term and would allow time served for the six months he had already been in prison. That meant Holmes would be a free man by October.

There were no other charges that could be pinned on him – he was convinced of that. Holmes leaned back comfortably in his chair while he waited for the prison wagon, his legs outstretched, and his fingers laced behind his head. Anyone who saw him would think he didn't have a care in the world.

But all that changed when the door burst open, and a harassed-looking clerk hurried inside. He had a message – District Attorney Graham wanted to see Holmes and his attorneys in his office right away.

The three men were taken to Graham's office and were seated on one side of a long conference table. Seated across from them were Graham and Thomas Barlow, who'd been named as special assistant district attorney earlier that day.

Graham was about to speak when the door to the office opened, and two more men stepped into the room -- Police Captain Miller and the detective that Graham had asked to be in the courtroom that day. He was a large, burly man with brown hair and a thick mustache. His name was Frank Geyer.

The men were followed into the room by the clamor of reporters in the hallway. One of the reporters asked Captain Miller what was happening, and Miller replied that he had no comment.

He slammed the door closed, walked around the table and sat down next to D.A. Graham. Detective Geyer remained standing but leaned against the wall, his eyes on Holmes.

Graham now got to the reason for the meeting. He told Holmes that he was dropping all charges against Carrie Pitezel and was going to set her free without delay. The poor woman had suffered enough, he said and added, "The uncertainty of the fate of Alice, Nellie, and Howard, coupled with the death of her husband, has almost dethroned her reason."

Frank Geyer - if there is a true hero in this story, there is no question that it was the dedicated Philadelphia detective.

Graham stared at Holmes, making it clear that he believed that Holmes had not only murdered Ben Pitezel, but his three children, too.

Holmes opened his mouth to protest, but Graham silenced him with an upraised hand. He went on speaking. "The best way to remove this suspicion is to produce the children at once," he said, leaning forward on the table toward Holmes. "Now, where are they? Where can I find them? Tell me and I will use every means within my power to secure their early recovery. It is due to Mrs. Pitezel - and to yourself - that the children should be found. When you were arrested in November, you said that the children were in South America with their father. It is now May, and we have heard nothing from them. You subsequently said that you gave the children to Miss Williams."

Graham stepped back and fixed Holmes with a cold stare. "I am almost persuaded that your word cannot be trusted, Holmes," he said.

Holmes remained silent.

Graham shook his head, still looking at the man in front of him. "Even so, I am not averse to giving you an opportunity to assist me in clearing up the mystery which surrounds their disappearance and their present abode. I now ask you frankly and truthfully – where are the children?"

Holmes looked at Graham. His eyes didn't blink. He first thanked the district attorney for the chance to restore the children to their mother and then as he started to speak further, his eyes filled with tears. With a quaver in his voice, he choked out his next words, strongly denying that he had killed Ben Pitezel or had done harm to the children.

"Why should I kill innocent children?" he demanded.

The prosecutor snapped, raising his voice for the first time. "Then tell us what has become of them!"

Holmes took a moment to collect himself. Then, according to witnesses, speaking with every appearance of candor, he launched into a new story – well, new to everyone else. It was one that he had likely been rehearsing for weeks, just waiting for the moment to use it.

The last time I saw Howard was in Detroit, Michigan. There, I gave him to Miss Williams, who took him to Buffalo, New York, from which point she proceeded to Niagara Falls. After the departure of Howard in Miss Williams' care, I took Alice and Nellie to Toronto, Canada, where they remained for several days. At Toronto, I purchased railroad tickets for them to Niagara Falls, put them on the train, and rode out of Toronto with them a few miles, so that they would be assured they were on the right train. Before their departure, I prepared a telegram, which they should send me from the Falls if they failed to meet Miss Williams and Howard. I also carefully pinned inside Alice's dress $400 in large bills, so Miss Williams would have funds to defray their expenses.

And they did join Miss Williams and Howard at Niagara Falls, from which point they went to New York City. At the latter place, Miss Williams dressed Nellie as a boy and took a steamer for Liverpool, whence they went to London. If you search among the steamship offices in New York, you must look for a woman and a girl and two boys, and not a woman and two girls and a boy.

This was all done to throw detectives off the track, who were after me for insurance fraud. Miss Williams opened a massage establishment in London, and I have no doubt the children are with her now, at that place.

There was a long moment of silence as Graham and his colleagues considered another of Holmes' complicated stories. Thomas Barlow – whose face clearly reflected his skepticism – was the first to break the stillness. He asked Holmes for the name of a single, respectable person in Detroit, Buffalo, Toronto, Niagara Falls, or New York who would vouch for the fact that Miss Williams and the three children were together.

Holmes feigned a look of insult and sputtered, "Your question seems to imply a disbelief in my statement." he said.

But Barlow didn't want Holmes to misunderstand. He wasn't implying anything. He flat out didn't believe him at all. Barlow told him, "It certainly does. Indeed, I believe your entire story to be a lie from beginning to end."

Holmes angrily insisted that the story was true – and that he had a way to verify it. He and Miss Williams had worked out a way by which they could communicate in case of an emergency. This involved placing a coded advertisement in the personal column of the *New York Herald*. To prove that he was telling the truth, Holmes offered to furnish Graham with the code, who could then plant a decoy message that would flush Minnie Williams out of hiding.

Graham considered this for a moment and then decided to give Holmes one more chance to prove he was telling the truth. Fearing he would end up regretting it, he told Holmes to provide the cipher by the following afternoon.

Holmes was returned to his county prison cell and the next afternoon – which was Wednesday, May 29 – Graham received the following letter from Holmes:

Dear Sir – The advertisement should appear in the NEW YORK SUNDAY HERALD and if some comment upon the case can also be put in the body of the paper stating the absence of children and that advertisement concerning appears in this paper, etc., it would be an advantage. Any words that you may see fit to use will do ... only one sentence need be in cipher as she will know by this that it must come from me as no one else.

The NEW YORK HERALD is (or was a year ago) to be found at only a few places regularly in London.

Very Respectfully,

H.H. Holmes

The code that Holmes sent along with the letter was a simple cipher that was based on the single word REPUBLICAN. Spelled out in capital letters, the word corresponded to the first 10 letters of the alphabet. In lower-case letters, the word represented the next 10 letters. The final six letters of the alphabet remained uncoded. Holmes wrote out the cipher for him and to show how it worked, he spelled out his own name in code.

Following Holmes' instructions, Graham immediately contacted the Philadelphia correspondent for the *Herald*, who prepared an article about the case. It was published on Sunday, June 2, 1895.

In the same edition, a coded advertisement appeared in the newspaper's personal column. Graham prefaced the ad with the names "Adele Covelle" and "Geraldine Wanda," which Holmes claimed were aliases that Minnie Williams sometimes used. The coded part of the message read:

> Important to hear before 10th Cable.
> Return Children at once... Holmes.

While the ad was placed and printed, Graham also contacted Scotland Yard, supplying them with details of the case and requesting their assistance in tracking down Minnie Williams, who was currently the owner of a massage establishment in London.

Graham received a quick reply from Scotland Yard, and he was not surprised to learn Scotland Yard detectives also had no luck in finding anyone named Minnie Williams or a woman using the other two aliases that Holmes had provided.

And despite Holmes' insistence that Minnie Williams would respond to the coded newspaper advertisement "without delay," two weeks passed without an answer – which again surprised no one in the district attorney's office.

On June 17, Holmes wrote another letter, this time a lengthy note to Carrie Pitezel, in which he repeated the lies that he told to Graham and the others. He began with a graphic account of Ben's

The legal nemesis of H.H. Holmes – District Attorney George S. Graham

erratic and suicidal behavior in the months before his death.
Holmes wrote:

> *Facts you should know are as follows. Ben lived out west, and while drunk in Fort Worth, Texas, married a disreputable woman named Mrs. Martin... When he became sober and found what he had done, threatened to kill himself and her and I had him watched by one of the other men until he went home. When he straightened up the bank account, he had been robbed by her of over $850 of the money we needed so much.*
>
> *Later, he wanted to carry out the insurance work in Mississippi, where he was acquainted, and I went there with him, and when I found out what kind of place it was, would not go any further with it there and told him so, and he said if I did not, he would kill himself and get the money for you, etc...*
>
> *To get him out of the notion, I told him I would go to Mobile and if I could get what was wanted (which was the substitute corpse) would do so, if not, I would go to St. Louis and write for him to come...*
>
> *When I reached St. Louis I wrote him, and in the letter left for me after he died, he said he had tried to kill himself with laudanum there, and later I found out this was so.*

In the letter – which must have been another stab to the heart of the poor woman – Holmes presented himself as an old family friend who had always had her best interests at heart. Holmes urged Carrie to trust in her common sense and not to believe in the cruel accusations that had been made against him by strangers.

He tried to assure her:

> *I was as careful with the children as if they were my own and you know me well enough to judge me better than strangers here can do. Ben would not have done anything against me, or I against him, any quicker than brothers. We never quarreled. Again,*

he was worth too much for me to have killed him, if for no other reason not to. As for the children, I never will believe, until you tell me so yourself, that you think they are dead or that I did anything to put them out of the way. Knowing me as you do, can you imagine me killing little and innocent children, especially without any motive?

He continued to try and convince her that Alice, Nellie, and Howard were in the care of Minnie Williams. He wrote:

So far as the children's bodily health is concerned, I feel sure I can say to you that they are as well today as though with you, also that they will not be turned adrift among strangers, for two reasons. First, Miss W., though quick-tempered, is too soft-hearted to do so; second, if among others where their letters could not be looked over and detained, they would write to their grandparents.

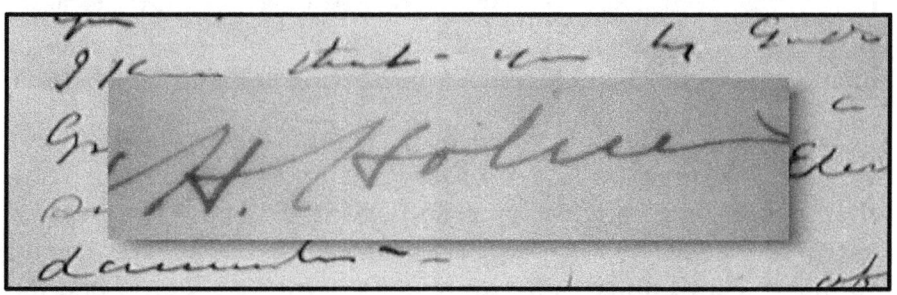

He concluded by saying that his most immediate concern – far outweighing any concern he had for himself – was to see Carrie set free. He added the hope that her suffering was nearly ended.

But Carrie's suffering was far from over. In fact, in the coming weeks, her life would be utterly destroyed. The only good news was that she was at least out of jail.

On the same day that she received the letter from Holmes, D.A. Graham, making good on his promise, arranged for her immediate release. Carrie was led down the front steps by her two

MRS. PITEZEL NOW FREE

Discharged From Moyamensing Prison and Will Now Look for Her Children.

NO ONE KNOWS WHERE THEY ARE

A Mother's Pitiable Story of the Results of an Acquaintance With Holmes.

AN ATTEMPT TO TAKE HER LIFE

Pictures of the Missing Ones That May Yet Lead to the Unraveling of the Mystery.

With the aid of pictures secured from a group taken when they were pupils in the D. S. Wentworth School in Chicago, two years ago, traces have been discovered of the three missing Pitezel children, whose whereabouts have been a great mystery ever since the unearthing of the big conspiracy against the Fidelity Mutual Life Association. The traces break off as suddenly as they crop out, and leave the theory of triple murder even stronger than before.

Yesterday a woman, tall and thin, whose deeply marked face showed

IN SEARCH OF HER CHILDREN

Mrs. Carrie A. Pitezel Believes That Both Her Husband and Little Ones Are Dead.

Mrs. Carrie A. Pitezel, who was arrested and confined in Moyamensing Prison as a witness in the famous Holmes-Pitezel insurance conspiracy, has been discharged from custody and has gone to her father's home in Illinois.

She left Philadelphia yesterday afternoon at 4.30 o'clock. Mrs. Pitezel said she was anxious to find her three children, of whom she has been unable to learn anything since she was committed to prison. She was accompanied by her oldest daughter, Derra, and her 2-year-old baby, both of whom have been cared for by the Society to Protect Children From Cruelty.

Mrs. Pitezel said she believed her children are dead, and claims she would have heard something from them were they alive. She also expressed her belief that her husband is dead.

---

oldest friends, who had made the trip from Illinois to lend their support. They took her to the office of her attorney, Thomas A. Fahy.

Dessie and Wharton, who had spent the last six months as wards of the Society to Protect Children from Cruelty, were waiting for her in Fahy's office. After an emotional reunion, Carrie and the children spent several hours with Fahy. He had reserved a hotel for her and before they went there, Carrie agreed to speak to a reporter from the *Philadelphia Inquirer*. It was the first interview that she had granted since her arrest.

Sitting across from her, the reporter later noted that he was struck by how haggard she appeared. Despite her still-dark hair, she looked as worn as an old woman. He found it hard to believe that the toddler she held in her arms was her own child and not that of 18-year-old Dessie, who was sitting next to her.

The reporter began by asking her opinion of Holmes. Did Mrs. Pitezel believe that he was telling the truth about her missing children?

Carrie replied bitterly, "Holmes would do anything. He is a smooth-tongued scoundrel. He has lied to me and cheated me, and I would not put it past him to make away with the children if it would do him any good."

The reporter asked about her husband. Did Mrs. Pitezel harbor any hope that he was still alive?

Carrie answered, "I believe that the body was that of my husband, for if Mr. Pitezel was alive, he could certainly come back here and make Holmes take back some of the things he said."

The reporter softly asked, "And the children...?"

Carrie began to cry. "What has become of them, I don't know. I feel like tramping all over the world to see if I can find any trace of them."

Carrie gasped, as if in pain, and it was a full minute before she could speak again. When she did, it was horrible.

"Even knowing they were dead would be a relief," she said quietly.

FOR DISTRICT ATTORNEY GRAHAM, FINDING CARRIE PITEZEL'S children had become a mission of the utmost importance. His motives were partly out of sympathy for Mrs. Pitezel. His heart went out to her. He knew that until the children were found – one way or another – she would be condemned to a life of tortured uncertainty.

But he was determined to find the children for an even more pressing reason. Graham had come to believe that, in capturing H.H. Holmes, the police had nabbed someone much bigger than just an insurance swindler. He had no intention of letting him go but to be able to keep the man behind bars, there was more evidence to collect.

By the time that Carrie was released from prison, Graham, along with his assistant, Thomas Barlow, and Police Superintendent

Linden, had decided to start one final, painstaking search for the missing children. Many of Linden's officers saw this undertaking as hopeless – a waste of the department's time and money.

William Gary and his fellow insurance detectives, they pointed out, had been hunting for the children with no results since the previous November. The consensus among the police officers was that Holmes had killed the children. It didn't seem possible, as one officer put it, "that such an astute and wily criminal would leave a trace behind."

They surmised that he had sunk the bodies in a lake somewhere, as he'd initially claimed he had done with the corpse of Nannie Williams.

Graham, Barlow, and Linden heard all the arguments against the new search but decided to ignore them. Graham believed that the failure of the insurance detectives to find the children was because their investigation had not been conducted with the skill of veteran, highly trained police officers. Graham was not yet convinced the children were dead, but if they were, he knew that a careful and patient search would inevitably discover the one mistake that Holmes had made that would lead to his downfall. It was, he believed, simply impossible in such a modern day and age for a man to get away with the murder of three children.

The daunting task of finding Alice, Nellie, and Howard, though, would require the skills of a very clever and resourceful detective – a dogged man who would never stop until he reached his ultimate goal.

It was fortunate for the district attorney that he had just such a detective at his disposal. It was the man he'd asked to observe Holmes in the courtroom on the day of his conspiracy trial -- Detective Frank Geyer.

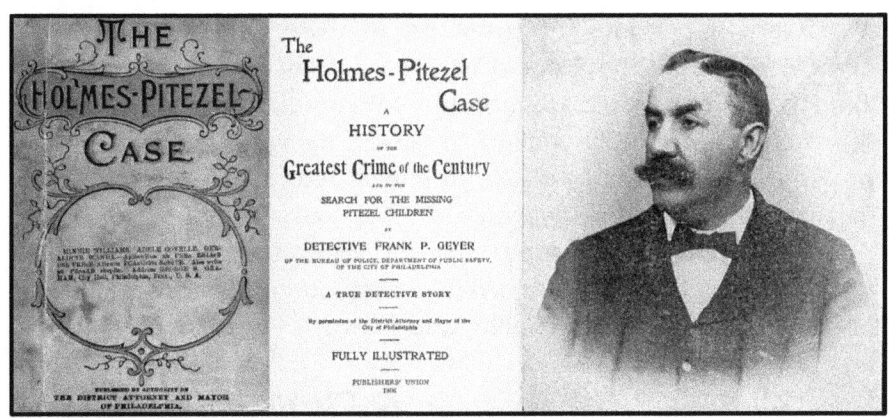

14

IF THERE WAS ANY ONE MAN WHO BECAME THE HERO OF THE tangled and twisted mess that was the H.H. Holmes case it was Detective Frank Geyer. With his beefy frame, balding head, bushy mustache, and thick eyebrows, he was almost a caricature of a policeman of the 1890s. But Frank Geyer was no cartoon character. He was a dangerous and formidable man – an honest cop and 20-year veteran of the Philadelphia Bureau of Police with a hard-earned reputation as the city's top detective.

But in the spring of 1895, Detective Geyer was at loose ends. His professional career had been slightly derailed by personal tragedy. In March 1895 -- just three months before District Attorney Graham began the all-out search for the Pitezel children – a fire had broken out in the Geyer home, killing Frank's wife, Martha, and their only child, a 12-year-old girl named Esther.

Even though Geyer would have accepted Graham's mission under any circumstances, the search came at the perfect time for him – and it became an obsession. His own tragedy had taught him there was nothing worse than the loss of a child. That a man like H.H. Holmes would deliberately inflict such grief on a mother seemed unimaginably wicked to Geyer. He wouldn't rest until he provided the answers that Carrie Pitezel was seeking – nor would he rest until Holmes answered for his crimes.

And so, on Wednesday, June 26, 1895, Detective Frank Geyer packed a bag, purchased train tickets out of Philadelphia, and began looking for Alice, Nellie, and Howard Pitezel.

FRANK GEYER HAD LITTLE TO GO ON WHEN HE STARTED HIS search. He had compared notes with Fidelity Mutual investigators and District Attorney Graham until he knew every aspect of the case, from Holmes' movements in the fall of 1894 to when the children were last seen. He was given money and various photographs – some of which were of the children and others were of trunks the children and their mother had used during their travels.

Geyer planned to make a valiant effort but deep down, neither her nor the district attorney held out great hope that he'd find the children or even what happened to them, but Geyer and Graham were determined to make one last effort for Carrie's sake.

Geyer was not entirely without clues. The dozen or so letters that had been written by Alice and Nellie – which Holmes had saved for his own devious purposes – had been found in a tin box among his possessions when he was arrested. The writings were filled with a lot of bad spelling and grammar, but each was headed with the date and the city from which it was written.

Thanks to this, though the insurance investigators had no luck in finding the children, they had managed to map out the route that Holmes had followed the previous fall when he was on the run with the children. He had traveled from Cincinnati to Indianapolis, Detroit, Toronto and finally, Burlington. Geyer knew that the answers that he was seeking were somewhere along this route and he knew that to find them, he had to start at the beginning.

Geyer arrived in Cincinnati on the evening of June 27. Tucked into his coat pocket were mug shots of Holmes and photographs of the three Pitezel children, which had been taken when they were students at the D.S. Wentworth School in Chicago.

He checked into the Palace Hotel, had a quick dinner, and then went to the local police headquarters, where he ran into an old friend, Detective John Schnooks. The two men chatted about old times for a bit and then Geyer

Geyer's old friend, Detective John Schnooks, who assisted him in Cincinnati

explained the reason for his visit. Schnooks suggested that he return the next day and speak with his chief, Superintendent Philip Dietsch.

The next morning, Geyer had a hearty breakfast and then went straight to police headquarters. The superintendent listened to the facts in the case and then summoned Detective Schnooks and directed him to help Geyer however he possibly could. The resources of the Cincinnati police were placed at his disposal.

The two detectives headed out into the city. The "Great Search," as Geyer came to think of it, had begun in earnest.

The detectives began by checking hotels near the train station. By late morning, they had located two hotels – the Atlantic House and the Palace – where Holmes had taken rooms for himself and the children under the name of Cook. Geyer knew that this was the same alias that he had made Carrie Pitezel use in Burlington. A desk clerk at the Palace, W.L. Bain, positively identified Holmes and the children from Geyer's photographs.

Knowing that Holmes had habitually rented houses in the cities that he passed through, Geyer decided to also concentrate on real estate agencies. He and Schnooks combed the city, fruitlessly talking to scores of rental agents, before finally entering the office of J.C. Thomas, whose clerk, George Rumsey, had no trouble recognizing the photographs of Holmes and Howard Pitezel. He had thought they were father and son and mostly remembered them because he'd noticed that the father wore an expensive tailored suit and yet, dressed his son in ragged clothing.

Unfortunately, though, Rumsey could offer no information about the house that Holmes had rented because the records were locked up in Mr. Thomas' office and he had gone home for the day. He urged them to return the following morning, when he could be of more assistance.

They were waiting on the real estate office doorstep when Mr. Thomas arrived the next day. Like his clerk, he immediately recognized the photographs of Holmes and Howard. Thomas didn't even need to consult his records for the information the detectives were looking for.

He clearly remembered that Holmes had paid a $15 advance for a vacant house at 305 Poplar Street and then abruptly disappeared two days after renting it. Thomas had no idea what had become of the man. He suggested that the detectives speak to Miss Henrietta Hill, who lived next door to the rental property. She had been in the neighborhood for years and might be able to offer additional information.

When the detectives called on Miss Hill, she did indeed have a vivid recollection of the odd tenant who abandoned the neighboring house within days of moving in – not that he had much to move into the house. What had puzzled her, in addition to the lack of furniture, was the enormous stove that he brought with him. It had been far too large for such a modest-sized house and strangely, the man had abandoned it when he left.

The detectives thanked Miss Hill for her assistance and went on their way. Geyer was pleased with what he had learned. Not only had he tracked down the places where Holmes had stayed while in Cincinnati, he had discovered two aliases that he had used as well – Cook and Hayes. He was already starting to feel more confident about his mission.

Geyer did ponder one thing that Miss Hill had told him, though. That bit about the enormous stove was intriguing, but he couldn't imagine how it would be relevant to his case.

A few weeks later, though, Detective Geyer would learn just how significant that detail had been.

FOLLOWING THE ROUTE PROVIDED BY THE CLUES IN THE children's letters, Geyer said goodbye to his old friend John Schnooks and departed for Indianapolis later that same day. He arrived there around 7:30 on Saturday evening, June 29. After registering and eating supper at the Spencer House, we went to police headquarters and introduced himself to Captain Spalnn, the head of the detective bureau.

Before Geyer could explain his investigation, the captain was called away to investigate a reported murder in the northern part of the city. Geyer waited around the station and ended up getting a lucky break. He was introduced to Police Superintendent Powell, who like his counterpart in Cincinnati, offered Geyer his department's full cooperation. He assigned a detective named David Richards to aid him in his search.

David S. Richards was a patrolman who was shot in the line of duty in 1879 and had moved up the ranks to detective by the time Geyer needed his help in Indianapolis.

Over the course of the next few days, Geyer and Richards followed the same method used in Cincinnati. They started with the hotels around the train station and then moved into the neighborhood known as the Circle. It was at the Hotel English that the children turned up in the registry. Using Geyer's photographs, the clerk on duty quickly identified Holmes as the man who rented a room for the children on the evening of September 30. He checked them out again the next morning.

They found no sign that they moved to another hotel downtown. Undeterred, they tried boarding houses but still had no luck. Over lunch, though, Richards recalled a small hotel called the Circle Hotel, which had been operating in September 1894, but had since gone out of business. They decided it might be worth a try to track down the owner – Herman Ackelow, who they discovered now operated a tavern on the west side of town.

Herman had no trouble remembering Alice, Nellie, and Howard. His entire family had interacted with the sad, grief-stricken children who had remained shut up in their room for days on end. He also recalled Howard's hysterical outburst in the hotel lobby after a rare, midday outing with the man who was keeping them at the hotel. He recalled for Geyer and Richards his subsequent conversation with the man, when he talked about sending his nephew to live with a farmer or be placed in an institution. The boy, he told Herman, "was a bad one from the day he was born."

However, Herman believed the boy wasn't bad. It was just that the man wanted to get rid of him.

Those words sent a chill up Detective Geyer's spine. He had the sudden thought that Howard might not have left Indianapolis alive. It was a feeling he couldn't shake, even those Fidelity's investigators had information that Holmes and the boy were seen together in Detroit, the next city on Geyer's list.

But Geyer didn't go directly to Detroit. In his hotel room that night, he considered his options, believing that he was missing something. From Carrie Pitezel, Geyer had been given a detailed description of the trunk that Nellie and Howard were using when they left St. Louis with Holmes. The trunk had since vanished.

When Geyer asked Holmes about the trunk, he claimed he'd left it in a hotel on West Madison Street in Chicago. Although he knew that little Holmes said could be mistaken for the truth, Geyer became eager to find the trunk, believing it might hold clues about the whereabouts of the children.

Just before noon on Monday, July 1, Geyer left Indianapolis by train and headed north to Chicago, where he spent two pointless days searching for the trunk. He didn't find it. He didn't even find the hotel where Holmes said he left it. It didn't exist. Holmes had made the whole thing up to slow him down.

But the trip wasn't a complete waste of time. Geyer met with one of Holmes' attorneys, Wharton Plummer, and he pressed him for information. Plummer said that he'd never seen the Pitezel girls, but he had met with Holmes around the time he was alleged to be in the city. However, it was not at a hotel on West Madison Street – it was at a rooming house on Division Street, somewhere on the north side.

Accompanied by Detective Sergeant John C. McGlinn, who had been assigned to assist him, Geyer tracked down the boarding house, which was owned by a woman named Jennie Irons. She didn't recognize the photographs of the children, but she immediately identified Holmes as a man she knew as Harry Gordon. He had occupied rooms in her lodging house. She thought he had been with a young woman – identified as Minnie Williams – but she might have been mistaken, at least about the woman.

There would be a lot of witnesses like her in the coming weeks – certain they had seen Holmes or one of the missing women or children but turned out to be wrong. But according to his lawyer, Holmes had been to the boarding house. He might have used the place for a rendezvous with one of his assorted wives and mistresses, or as a place for meetings with some business associate. Who can say?

Before leaving Chicago, Geyer decided that he wanted to see Holmes' business building for himself. After breakfast on Wednesday, July 3, he and Detective McGlinn boarded a cable car for Englewood. They were on their way to interview Patrick Quinlan, the man some claimed had been an accomplice to Holmes.

Geyer was bothered by the dark, derelict-looking building that Holmes had once called his "Castle" in Englewood

When the men arrived, Geyer noted the grim, almost derelict look of the place and after climbing a dark staircase to the second floor, they found their way to Quinlan's apartment.

The detectives knocked, identified themselves, and were invited inside by a voice behind the door. They entered and found Quinlan, a pale, slim man of medium height with curly hair and a sandy mustache. Geyer guessed him to be in his thirties. He gave him his card, and Pat took it, then invited the detectives to sit down.

Geyer immediately got to the point. He explained who he was and what he was doing. He grilled Pat about Holmes and the children but stopped short of accusing him of helping Holmes carry out his crimes. He did make it clear, though, that he believed Pat knew something about the missing children.

But Pat denied everything. He admitted that he knew Ben and his family very well but insisted that he hadn't seen any of them in nearly a year. He was willing to help in any way that he could – but as to the whereabouts of Alice, Nellie, and Howard, he knew nothing.

Geyer later wrote that he was inclined to believe the man. Patrick Quinlan was a father himself and therefore unlikely, the detective believed, to have schemed against innocent children. Even more to the point, it was clear to Geyer that Pat harbored many resentments against Holmes. He let it slip that his employer was a "dirty, rotten scoundrel." He had been following the newspaper stories about Holmes' crimes and nothing that he'd read had surprised him. He believed the man was capable of anything.

Pat came out and told him, "If that corpse they found in Philadelphia really was Ben Pitezel, you can wager good money that Holmes was the one who done it. And if he done for Pitezel, then he murdered the children, too."

Geyer once again had the same unsettling feeling that he had experienced in Indianapolis. Something terrible had happened, he just knew it. But he knew Pat Quinlan couldn't tell them anything else. He and McGlinn got up to leave, and Pat followed them to the door.

Pat Quinlan

Geyer was just stepping out into the dim hallway when Pat reached out and grabbed him by the arm. He spoke to the detective, "If you find out those little ones are dead, I hope Holmes swings for it. And when they day comes, I'd be glad to be the man who springs the trap."

ON THURSDAY, JULY 4, WHILE THE REST OF THE COUNTRY WAS enjoying the holiday, Frank Geyer was on his way to Detroit, the next stop following in the footsteps of H.H. Holmes.

Driven by his own grief and his anger over the things that he'd learned so far about the evil deeds of Holmes, he was unable to stop until he learned the fate of the Pitezel children.

Detective Geyer checked into the Hotel Normandie that evening and skipped supper to go straight to police headquarters. He had another old cop friend in Detroit, Detective Thomas Meyler, who introduced him to his captain. He arranged for Geyer to meet Superintendent Starkweather the next morning after breakfast.

Starkweather, like the other police officials that Geyer had encountered in his search, offered any assistance he needed. He

Police Headquarters in Detroit in the 1890s, where once again, Geyer received help with his search

assigned a detective named Tuttle to help him with his local inquiries.

Their first stop was the local office of the Fidelity Mutual Life Association, whose investigators had turned up an important lead – the name of the real estate agent who had rented a house to Holmes the previous October.

From the agent, the detectives learned that Holmes had inquired about a rental house on the outskirts of the city and offered a $5 advance for a house on East Forest Avenue. The agent seemed to recall that Holmes had a little boy with him, probably nine or ten years old. His clerk remembered the same thing.

But Geyer wasn't convinced of that. He still had a nagging feeling that Howard had never left Indianapolis. He didn't know why. But now he had two men telling him that Howard had been with Holmes in Detroit. He couldn't just ignore that. He decided that when they searched the records of the city's hotels and boarding houses, he'd try and find some evidence that Howard made it to Detroit.

But he didn't.

After visiting numerous hotels, he and Tuttle did find an entry for "Etta and Nellie Canning" in the register of the New Western Hotel. The proprietor, P.W. Cotter, took one look at Geyer's photographs and immediately identified the Pitezel sisters as guests of the hotel and Holmes as the man who checked them in. But Cotter hadn't seen a little boy.

From Alice's last, sad letter to her grandparents, Geyer knew that the girls were taken next to Lucinda Burns' boarding house at

91 Congress Street. The landlady clearly remembered Alice and Nellie and said they were "quiet and reserved" and never left their room. They seemed to spend all their time reading and drawing. Like Cotter, Mrs. Burns stated that the girls had been alone. She had never seen the little boy in the photograph that Detective Geyer showed her.

Geyer knew that it was possible that Holmes, for whatever reason, had wanted to keep Howard close to him and did not put him in the rooms where the girls stayed. So, he and Tuttle started to try and track down where Holmes had been staying in Detroit. In the register of the Hotel Normandie, the detectives came upon an entry for "G. Howell and wife" and Geyer immediately recognized both the handwriting and the alias as belonging to Holmes.

After that lucky discovery, though, the detectives ran into a dead end. They searched through the records of every hotel in the city and failed to turn up any other trace of Holmes. They moved on to boarding houses. They spent an entire day walking the streets, ringing entry bells, and questioning landlords but none of them recognized photographs of Holmes or Howard Pitezel.

Detective Geyer was starting to think they were wasting their time but then, late that evening, they arrived on the doorsteps of May Ralston's rooming house at 54 Park Place. It was the place where Holmes – who was posing as "a member of the theatrical profession"– had stayed briefly with Georgiana. Mrs. Ralston clearly remembered the handsome couple. When Geyer asked her about Howard, though, she insisted that they did not have a child with them.

Geyer had spent two days reconstructing the movements of Holmes and the Pitezel girls in Detroit but only the real estate agent and his clerk claimed that Howard was in the city.

The trip to examine the house that Holmes had rented also seemed to be pointless – at first. The current tenant allowed them inside and the detectives carefully searched the place. They checked the cellar, inspected the furnace, and checked the entire yard, looking for a place where the ground had been disturbed – but they found nothing out of the ordinary.

But as they were leaving, the tenant mentioned something that he'd almost forgotten. He said that when he'd moved in, he'd discovered a very peculiar hole that had been dug in the basement. He had since filled it in. He speculated it had been dug by a previous tenant, perhaps as a place to store potatoes, but didn't really know.

Geyer and Tuttle exchanged a knowing look. The two detectives knew that the hole had been dug for a much more sinister purpose. They could only speculate about what had occurred that prevented Holmes from putting the hole to use.

Geyer now felt he'd done all he could do in Detroit. He was, though, still bothered by the mystery of the children's missing trunk. Before he left the city, he made every effort to find it. He questioned scores of liverymen and cab drivers, porters and bag handlers and visited every freight depot, storage company, and express office in the city. But even after all that, he found no trace of it.

And he was troubled by something else, too. The register at the Circle Hotel in Indianapolis stated that the Pitezel children had checked out on Saturday, October 6. According to the register at the Western Hotel, the girls arrived in Detroit on Friday, October 12. Geyer had a six-day gap between the two cities that he was unable to account for. He knew very well that it was a relatively short trip between Indianapolis and Detroit. It certainly didn't take six days. So, where had they gone?

He made one last stop in Detroit before continuing his journey. When he had interviewed Carrie Pitzel, he learned that when she had arrived in Detroit with Dessie and the baby, Holmes had checked them into the European Hotel. He wanted to find out more about their stay, so on Sunday, July 7, he stopped in and interviewed the housekeeper, Minnie Mulholland.

When she looked at Carrie's photograph, she immediately began to cry. She identified her as Mrs. Adams, a terribly sad woman that she had never forgotten. Geyer tried to get more information from her, but the housekeeper knew nothing else. She could only tell Geyer that her heart had broken for the poor woman, who seemed so upset and worried that she was practically an invalid.

Detective Geyer slowly walked back to his hotel, deep in thought. His route took him past Lucinda Burns' boarding house on Congress Street, where Holmes had kept the Pitezel girls for five days – while their mother was lodged only a few blocks away at the European Hotel.

As he passed the boarding house, he recalled from her letters how desperately Alice missed her mother, older sister, and baby brother. And all of them, as she was writing her last desperate letter to them, were only minutes away from her.

Even Frank Geyer, who had seen some horrible things during his many years as a police officer, felt a terrible pain in his heart for the poor girl.

He returned to his hotel, struck once again by the monstrous nature of H.H. Holmes – a heartless devil who had contrived to keep desperately homesick children away from their mother while he planned their deaths.

Geyer would see that he paid for his crimes if it was the last thing that he did.

LATER THAT SAME EVENING, GEYER LEFT DETROIT AND TOOK AN overnight train to Toronto, arriving in the Canadian city around 9:30 the next morning.

Geyer felt fortunate the trail had led him to Toronto. He had visited the city many times over the years with his family and had many friends on the police force, including Detective Alf Cuddy, who volunteered to assist him with the local investigation.

The detectives got off to a promising start. Within hours of starting their search, they traced Holmes first to the Walker House, then to the Palmer. They found evidence of Carrie, Dessie and Wharton at the Union Hotel and traces of Alice and Nellie at the

In Toronto, Geyer was assisted by another old friend, Alfred Cuddy, who later went on to become the Calgary Police Chief.

Albion. At the last hotel, Geyer heard a grim tale from chief clerk Herbert Jones. After looking at the photograph of Holmes, Jones identified him as the man who had taken the two girls out sightseeing every morning during their stay. The girls always returned in the late afternoon, well before suppertime. But on the morning of October 25, after paying their daily bill, Holmes had taken the girls out but had never returned. Jones said, "It was the last time they were seen by me or anyone at the hotel."

After tracking Holmes from city to city, Geyer was familiar with his habits. He knew that Holmes had abruptly left Toronto on October 26. Putting all the facts together with what he had found out from Jones, he drew a macabre conclusion, which he put into words in a letter to his superior, Police Superintendent Linden. He wrote:

It is my impression that Holmes rented a house in Toronto, the same as he did in Cincinnati, Ohio and Detroit, Michigan, and that on the 25th of October he murdered the girls and disposed of the bodies by either burying them in the cellar, or some convenient place, or burning them in the heater. I intend to go to all the real estate agents and see if they can recollect having rented a house about that time to a man who only occupied it for a few days and who represented that he wanted it for a widowed sister.

Even though Geyer had a daunting task ahead of him with this plan, he never considered giving up. He was determined to get to the bottom of the challenge that was now engulfing his life.

He never doubted for a moment that, as he later wrote, "perseverance and energy would bring forth some good result."

On Wednesday, July 10, Geyer arrived at police headquarters early. Over the next few hours, Cuddy and Geyer compiled a list of every real estate agent in Toronto from the most current edition of the city directory. Then, with the long list in hand, they went out into the city in search of their prey.

The detectives began in the business district. It soon became clear to Geyer that the job was going to take much longer than he expected. At every office on their list, he and Cuddy had to patiently explain the reason for their inquiry and wait while the agent checked through his records.

Time passed quickly and evening fell upon them. Soon, all the agencies were closed for the day. They had accomplished little, Geyer realized, and felt they needed a different approach. With a quiet chuckle, he suddenly had an idea, which he explained to his partner. As an avid reader, Geyer often pored over several newspapers every day. He knew that reporters loved a good story, as evidenced by the lurid and sensational accounts that had already appeared about the Holmes-Pitezel case. He and Cuddy needed help with their search, and they would soon have it. Geyer would call a press conference.

That night, Geyer's room at the Rossin House was jammed with reporters. They were quick to pounce on the dramatic elements of the story: a heroic detective on the trail of three missing children who had fallen victim to a fiend that had been making headlines for weeks. Geyer provided all the details of the case, passed around the children's photographs, and made a plea to "all of the good citizens of Toronto" for their assistance.

The tactic worked. The next morning, every newspaper in the city carried the story on the front page. This time, when Geyer and Cuddy made the rounds of the real estate offices, they found their job was much easier. There was no longer the need to explain the purpose of their visit at every office – the agents were all too familiar with the blood-curdling story. Most of them had already checked their records before the detectives arrived – all praying that they had not been the ones who had rented a house to the fiend.

But the day still turned out to be a disappointing one. Once again, the detectives returned to police headquarters empty-handed. To their surprise, though, the desk sergeant had a message for them from a local real estate agent who had read about the investigation in the newspaper. The man reported that, the previous fall, he had rented a house on the outskirts of the city to a man named Holmes. The house, located at Perth and Bloor streets, stood in the middle of a field and was surrounded by a tall fence.

Geyer didn't want to wait until morning to follow up on the report. He and Cuddy hurried to the house and found it occupied by an elderly couple and their 20-year-old son. Geyer explained to them why had had come, ending his story with his belief that Holmes had killed the children and buried them somewhere under the house.

The old man listened to the story and then looked at his son with a dawning realization. "That would account for that loose pile of dirt under the main building," he said. When Geyer and Cuddy exchanged a significant look, he told his son to go and fetch a shovel.

As the young man hurried away, the father led the detectives to a wooden door that led down to the crawlspace under the house. Pulling off their coats, the two men squeezed under the floor and quickly discovered a loose mound of dirt. The son, who had returned with the shovel, provided them with some coal lamps to illuminate the dank space. Geyer and Cuddy took turns digging, turning the dirt from a hole that was about four feet across and several feet deep. Sweating and barely able to breathe, they worked for hours and finally gave up – they found nothing.

The next morning, they sought out the real estate agent who had contacted the police. The agent studied Holmes' photograph for a few moments and then stated that he was not the man who

Geyer also took a side trip to Niagara Falls, knowing that Holmes had taken Georgiana there for some sightseeing.

had rented the house. He had no idea who the man in the photograph was.

Angry at himself for jumping to conclusions without having all the information, Geyer apologized to Cuddy and his friend joined him as they switched methods and began interviewing railway ticket agents in an effort to discover where Holmes had gone after leaving Toronto. By evening, Geyer felt sure that Holmes had traveled to Prescott. In a letter to his chief, he announced his decision to travel there next, "in the event of my not meeting success in Toronto." But Geyer added to the letter that he was firmly convinced that Holmes had disposed of the children in Toronto. "I cannot think of leaving until I have made a more extended search."

On Saturday morning, Geyer took a quick trip to Niagara Falls, where Holmes had taken Georgiana to go sightseeing. Geyer located their names in the registry of the King's Imperial Hotel. The desk clerk verified that the couple had been alone, without any children. Geyer believed that Georgiana knew nothing about the children and this information seemed to confirm it. Even though Holmes had betrayed Georgiana from the start, he thought, at least he had shielded her from the knowledge of his most horrific crimes. It was the single redeeming feature that Geyer was willing to consider about the man.

The detective returned to Toronto later that afternoon. He spent the rest of the day searching newspaper morgues, looking for ads that had been placed by private renters the previous fall. He planned to start calling on all of them on Monday morning.

Meanwhile, the newspapers continued to run stories and updates about the case. When Geyer met Cuddy on Monday morning, his partner told him that the police had just received word from a man named Thomas Ryves, who had read about Geyer's search in the newspaper. Ryves recalled that a man matching Holmes' description had a rented a house next door to him the previous October. The man had been accompanied by two young girls. But when he left suddenly about one week later, Ryves noticed that the girls were not with him. The house in question was located at 16 St. Vincent Street.

Geyer quickly looked through the lists of classified ads that he had copied from the newspapers. He discovered the listing for St. Vincent Street and saw that interested parties were asked to contact Mrs. Frank Nudel at 54 Henry Street. As luck would have it, Cuddy was acquainted with Frank Nudel, a clerk for the educational department of Toronto. Cuddy suggested that they go and see Nudel before proceeding to the St. Vincent Street House.

Frank Geyer readily agreed. He dared not allow himself to hope once again that a revealing clue had been discovered – although Ryves' recollection was the strongest lead to date. The detectives went immediately to the educational department and tracked down Nudel. The clerk's eyes grew wide as they explained why they wanted to see the house. He confirmed that he had rented it the previous fall, but it was abandoned a week or so later. He knew nothing else. The house belonged to his wife, and she took care of the rentals. The detectives would have to talk to her about it.

Geyer and Cuddy decided to first pay a visit to Thomas Ryves. When they showed him the photographs of Holmes and the girls, Alice was the only one that he had trouble identifying. But his story left little doubt that the stranger who had briefly been his neighbor was H.H. Holmes.

As Ryves told it, the man had dropped by one morning and explained that he was renting the house next door for his widowed sister, who would be arriving in a few days. He wanted to dig a place in the cellar where she could store potatoes and asked if he might borrow a shovel. Ryves agreed and later that afternoon, was looking through the window and saw the man moving a mattress, an old bed and a large trunk into the house. Several days later, he hauled away the trunk. That was the last time that Ryves had seen him.

Geyer was sure that he and Cuddy were on the right track. Telling Ryves that they would return within the hour, they quickly traveled to the Nudels' home on Henry Street. Mrs. Nudel immediately recognized the photograph of Holmes as the man who had rented the house last October, even though he had only occupied it a few days. He had given her a month's rent of $10 in advance, but she never saw him again after that.

Leaving Mrs. Nudel with a hurried thanks, the detectives rushed back to St. Vincent Street where Ryves was waiting anxiously on his front porch for them to return. Geyer asked for a shovel – probably the same one that Holmes had used – and the man retrieved it for him. The detectives then grimly walked to the cottage next door.

Ironically, it was a lovely little place. The quaint, two-story house had a single gabled window in front and a pleasant porch that was covered with flowering vines. Geyer paused at the front door and looked at the house. He later wrote that he wondered if the Pitezel sisters had truly met their fate at such a peaceful and pleasant place. It seemed hard to believe that it could be the scene of such horror – but tragically, it was.

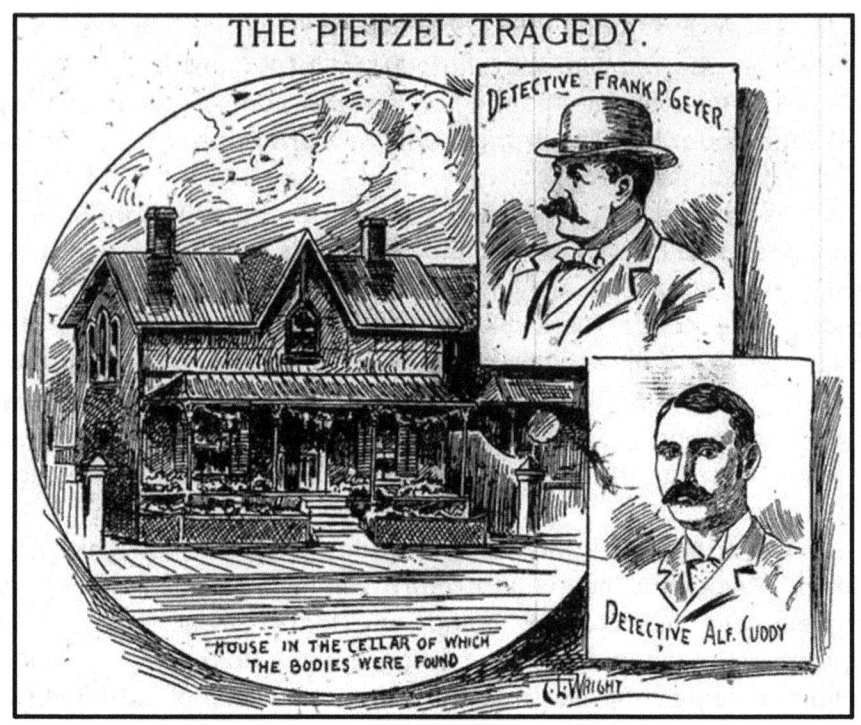

House in the cellar of which the bodies were found.
Detective Frank P. Geyer
Detective Alf. Cuddy

Geyer's knock was answered by Mrs. J. Armbrust, the current tenant. She was shocked when Geyer explained the reason for their visit. She quickly led the detectives into the kitchen and, lifting an oil cloth from the floor, she revealed a small trapdoor that was about two feet square. It was the only access to the cellar. Geyer raised the door and peered down into the darkness below. Mrs. Armbrust retrieved an oil lamp and handed it to Cuddy. The detective led the way down a narrow, steep staircase into the pitch-black cellar.

Cuddy held the light as Geyer walked around the low-ceilinged and cramped chamber. He poked the shovel blade into the ground here and there, searching for signs of recent disturbance. In the southwest corner of the cellar, he found what he was looking for. The shovel's blade sank into the soft earth and Geyer knew that the soil had been recently turned. Cuddy directed the light into the corner as Geyer began to dig. He found that the dirt was easily removed from a hole that had been carved from the packed soil around it. He had cleared away a section that was about a foot deep when the cellar began to fill with the stench of death. He dug down two more feet, and he saw a human arm, blackened by rotting flesh.

Cuddy gagged and backed away, placing the lamp on the floor. Geyer, struggling to breathe through his mouth, began scraping the dirt back into the hole, trying to keep down the putrid smell. He finally tossed the shovel and pushed Cuddy along with him as he climbed the stairs back into the kitchen above. Cuddy, his face ashen, rushed over to the window and gulped in great gulps of the fresh air from outside.

"We must get to a telephone," Geyer said, his voice tense with horror.

They found one at a telegraph office on Yonge Street. Cuddy called Inspector Stark, who congratulated the men on their discovery and instructed them to contact an undertaker who worked nearby, B.D. Humphrey. After ending the call, the detectives went to Humphrey's establishment and the undertaker agreed to accompany them back to the cottage to assist with the exhumation. Geyer described what he had seen of the bodies and Humphrey brought along three pairs of thick rubber gloves.

Back at the St. Vincent Street house, the men took a moment outside to prepare themselves and then descended through the trapdoor into the dank cellar. It took only a few moments for Geyer to uncover the bodies. Humphrey shouted upstairs to Mrs. Armbrust and asked her to send her teenage son to his establishment with orders to have his assistant bring two coffins to the house.

In the shallow pit, Alice Pitezel lay on her side. Nellie was face down in the grave, crossways to her sister, her legs resting on Alice's body. Both girls were naked.

The three men bent down and gently took hold of Nellie's corpse. Her flesh was so decayed that, as they lifted her body, her

Alice and Nellie Pitezel, whose body were found buried in the basement of the cottage on St. Vincent Street in Toronto

scalp – pulled free by the weight of her long, plaited hair – slipped wetly from her skull.

By then, a wagon had arrived with the coffins. The men placed Nellie's body on a sheet and carried it up the narrow stairs. They placed the small body into one of the coffins, then returned to the cellar and removed Alice's remains from the makeshift grave. The bodies were first taken to Humphrey's undertaking parlor and from there, to the city morgue.

Geyer later recalled, "By this time, Toronto was wild with excitement. The news had spread to every part of the city. The St. Vincent Street house was besieged with newspapermen, sketch artists and others. Everybody seemed pleased with our success, and congratulations, mingled with expressions of horror over the discovery, were heard everywhere."

That night, when Geyer returned to his hotel, the fetid stench of death was still in his nose, on his skin and soaked into his clothing. He bathed repeatedly, trying to wash it away. His suit was nearly impossible to clean. Worst of all, the sight of the bodies of the two girls refused to leave his mind. As he lay in the dark of his hotel room, trying to sleep, all he could see were those rotting remains – the putrefied remains of what had once been pretty young girls. He shuddered in the darkness and remained awake long into the night.

And as he lay there, he could only think about the fact that his task was not yet completed. Howard Pitezel had not yet been found. However, in less than three weeks of searching, Geyer had managed to solve a major portion of the mystery and in so doing, had accomplished something even greater than a remarkable feat of detection. It was that accomplishment that finally allowed him to sleep that night.

As he drifted off, he knew that H.H. Holmes was finally going to get what he deserved.

THE DISCOVERY OF THE PITEZEL SISTERS' BODIES IN TORONTO made front-page news across North America.

In Philadelphia, District Attorney Graham had been the first to get the word, having received a telegram from Geyer on Monday evening, July 15, the date of the discovery. Graham planned to keep the news from Holmes, intending to spring it on him during a private meeting the following day. He hoped that Holmes would be so rattled that he would break down and finally confess to the murders. On Tuesday morning, Graham telephoned the officials at Moyamensing and instructed them to withhold all of Holmes' daily newspapers.

But the telephone call came too late. Earlier that morning, a crowd of reporters had shown up at the prison, clamoring for an interview with Holmes. Suspecting that some major break had occurred, Holmes requested his usual newspapers. By the time that court officers Gentner and Alexander arrived to transport him to City Hall, he had already seen the headlines and was prepared for a brutal interrogation.

In shackles, Holmes was taken into the district attorney's office. He maintained a stubborn silence while Graham and Thomas Barlow pounded him with questions for nearly two hours. Holmes later claimed that he was not being difficult by refusing to talk. He claimed to be "speechless with grief over the killings."

He finally spoke as he was being led back to his cell, muttering to one of the guards, "I guess I'll hang for this."

WHILE HOLMES WAS BEING INTERROGATED IN THE DISTRICT attorney's office, Frank Geyer was doing everything he could to make sure that Holmes' prediction about going to the gallows was going to come true. Early on Tuesday morning, he and Detective

Cuddy set out to find evidence that would confirm the identities of the two murdered girls. The corpses had decomposed beyond recognition. Geyer, of course, was convinced they were the Pitezel sisters, but he still had to prove it.

By lunchtime, the two men had succeeded in locating the tenants who moved into the St. Vincent Street house immediately after Holmes had abandoned it. They were a family named McDonald, who now resided in a house on Russell Street. Mrs. McDonald told the investigators that, except for an old bedstead and mattress, the house had been completely empty when they moved in. However, her 16-year-old son produced a child's toy that he found in a closet -- a painted egg that concealed a little snake that sprang out like a jack-in-the-box when the wooden shell was opened.

Geyer removed a printed sheet from his coat. It was an inventory that he had received from Carrie Pitezel that detailed all the belongings the children had taken with them when they left on their journey with Holmes. Geyer scanned the sheet and then let out a small gasp. Included on the list was a toy egg that contained a spring-loaded snake. It had been one of Howard's favorite playthings.

Although Geyer still believed that Howard had been killed in either Indianapolis or Detroit, Thomas Ryves recalled that Holmes had moved a large trunk into the house at 16 St. Vincent Street. Perhaps, Geyer speculated, Holmes had killed the boy, stuffed him in the trunk, and carried him to Toronto for disposal.

He and Cuddy returned to the St. Vincent Street cottage with several other officers, and they spent the next several hours excavating the rest of the basement and making a thorough examination of the barn and outbuildings. They found only a few small bones, which turned out to come from chickens.

Geyer did obtain some additional information from Mrs. Armbrust, however. Shortly after moving in, she had gone to use the fireplace in the north front room and discovered that the chimney was blocked. Reaching her hand up into the chimney, she pulled out a mass of charred straw and partially burned rags. The rags turned out to be remnants of girl's clothing – a scrap of blue dress, a piece of a gray blouse and some reddish-brown material from a woolen garment. Someone had apparently tried to burn the clothing but had packed it too tightly inside the chimney, choking off the burning straw. In the box for storing wood next to the hearth, she also discovered a pair of girl's black, buttoned boots.

Unfortunately, none of this evidence existed anymore. Mrs. Armbrust had disposed of it many months before. But Geyer knew that the description was consistent with Carrie Pitezel's inventory of Alice and Nellie's belongings.

The bodies of the two girls, meanwhile, were at the city morgue, where Coroner Johnston and a trio of doctors performed a postmortem early on Tuesday morning. Although the extreme putrefaction of the remains made it hard for the physicians to determine a definitive cause of death, they believed that the girls had died of suffocation before being buried in the basement. This finding led to a lot of sinister speculation about Holmes' large trunk.

At the time of Holmes' arrest, the trunk had been recovered in his hotel room. The Boston police had inspected it thoroughly and discovered a small hole that had been neatly drilled in the lid. Geyer now surmised that Holmes had somehow lured the girls into the trunk, closed and locked the lid, then inserted some type of tube into the hole. The other end, he believed, was attached to a gas jet. He could have simply opened the valve and stood by as the girls were asphyxiated. But how had he gotten them into the trunk in the first place?

The findings of the postmortem were tentative, but given the condition of the corpses, Johnston and the other doctors felt confident about their conclusions. They were puzzled by one anomaly though – the feet of the smaller child were missing.

At first, they supposed that the feet had been accidentally severed by a shovel blade when the corpses were exhumed. But no trace of them were found during the subsequent search of the cellar. It was Detective Geyer who provided the solution to this grisly mystery. Having carefully questioned Carrie about any distinctive physical traits that her daughters might have, he knew that Nellie had been slightly clubfooted. The conclusion was inescapable -- Holmes had tried to hide her identity by cutting off her misshapen feet.

Later that night, the coroner's jury convened at the morgue to examine the bodies as part of the preliminary inquest. Geyer was there, too, having been asked to attend by Corner Johnston.

By that time, the people of Toronto were in such an uproar about the gruesome discovery that Geyer, he later wrote, "felt sure they would have made short shrift of Holmes had they been furnished with the opportunity."

The public had started clamoring for Holmes' extradition to Canada. When he met with reporters before the opening of the inquest, Geyer assured them that Holmes would certainly stand trial in Canada for the murders of the Pitezel children if he somehow escaped the hangman in Philadelphia for the murder of their father.

While Geyer remained in the waiting area, Coroner Johnston led the jury members, all respected city merchants, into the morgue to view the girl's bodies. Moments later, the jurors came hurrying out of the room, overwhelmed by the horrible sight and by the ghastly stench of the remains.

The following evening, the inquest resumed at the police court in City Hall. Thomas Ryves was called as a witness and he testified that the girls in Detective Geyer's photographs were the same children who had lived next door to him for a short time the previous autumn.

Geyer followed him to the witness stand and spent more than two hours offering a history of the Holmes-Pitezel case, concluding with details about his search for the missing children.

At that point, the inquest was adjourned. Although no one doubted that the corpses in the morgue were those of Alice and

Nellie Pitezel, there was still no actual proof of their identities. There was only one person who could offer that proof and so Carrie Pitezel was sent for.

The inquest would have to wait until she arrived in Toronto, when she would be faced with the gruesome and heartbreaking task of viewing what remained of her two youngest daughters.

LIKE HOLMES, CARRIE HAD LEARNED THE DEVASTATING NEWS about her daughters from the newspaper. The previous week, she had traveled to Chicago from her parents' home in Galva, Illinois, to pursue her own inquiries into the children's whereabouts. She was staying with old friends, the Haywards, when the newspaper arrived.

When she saw the horrific headline, she literally collapsed. She was in such a state of hysterical grief that her friends sent their eldest son to fetch the family physician. With the help of "quieting mixtures," the doctor temporarily tranquilized the grieving woman and had to return twice more than day to administer additional medicines. Finally, the drugs caused her to lapse into a troubled and fitful sleep.

When she awoke later that night, she found a telegram from District Attorney Graham, informing her of the trouble faced by the coroner's jury in Toronto. They were unable to proceed without a positive identification of the bodies. So, early Thursday morning, July 18, Carrie set off by herself for Toronto.

She went unrecognized during the train ride, although her black mourning clothes and tear-streaked face attracted many curious looks. In Toronto, however, a crowd of several hundred people gathered at the railway station to greet and stare at her as she stepped off the train. Fortunately, Detective Geyer was there, as well. When she stepped down from the train, he took her by the arm and led her through the curiosity-seekers and reporters to a waiting carriage. He drove them to the Rossin House, where he had been staying while in the city.

By the time Geyer got her to a room, directly across the hall from his own, Carrie was on the verge of collapse. Emotionally ravaged and exhausted, she fainted as he led her toward the bedroom. Geyer, who arranged to have smelling salts brought to the room, immediately administered the restoratives. Carrie's eyes fluttered open and she focused on Geyer's kind face. She moaned, "Oh, Mr. Geyer, is it true that you have found Alice and Nellie buried in a cellar?"

Geyer took her by the hand and, in a soft, calming voice, warned her that she must prepare for the worst. Through her tears, Carrie said that she would do her best. Geyer reluctantly told her that her daughters were dead, although he stopped short of revealing the condition of their bodies or exactly how they had been discovered. After arranging for a hotel maid to care for Carrie, Geyer returned to his room for the night.

Carrie seemed slightly improved when Geyer stopped in to see her the next morning. He was on his way out, he explained to her, to make arrangements for her to view the bodies.

Geyer met Detective Cuddy at police headquarters, and the two men went to the home of Coroner Johnston, who informed them that the remains would be ready for viewing at 4:00 that afternoon.

This photograph was taken in the 1950s but shows the old 1877 morgue on Lombard Street in Toronto. It was here where Carrie was taken to view the corpses of her daughters.

When they returned to the hotel, Geyer and Cuddy did what they could to try and prepare Carrie for her coming ordeal. Geyer tried to be as gentle as possible, but he could no longer conceal the terrible truth about the condition of the children's bodies. When he told her, "it would be absolutely impossible for her to see anything but Alice's teeth and hair, and only the hair that belonged to Nellie," Carrie nearly fainted again.

The two detectives stayed by her side until the carriage arrived at 4:00 P.M. Then, bringing with them a bottle of brandy and smelling salts, they escorted the trembling woman to the waiting cab. There was a small crowd milling about outside the city morgue as Geyer and Cuddy hurried Carrie inside. They left her in the waiting area as they went into the room where the bodies were to make certain that everything was ready. Later, Geyer wrote a graphic account of the scene that followed:

I found that Coroner Johnston, Dr. Caven and several of his assistants, had removed the putrid flesh from the skull of Alice. The teeth had been nicely cleaned and the bodies covered with canvas. The head of Alice was covered with paper, and a sufficiently large hole had been cut in it, so that Mrs. Pitezel could see the teeth. The hair of both children had been carefully washed and laid on the canvas sheet which was covering Alice.

Coroner Johnston said that we could now bring Mrs. Pitezel in. I entered the waiting room and told her we were ready, and with Cuddy on one side of her and I on the other, we entered and led her up to the slab, upon which was lying all that remained of poos Alice. In an instant she recognized the teeth and hair as that of her daughter, Alice. Then, turning around to me she said, 'Where is Nellie?' about this time she noticed the long black plait of hair belonging to Nellie lying on the canvas. She could stand it no longer, and the shrieks of that poor forlorn creature are still ringing in my ears. Tears were trickling down the cheeks of strong men who stood about us. The sufferings of the stricken mother were beyond description.

We gently led her out of the room and into the carriage. She returned to the Rossin House completely overcome with grief and despair and had one fainting spell after another. The ladies in the hotel visited her in her room and spoke kindly to her and expressed their sympathy with her in sad bereavement, and this seemed in a measure to ease her mind.

Later that afternoon, Geyer received a message from Coroner Johnston, asking that Carrie testify at the inquest that evening. Although somewhat taken aback by this demand, Geyer told Carrie, and she replied that she wished "to go and get through with it."

She remained on the stand for a grueling two hours, answering questions in a shaking, barely audible voice. When the Crown's Attorney dismissed her around 10:00 P.M., the strain of the day finally broke her and she gave way to her grief, shrieking wildly for Alice, Nellie, and Howard. Several doctors in attendance did their best to calm her down. She was returned to the hotel in the care of a nurse, who remained at her bedside throughout the night.

The remains of Alice and Nellie Pitezel were buried in St. James Cemetery the following afternoon, Saturday, July 20, 1895. The funeral expenses were paid by the City of Toronto.

Carrie bore her pain as best she could. She had lost her daughters but still had hope that Howard was alive. Detective Geyer did not share her hope, but he kept that opinion to himself. No matter what, though, he was determined to discover the little boy's fate.

On Sunday morning, July 21, the pair boarded a train that would take them back to the United States. Carrie was bound for Chicago, where the women of the Christian Endeavor Society helped take care of her.

Frank Geyer left the train at Detroit. His quest was not yet over.

WHILE THESE THINGS WERE OCCURRING IN FAR-OFF TORONTO, Holmes continued to claim that he had nothing to do with the deaths of Alice and Nellie. He was "as innocent as a newborn babe of murdering the Pitezel children," he protested.

Then, on Thursday, July 18, a mysterious stranger came forward to claim that he was telling the truth. The man's name was Francis Winshoff, and he walked into the office of Holmes' attorney, William A. Shoemaker, that day and announced that he was an "old pal" of the accused criminal. He had been with Holmes in Toronto, he said, and "knew the children well." He was willing to swear to the fact that "Holmes had no hand in the murder."

The reporters covering the case were dubious about Winshoff from the start, partly because he was such an odd-looking character. He was short and shaggy-browed, with dark, maniacal eyes, thick, bushy black hair and thick lips surrounded by unkempt whiskers. He was very excitable, speaking with waving hands and wild gestures. He claimed to be a Canadian and spoke with a thick French accent. The newspapers reported his stories in tones that ranged from skepticism to outright scorn, deriding him as a half-crazed publicity-seeker. Attorney Shoemaker, of course, confidently declared the man to be a "living witness" who knew "just who killed the children" and would positively "clear Holmes of complicity" in the crime. But what else was the defense attorney supposed to say?

As it turned out, the newspapers were right about Winshoff. By the following afternoon, he was revealed to be a fifty-year-old Russian immigrant and "Spiritualist crank." He made his living conducting séances for a small but devoted following and in his spare time, sold his own patent "nerve medicine." He also attempted, by using his occult powers, to transform clay balls into diamonds by rolling them around in his hands.

Winshoff later confessed that he had never actually met Holmes but insisted that he had received his information from reliable sources in the spirit world.

The fact that a crackpot like Winshoff could attract so much attention – along with several days' worth of newspaper stories – was evidence of the public's continuing fascination with the Holmes case. At that point, it was still comparatively mild. Fueled by the yellow press, though, it was about to turn into a feeding frenzy.

The Holmes-Pitezel came into the public eye at a particularly bitter moment in American history. The country's economy was in a terrible state, brought about by the devastating bank panic of 1893, which effectively ended the Gilded Age. It was a time of widespread industrial collapse, massive unemployment and violent labor strikes. Chicago saw some of the worst of it, including the bloody Pullman strike of 1894, which ended with 30 deaths and $80 million in damages.

The public's obsessive interest in Holmes came about in part because of the grim economic conditions of the day. To many, Holmes personified everything that had gone wrong with the country. He was a symbol of the corruption that was at the heart of the American "success ethic." Poet Walt Whitman would call it the "depravity of the business classes." Holmes was the incarnation of "money lust," of the evils to which the rabid pursuit of individual wealth could lead.

In late July 1895, however, the public's perception of Holmes underwent a dramatic change. Suddenly, he was seen as something much more diabolical than a bold, ruthless schemer who had killed an accomplice to cash in on an insurance policy. Partly, this change resulted from the discovery of the murdered Pitezel girls – deaths that could not be attributed to simple greed.

But there was something else that occurred at this time, too. Holmes began to be seen not merely as the "boss crook of the century," but as a creature of monstrous, perhaps even mythical, proportions.

It was at this time that the legend of Holmes was truly created – a legend that continues to grow today. The transformation from "swindler" and "fiend" to "monster" literally occurred overnight. For on Friday evening, July 19, 1895, the Chicago police finally began exploring the Castle of H.H. Holmes.

15

IN 1914, THE NEWS OF A SUICIDE IN THE SMALL TOWN OF Portland, Michigan, was barely noticed by the newspapers. The dead man's name was Patrick Quinlan, a poor Irishman who mostly kept to himself. Even the strange circumstances of his death failed to attract any real attention. Quinlan had taken a fatal dose of poison and left a note lying on the floor next to his body. On the scrap of paper, he had scrawled just four words: "I could not sleep."

Few remembered Quinlan's claim to infamy as the accused accomplice of a man named H.H. Holmes, one of the most notorious murderers in American history. Shortly after Holmes' arrest, Quinlan, who had worked as a caretaker at Holmes' "Murder Castle," was also taken into police custody. He was later released and forgotten, mentioned mainly as an afterthought in the writings that have since appeared about the murderous life of Holmes.

But was Patrick Quinlan really as innocent as the police said he was? There were many who didn't believe so, including a Chicago chief of police, neighbors who believed that he disposed of damning evidence --- and perhaps even Quinlan himself.

What really led to his suicide? Guilt over what he had done while in the employ of Holmes or was he, as some would later claim, hounded to his death by the ghosts of his victims?

H.H. HOLMES WAS ARRESTED IN NOVEMBER 1894 BUT HIS LINKS to Chicago and his infamous "Murder Castle" – as it first became known at this time – were not fully explored until the following summer. As more of his crimes were revealed, the authorities finally investigated his Chicago property.

The only excuse for this was the innate corruption found in the Chicago Police Department at the time. It wasn't because Holmes was paying anyone off but because it seemed every other criminal and politician in the city was. It wasn't until the bodies of Nellie and Alice Pitezel were found that the Chicago police got involved in our story. Before that, they paid little attention to the man the newspapers called "the king of crime," except to serve him a court summons when he was sued. Even the speculation that he might have killed the missing Williams sisters, didn't prompt any legwork by the Chicago police.

Between the time of Holmes' arrest and the discovery of Alice and Nellie's bodies, though, the police force had been reorganized. That may not have made it that much better, but a clear effort was made to bring in a new man and clean up the force from the top down. Once the bodies of the two girls were found by Detective Frank Geyer, all eyes turned to the strange building that Holmes had constructed in Englewood.

For the next few weeks, the police tore the place apart looking for clues and putting Holmes on the front page of newspapers every day.

The new chief John J. Badenoch chose Detective John W. Norton and Inspector John E. Fitzpatrick to lead the search under his direction. These two men, assisted by a handful of other cops and a legion of reporters who took a hands-on role in the investigation in a way that would be unthinkable today, entered the building on Friday, July 19.

A side view of Holmes' Castle from Wallace Street. The Chicago Police finally decided to investigate the building in July 1895.

E.H. Robinson, the druggist, took Norton and Fitzpatrick down into the cellar. He later told a reporter:

There was a stench down there which I had never before observed. The basement would naturally be foul but the odor which I noticed was one which I have never experienced without causes other than natural.

In other words, it smelled like death.

He also showed them a walk-in safe upstairs. The door was opened to reveal another set of doors, which were opened with crow bars. The interior of the vault was empty but was lined with asbestos panels.

Inspector Fitzpatrick questioned what the purpose of those panels could be, but no one could answer, other than to say it would have muffled the sounds of anyone locked inside of it. And when they were joined by the always-chatty jeweler Charles Davis, they found out that this was exactly what Holmes used it for.

Davis also showed them what he called a "dummy elevator" that ran between floors. It was the size of a dumbwaiter but had never been used for the restaurant on the first floor. He took them to the third floor and showed them a room that Holmes had used as an office. It contained another walk-in safe and a

This stove, moved from the third floor, was the one that Charles Davis suspected had been used to try and burn down the building.

huge stove. Davis believed that the stove had been the cause of the fire Holmes had started in the building when fleeing Chicago and trying to cash in the insurance policies he'd purchased for it.

In addition, he claimed that Patrick Quinlan had investigated the stove in the months since Holmes left Chicago and when he thrust his hands inside, he found a watch chain and some buttons. Davis stated that the chain belonged to Minnie Williams. He had once repaired it for her and would recognize it anywhere.

Fitzpatrick asked him, "Do you think Minnie Williams was murdered and her dismembered body burned in that stove?"

Davis replied, "Draw your own conclusions but I am satisfied that Minnie Williams has been murdered."

After the first day's investigation, Chicago newspapers confidently announced that Minnie and Nannie Williams had been burned to death and cremated in the stove. Of course, there was no evidence of this. It *could* have happened but there was no way to know, which is a good reason to be careful about believing

Crowds gathered outside the "Murder Castle" while the police, reporters, and city officials investigated the building. The crowds spread lurid tales even faster than the newspapers could.

every story you might read about Holmes in the newspapers of the day.

That's easy to say in hindsight, of course, because one thing that is sure is that readers of the day weren't skeptical about *anything* they read about Holmes in the papers of the day.

Crowds who'd seen the morning headlines gathered outside the building and officers were sent to try and hold them back. The crowds would continue to gather, in ever-growing numbers, throughout the search of the building.

Meanwhile, a team of laborers were brought in to start digging up the basement. Using picks and shovels, the men searched for any likely spot where Holmes might have disposed of his victims. As the workmen made their way along the south wall, they discovered a hollow spot about 25 feet from the Wallace Street side of the building.

The large wooden tank that was found inside of the wall. Despite the fumes that came from inside, the contents of the tank were never determined.

The bricks came down easily when hit by picks and shovels. Peering into the darkness, they could see a large, U-shaped wooden tank. The workmen picked at it carelessly, chipping away at the zinc lining, until a foul-smelling gas began rushing out of it.

The men decided to take a lunch break to let the smell dissipate and when they returned, one of the workers approached the tank with a lit candle. And suddenly, there was a blinding flash of light and a loud noise and three of the workers were knocked to the ground. They had to be carried out of the basement and then were sent home.

Fire Chief Joseph Kenyon was brought in to examine what turned out to be a tank within the tank. He ordered the men to haul out the interior tank, but the workers couldn't get close to it without being overcome by the fumes. Most recovered quickly but Kenyon himself was knocked unconscious. He finally ordered the tank flooded with water and boarded up.

What the gas might have been, or what the mysterious tank might have been used for, remains unknown.

MEANWHILE, ABOVE GROUND, INSPECTOR FITZPATRICK AND Detective Norton were continuing the tour of the building, leading a procession of reporters behind them. They were baffled by the narrow, winding passages, doors that opened to brick walls, hidden stairways, secret panels, hidden passages, and trapdoors.

It was documented that there were 35 rooms of all sizes and shapes, six gloomy and dark halls – some wide and roomy and others barely wide enough to fit through – and 51 doors that were cut into the walls in every conceivable place. It was noted that there was a dozen different ways to go from one end of the floor to the other.

They found a bankbook that belonged to a woman named Lucy Burbank, a bottle of carbolic acid, and what appeared to be bones in the large stove that was in Holmes' office. Whether they were human – or even bones at all – would later be argued, but we do know that when reporters took apart the stove, they found a large quantity of singed human hair – so make of that what you will.

Workers digging along the Wallace Street wall of the basement found a barrel that contained a woman's dress with a white ribbon design on the front, as well as part of a porcelain teapot. The dress was stained with something that looked like rust and was immediately thought to be blood. The dress, of course, does not survive today, so there's no way to know either way.

Some of the stories that emerged from the Castle were believable and others, not so much. A reporter printed a rumor that Holmes had an affair with Mrs. Warner, who was married to the namesake of the Warner Glass-Bending Company, and that he killed her. However, she later turned up alive and well.

Better sourced was the story of Julia Connor, whose account reporters had started to piece together based on interviews with neighbors who now realized they hadn't seen Julia or her daughter since late in 1891.

Discovering the fate of Julia Connor soon became as important to the investigation as the fate of the Williams sisters. Detective Norton, reading through papers in Holmes' office, found a letter from Julia's mother, mailed from Davenport and dated October 1, 1892. The contents suggested that Mrs. Smythe had tried to contact Julia in Englewood and had received a letter from Holmes' claiming that he had no idea where she was. Mrs. Smythe had written back to him, telling him that his letter "surprised us very much as we supposed our daughter Julia was in your company. We are very anxious to know her whereabouts, and her daughter also, and by answering this letter and telling us where she is you will greatly relieve her poor old gray-haired father and mother."

The police felt certain that Holmes had murdered his former mistress, as he had Minnie and Nannie Williams, although they had no real evidence to back up their suspicions. On Tuesday afternoon, July 23, though, one mystery might have been solved, though -- the fate of Julia's daughter, Pearl.

The size of the workforce in the basement had been increased and around 1:00 P.M. on Wednesday, July 24, a workman named Pat McGovern was digging about two feet underground and discovered bones in a bed of quicklime – calcium oxide that was used in making concrete but also conveniently known to criminals as a chemical that speeds up the process of decomposition for human remains.

There were about 18 bones in all, appearing to be ribs, a pelvis, and part of a jaw. Blackened and slimy, they were buried near some pieces of clothing, chunks of matted hair, some broken glass, and part of a ruined suitcase.

The bones were taken upstairs to Dr. Robinson in the drugstore, who said they appeared to be the bones of a human child between six and eight years of age – just the age of Pearl Connor when she was last seen around Christmas 1891.

THE SEARCH OF THE BUILDING CONTINUED AND MORE gruesome discoveries were made. However, the efforts of the police continued to be hampered by the curiosity-seekers who swarmed the structure, drawn by the lurid newspaper headlines. Some of them even broke into the building while the investigation was being carried out. The police managed to kick them out, but not before many of them had helped themselves to souvenirs, including personal letters and files from Holmes' private office.

Further discoveries included a woman's shoe, the broken lid of an opera-glass case, and more human bones, hidden under some rotten boards. Holmes's defense attorney tried to brush off the discovery of the bones, saying that Holmes was a medical man and that it was quite common for him to have skeletal pieces in his possession. But the police weren't convinced by his claims and the public wanted, perhaps even needed, for Holmes to be the monster that he was being portrayed in the newspapers.

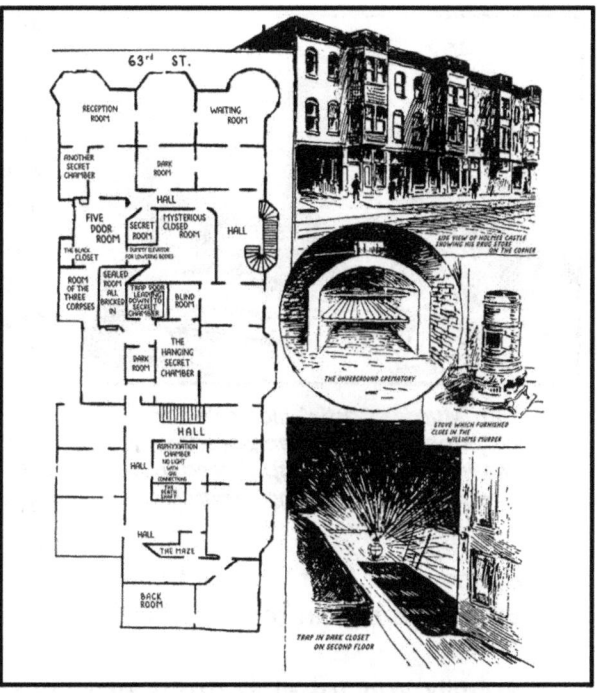

Illustrations from Chicago Tribune reporters, based on the discoveries made inside the "Castle."

As news of the macabre discoveries spread, people began to realize that Holmes was something the authorities had never dealt with before – a killer so unique in their experience that they were unable to define him. A Chicago journalist came up with the term "multi-murderer," but it would be nearly a century before criminologists coined the term "serial killer" to describe someone like H.H. Holmes.

He certainly wasn't the first of his kind in American history, but he got more attention than any other killer of the era. And it seemed with each passing day, Holme' list of victims – and possible victims – seemed to grow.

The lists were splashed across newspaper pages and while most of the victim's names were guesswork and others who were

The "Murder Castle" illustrated for newspapers by a contemporary artist shows the crowds that appeared in the wake of the building's search.

allegedly killed turned up alive and well, there were some who were never seen again. There was no evidence that Holmes had killed them, but the idea that he might have killed them created the mythology that still surrounds him today.

In many ways, it has been impossible to determine just what part of Holmes' story was legend and what part was fact.

Even with that in mind, his list of alleged victims included:

* Emily Van Tassel, a pretty grocery store cashier who had vanished soon after striking up an acquaintance with Holmes in 1893.

* There was also Wilfred Cole, a wealthy lumberman from Baltimore who had traveled to Chicago on unspecified business with Holmes and was never seen again.

* A physician named Russler, who was allegedly a close friend of Holmes and had vanished in 1892.

* Harry Walker, a young man who had gone to work as a private secretary for Holmes had disappeared in 1893, a few months after a $15,000 life insurance had been taken out on him with Holmes as the beneficiary.

* The police also wondered about the whereabouts of a wealthy and attractive widow named Mrs. Lee, who had kept company with Holmes and then vanished.

* The list also included three missing members of the Gorky family: a middle-aged widow named Kate, who ran a restaurant

on the first floor of Holmes' building during the time of the Columbian Exposition; her sister, Liz, and her pretty teen-aged daughter, Anna.

* There were also an indeterminate number of female clerical workers who had allegedly vanished after taking jobs at the Castle, including a Boston girl named Mabel Barrett, a 16-year-old stenographer named Miss Wild, a bookkeeper named Kelly and perhaps dozens of others.

* One report stated that Holmes had "employed more than 100 young women during his years in Englewood." He didn't, but he did employ a few and how many of them were never heard from again remains a mystery.

And then, of course, there was Emeline Cigrand, the pretty young woman that Ben Pitezel had met while trying to stop drinking at the sanatorium in Dwight, Illinois.

The police first learned about Emeline when Doctors B.J. and P.J. Cigrand came to them to file a missing person complaint. They explained about her time at the Keeley Institute and then her move to Chicago to work for HH Holmes. Then, according to a note received by her parents, she married a man named Robert Phelps on December 7, 1892. She hadn't been heard from since, but the doctors had immediately recognized a photo of Holmes that had recently appeared in the newspaper, along with his building – which Dr. B.J. Phelps had toured in the fall of 1892 when he'd visited Emeline.

Chief Badenoch was startled to have a case presented directly to the police and said:

I wouldn't be surprised if we found the bones of 10 or 15 persons in the basement of Holmes' Castle. The deeper we go into this case, the more horrible it becomes. Every hour brings forth some new and startling phase of Holmes' black career, and he is undoubtedly the greatest criminal that ever lived.

He may have been overstating things just a bit, but you get the idea.

The chief ordered his men to find Dr. Robinson, the Lawrences who lived in an apartment in the Castle, and jeweler Charles Davis, who could always be counted on for good gossip about Holmes, and bring them to headquarters. Since all of them had been in the building in 1892, he assumed they knew Emeline Cigrand.

Reporters reached Mrs. Lawrence before the police did. She was eager to talk:

I have said 100 times there is something wrong with the departure of Miss Cigrand. I have not the slightest doubt that Holmes killed her.

She recalled that after the last time she and her family saw Emeline, Holmes' office was kept locked, and no one went inside but Holmes and Pat Quinlan – who you might recall she once dubbed that "dirty Irishman" – and that evening, Holmes asked two men who were living in the building if they would help carry a trunk downstairs from his office. Holmes seemed nervous and warned them several times to be careful with it. It was placed in a wagon and taken away.

A few days later, Holmes brought them cards announcing Emeline's marriage to Robert Phelps, but the Lawrences had never heard her mention a man by that name. Mrs. Lawrence took the card from him with no comment but remained suspicious of Holmes until the stories of his crimes began appearing in the newspapers.

After that, any doubts that she had about him killing Emeline were gone.

AS FAR AS MOST NEWSPAPER REPORTERS AND EDITORS WERE concerned, the Chicago Police Department had a lot answer for when it came to their handling of the Holmes case – even blaming them for the deaths of those who were killed by Holmes after he left the city. If they had been doing their jobs, Holmes would have been arrested for the murders of the Williams sisters, or someone else, and never fled Chicago at all.

This forced the department into stepping up their efforts and, as Chief Badenoch was fond of ordering, arresting all known crooks and thieves on sight, whether they'd committed any new crimes or not. In this case, the "known crooks and thieves" were anyone associated with Holmes.

This put Patrick Quinlan high on the list of men to arrest. He was grilled for hours and often seemed nervous and high-strung to the detectives. The chief himself sat in on the interviews, and it was reported that his exasperated shouts of frustration could often be heard outside the room. Reporters in the corridor could only hear parts of the interview, but they scribbled down what they could make out. They heard Pat say that Holmes told him Julia Connor had married a North Side doctor and went to live in California and that Holmes had wanted to insure the life of Pat's wife.

No one heard his reply to that, but I'll assume it was NO.

The chief asked, "Do you know anything about the murder of the child whose bones were found in the cellar of the building?"

Pat said he didn't.

"Isn't it true that little Pearl Connor was murdered and buried in that basement?"

Pat replied, "I don't know if she was."

"If you don't tell the truth, we can and will make you!" the chief warned him.

"I am telling all I know!" Pat insisted.

Badenoch scoffed, "You are not."

The chief told reporters that the interrogation of Patrick Quinlan would continue until they had gotten the truth out of him – no matter what that took. It's worth noting that Chief Badenoch was new to law enforcement. He'd been a city commissioner before he'd been named to the job and, most likely, had little knowledge about what was legal and what wasn't.

Not that this would have concerned the Chicago police, though. Pat's treatment while in custody was so brutal that he would eventually attempt to sue Chief Badenoch and Inspector Fitzpatrick.

Trying to get Quinlan to talk, the police arrested his wife, Ella, and hauled her into the station. When she saw her husband in shackles, she broke down, which was exactly the reaction that Chief Badenoch wanted. In tears, she confessed to her and her husband's knowledge of at least some of Holmes' insurance scams. Rumors among reporters were that she also admitted to impersonating Minnie Williams at a LaSalle Street bank when Minnie's signature was required. She was placed in a separate cell from her husband, who was still refusing to admit anything.

After one interrogation, the pale and bruised man told reporters:

I am innocent. I knew Holmes and worked for him. All these people you say were murdered, I knew, and when they went away, as Holmes claimed, I thought it was funny. You say I helped him to commit murder, but I did not. I am innocent and I cannot tell you what you claim I know. Let me alone. I am innocent!

Chief Badenoch disregarded Pat's claims of innocence. He stated flatly that the man was a murderer. At the time of his arrest, the janitor had been carrying a big iron ring that held 37 keys to various locks throughout the building, including the rooms that the police speculated were murder scenes. They maintained that someone with that sort of access to the building was undoubtedly aware of its secrets. Pat was either a willing accomplice or one of the stupidest human beings on earth.

What made things worse is that the police were getting help building a case that Patrick Quinlan was an accomplice of Holmes' from an unlikely source – H.H. Holmes himself.

When police searched the Quinlan apartment, they found a letter from Holmes that had been mailed from his prison cell in

Philadelphia. The letter was written on two scraps of paper and looked suspiciously as though it was meant to be found and read by the police. In it, Holmes made it look as though Pat knew that Minnie Williams had killed her sister, Nannie, but Holmes didn't ask him to help cover it up.

In the letter, of course, Minnie was alive and well and had the Pitezel children with her. I should note that it was dated just one day before Detective Frank Geyer discovered the bodies of the Pitezel girls in that shallow grave in Toronto.

The discovery of the letter, despite its claim that Pat was not involved in anything illegal, made the police even more convinced that he was a willing participant in Holmes' crimes.

Chief Badenoch told reporters on July 27:

I think I will be able to wrest a confession from Quinlan before long. I do not intend to let him turn state's evidence, if I can help it, although I believe he is weakening to such an extent that should such a suggestion be made to him, he would grasp it eagerly and at once.

The next day, the police believed they had him. A new witness had been found whose testimony seemed to firmly cement Pat's role as an accomplice in Holmes' crimes. The statement initially convinced the police of his guilt but eventually, it would be what freed him from custody.

According to newspaper reports that appeared that afternoon, Detective Fitzpatrick had tracked down four skeletons that had been removed from the Castle under the direction of Holmes and Pat Quinlan. They were skeletons that had been prepared by Myron Chappell.

Chappell told the police all he knew about the skeletons that he had handled for Holmes. Perhaps most damning in his allegations was the testimony that he gave against Patrick Quinlan, whom Chappell claimed knew all about Holmes' illegal activities. Chappell stated that while he was working on the remains for

Holmes, Quinlan was on the premises and appeared, in Chappell's mind, to be Holmes' "trusted man."

Chappell also led the police to another witness who could vouch for Quinlan's involvement with Holmes' crimes. This second witness was express wagon driver Cephas Humphrey. Humphrey told detectives that one day in June 1893, Holmes summoned him to the Castle and asked him to take a trunk and a box to Union Station. Holmes told him to come after dark, so no one saw him take them away.

When he returned that evening, he claimed he was taken to a dark room on the second floor of the building by none other than Patrick Quinlan.

Humphrey was shown a large box – about the size of a coffin – which he carried downstairs and stood on its end while he opened the wagon gate. As he did this, he heard a sharp tapping sound coming from above and behind him. He looked up and saw Holmes peering out of a second-floor window. He told Humphrey not to stand the box on end but rather to lay it down flat.

Newspaper illustration of Patrick Quinlan that appeared in 1914

After loading the box into his wagon, Humphrey retrieved the trunk and then was instructed to take them both to Union Station and leave them on a certain platform. He was told not to say anything to anyone but simply leave the packages. A man there was expecting them and knew what to do with them. The express driver vaguely remembered that the box was supposed to go to Philadelphia, but he could not remember where the trunk was sent.

According to the newspapers, the police were excited to hear of these new developments and felt they now had Pat dead to rights.

Chief Badenoch publicly stated that he believed Holmes had corrupted Quinlan, who was known as an honest man before he met Holmes. He had worked for Holmes for $2 per day but rarely did any real labor, acting more as a confidential agent. This was the reason, detectives believed, that he was aware of what Holmes was doing. Badenoch felt that with the new information that they had received, Quinlan would soon confess his role in the many murders of H.H. Holmes.

Chief Badenoch had no idea at the time that he made these statements that he would be forced to release Pat Quinlan from custody a few days later.

IN EARLY AUGUST, THE POLICE WERE FINALLY WRAPPING UP their search of the Castle. They were convinced that the building had yielded its darkest secrets. The only question now seemed to be – what should be done with the place?

Some called for its immediate demolition. The building was a "death trap" and not just for the unlucky victims who never left the place. E.F. Laughlin, an inspector for the Chicago Department of Buildings, took a tour of the Castle and was appalled by its shoddy construction. He wrote in a report:

The stores are the only habitable part of the building. The rest of the building should be condemned. The structural parts of the inside are all weak and dangerous. Built of the poorest and cheapest kind of material. All dividing partitions between flats are combustible. The sanitary condition of the building is horrible.

And the stores weren't doing that well either. Annoyed by the traffic and constant sightseers, Dr. Robinson sold his drugstore and moved out. The owner of the candy store closed, too. Only Charles Davis seemed to enjoy the attention.

The public calls for the building to be torn down seemed a terrible waste to many people. Robert Corbitt, a playwright and amateur detective, was working on a book about Holmes' Castle and became a thorn in the side of the police.

Corbitt was regarded as a shiftless, incompetent, and unscrupulous man whose divorce record painted a picture of a man so cruel that he beat his wife while she was still in bed recovering from childbirth. He was frequently evicted from apartments but refused to find real work, however, something about the Holmes story had inspired him to become more enterprising. He managed to weasel his way into the investigation, posing as a reporter, and ended up with piles of Holmes' letters, documents, and personal effects that he stole from the Castle.

In just a matter of a few weeks, he published his "book," *The Holmes Castle*, which had little in it that readers couldn't find in the newspapers. It also included Corbitt's rambling theories that Holmes was innocent of murder. He claimed that at one time, he had his hands on a canary-yellow envelope addressed to Holmes from Minnie Williams, dated 1894, but Detective Norton had taken it away from him. He suspected it would shed light on the whole mystery if the contents were released. If the envelope existed at all – which is very doubtful – the information inside was never made public.

Corbitt saw the Castle as a vein of gold just waiting to be mined, but so did others. The building might not be fit for habitation, but many believed there were other uses to which it might be put.

On one day in late July alone, nearly 5,000 people had flocked to Englewood, hoping for a glimpse of the Castle's interior and its "torture chamber," "suffocation vault" and "burial cellar."

There was good money to be made from such morbid fascination and an enterprising former policeman named A.M. Clark was convinced he was just the man to do it. Even before the police had called a halt to the search, Clark had been in touch with Frank Chandler, the man who essentially owned the building – or at least held the largest of the many mortgages on it – and arranged to lease it.

On Sunday, August 11, he made an announcement to the press. Beginning that week, the Castle would be opened as a "murder museum" with an admission charge of 15-cents and guided tours conducted by police detectives with first-hand knowledge of the case.

WHILE CLARK WAS PREPARING TO OPEN HIS NEW "MURDER Museum," the case against Patrick Quinlan was falling apart.

Pat and Ella were in the middle of their third week in custody but no matter how relentlessly the police questioned them, both refused to admit to any part in the murders that Holmes had committed. Ella had confessed to knowing about Holmes' insurance schemes, but her husband was adamant about the fact that he had done nothing illegal. Detectives were sure that the witness statements from the machinist, Myron Chappell, and the express driver, Cephas Humphrey, would be enough to push Quinlan into a full confession, but they couldn't have been more wrong.

It would be the family of Myron Chappell who called his testimony into question. Aside from the fact that the police had no evidence the skeletons they had found had actually come from the Castle, there was no evidence that Chappell had articulated them, and Chappell's own family was now dismissing his statements to police as the ramblings of a delusional drunk.

They claimed his story was nothing more than a fantasy he made up in hopes of getting free drinks for repeating the tale he'd told the police. Chappell had done some work for Holmes, but no one knew if he had really assembled as many skeletons for him as he claimed.

This caused authorities to question his identification of Pat Quinlan as Holmes' "trusted man," as well. With nothing more than suspicion, the police were forced to let Pat go. He never confessed to any wrongdoing and no hard evidence ever emerged against him.

When he later tried to sue the police for false arrest, the case was dismissed by the courts. Could it have been because the judge felt just as the police did -- that Patrick Quinlan knew much more than he was saying, even though no one could prove it? It seems possible and, in fact, questions have continued to be raised about the role that Quinlan had in Holmes' crimes, especially because of what happened next.

Less than two weeks after it was vacated by the police, H.H. Holmes' "Murder Castle," which had been newly remodeled as a tourist attraction under the management of ex-policeman A.M. Clark, was ready to admit its first paying customers. However, around midnight on Monday, August 19, just days after Pat Quinlan was released from custody, Clark's get-rich-quick scheme literally went up in smoke.

The building was not destroyed, as is commonly believed, but it was badly damaged. The second and third floors were wrecked, so if any evidence remained there from the crimes of H.H. Holmes, it was now gone. No cause for the fire was ever determined, but it did put an end to the dreams of a "Murder Museum."

The upper floors were rebuilt, and the building was renamed the "Chandler Block" for Frank and Peyton Chandler, the official owners. Newspapers – and the public – would refer to it as the Holmes Castle for decades, though, even though the first floor and basement of the original were all that remained.

The ground-floor shops remained in business and new tenants came and went. A second fire, in 1903, was caused by a lamp exploding in a second-floor apartment. There was another fire in the building in 1907.

By the 1930s, the Castle was in rough condition and in January 1938, the city of Chicago purchased it with the intention of tearing

One of the last photographs taken of the former "Murder Castle," shortly before it was demolished in 1938.

it down to put up a post office on the site. It was finally demolished in May of that year.

Over the years, the post office has gained a reputation as haunted. These stories of restless spirits may or may not have merit, but the Castle itself was said to be haunted when it still stood.

When the structure was rebuilt after the fire, the second and third floors were turned into apartments and in 1902, a newspaper story noted that tenants rarely stayed long in the place. They left after hearing unearthly noises and seeing ghostly apparitions. If the site really was haunted, then it's likely it still is – especially since the foundation of the building is the SAME foundation used for Holmes' Castle.

People who walked their dogs past the new building claimed the animals would often pull away from it, barking and whining at something only they could see or sense.

Postal workers in the building have had their own encounters, often telling of strange sounds and feelings that they couldn't

The U.S. Post Office at 63rd and Wallace in Englewood, the former site of H.H. Holmes' "Murder Castle." Stories say that the Castle was haunted in its later years and many believe its restless spirits linger here today.

easily explain. There are also reports of lights turning on and off at night when the building is empty and seeing strange figures looking out the windows of locked and empty rooms.

The location certainly has the potential for being haunted and, if the stories are true, then it just might be.

PATRICK QUINLAN DID NOT FARE WELL AFTER HIS RELEASE FROM police custody.

Naturally, he was the first suspect of the mysterious fire that occurred at the Castle on August 19. It was assumed he was trying to destroy any evidence that hadn't been found by the police. But Pat had an alibi, and they couldn't make the charges stick, so they had to let him go – again.

To this day, we'll never know just how much Pat knew about Holmes's crimes – or if he took an active role in them. In my opinion, he was as guilty as Ben Pitezel, another not-so-bright guy who got pulled into Holmes' world and believed he could straddle the line between crimes involving money, where no one got hurt, and crimes that led to murder.

The Chicago police were convinced that Pat was a killer, despite the way he publicly maintained his innocence. He lived and worked at the Castle, and he admitted that. He'd helped to build parts of it but never knew what Holmes intended to do with some of the rooms or how he planned to use those secret passages between the walls. He hadn't killed anyone and if he knew for a fact that Holmes had committed murder, he'd have turned him in.

Or so he claimed.

After his unsuccessful lawsuit against the police department, Pat left Chicago and returned to Portland, Michigan. There, he tried to settle into a quiet life but one that was continually plagued by other people's curiosity. He often told Ella and his friends that he was constantly being stared at on the streets. People watched him and wondered about what terrible things he'd done. Pat said that while the rest of the world would forget about H.H. Holmes, the curiosity-seekers of Portland, Michigan, would never forget about Pat Quinlan.

For 19 years, Pat was unable to sleep. His daughter, Cora, later said that, at night, he would wake with a start and find himself covered in sweat. He would call for help and when a light was

DIES, KEEPS SECRET OF CRIME CASTLE

Carpenter, Police Think, Goes to Grave Hiding Mystery of House He Built.

Trap Doors, False Partitions and Wires Baffle Detectives.

CHICAGO, March 7. — Patrick Quinlan, said to be one of the few men who might have explained the mysteries of "Holmes castle," famous in the annals of Chicago crime, is dead at his home near Portland, Mich., according to dispatches received here today. Before his death he told physicians he had taken poison.

Quinlan, a carpenter, was employed by Herman W. Mudgett, better known as Dr. J. J. Holmes, to build the structure which later became known as the "castle."

The police held him for a time as a possible accomplice in the five or six murders for which Holmes was convicted. Quinlan acted as agent for the "castle" until Holmes was hanged.

Trap doors, false partitions and wires were part of the equipment found in the "castle."

Except for several bones, not proved to be human, found in the furnace, there was no evidence that any of Holmes' crimes had been committed there.

"He couldn't sleep," was the reason given by relatives for Quinlan's suicide.

turned on, he would recount how he was attacked in his sleep by strange hallucinations -- ghosts of the many victims of H.H. Holmes.

Finally, when he could stand it no more, Quinlan wrote a note declaring: "I could not sleep," swallowed a bottle of poison, and died on the floor of his home, his hastily scrawled note by his side.

Was he an innocent man, driven to suicide because of guilt over what he should have known or a guilty man, who was, as the newspapers would claim, hounded to his death by the spirits of those he helped send to an early grave?

The truth will likely never be known.

AS THE DRAMA ABOUT THE DISCOVERIES INSIDE HOLMES' Castle was filling the pages of newspapers, another drama was taking place in Michigan and Indiana.

During the trip from Toronto with Carrie Pitezel, Detective Geyer had left on his own for Detroit. He had arrived on the evening of July 21, too late to do anything more than drop in on his old friend, Thomas Meyler, who insisted on buying him a steak at a local chophouse to celebrate his recent success in Toronto.

The next morning – once again accompanied by Detective Tuttle – Geyer sought out the two witnesses who claimed to have seen Howard Pitezel in Holmes' company. The men were questioned more closely this time, and both admitted that they might have been mistaken. The detectives also returned to the house that Holmes had rented and made another thorough search of the premises, including the cellar, barn, and outbuildings. They found nothing that suggested that Howard had been murdered there. They did find an enormous furnace in the basement, which would have been a convenient place to dispose of a child's body, Geyer thought, but found no evidence that it had been used in such a manner.

The only disturbing clue remained the mysterious hole, which the current tenant had discovered in the cellar shortly after moving in.

In his hotel room that night, Geyer reviewed all that he had learned. Now that the two witnesses had revised their story, there wasn't a shred of evidence that Howard had been with Holmes in Detroit. This made the letter that Alice had written in October 1894 even more heartbreaking when she said that "Howard is not with us now."

He also knew something else – that the hole that Holmes had dug in the cellar in the Detroit house was the same size as the makeshift grave in Toronto. He surmised that the hole had been intended for Alice and Nellie, not Howard. When something unexpected occurred, forcing Holmes to leave Detroit, he had abandoned his plans and spirited the girls away to Toronto. It was there that he killed them.

Geyer was now convinced that by the time Alice and Nellie checked into the Western Hotel on October 12, they were alone. Howard had never made it to Detroit.

When Geyer woke the next morning, he dressed and went to the telegraph office to send a wire to Philadelphia. He informed them he was on his way back to Indianapolis.

On July 24, Frank Geyer marched through the doors of the Indianapolis Police Department headquarters and within 20 minutes was conferring with Superintendent Powell, who detailed Detective Richards to assist him again. Geyer knew exactly what they should be searching for – a house that had been rented in early October 1894 by a man who claimed that he was taking it for his "widowed sister." It was the same story that Holmes had used in Cincinnati, Detroit, and Toronto.

Using a city directory, Geyer and Richards put together a list of every real estate agent in Indianapolis and began visiting every one of them. While this was taking place, the newspapers were running front-page stories about Geyer's search, complete with pictures of Holmes and Howard.

As in Toronto, the public was fascinated with the story. Countless leads began pouring in from all over the city and the surrounding region, but all proved to be worthless.

Day after day, in the sweltering sun of what was one of the hottest summers in memory, the two detectives walked and rode trolleys all over the city. They found nothing. By month's end, even Frank Geyer was starting to give up hope, fearing that the disappearance of Howard Pitezel would never be solved.

Just as Geyer's faith was starting to falter, his spirits were buoyed by a letter from Assistant District Attorney Thomas Barlow, who continued to feel certain that "skill and patience would yet win." After analyzing letters written by Alice and Nellie Pitezel, Barlow had come to believe that the children couldn't have possibly checked out of the Circle Hotel on October 6, as the proprietor, Herman Ackelow, had claimed.

This was that missing week that had been bothering Geyer so much and making the search for Howard so difficult. Now it looked like the prosecutor had figured out the solution to the puzzle.

Geyer managed to track down the registry for the hotel, and he discovered that Barlow was right – the last payment for the Pitezel children's board had been made on October 10. Since Geyer had already discovered that Alice and Nellie had arrived in Detroit on the evening of October 12, he now felt sure that he was very close on Holmes' trail, with only 48 hours to be accounted for, not six days as he had previously thought.

At some point during those 48 hours, Howard Pitezel had disappeared either in Indianapolis or between there and Detroit.

Before he could look any further, though, his search was interrupted by a telegram informing him that a child's skeleton had been found in the cellar of Holmes' building in Englewood. He was needed in Chicago at once.

Geyer arrived there before breakfast the next morning, conferring with Chief Badenoch and Inspector Fitzpatrick. It soon became clear, though, that the remains were not those of a little boy.

After another side trip to Philadelphia – where he updated the district attorney on the case, spoke to reporters, and got some much-needed rest – Geyer was back in Indianapolis on August 7.

This time, he was accompanied by another skilled investigator – W.E. Gary, from the Fidelity Mutual Company. He had been involved in the Holmes case even longer than Geyer and was just as adamant about seeing the man brought to justice.

They began the next leg of the search in Chicago -- not because they thought Howard was there but to interview Pat Quinlan again and to speak with his wife, Ella. They maintained their ignorance about the Pitezel children and Geyer was still inclined to believe they were telling the truth.

The search now took them to the towns that lay between Indianapolis and Detroit. They traveled to Logansport, and from there to Peru, Indiana, Montpelier Junction, Ohio, and Adrian, Michigan. In each of these towns, they spent several days talking to the owners of hotels and boarding houses and interviewing real estate agents, but nothing turned up.

Geyer now decided that he would return to Indianapolis and would search there until District Attorney Graham told him to stop or until the boy had been found.

This was Geyer's third trip to Indianapolis and by now, he was feeling discouraged again. The newspapers were still trying to help by printing stories about the search and the detectives continued to be inundated with leads and tips about mysterious people who had rented houses for a short time and then disappeared. Geyer and Gary ran down each of these leads. They also made a list of all the newspaper classified advertisements from October 1894 that offered private houses to lease. Altogether, the two men – plus a small team of detectives loaned to them by the police department -- checked out no less than 900 locations without coming any closer to a solution.

Feeling as though they had exhausted every possibility in Indianapolis, Geyer asked one of the local detectives about small towns that were nearby. He was told there were two they hadn't investigated – Irvington and Maywood. They tried Maywood first but struck out, so on Thursday August 27, Geyer and Gary took a trolley to the small town of Irvington.

There were no hotels in town for the detectives to check, so they turned their attentions to real estate agents. Near the trolley stop, Geyer saw a sign for an agency run by a man named Samuel Brown.

When they entered the office, Geyer asked Brown if he knew of a house in town that was rented in October 1894 by a man who wanted it for his widowed sister. He removed the now-worn photograph of Holmes from his coat pocket and handed it to Brown. The old man adjusted his glasses and stared at it for a long moment.

He looked up at Geyer and nodded. He did remember the man. He was not the leasing agent for the house – that was J.C. Wands – but he did have the keys for it. He told Geyer about how rudely Holmes had stomped into his office and demanded the keys and about the boy who was with him. He only remembered the pair because the man had been so disrespectful.

For a few moments, Geyer and Gary were both speechless. They stood there, feet frozen in place before finally exchanging a look and sinking down into the two chairs that were placed in front of Brown's desk.

The two detectives were in shock, but they recovered quickly and sprang out of the seats. Seeing the urgency in their faces, Brown volunteered to take them immediately to the home of Dr. Thompson, the owner of the rental property. The physician, who lived only a short distance away, was in his office when the three men arrived. Dr. Thompson took one look at Geyer's photograph and quickly identified Holmes as the man who rented his home the previous fall. He also told Geyer that a boy in his employ – Elvet Moorman – had seen and spoken with Holmes at the time.

At Geyer's request, Dr. Thompson sent his young daughter to fetch Elvet, who arrived a few minutes later. The teenager looked at the photograph and exclaimed, "Why, that's the man who lived in your house... the one who had the small boy with him."

When Geyer showed him Howard's picture, Elvet confirmed that it was the boy he had met. There was no doubt about it.

By this time, Geyer and Gary could hardly contain their excitement. With Thompson leading the way, they hurried to the house, which stood a little distance from Union Avenue on the east side of town. The detectives went directly to the cellar, which was divided into two parts. In the rear section, which was evidently intended as a washroom, the floor was made of cement. The floor in the front section was hard clay. Just by a glance, they could see that both floors were undisturbed. They decided to search outside the house.

The two detectives poked around the house while the others watched, trying to stay out of the way. Geyer walked along the small wooden porch that extended from the right side of the house. The sides were enclosed with thin, wooden latticework. As Geyer peered through the crosshatches of lattice, something caught his eye. Prying off the porch steps, he squeezed himself underneath and began dragging a wooden trunk out into the sunlight.

For many weeks, Geyer had been bothered by the mystery of the children's missing trunk, but now he was certain that the mystery had been solved. The trunk had been found – but what was inside?

He carefully opened it, only to find the trunk was empty. Geyer carefully examined it and noticed a strip of blue calico, about two inches wide and printed with white flowers, which had been pasted along an inside seam, evidently as a patch. There was nothing else about it that was out of the ordinary.

This meant that Howard had likely been buried somewhere on the property. Crawling back under the porch again, Geyer noticed a place where it looked as though the dirt had been disturbed. Excited, he called for help and a few men with shovels crowded into the cramped space and began to dig. They moved

The cottage in Irvington that Holmes had rented with Howard Pitezel – who went missing soon after

several feet of dirt before Geyer called a halt – they would have been able to smell human remains by then.

Geyer, Gary, and their team searched for the next several hours without turning up anything but the trunk. By then, there were reporters at the scene and news was starting to spread. A crowd of a few hundred people had gathered near the house, milling about, gawking, and seriously impeding the investigation. The detectives planned to leave, regroup, and return to the house that evening to begin an all-night search.

On their way to dinner, they stopped at a Western Union office and sent a message to Carrie Pitezel in Illinois:

DID MISSING TRUNK HAVE STRIP OF BLUE CALIFO OVER SEAM? STOP. WHITE FIGURE ON BOTTOM. STOP. PLEASE REPLY AT ONCE. STOP.

They were waiting for a reply when a telephone call came in from the *Indianapolis Evening News*, requesting that the detectives come immediately to the newspaper's office. When he arrived, the city editor told him that he had an urgent message from a doctor named Barnhill – Dr. Thompson's partner. Barnhill was on his way with something important and wanted Geyer to wait for him at the newspaper office.

A short time later, Dr. Barnhill hurried in. He was carrying a little bundle, and he unwrapped it on the city editor's desk. Inside of the paper were several charred fragments of human bone –

part of a femur and a chunk of skull. Barnhill was convinced that the remains were those of a child between the ages of eight and twelve.

He explained that after the detectives had left, he and Dr. Thompson had continued to search the premises. At the same time, a pair of neighborhood boys named Walter Jenny and Oscar Kettenbach decided to "play detective" in the cellar. There was a chimney located in the rear part of the cellar and, sticking his hand into the pipe hole, Walter pulled out a big handful of ashes. Among those ashes was a burned chunk of bone. Reaching in again, he pulled out more ashes and bones. At that point, the boys ran to fetch the doctors.

The detectives rushed to the house to investigate the chimney at once but when they arrived, the cottage was surrounded by hundreds of people. The town marshal was there, trying to maintain order, but he was not having much luck. It took them several minutes to get inside.

Once in the basement, they sifted through the pile of cinders, soot, and debris, separating out charred bones, buttons, pieces of scorched cloth, burned tintype pictures, and locks from a small box, the sort that Howard might have had to carry little toys and keepsakes in. And there were teeth – teeth that Dr. Barnhill confirmed were human and those of a child.

After two months of hell, Frank Geyer had at last found Howard Pitezel.

The evidence was carefully packed for the coroner, although one newspaper later

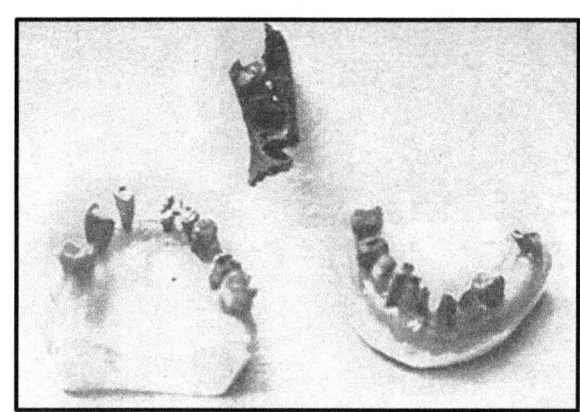

The scorched teeth of Howard Pitezel, which were found in the Irvington cottage.

claimed that the ashes from the furnace were tossed into the yard, where ghoulish spectators picked out small bits as souvenirs.

Geyer planned to turn the rest of the evidence over to the authorities, to be used against Holmes in case he beat the prosecutors in Philadelphia or Toronto.

Even though the discoveries of the day would have been the stuff of nightmares for most men, Frank Geyer slept peacefully that night, for the first time in two months.

But he wouldn't rest for long. The mission to find Howard Pitezel had been completed. He'd found the boy, peace, and a small measure of fame, but the overall task had not yet been concluded. As Frank Geyer later wrote:

All that had been unearthed would count but for little if Holmes were permitted to elude the firm grasp of the law or to avoid punishment.

The most important part of all this remained – H.H. Holmes still had to answer for the crimes that he had committed.

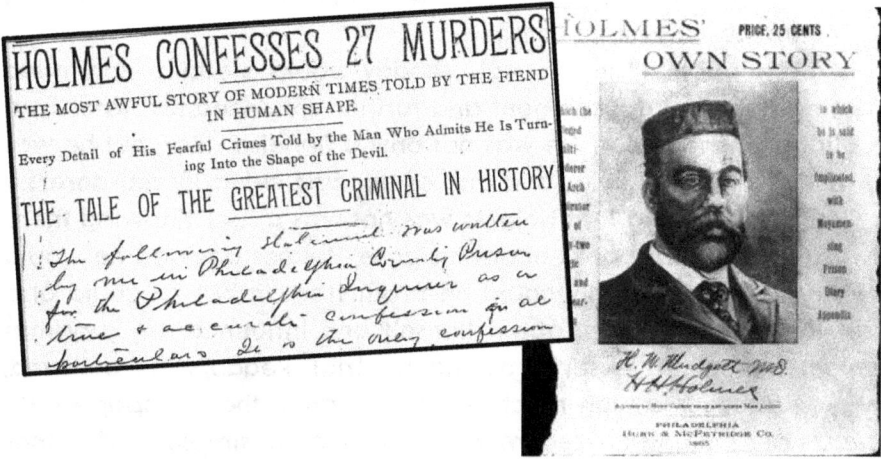

16

EVEN THOUGH THE "MURDER MUSEUM" PLANNED FOR Holmes' Castle in Chicago went up in smoke, this wouldn't be the last attempt to try and cash in on the infamy of H.H. Holmes.

In Philadelphia, for example, a man who operated a dime museum of freaks and wonders, drew in large crowds that summer by converting his establishment into a "Holmes Museum." Included in the exhibits were a scale-model replica of the Castle, phrenology charts that illustrated Holmes' cranial abnormalities, and a human skull that was allegedly identical to that of Ben Pitezel's.

For readers whose interest was not satisfied by the weeks of front-page newspaper coverage, the bookshops offered true-crime books on the case. Most were simple rehashes of what had already appeared in the papers, but others – like *Sold to Satan: A*

Poor Wife's Sad Story – offered new -- and completely fabricated -- stories about Holmes' career.

The publication of such shoddy books steadily continued during Holmes' imprisonment and further enhanced his status as a cultural phenomenon. He was not only a fiendish killer, but he was America's fiendish killer and one of our first celebrity murderers.

But one thing that Holmes was not was a fool. Knowing there was a market for books about his case, Holmes decided he would write his own. Not only could he profit from it, but he could also set the record straight about himself and influence any jury that might be called to serve during his trial. Readers, he believed, would discover a man much different than in the newspapers. He was not a blood-crazed monster; he was a simple and rather unsuccessful crook. He was "a swindler, yes, but innocent of murder." The book was allegedly an autobiography, but it was really just a public relations campaign started by Holmes and a freelance writer named John King. Written quickly over the summer, a book called *Holmes Own Story* was already on bookshelves by early Fall 1895.

The book sold for 25-cents and followed Holmes' criminal career from boyhood to imprisonment and was almost unreadable. It truly had no literary merit at all, and in the end, was mostly fiction. It was overwritten, self-serving, melodramatic, and wildly silly. To make matters worse, if readers were hoping for a lurid and bloody account of Holmes' crimes – and you can bet that just about every one of them was – they had to look elsewhere to find it.

It was filled with stories that have since become part of Holmes' mythology – in other words, outright lies, concocted by Holmes, that have since become accepted as fact because modern writers have forgotten the source of the information was an unrepentant liar.

If *Holmes Own Story* had any distinction at all, it was in the book's stunningly self-justifying quality. The book managed to rationalize everything that Holmes admitted to doing. For 200 pages, the reader couldn't help but be amazed as Holmes managed to avoid blame for everything he ever did. And when the irrefutable facts made it impossible for him to do so, he did the same thing each time – he refused to acknowledge their existence. Because of this, he made no mention of his first wife, Clara Lovering, or even his second, bigamous marriage to Myrta Belknap.

He admitted to cheating insurance companies with phony corpses but shrugged it off. Such stories were recounted as comedies of error, trying to give the reader that idea that Holmes was being open and honest with the reader but managed instead to convey a smirking, self-satisfied tone that crept into the narrative in a way that made it obvious he thought he deserved credit for the ingenuity of his schemes.

Honestly, though, Holmes just came across as a sociopath and made it clear why laws have since been passed that make it illegal for criminals to publish things like this and profit from their bad acts.

Some of the stories were so convoluted that I can't even paraphrase them to make sense, but he did present a very bad image of Ben Pitezel – calling him a bitter, hopeless failure who neglected his children, abused his wife, and eventually took his own life in a fit of drunken despair. Holmes did this, he said, to counter the "horrible aspersions cast upon himself" by casting horrible aspersions on a dead man who considered Holmes a friend.

Even more insulting was the image he created of Minnie Williams as a hardened sophisticate with a very checkered past. Holmes claimed that she had been seduced and betrayed by various lovers, suffered a nervous collapse after aborting an illegitimate child, killed her own sister in a jealous rage, and ultimately fled to London to open a "massage establishment."

What the book also succeeds in doing was that managed to show that Holmes was no criminal mastermind. He believed that he was a genius, but he wasn't. His schemes were largely ridiculous and transparent and only worked because he was convincing enough to fool people who were even less clever than he was. He took advantage of those who believed in him and for a time, he got away with it. His book was poorly written, painfully bad, and an obvious example of Holmes' belief that he was much smarter than he was.

Shameless to the final page, Holmes concluded by nobly insisting that his own fate was a matter of indifference to him, and that his only concern was to see justice served.

Prosecutors apparently felt the same way. The book was still on the shelves in local stores on September 23, 1895, when Holmes was finally arraigned in Philadelphia criminal court and his trial date had been set for October 28.

He was now officially running out of time.

THE TRIAL OF HERMAN MUDGETT, A.K.A. H.H. HOLMES BEGAN IN Philadelphia just before Halloween 1895. It only lasted for six days but the newspapers claimed that it was one of the most sensational trials of the century.

Holmes' notoriety had spread overseas and newspapermen from every corner of America were joined in Philadelphia by a contingent of correspondents from all over Europe. Local dignitaries, including the city's mayor, occupied front-row seats. Many of Philadelphia's most prominent clergymen were also in attendance, drawn perhaps, by the opportunity to get a firsthand glimpse of a man so evil that he must be in league with the Devil himself.

A crowd of onlookers began gathering outside of the courthouse before dawn, hoping for seats in the gallery. But the trial was the hottest ticket in town and anyone without some sort of political pull found it impossible to get inside. A squad of police officers was stationed in the entryway to maintain order and to screen those who came inside.

For the most part, ordinary citizens had to content themselves with reading the newspaper accounts. The front pages of every

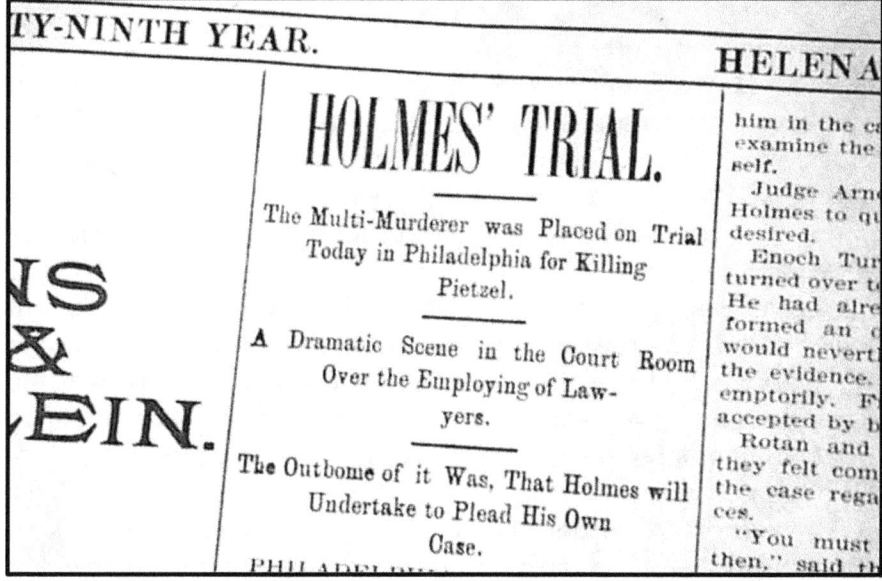

paper in the country were filled with blazing headlines, sounding a lot like the popular melodramas of the day, using phrases like "Holmes Fights for His Life," and "Mrs. Pitezel's Sad Story."

And indeed, the Holmes trial would offer the public a full range of theatrical experience, from tragedy to farce, with starring performances by characters people had been reading about. Anyone who came to the courtroom looking for a sensation didn't go home disappointed.

The judge presiding over Holmes' trial was Michael Arnold. The 55-year-old Arnold had graying hair and penetrating eyes that peered out from beneath bushy black brows. He entered the courtroom in a flowing black robe and took his seat on the bench.

No sooner had Judge Arnold arrived than an equally compelling character entered from the courtroom's side door, led in by a pair of grim-faced bailiffs.

All eyes turned to see H.H. Holmes as he took his place in the prisoner's dock, a waist-high enclosure of heavy wire mesh that was positioned next to the defense table.

During Holmes' imprisonment, he had put on a great deal of weight and had grown his facial hair into a heavy beard. But recently, he had transformed back into the sinister character that most expected to see. Thin once more, he wore a black, double-breasted suit that emphasized his jailhouse paleness. His mustache had been carefully trimmed, and he wore a neat Vandyke beard – looking a lot like the Devil that had supposedly been at his side when he was born.

After he placed his derby hat on the floor, he cast a defiant look around the crowded courtroom. Later, some would claim he was nervous and agitated when he sat down but if that was the case, he must have recovered quickly because he was about to put on one of the most remarkable displays of self-confidence that his audience had ever seen.

The trial's first order of business was jury selection. Before the first prospective juror could be questioned, one of Holmes' lawyers, William A. Shoemaker – who had rushed into the courtroom only moments before, having somehow managed to be late to the opening of the most important trial of his career – jumped to his feet. Speaking in a thin voice that could barely be heard in the restless courtroom, Shoemaker requested a continuance, arguing that he hadn't enough time to prepare.

Judge Arnold looked over at the prosecutor's table and addressed District Attorney George Graham. He asked, "Do you agree to this postponement?"

Graham rose to his feet. He replied emphatically: "I do not."

With his black suit and thick mustache, the tall and dashing Graham was an imposing figure. He was extraordinarily popular in the city, currently serving his fifth three-year term as district attorney. He added, "This motion comes within no rule of the court, except that it may be an appeal to Your Honor's discretion, and I strenuously oppose the motion for a continuance."

Unlike Shoemaker, who had to be told repeatedly by the judge to speak louder, Graham required no instruction. His voice carried to every corner of the room. He continued speaking to the judge:

Witnesses have been gathered from states far distant from here who are voluntarily in attendance and have come simply because of their duty to the cause of justice. I cannot compel their attendance, and I am quite sure I will never be able to get these witnesses here again. If a continuance is granted, it means the absolute destruction of the Commonwealth's case.

There is one person who has been subjected to an unusual – nay, an awful! – strain, and that is Mrs. Pitezel, the widow of the deceased. Her condition is such that it is absolutely perilous to the Commonwealth's case to permit it to go over again. These gentlemen had full and complete time for preparation. No legal grounds have been laid, and therefore I object to the continuance."

No sooner had Graham finished speaking than Holmes' other attorney, Samuel Rotan, a chubby young man with a face that was continually flushed red, leapt to his feet. He began barking out a protestation, "May it please this honorable court! This man is charged with a crime which is the highest known to the law! It is the purpose of the district attorney, as stated in the newspapers...."

Graham interrupted him. "I beg your pardon," he snapped at the other lawyer, "but my purpose has not been stated in the newspapers. On the other hand, the statements of the defense have been numerously and copiously quoted."

Rotan retorted, "I have only to say that I will leave it to those who read the newspapers to say where those purposes come from."

Judge Arnold banged his gavel and spoke up loudly, "We are not trying this case in the newspapers. The motion to continue the case is overruled. Let the jury be called!"

After this, Shoemaker cleared his throat and addressed the bench. His voice was still so soft that many of the spectators strained to hear him. The courtroom fell into a deep hush and his words drifted across the crowded space – with regret, he said, he needed to withdraw from the case. As soon as the words left his lips, an astonished murmur swept through the courtroom.

Judge Arnold again rapped the wooden bench with his gavel, demanding silence in the courtroom. He then turned and looked sternly at Shoemaker as he spoke, "Counsel, in a case like this have no right to withdraw. Your duty is to remain. Of course, I cannot force you to stay and do your duty. The remedy of the Court is – if counsel withdraw upon the eve of a murder trial without consent – to enter a rule on them to show just cause why they should not be disbarred."

Standing next to his colleague, Rotan jumped into the argument. Without a "reasonable" delay to permit them to gather the necessary witnesses, the trial, he insisted, would be a "farce."

But Judge Arnold was not swayed, and he ordered the bailiffs to call in the first prospective jurors.

The first juror questioned by Graham was a streetcar conductor named Enoch Turner. When he responded to Graham's initial question, Turner acknowledged that, based on what he read in the papers, he had already formed an opinion about Holmes' guilt.

Graham asked him, "Could you, notwithstanding that opinion, enter the jury box, and under your oath as a juror, try this case upon the evidence as you hear it in the courtroom, aside from what you might have read in the papers?"

Turner shrugged, "Well, I might."

"Don't you know whether you could or not?"

"I don't know that I could."

Graham sighed with irritation. He looked at Turner. "You are called as a juror in this case to try it according to the evidence. What I want to know is this: Can you not take your place under the obligation of your oath and try this man fairly and impartially according to the evidence as you hear it in the courtroom?"

Turner paused and appeared to be thinking hard before he replied, "Well, I hardly know."

Graham then asked sharply, "Haven't you the strength of mind enough to try this case according to the evidence as you hear it in court and lay aside these outside objections?"

Turner, his face red with shame, sheepishly mumbled, "Yes, sir."

He had finally said the right thing. Graham approved him for the Commonwealth.

During this questioning, Holmes had been huddling with his attorneys. None of them had been paying attention to what was occurring on the stand. When Graham was finished, Rotan turned to the bench and announced that his client wished to make a statement.

Holmes stood in the dock and addressed the judge, "May it please the Court, I have no intention to ask Mr. Rotan and Mr. Shoemaker to continue in this case when I see it is against their own interests. Bearing that fact in mind, I ask you to discharge them from this case. These gentlemen have stood by me during the last year, and I cannot ask them at this time to stay when it is against their interest..."

Rotan interrupted him, "We do not want the Court to receive the impression we are deserting this man. He now states that he would rather go on with the case himself."

Ignoring Rotan, Judge Arnold spoke directly to Holmes, "You cannot discharge them, Mr. Holmes. That is for the Court, and if they decide to withdraw from this case, they will be punished."

But Holmes implored the judge in a voice filled with sorrow, "If Your Honor will only give me until tomorrow to secure additional counsel."

A ripple of voices was heard in the courtroom and Judge Arnold again called for order. There would be no more debate. The judge turned to Holmes' attorneys and asked if they planned to examine the juror. If not, he would go into the jury box.

PROMINENT FIGURES IN THE HOLMES TRIAL.

But Rotan refused. The courtroom was shocked until he explained that Holmes wanted to examine the potential jurors himself. A surprised murmur now went through the crowd.

Rotan and Shoemaker returned to their seats at the defense table and Holmes placed his hands on the dock rail and leaned toward the witness stand. After putting a few questions to Turner – who admitted again that he had already formed an opinion about the guilt or innocence of the defendant – Holmes used one of his 20 challenges to have the man dismissed.

Once again, Rotan spoke up, "May it please Your Honor, there is no use at all for Mr. Shoemaker and me to stay here. The defendant is going on and will not allow us to do anything. We ask leave to withdraw. We do so reluctantly, and at the same time, it is with full appreciation of what we are doing."

HOLMES HIS OWN LAWYER

His Counsel Resign and He Refuses Court Appointments.

QUAKER CITY COURT SCENE

Beginning of the Case of the Man Who, If All That Is Suspected Be True, Will Be Found to Be the Most Horrible Impostor and All-Round Criminal of Modern Times.

Philadelphia, Pa., Oct. 28.—Herman W. Mudgett, better known as H. H. Holmes, the self-confessed life insurance swindler and the alleged multi-murderer, whose supposed crimes have been a topic for general discussion during the past several months, was placed on trial this morning in the court of oyer and terminer on the charge of having murdered Benjamin F. Pitezel. Judge Arnold presided.

The Commonwealth was represented by District Attorney George S. Graham and Assistant District Attorney Thomas W. Barlow and the defense was conducted by W. H. Shoemaker and Samuel P. Rotan.

In addition to the murder of Pitezel, the prisoner is also accused of the murder, at Toronto, Ont., of Pitezel's two young daughters, Alice and Nellie; of the murder, at Irvington, Ind., of the young son, Howard Pitezel, and also of the murder of various other persons in the famous Holmes castle at Chicago.

STORY OF THE ARREST.

Benjamin F. Pitezel's body was found in a house at 1316 Callowhill street on September 3, 1894. A shattered lamp was found by the side of the body which bore evidence of having been burned, and the coroner's jury concluded that the oil lamp had exploded and that Pitezel, who was at the time known as B. F. Perry, had been burned to death, and accordingly rendered a verdict of accidental death.

There was no claimant for the body and it was buried in Potter's field. Subsequently an assertion came from Mrs. Pitezel's lawyer at St. Louis, Mr. Jeptha Howe, that the body was that of Benjamin F. Pitezel, and a claim was made on the Fidelity Mutual Life Association of Philadelphia for $10,000, which that company carried on Pitezel's life.

The insurance company paid the claim.

The judge let out a loud sigh of resignation. He shook his head and then waved away the two defense attorneys as though tired of the sight of them. "Very well," he said. "But you will have to bear the consequences – and you know what they are."

At that point, as the spectators looked on in amazement, the two attorneys picked up their briefcases, put on their hats, and marched out of the room with their mouths set in a grim line. They looked straight ahead as they pushed open the doors and disappeared into the corridor.

It took a moment for the judge to restore order. When everyone had settled down, he turned to the defendant and said, "Mr. Holmes, you have discharged your attorneys. We intend to go on with the case, and you may as well cease your efforts to force a continuance. You are now your own lawyer."

With this pronouncement, Holmes began his performance. With a pencil and pad of paper in hand, he underwent an amazing transformation. From the humble man who had been choked with emotion just a few minutes before, he turned into a cool and collected figure who witnesses claimed would have done credit to the most experienced lawyer in the bar.

He worked his way through the jury pool, focusing mostly on the publicity that surrounded the case. He dismissed those who'd read too much about it but once challenged a juror for the opposite reason. A railroad watchman named James Collins made the outrageous claim that he had never read a single word about it. After the man was dismissed, Holmes turned to the spectators with an expression of such exaggerated disbelief that it brought chuckles from almost everyone in the gallery.

District Attorney Graham saved most of his challenges for those with a bias against capital punishment – making it clear what direction he planned to take the trial.

By 2:00 P.M., the panel had been sworn in. All of them, of course, were men. Women were not allowed on juries in those days.

After lunch, District Attorney Graham gave a nearly two-hour opening statement, offering a detailed account of the crime that began with the discovery of Ben Pitezel's body. He walked the jury through the exhumation at potter's field, the payment of the insurance policy, and the division of the money. Graham maintained that greed was not Holmes' only motivating factor in carrying out the murder of his accomplice. Pitezel's drinking had become so bad that Holmes feared that he might spill the secrets of Holmes' crimes. For this reason, Holmes had to make sure that his friend did not talk.

Next, Graham spoke of Holmes' fateful encounter with Marion Hedgepeth, of the double cross that provoked the notorious robber into betraying the insurance scheme to the police, and of Holmes' bizarre journey across the Midwest and into Canada with the helpless Pitezel family under his power and Pinkerton agents on his trail.

Graham explained to the jury how Holmes had moved himself, Georgiana, Carrie, and the Pitezel children around the country, making sure that each group was ignorant of the others. For the most part the story was a familiar one to the jurors since all of them had admitted they'd kept up with the case in the newspapers, but Graham managed to shock them when he insinuated that, during the night they had spent in Philadelphia at

Adella Alcorn's rooming house, Holmes had violated the innocence of Alice Pitezel. This suggestion brought gasps from many of the women in the audience.

Holmes, whose face had been set in stone as he made notes on a pad of paper, jerked his head up at this and started to rise from his seat, as though he was about to raise an outraged objection. After a moment, though, he seemed to think better of it, sank back into his chair, and returned to his notes.

Graham caused another sensation in the courtroom later when he recounted Holmes' failed attempt to kill the rest of the family with a bottle of nitroglycerin, a part of the sordid tale that had not been made public before.

Graham concluded his opening statement just as he had started it, by repeating that there was only one charge that the jury could bring against Holmes: murder in the first degree -- "the punishment for which is death."

By this time, with the clock approaching 5:00 P.M., Judge Arnold started to adjourn court for the day, instructing everyone to return at 10:00 A.M. the next morning. The bailiffs went to the dock to escort the defendant out of the room, but Holmes was not yet finished with his performance on the first day of his trial.

He spoke up, "May it please Your Honor, I am forced to ask that certain privileges be accorded me in prison. They are not very extensive privileges."

He explained that his cell lacked sufficient light for him to work at night and so he needed a lamp, along with his paper and writing materials so that he could continue to prepare his case. Then, looking defiantly at the district attorney, he demanded that he be permitted to interview a certain party - his wife.

Graham was ready with a quick retort, "Which wife?"

Holmes indignantly turned to the district attorney, "You well know who I mean, Mr. Graham."

Graham shrugged, pretending to be confused, "I don't know. I know you have a wife in New Hampshire and another in Wilmette, Illinois, and then there is Miss Yoke in this city."

Holmes replied, as if his pride had been wounded, saying that Graham knew he meant Miss Yoke and he wanted to see her.

But Graham told him that he'd had that opportunity, but that Georgiana wasn't interested and besides, they weren't legally married anyway. But Holmes insisted they were. They had been married and the only separation that had occurred between them since their wedding had been forced by the law.

Holmes insisted that Georgiana send him a letter so that he could see – in writing – that she did not want to see him. Judge Arnold interrupted their bickering by allowing Holmes to write a letter to her that would be delivered by a court officer. If she answered, it would be delivered to him.

Holmes answered, "I do not want it to be taken by any officer who is in any way connected with the district attorney."

After that remark, Judge Arnold grew angry, "Well, you can't get that. You can't have everything. You can't have the world. We have sworn officers of the court here. All you have to do is write her a letter and it will be taken to her by an officer."

Holmes grudgingly agreed, then made the claim that D.A. Graham had been intercepting letters that Georgiana had been writing to him for weeks. Graham denied the allegations and the judge piled on, suggesting that perhaps Holmes had received no letters from his wife because she hadn't written any to him. But he added that Holmes could write his letter and only Georgiana would see it.

Graham, though, couldn't help but get a final dig in, "If you don't hear from her, I'll have her in court tomorrow anyway."

Before the two men could start arguing again the judge assured Holmes, he would have a lamp and writing materials delivered to his cell. Holmes bowed and thanked him, and court adjourned for the day.

What was Holmes trying to accomplish with his final performance that day? Few believed he merely wanted to see his wife and fewer still believed that he was protecting Georgiana's honor by insisting they had been legally married. Many believed he had a different motive – by establishing that his marriage was legitimate, Holmes knew full well that a wife could not testify against her husband without his consent.

ON THE SECOND DAY OF THE TRIAL, HOLMES ENTERED THE courtroom through the door usually reserved for lawyers and took a seat at the defense table, not in the box for the accused. He was already making himself comfortable in his new role.

The antagonism between Holmes and Graham began before the first witness was even called. Holmes demanded maps and drawings of the Callowhill Street building where Ben Pitezel died. He also asked for a sample of the alleged nitroglycerin that was found in the Pitezel's rented house in Burlington so he could have it analyzed.

But Graham told him that he didn't have the liquid so there was nothing he could do. When Holmes claimed he lied about its existence, Graham reminded him that he had told the story about trying to destroy the house – with the family inside – in one of his many confessions.

Holmes dropped that part of his argument and Graham called his first witness of the day – Dessie Pitezel.

Wearing a dark gray dress and looking surprisingly self-possessed, Dessie only stayed on the witness stand for a few minutes. The 17-year old's testimony only consisted of her identifying a photograph of her father. Graham, however, stunned the courtroom when – after showing the picture to the girl – whirled around and shoved it in Holmes' face.

"Do you wish to look at it, sir?" he asked.

But Graham would have to do better than that. If he had hoped to unsettle Holmes, he was disappointed by his reaction. The defendant gave the photograph a brief, unblinking look, and then turned and asked Dessie a few simple questions. She answered them curtly and then was excused from the stand.

Holmes didn't go on the offensive until Eugene Smith was called to the witness stand later that morning. Under Graham's questioning, the carpenter and amateur inventor who had discovered Pitezel's body explained his part in the affair, beginning from the day that he brought his invention into "B.F. Perry's" patent office and concluding with his trip to potter's field to help identify the corpse.

Smith appeared to be comfortable on the stand, only becoming slightly timid when he confessed that he had recognized Holmes during the trolley ride to the cemetery but had failed to alert the authorities because he was afraid to say anything. More than one observer, after hearing Smith's testimony, was left with the grim conclusion that if the carpenter had spoken up with his suspicions about Holmes, tragedy might have been averted.

Holmes took over the examination from the district attorney and quickly scored minor points by compelling Smith to retract one of his statements. The man had testified that, on his second visit to the patent office, he had seen Holmes enter the office then proceed upstairs after gesturing to "Perry" to follow him. Holmes got him to admit that he'd seen two men enter the stairwell but had not actually seen them go up the stairs.

It was a nit-picking point and eyes rolled in the courtroom. The admission struck the audience as less damning to Smith's testimony than the self-satisfied smile on Holmes' face suggested.

During the rest of the time that Smith was on the stand, Holmes did his best to shake him up, but Smith stuck to his original statements.

Things between Holmes and Graham blew up again when the D.A. called his first medical witness, Dr. William Scott. Before the district attorney could ask his first question, Holmes stood up and asked that all the other witnesses be excluded from the room during Scott's testimony. He stated that he did not think that it was fair that the other witnesses should sit in the courtroom and receive the full benefit of the questions that were asked so that they could consider them and arrange their own answers.

Graham objected but the judge agreed to have any witnesses about what took place at the patent office or the potter's field removed from the courtroom until it was their turn to testify.

At Graham's direction, Assistant District Attorney Thomas Barlow picked up a sheet of paper and read off the names of the relevant witnesses, who filed out of the room. Holmes was still unhappy and insisted on seeing the roster since he didn't have his own list. He was convinced he was being tricked in some way.

Graham snapped impatiently, "I wish I could get this prisoner to understand that everybody is acting honestly in this case."

Holmes ignored the remark. He asked, "Is Jeptha Howe here?"

Graham replied, "Mr. Howe is in St. Louis, but he may be here later."

"And in regard to my wife?"

Graham snidely asked again, "Which one?"

Holmes face flushed with anger, and he spoke through clenched teeth, "The one you designate as Miss Yoke, thereby casting a slur upon her, as well as myself."

Graham shook his head, "That is how she wants to be designated herself. The man who laid the foundation of the slur is the man who married her with two other wives living."

Holmes barked out, "I shall challenge you to prove that!"

Graham smiled thinly, pleased that he had gotten a rise out of Holmes. "That we shall do" he said.

Holmes composed himself. When he spoke again, his voice had returned to its normal volume, "I ask if my wife is to be a witness and ask her to be excluded."

Graham still wasn't finished antagonizing Holmes. "If you are speaking of Miss Yoke – and that is the name she gave me, for she has the right to say which name she prefers -- I decline to inform you whether she will be examined as a witness or not. But she is in the courtroom, if that is a matter of any satisfaction to you."

Holmes sarcastically thanked Graham and took his seat.

After that, the examination of Dr. Scott began. Graham walked him through his first look at Pitezel's body, the condition of it and the contents of the second-floor bedroom in which it was found. It was clear that Graham wanted to use Scott's testimony to show that Pitezel's death could not have been caused by a chemical explosion or suicide. Scott agreed with this, stating that the evidence was not consistent with an accident.

Scott had also attended the postmortem, and he described the findings, all of which – the drained heart, empty bladder, paralyzed sphincter and congested, chloroform-filled lungs – pointed to one sensible conclusion: "sudden death through chloroform poisoning."

Graham asked him if a person who took chloroform could arrange his own body in the way it was found. Scott insisted it was impossible.

Holmes launched into a brisk cross-examination of Dr. Scott when the trial resumed at 2:30 P.M. He handled himself so professionally that even Judge Arnold nodded in approval at several of the points that he made. Even so, he failed to score any points in his favor against the druggist's testimony.

By the time the next witness was called – the coroner's physician Dr. William Mattern – Holmes began to seem under pressure. Pleading exhaustion, he begged for a continuance until the following day. He claimed that he did "not feel up to the strain" of cross-examining another major witness that afternoon. But Graham refused to agree to this motion and proceeded with his questioning of Mattern, whose testimony about the autopsy findings agreed with Scott's.

When Holmes took over for the cross-examination, it was soon painfully clear that no matter how shrewd and clever he was, he had reached the limits of his legal abilities. He hammered away at Mattern in a desperate attempt to find some vulnerable spot in the physician's testimony, but everyone in the room could see that Holmes was flailing about with no clear plan in mind.

Nearly two hours into the plodding cross-examination, Holmes began dwelling on such a small, insignificant detail – the size of the lancet that he used to remove the wart on Pitezel's neck during the exhumation at potter's field – that Graham could contain his impatience no longer. He bolted from his chair and angrily protested that Holmes was wasting the court's time on trivialities. Judge Arnold agreed and Holmes brought the cross-examination to an end.

By the time that Graham finished with Dr. Henry Lefferman, professor of toxicology at the Women's Medical College of Pennsylvania and one of the country's leading chemists, Holmes seemed like a defeated man. Lefferman acknowledged that people had been known to kill themselves with chloroform, but he insisted that it would be impossible for someone to do so and then "compose himself" in the way that Pitezel's body had been found.

When he cross-examined the witness, Holmes limited himself to a few dispirited questions. To the onlookers, he seemed like a different man from the confident one who had sparred with Graham earlier that day. The fight had gone out of him, and he seemed on the verge of surrender. When Judge Arnold announced his intention to continue the trial after a one-hour supper recess, Holmes begged him to reconsider. He claimed he had been suffering from a migraine all day and was becoming sick.

But the judge had no sympathy – the trial would continue.

THERE WERE MANY MORE EMPTY SEATS IN THE COURTROOM when the trial reconvened at 7:30 P.M. Most of the audience had gone home for the night – unaware that the trial, which was already filled with dramatic turns, was about to take another surprising twist.

The session started slowly that evening. Graham and his assistant ran late and kept the court waiting. After apologizing, the district attorney called for his next witness, but the bailiff misread the name, and it took several minutes to straighten the matter out.

During the confusion, Holmes suddenly rose and made a sensational announcement. He admitted that he had been slow examining witnesses all day because of his illness and, because they had been accused of deserting him, he'd asked his attorneys to return to the case. At that moment – like actors responded to cues – Rotan and Shoemaker strolled into the courtroom as audience members began to murmur. Walking to the bench, Rotan loudly began a long and involved explanation of events to Judge Arnold, but the judge silenced him with a wave of his hand.

Holmes reclaimed his seat in the dock, going from criminal attorney to just accused criminal in a matter of seconds. He breathed a sigh of relief.

The evening provided one more bit of final drama during Graham's questioning of Adella Alcorn, the owner of the boarding house where Holmes and Alice had stayed on the night of September 22, 1894, following the identification of her father's body. The landlady testified that after the pair had departed the next morning, she had gone upstairs to clean their rooms and had found a nightshirt in one of the beds and something else that was scandalous and that she insisted did not belong to her.

At this point, it was obvious to everyone in the courtroom that Graham was going to try and prove the insinuation that he had made during his opening remarks that Holmes had slept with the 15-year-old girl.

But what was the object that she found? The judge called the lawyers over for a whispered sidebar. As the lawyers approached the bench, the audience puzzled over the meaning of the mysterious testimony. Clearly, Dr. Alcorn had discovered something suspicious, even shocking, in Holmes' bedroom. Considering her comment that "it was not mine," some courtroom watchers surmised that the incriminating item was a female undergarment, which would have been "unmentionable" at the time.

But we will never know what was found. After briefly consulting with the attorneys, Judge Arnold rejected that portion of the testimony. A few minutes later, Dr. Alcorn stepped down from the stand, leaving the audience – and of course, the jury – to imagine the worst.

FOR MANY SPECTATORS, THE RETURN OF ATTORNEYS ROTAN and Shoemaker meant that the trial had lost the novelty of Holmes as his own attorney. But all was not lost in terms of entertainment value, for day three of the trial turned out to be the dramatic high point of the proceedings.

But until that moment took place, the day offered very few diversions. A succession of witnesses was called to the stand, including O. Forrest Perry and William Gary of the Fidelity Mutual Company. Their dry testimony, while important to the prosecution's case, had the audience stifling yawns.

The spectators stirred a little when Orinton M. Hanscom, deputy superintendent of the Boston Police Department, took the stand. Hanscom was something of a celebrity, having played an important role in the Lizzie Borden case a few years earlier as a detective for the defense. He was a dashing figure, but his testimony was as boring as the insurance officials' statements had been.

At the end of his testimony, Assistant District Attorney Barlow was asked to read the transcript of the statement that Holmes had made to the authorities following his arrest in Boston. Barlow got to his feet and read from what turned out to be merely the first of Holmes' confessions in a deep, dramatic voice.

He was roughly halfway through the document when a side door opened, and three figures entered the courtroom. One of them was Dessie Pitezel, dressed in the same gray outfit that she had worn the day before on the witness stand. The other was a stout, matronly woman, whose manner made it clear that she was a professional nurse. In between the two of them was a frail, deathly pale figure, wearing funeral black. Excited whispers ran through the audience – Carrie Pitezel was in the courtroom.

The audience members in the back of the room half-stood, craning their necks for a better look. However, their view was obstructed by the district attorney, who walked over to have a brief, whispered conversation with Carrie. A few minutes later,

Barlow reached the end of the document and Graham called Carrie to the witness stand.

On that day – Wednesday, October 30, 1895 – Carrie was just three months shy of her 37th birthday, but you'd never know it. Tragedy had drained all the youth from her face. Even if she never spoke a word in court, her appearance was damning proof to almost everyone of what a villain Holmes was.

One reporter wrote that she was "the very picture of human misery. Despair was written in every lineament of her colorless face. Big, dark circles marked her eyes, and heavy lines furrowed her cheeks – the indelible evidence of ceaseless sorrow and worry."

As she settled onto the witness stand, Carrie looked over at Holmes with a glare of bitter hatred in her eyes. At that instant, Holmes looked up from where he was furiously scribbling notes. The courtroom was absolutely silent for a moment. All seemed poised for a confrontation to occur between them.

But Holmes just looked indifferently at Carrie for a moment as if she was someone he barely knew and then nonchalantly returned to his writing. It was a cold, chilling moment for even the most hardened spectators and court officers in the room.

Carrie's testimony lasted for several hours. During her time on the stand, her voice was so choked and feeble that a bailiff often had to stand next to the witness box and repeat her replies in a louder voice. At various times, she became so overwhelmed that she had to be revived with smelling salts, administered by the nurse who stayed close at hand. Several times during the afternoon, her physician, Dr. Thomas J. Morton, stopped by the courtroom to see how she was holding up to the strain.

Meanwhile, Holmes was totally disengaged. He took notes of the proceedings, occasionally read from a book, and chatted breezily with his attorneys. He seemed entirely indifferent to the heartbreaking spectacle that was taking place just a few steps away – even when virtually every other eye in the courtroom was wet with tears.

MRS. PITEZEL TESTIFIES

Four Long Hours She Was on the Stand.

Her Pitiful Narrative Frequently Interrupted With Tears.

She Tells How Her Husband Was Spirited Away and Murdered.

How She Bade Her Little Ones Goodby, Confiding Them to Holmes.

Throughout the Shocking Story the Arch-Criminal Sits Unmoved.

Philadelphia, Oct. 30,—Four long hours to-day, under the scrutinizing gaze of a

MRS. B. F. PITEZEL AND DAUGHTER.

If Holmes was trying to appear innocent by not being affected by Carrie's suffering, he failed miserably. Instead, he gave the spectators – and the jury – a clear look at a cold-blooded, unsympathetic monster.

Gently guided by the district attorney, Carrie told the story of Ben, his death, and then in a barely audible voice, often interrupted by sobs, she described how Holmes had taken away Alice, Nellie and Howard, then kept her moving from city to city until – crazed by confusion and worry – she found herself arrested by the Boston police.

It was a familiar story to everyone who had been reading the newspapers over the course of the past several months. The details had been repeated endlessly by the press. But there was something different – something tragic and horrific – about

Victims of H.H. Holmes – The Pitezel family of Ben, Alice, Nellie, and Howard

hearing the story first-hand in the words of the tormented wife and mother who had lived through it.

Graham – who obviously considered Carrie Pitezel as the prosecution's trump card – handled the examination so skillfully that the evening headlines described the afternoon as a "field day for the Commonwealth."

At one point, he stepped over to the prosecution table, picked up something in each hand, and returned to the witness stand to offer the objects for Carrie's inspection. They were two small, faded pieces of cloth. At first glance, they were nothing remarkable but in truth, there was nothing ordinary about them. Many people, who knew where the scraps had come from, would have refused to touch them. Few would have held them in their hands, as Graham was doing, without a feeling of dread.

The objects were pieces of Ben Pitezel's grave clothes, removed from his moldering corpse during a second exhumation of his body in early September.

Graham spoke in a somber tone. "Mrs. Pitezel, I show you two portions of garments taken from a corpse in potter's field, this city, but since laundered. Do you recognize the material?"

Carrie's bottom lip quivered, and she began to weep into her handkerchief. It took a few moments for her to regain her composure and speak. She choked out her words: "That blue. It's the same color as my husband's trousers when I last saw him – when he left St. Louis."

She pointed shakily at Graham's other hand: "And that checked good. I made him a shirt out of goods just like that."

It was a powerful moment in the trial, and it produced its desired effect. Several of the jury members were fighting back tears and one or two of them cast dark looks at Holmes.

A few minutes later, Graham tore out the heart of every spectator in the room when he held up some of the letters that Carrie's homesick children had written, but Holmes had never mailed. He spoke again to Carrie, "Mrs. Pitezel, I wish to show you these letters at this time, solely for the purpose of identifying the handwriting. Look at them and hand them back to me."

He passed her a letter and asked her to identify the handwriting. Her hands shook as she examined the sheet of cheap paper: "Oh my God, Mr. Graham. That's..."

She could not finish the sentence. Overwhelmed by grief, she broke into wailing sobs. It was not until the nurse came to her side and administered several spoons filled with medicine that Carrie was able to identify the handwriting as that of her daughter, Alice.

But the most harrowing moment in her testimony was still to come.

Standing next to the witness box, Graham asked Carrie if she had seen her husband after he had left from St. Louis for Philadelphia in the summer of 1894. She said that she had not. The last time she saw him was on July 29. He then asked, "Have you seen or heard from Alice, Nellie or Howard since this man got possession of them and took them away from you?"

Carrie wiped her tear-soaked eyes before she replied, "No sir. I have not heard from them."

Graham then asked. "And have not seen them since?"

At this moment, Rotan raised a strenuous object to this line of questioning, insisting that it was irrelevant and would hopelessly prejudice the jurors against his client. Judge Arnold, however, ruled the testimony admissible, and Graham repeated the question.

"Have you seen your children since?" he asked.

Carrie's reply came in a pathetic, broken voice, "I saw them in Toronto. In the morgue. Side by side."

The audience, who had been straining to hear her answers, had remained utterly silent during her reply. All at once, cries broke out in the courtroom, jury members wept openly, and Judge Arnold reached into his robe for a handkerchief and wiped his eyes with it.

Rotan objected again, even though he seemed shaken and upset. His usually loud voice wavered and cracked, "I cannot see what motive there is to bringing in these children."

Graham wasn't putting on an act when he became angry and turned on the defense attorney. His voice raised in indignation, he demanded, "Was there not a motive for him to take Alice and put her out of the way – the girl that he sent to identify her father who was buried in potter's field? Was there not a motive for him to kill the child? How can we tell but what those children together had talked over what had taken place? Was there not a motive for him to have destroyed the lives of all three of them?"

Graham spun on his heel and pointed a shaking, accusing finger at Holmes, but the killer's face registered nothing but indifference. As they looked at him through their tears, more than a few of the spectators shook their heads in bewilderment and wondered once again what kind of monster he was.

ON THURSDAY, OCTOBER 31, THE LARGEST CROWD SO FAR CAME to City Hall, hoping to be admitted to the trial. The throng was hoping for a big show and Holmes gave it to them. By the end of the day, though, the spectators were sharply divided over what they had seen. Some were convinced that it had been Holmes' most remarkable performance so far. Others felt sure that, for once, he had not been acting at all.

Holmes' dramatic display was the result of Georgiana Yoke's long-awaited appearance on the witness stand. Before she could testify, Graham had to clear up the issue of her marital status. To that end, he first recalled William E. Gary, who had visited the

Holmes residence in Wilmette as part of his insurance company investigation and testified that the woman he met there – Myrta Holmes – was Holmes's actual wife. He also produced letters from Holmes in which he referred to Myrta as his wife.

Graham was still reading these letters when the door behind the jury box opened, and a young woman slipped silently into the room. Every head in the audience seemed to swivel at once in her direction. She was a captivating figure, clad in a stylish black gown, a black, broad-brimmed hat, trimmed with velvet and matching gloves. Holmes looked at her too – and a peculiar, stricken expression passed over his face.

Graham finished reading the letters, knowing that he had lost the attention of everyone present. But he had made his point. Over Rotan's objections, Judge Arnold announced his intentions to allow Georgiana to testify against Holmes. Holmes had called Myrta his wife and as far as the law was concerned, he and Georgiana were not married.

Interestingly, the judge did not even delve into the fact that Holmes had already been married to Clara Lovering when he married Myrta Belknap. This would have made his marriage to Myrta unlawful, too.

But on that day, Georgiana Yoke took the stand. The audience was transfixed by her charming appearance, and the reporters were absolutely enraptured by her.

It would have taken something extremely riveting to draw the audience's attention away from her – and at just that moment, the riveting event occurred. Something very strange was occurring in the prisoner's dock. H.H. Holmes was uncontrollably weeping.

The newspapers splashed Holmes' bizarre behavior across their front pages the following day. Holmes' nerve had finally deserted him, they claimed. As Georgiana took the stand, his eyes filled with tears and then he dropped his head down on his arm and began to sob. Two of three audible moans escaped his lips, and it took him several moments to regain his composure.

In hindsight, many came to believe the whole spectacle was simply another of Holmes' performances – that Holmes had been acting on the advice of his attorneys, who had urged him to show a bit of human emotion after his shockingly callous response to Carrie Pitezel.

Others, especially many of the women in the courtroom, contended that the outburst could not have been faked. One reporter said, "The emotion could scarcely be assumed. The heaving chest, the panting lips, were too real for that."

And perhaps his tears and panic were real – but I don't think that they had anything to do with love. Holmes's panic was caused by fear. Taking the witness stand in his trial was the only living person who could still expose secrets that the authorities were unaware of. None of the others survived. If Holmes truly believed he might be acquitted in the case, this was the one person who could make sure that this didn't happen.

Whatever the reason for his outburst, Holmes' reaction sent a wave of whispers through the audience.

The judge called for order, rapping his gavel on the bench, and once he regained control over the courtroom, Graham began his examination. Holmes dried his eyes and watched glumly as Georgiana began to testify.

During her testimony, Georgiana recalled her experiences with Holmes. She gave particular attention to his odd behavior on the afternoon of September 2, 1894 – the day of Ben Pitezel's death – when he had returned to their rooms, flushed and breathless, and insisted that they leave Philadelphia right away.

By now, Holmes had regained his composure and held an urgent, whispered conference with his attorneys. As soon as Graham finished his questions, Rotan stood up and informed the judge that the defendant insisted on cross-examining the witness himself. The judge did not object. Holmes slowly got to his feet and placed his hands on the dock rail. For a moment, it seemed like he might start crying again. He swallowed hard and dabbed at his eyes with his handkerchief.

> **HOLMES' WONDERFUL NERVE AND COOLNESS FORSOOK HIM YESTERDAY.**
>
> ## HIS WIFE TURNED AGAINST HIM
>
> And She Never Bestowed a Glance on the Man She Once Had Loved as, for One Hour and Forty Minutes, She Related a Story that Slowly but Surely Tightened the Noose Around His Neck--Holmes Conducted the Cross-Examination Himself.
>
> PHILADELPHIA, Pa., Oct. 31.—For about thirty minutes to-day, the nerve at which all men have marvelled forsook Holmes, and, bowed and broken, he sank his head into his hands and sobbed like a child. Meanwhile, the woman he persists in calling his wife, and upon whom he had pinned his highest hope, sat two yards away, relating a story

It was a disturbing sight – though its authenticity was undermined by a remark that he had let slip to his attorneys. As he was rising from his seat, a newspaper reporter that was sitting nearby overheard him mutter, "I will now let loose the font of emotion."

Holmes did his best to appeal to Georgiana by rehashing memories of their shared days of travel, but it did him little good. Georgiana remained aloof. She refused to meet his gaze and replied to his queries with short, cool, and formal answers. The cross-examination turned out to be a brief and undramatic affair, notable only for the theatrical quavering of Holmes' voice, as if he were struggling to keep his emotions in check. He seemed happy to finally dismiss the witness, most likely convinced that her testimony did little damage to his case.

Georgiana was followed to the stand by Detective Frank Geyer, which caused another buzz of excitement to run through the crowd. They expected a dramatic, first-hand account of the intrepid detective's grueling search for the Pitezel children – but they were in for a disappointment.

The defense argued that there was no clear evidence that Alice or any of the Pitezel children were killed because there were witnesses to the murder that Holmes was being tried for. In short, there was no reason for Frank Geyer to take the stand. DA Graham put on a passionate defense that the witness needed to be heard but, in the end, the judge agreed with the defense.

Judge Arnold said to Graham, "If he is found guilty of the one murder for which he is indicted, he may be sent to Canada or Indiana. But he cannot be tried for these extraneous offenses now."

This ruling meant that nearly three dozen witnesses – from Detroit, Indianapolis, Toronto, Vermont and elsewhere – had traveled all the way to Philadelphia for nothing. There was also a box filled with gruesome evidence – including the charred bones of Howard Pitezel – that would never be shown to the jury.

The decision was a serious blow to the prosecution and a disappointment to the spectators that were crowded into the courtroom.

Rotan and Shoemaker, on the other hand, were visibly elated. They had scored a major victory, the first one that they could legitimately claim in the case. Their tremendous win gave Holmes and his lawyers a sense of confidence that would prompt them to make a tactical move that would provide the final sensation of the trial.

HOLMES WAS COCKY AND SURE OF HIMSELF WHEN HE STROLLED into the courtroom at the start of Friday's session. He was relaxed, grinning and confident, sure that the damage his attorneys had done to the Commonwealth's case would win him an acquittal. He had recovered his old arrogance, and he cast a defiant look around the courtroom as he stepped into the prisoner's dock and sat down.

The prosecution spent most of the morning tying up loose ends. Both Carrie Pitezel and the coroner's physician Dr. William Mattern were briefly recalled to the stand – the former to identify her dead husband's shirt cuffs and the latter to confirm that involuntary movements of the bowels could occur "at or immediately after death," not "after rigor mortis sets in."

As soon as Dr. Mattern left the stand, Graham rested the prosecution's case. By then, it was time for lunch.

When the court came back into session at 2:00 P.M., the room was jammed to overflowing. Those who could not find seats pushed their way into every bit of standing room available. They had come to watch the defense start its case. According to rumor, Holmes himself was slated to appear as the first witness, perhaps that very afternoon.

Ten minutes passed, but the defense table and the prisoner's dock remained empty. The crowd grew more restless with each passing moment. Finally, at 2:12 P.M., Holmes entered and was taken to his seat. He was followed a few minutes later by Rotan and Shoemaker. The former looked flushed and nervous as he offered a bumbling apology to the judge, who accepted it with an impatient nod.

Three more tense minutes passed as Holmes' lawyers held a whispered conversation. Then, Rotan stood and addressed the judge, asking for a directed verdict, claiming that the prosecution had not made its case. They had proved Ben's body was present at the scene, but they had not proved beyond a reasonable doubt that anyone had killed him. In short, they were asking the judge to acquit Holmes of murder.

But the judge refused to consider it, "I decline to make any such ruling. The jury must find a verdict for itself. I will not express any opinion."

After another hurried conversation, the defense attorneys asked for another consideration from the judge – they needed a recess to decide what kind of defense they were going to present.

Judge Arnold let out an exasperated sigh and agreed to a half-hour recess. As Holmes and his lawyers made their way out of the room, a murmur went through the crowd. Something extraordinary was about to happen; they just knew it. And they were right.

About 45 minutes later, well past the judge's allotted time, Holmes and his attorneys returned. As Shoemaker sat down at the defense table, Holmes took his place in the dock. Rotan remained on his feet. He stood there for a moment, swaying slightly, and then he approached the bench and did something that no attorney in his right mind should have done under those circumstances. He announced that the defense was closing the case without calling any witnesses.

He announced, "We feel that – owing to our inability to bring in a number of important witnesses from other places – it is advisable for us to close the case now. We do this, Your Honor, also from the fact that we feel that the Commonwealth has failed utterly to make out its case."

It was the final – and perhaps most astonishing – turn in this already unusual trial. The defense was calling no witnesses on Holmes' behalf. It would submit its case on the final argument alone.

When the attorney's words became clear to the spectators, they let out a groan of disappointment. Judge Arnold loudly banged his gavel and announced that court was adjourned until 10:00 A.M. the following morning, when closing arguments would be heard.

BY 7:00 ON SATURDAY MORNING, THE HALLWAY OUTSIDE THE courtroom was already packed with hopeful audience members. Men, women and even some children pushed, shoved, and elbowed one another in a struggle to get close to the doors. No one wanted to miss an event they would be likely to remember for the rest of their lives. When the large double doors opened at 9:45, the crowd surged forward with a roar. Many of those who made their way inside only managed to do so by not being one of the unlucky ones who were pushed down or fell to the floor.

For the first time since opening day, the upstairs gallery was made available to spectators, and it was filled to capacity in less than a minute. A few of the female spectators had brought opera glasses and were perched on their balcony seats, hoping for a glimpse of the dashing defendant.

Holmes was seated at his usual spot, inside the prisoner's dock. He tried to write something on his worn note pad, but his hands shook so badly that he was forced to give up.

Just before 10:00 A.M., District Attorney Graham strode into the courtroom, but not surprisingly, Holmes' attorneys provided some last-minute melodramatics.

At 10:15, Judge Arnold began drumming his fingers loudly on the bench, staring at the empty defense table. Suddenly, Rotan rushed in to announce that he had just received word that his partner was ill – and he'd be right back.

He returned in five minutes and claimed that he had gone over the drugstore and found Shoemaker under the care of a physician, who said the attorney was in a state of complete nervous prostration. Rotan exclaimed, "Mr. Shoemaker says he is willing to leave the entire matter in charge of the court – that if the court feels the case should go on, he has no objection at all. I express the sentiment myself, but at the same time, of course..."

And here the ruddy-faced, out-of-breath lawyer paused: "I recognize that the defendant by law is allowed the right to have two speeches."

Once again, the courtroom was in an uproar. A brief battle followed in which Rotan insisted on his right to make both the opening and closing statements with Graham's final remarks stuck in between. Judge Arnold disagreed with his interpretation of the law, asserting that it was the prosecution's right to present the closing argument.

It was Graham who settled the matter, giving the crowd the impression that he was both generous and fair. Standing, he graciously nodded to Rotan and stated that since Shoemaker was ill and Rotan was in court by himself, "I propose on behalf of the Commonwealth to voluntarily waive my right to close the case. I will make the opening speech to the jury and leave Mr. Rotan the closing argument."

With this settled, Graham shuffled together a stack of papers and stepped in front of the jury box. He had a well-deserved reputation as a spellbinding orator, and his final statement was a masterful demonstration of his skills. He walked the jurors through the facts of the case, following a simple chronological path through the trial, paying close attention to medical experts, those who contradicted the idea of Ben committing suicide, the evidence of poisoning, the many confessions of Holmes, and of course, Carrie Pitezel's turn on the witness stand.

With withering scorn, Graham spoke of Holmes' initial statements to the police, calling them "wonderful statements, with scarcely an element of truth in them." He also described the myriad of lies that Holmes told to Georgiana, convincing her of his past, his "real" name of Henry Howard, his various aliases, and trips around the country.

His voice rose in indignation, "Think of it! Think of the deception and falsehood! Think of his deceit to her!"

Turning away from the jury box, he stabbed an accusing finger in the direction of the prisoner, who visibly flinched when Graham shouted his next words, "Upon every step, from point to point, as we go through this evidence, we find Mudgett, alias Holmes, a fabricator and a falsifier!"

Graham's speech ended quietly, as though after producing such compelling evidence of Holmes' guilt he no longer needed to be eloquent. He confessed that the story was strange and had many dramatic elements, but it boiled down to the fact that Holmes had committed murder. If the jury believed the Commonwealth had proven that fact, then it was their duty to find a verdict of murder of first degree against him.

He told them, "There is no middle ground. If this man was poisoned, then there was a purpose to kill, and it was a willful, premeditated, and deliberate murder, and this prisoner is responsible for the highest form of verdict you can render."

Graham's body visibly slumped. After thanking the jury for their patience and earnest attention, he gave a quick bow and returned to his seat. The appreciative murmur of the crowd made it clear that if the courtroom had been a theater, Graham would have received a resounding round of applause.

Samuel Rotan's closing argument did not begin until 3:00 P.M., following a one-hour break for lunch. In addition to their meal, the jurors had a lot of information to digest from Graham's enthralling presentation. Rotan's speech turned out to be a good deal shorter than the prosecutor's and was not nearly as accomplished. When it was over, though, the young lawyer still received good marks from the listeners for presenting a worthy performance in the face of overwhelming odds.

Rotan knew that he was battling not only against the more experienced Graham, but also against the allegations and accusations that appeared in the press. He began by reminding the jurors that Holmes was entitled to a presumption of innocence. He could not be judged by what had appeared in the newspapers.

Cleverly – and very necessarily, since the defense presented no case of its own – Rotan used the Commonwealth's witnesses to his own advantage. He didn't challenge their testimony. Instead, he freely conceded that they were telling the truth but argued that their statements bolstered the defense's position that Ben Pitezel had taken his own life. Holmes hadn't killed him.

Rotan also admitted that Holmes had manipulated Carrie Pitezel by promising to reunite her with her husband. But here, too, he argued, there was nothing to suggest that Holmes was guilty of any crime worse than insurance fraud. Holmes was simply trying to maneuver Carrie to get her out of the country. Since she knew of the insurance scheme, he could not very well have left her in St. Louis, or at her parents' home in Illinois. She could have been found by the police and could have been turned against him as a witness to fraud. He couldn't tell her that her husband was dead – having killed himself, of course – because she might be then unwilling to come along with him.

He also claimed that Holmes had voluntarily returned to Philadelphia to try and sort out the matter of Ben's death. Would a murderer do something so risky?

Rotan began bringing his argument to a close and he pointed to Holmes, sitting in the prisoner's dock before he urged the jury to only consider the evidence they heard in court when determining his client's fate – not the windy performance of the district attorney or the lies printed in the newspapers.

Rotan then spoke his final words with all the assurance that the nervous, sweating young man could muster:

I now let this case go to you with a great deal of confidence – so much confidence that we have not put on a defense. We feel that the Commonwealth has failed in removing the reasonable doubt to which the prisoner is entitled, and that we can safely rely upon this case going to you and you rendering a verdict of not guilty.

The judge followed the closing with his instruction to the jury, explaining that that while the jurors had it in their power to find Holmes guilty of second-degree murder or manslaughter, neither of those verdicts would be in accord with the evidence. He could either be acquitted or found guilty of murder in the first degree.

When he finished, Judge Arnold removed his reading glasses and placed his notes on his desk. He looked gravely at the men in the jury box before he spoke, "Consider this defendant's case calmly, considerately, patiently. I have no doubts that if you do that, if you adhere to the evidence, you will have no trouble in reaching a righteous verdict."

It was almost 6:00 P.M. when the jurors were escorted out of the courtroom by a contingent of officers. As soon as they were locked away in seclusion, Graham – keeping a promise that he had made to the press corps a few days before – led the reporters into his office and allowed them to examine a cache of evidence that, as one reporter stated, "left no doubt that Holmes was a scoundrel unworthy of human form."

These grisly items, which had been barred from the trial by Judge Arnold's ruling, included Howard Pitezel's charred jawbone and several of his teeth, the stove in which the boy had been cremated, and the spade which Holmes used to bury the bodies of Alice and Nellie. Graham also displayed Ben Pitezel's skull, which had been removed from the corpse during the most recent exhumation, when the authorities had also retrieved the pieces of his clothing identified by Carrie.

As the relics were examined and passed around the room, Graham noticed an unfamiliar face among the reporters. The man was closely examining Pitezel's skull. Graham confronted the man, who turned out to be C.A. Bradenburgh, proprietor of the local Holmes Museum. He had slipped into the room with the reporters. He had been making a fortune over the past few months displaying a replica of Ben's skull – would the Commonwealth be interested in selling him the original?

Graham cried out, "Indeed not!"

He snatched the skull out of the man's hands and showed him unceremoniously to the door.

Holmes, meanwhile, had been taken to a cell in the basement of City Hall to await the verdict. Although he was disinterested in the supper that he was offered, he seemed remarkably confident for a man whose fate was in the hands of 12 strangers. He chatted with his jailers and passed the time flipping a coin, thumbing it into the air, catching it on his palm and slapping it onto the back of his opposite hand.

When one of the guards asked him what he was doing, Holmes replied that he was trying to predict the verdict with a coin toss. Altogether, Holmes flipped the coin ten times.

It came up heads – "not guilty" – every time but one.

At precisely 8:45, an announcement was made that the jury was about to return. Judge Arnold was the first back in the courtroom, followed by Graham and his assistant, Thomas Barlow.

Rotan and Shoemaker quickly followed, the latter bundled into an overcoat and shivering as though he was seriously ill. Finally, the prisoner was ushered in and led to the dock.

The silence in the courtroom was almost oppressive. Every eye was focused on Holmes, who stood in the dock, with his hands behind his back. He showed no signs of nervousness, although spectators sitting directly behind him later reported seeing how tightly he gripped his wrist, as evidenced by the whiteness of his knuckles.

A few moments later, the jury filed in. None of them looked in Holmes' direction as they took their places. When Holmes saw the grim expressions on their faces, his own face turned a deathly shade of white. He let out a few dry, choking coughs, raising a trembling hand to his mouth.

The clerk asked the jury if they had reached a verdict and the foreman replied that they had. Judge Arnold nodded and the clerk turned back to the jurors and asked them to rise.

The jury all rose to their feet. The clerk then asked, "Gentlemen of the jury, how say you? Do you find the prisoner at the bar, Herman W. Mudgett, guilty of the felony of murder, whereof he stands indicted, or not guilty?"

Without hesitating, the foreman spoke, "Guilty of murder in the first degree."

Holmes compressed his lips into a thin line and then sank into his seat.

When it was over, one of the jurors told a reporter that he and his colleagues had arrived at their fateful decision before the door of the deliberations room had even been closed behind them. But – believing that it didn't seem proper to send a man to the gallows without even the appearance of due consideration – they had decided to have supper and discuss the case before delivering their judgment.

HOLMES FOUND GUILTY.

JURY AGREED WHEN IT LEAVES THE COURT-ROOM.

Brings In a Verdict of Murder in the First Degree After Remaining Out of the Court-Room Some Time for Decency's Sake—Murderer Gives No Sign of Nervousness and Complains of Injustice—Only Two Speeches Made—Motion for New Trial Nov. 18.

As the trial was adjourned, Holmes was returned to the basement holding cell. A mob of reporters quickly gathered outside of the iron door, pleading for comment.

He told them he had nothing else to say.

A few minutes later, he was taken to a van and returned to Moyamensing prison. By the time he was back in his all-too-familiar cell, he had found his words. He sat down at his small writing desk and composed a formal statement.

He did not blame his lawyers for their work – he blamed the system in which an innocent man could be tried and still be found guilty. He trusted in the appeal process, he said, believing he would be given a new trial. He wrote:

I did not murder Pitezel. He committed suicide. I am innocent of the charge against me. I cannot possibly be condemned for a crime which I did not commit.

This statement of innocence was published in newspapers all over the country the next day, but it would not be Holmes' final word. A few months later, he would write another, very different statement – and it would be one that would shock the entire country.

HOLMES CONFESSES TO MANY MURDERS!

That's what the headline of the April 10, 1896, edition of the *Philadelphia Inquirer* practically shouted at readers when they picked up the morning paper. The stunning story took up half of the front page and sold so many newspapers that day that the publishers set a new sales record for a single edition.

After spending months proclaiming his innocence and blaming his conviction on a district attorney who had railroaded him to the gallows because of his own political ambitions, H.H. Holmes had experienced a change of heart.

Some believed that perhaps he wished to unburden himself before going to meet his maker, while those with first-hand knowledge of Holmes's devious nature suspected his motives weren't so pure.

As it was, Holmes had nothing to lose. His appeals had all been rejected and his sentence to hang was upheld. The date for his execution had been set for May 7.

He had nothing to lose but he did have something to gain from publicizing his crimes. A month earlier, he had been visited by a representative of newspaper owner William Randolph Hearst. He was offered $7,500 for exclusive rights to his confession, which was a considerable sum in 1896. Holmes planned to give the money to Myrta so she could care for herself and their daughter, Lucy. Hearst was offering a lot of money and Homes planned to make his new confession worth every penny.

But money was only part of the motive. Holmes had another, even more powerful need that was more in keeping with his twisted personality. A newspaper reporter who had recently visited Holmes in his cell had noted that Holmes seemed desperate to be great in some way – a villain of the highest degree.

His arrangement with Hearst had been accurately predicted months earlier by District Attorney Graham, who told the press that he was convinced that Holmes would confess fully when he realized all hope of escape was gone. Before he died, Graham had said, he would make a confession that would help him achieve the highest possible rank of criminal.

And on that April Sunday, Holmes announced himself as the most monstrous criminal of the day, a notorious killer whose record of murder might never be topped. Whether largely truth, mostly fiction or – most likely – a mixture of both, Holmes' final confession guaranteed that his name would live on for decades to come.

ONCE THE INNER WORKINGS OF THE "MURDER CASTLE" IN Chicago were revealed to the world, Holmes hysteria peaked, and the newspapers began making all kinds of claims about the number of victims the killer had dispatched during his bloody career. The numbers ranged from dozens into the hundreds.

Even today, when more valid research is available, many sensational writers still try to thrill their readers with claims of 300 or even more.

Or they claim he was Jack the Ripper, so it could be worse, I suppose.

But we'll never actually know for certain how many people Holmes killed. According to his final confession, the number of victims he claimed was much smaller than anything printed in the newspapers of the era – but even so, it still made him one of the most prolific murderers in American history.

Because, according to H.H. Holmes, he had killed 27 men, women, and children.

Although Holmes promised to reveal the motive for his crimes in his final printed confession, he never actually did so. Instead, he simply listed his victims, starting with a friend and schoolmate named Dr. Robert Leacock, who he said he murdered in 1886. His life had been insured for a large sum.

Another physician, a man named Russell, became Holmes' second victim. Russell was a tenant of the Castle who had fallen behind in his rent. During a heated argument over the matter, Holmes struck him with a heavy chair and killed him. Russell's corpse became the first of many that he sold to an acquaintance at a medical college.

Julia Connor and her four-year-old daughter, Pearl, were next. Holmes is vague about Julia's murder, hinting that her death was due to a criminal operation, which we can assume was an abortion. He did away with the little girl to get rid of a potential witness. He had poisoned her because he believed that she might be old enough to remember her mother's death.

The fifth murder was the cold-blooded killing of a man identified only Henry Rogers, a fellow tenant of a boarding house in Morgantown, West Virginia, where Holmes was staying for a few weeks during a business trip. He stated that after learning the man had some money, he convinced him to go on a fishing trip with him and then ended his life by hitting him over the head with a boat oar.

His sixth victim also died from a fractured skull, although in this case, Holmes claims that the fatal blow was struck by an accomplice. The dead man was a speculator named Charles Cole, who Holmes had enticed to the Castle as a possible investor in one of his phony devices. While in the

cellar, the man was struck in the head with a gas pipe by an unnamed accomplice. Holmes' only regret was that the blow had rendered the man's skull unusable as a medical specimen. He admitted that while he did not kill the man with his own hands, he considered himself responsible for his murder.

A domestic servant named Lizzie was his seventh victim. She had worked in a restaurant at the Castle. Pat Quinlan – a married man with several small children – had become infatuated with the girl and, concerned that his indispensable assistant might run off with the young woman, Holmes had killed her. He brought her into his office and locked her in the airtight vault, where she suffocated. Before her death, he had forced her to write letters to her family and to Quinlan stating she had left Chicago for a western state and would not return.

During the exposure of the Castle, Holmes was presented as a Bluebeard-type character – a legendary lady-killer who butchered each of his successive brides when she opened a forbidden door and discovered the corpses of her predecessors. Holmes' accounting of his next crimes makes the analogy seem disturbingly fitting.

The murders that Holmes next described occurred immediately after Lizzie's killing – in fact, on the very evening that Holmes was getting the corpse of Quinlan's sweetheart ready to be sent to a medical college. Among the tenants of the Castle at that time were a man named Frank Cook, his wife, Sarah, and Sarah's niece, Mary Haracamp of Hamilton, Canada, who shortly after arriving in Chicago, became a stenographer for Holmes.

For reasons that Holmes never explains, Sarah and her niece had access to all the rooms in the Castle by means of a master key. On the evening in question, Holmes was busy preparing Lizzie's body when the two women opened the door of the room where he was working and walked in.

When they saw the body, they were horrified. Holmes overpowered them and forced them into the same airtight vault where Lizzie had died. What made the crime even more horrible was that Sarah was pregnant at the time. Counting that unborn child, Holmes' murder count had now reached 10.

The lovely Emeline Cigrand became victim number 11. For the first time, Holmes confirmed what the police had suspected for months -- that he had murdered the young woman by suffocating her in his vault. He had done this, he claimed, because Emeline had become engaged, and Holmes could not stand this because was not only his secretary but his mistress.

On the day that she was supposed to get married, Emeline came to Holmes' office to say goodbye. Tricking her into the vault, he locked the door behind her, only promising to release her if she wrote a letter to her fiancé and called off the wedding. She wrote the letter, but Holmes never let her out.

It was, in his mind, a fitting punishment for her betrayal.

Holmes then goes on to describe a botched attempt at a triple murder. Apparently hard up for cash and eager to collect the money that was paid to him by his agent for medical cadavers, he attempted to kill three young women who worked for him in his restaurant on the Castle's ground floor.

Late at night, he sneaked into the Castle rooms where they stayed and attacked them in their sleep using chloroform. He tried to kill them all at once and they fought back, overpowering him. They ran screaming into the street, clad only in their nightgowns.

Holmes was more successful with his next victim, a beautiful young woman named Rosine. After living with her for a time at the Castle, he poisoned her and then buried her remains in the basement.

In the confession, Holmes claims that his bloodlust grew stronger with every murder, and this seems to be true, at least based on the sadistic cruelty of his next murder. This victim was a one-time Castle employee named Robert Lattimer, who knew about some of Holmes insurance schemes and tried to blackmail Holmes with the information. Holmes confined him in one of the Castle's many secret rooms and slowly starved him to death.

When he needed the room for some other, likely diabolical, purpose, he unlocked the door and found that the man had literally tried to claw his way through the walls, destroying his fingers as he flailed at the solid brick and mortar.

Suffocation, starvation, and chloroform poisoning were revealed to be Holmes' favorite methods of murder, which he also used to dispatch several other victims in the Castle – a woman identified only as "Kate;" a young Englishman, who had partnered with Holmes in several real estate scams; a wealthy widow whose name he could not remember, and a man who came to Chicago to visit the Columbian Exposition.

For the sake of convenience, or perhaps variety, he occasionally used other methods of eliminating his victims. He killed two women – Miss Anna Betts and Julia Connor's sister, Gertie – by substituting poison for prescription medicines.

He claimed to have killed a man named Warner – the "originator" of the patented "Warner Glass-Bending Process" – in an especially gruesome way. In the basement of the Castle, Holmes had installed a massive kiln, capable of producing great heat, because he was interested in going into the glass-bending business himself. Under the pretext of making some adjustments to the furnace, he managed to lure Warner inside it.

As soon as he stepped in, Holmes bolted the door and turned on both the oil and steam to their full extent. He wrote, "In a short time, not even the bones of my victim remained."

Victims number 21 and 22 were the William sisters. Holmes had finally stopped pretending that Minnie Williams was alive and admitted that his tale about her murdering her sister was a lie. Holmes apologized for casting aspersions on the young woman's good name and attested to her "pure and Christian life."

Prior to meeting Holmes in 1893, he stated, she was a virtuous woman. Soon after her arrival in Chicago, Minnie came to work for Holmes and it wasn't long before he persuaded her to turn over large sums of money to him, including her inheritance. He also induced her to into having sex with him, which he was able to accomplish, he said, because she was so innocent and child-like and didn't know her behavior was wrong.

Correctly perceiving that Minnie's younger and worldlier sister, Nannie, would be a potential threat to his schemes, Holmes invited her to Chicago, brought her to the Castle, and killed her in the vault. He writes, "It was the footprint of Nannie Williams that was found on the painted surface of the vault door, made during her violent struggles before death."

Minnie was murdered soon after. According to this version of the story, Holmes took her on a trip to Momence, Illinois, and in an abandoned house on the edge of town, he poisoned her and buried her in the basement.

But Holmes was not yet finished with the Williams family. After Minnie's death, he discovered an insurance policy in her papers that was made out in favor of her brother, Baldwin Williams of

Leadville, Colorado. Holmes traveled there in early 1894 and murdered him. He justified this by saying that it was self-defense because if the brother had learned of the fate of his sisters, he might have murdered Holmes or offered his suspicions about him to the authorities.

It should come as no surprise that Holmes devoted the largest space to the crime for which he was condemned to death. After two years of denying his guilt, he finally admitted to Ben Pitezel's murder.

But he went even further than a simple confession. For reasons that we may never understand – perhaps a need to live up to the devilish billing that he'd given himself, or a showman's desire to make sure the reader got his or her money's worth, or possibly even a sincere need to confess – he portrayed himself in the confession as having been much crueler than even his prosecutors had suggested.

Holmes stated:

It will be understood that from the first hour of our acquaintance, even before I knew he had a family who would later afford me additional victims for the gratification of my bloodthirstiness, I intended to kill him.

He went to great pains to exonerate his late accomplice of any involvement in murder, declaring that Ben neither knew about nor had any knowledge of Holmes' murders. Of course, this just makes Ben's death seem even more undeserved.

And that murder, as Holmes described it in his confession, was far more horrific than anyone ever suspected.

Holmes recounted the two men's travels to Philadelphia and Pitezel's arrangement of the patent office, where he believed that a fake accident was going to be staged. Holmes then picks up the story on the morning of September 2, when he planned to commit the murder, since he had been waiting for Pitezel to be found in a drunken stupor.

According to Holmes, he had gone to the patent office, quietly unlocked the door, and went silently to where Ben was passed out drunk on the second floor. To keep him from fighting back, he tied Ben's hands and feet and then burned him alive by pouring a flammable liquid called benzine on his clothing and his face. He then lit a match.

Ben screamed in pain and Holmes admitted that it was so terrible to watch that he almost lied in his confession to make the death seem more humane.

Holmes' description of the death of young Howard Pitezel is just as shocking.

After purchasing drugs to poison the boy with, he took Howard with him to pick up surgical knives that he'd left at a shop to be sharpened. When they returned to the Irvington cottage, he gave him a dose of poison and put him to bed.

As soon as Howard stopped breathing, he cut his body into pieces and using gas and corncobs for fuel, he proceeded to burn the remains. He said did it "with as little feeling as though it had been some inanimate object."

As for his final victims, Alice and Nellie Pitezel, Holmes confirmed the theory that he murdered the girls by locking them in a trunk. He then inserted a rubber tube into the hole that he opened for the purpose, connected the opposite end of the tube to a gas jet, and asphyxiated them.

He said that when he opened the trunk, he looked down at their blackened and distorted faces and felt no remorse at the time. He also didn't regret digging shallow graves for them in the basement of the house, stripping off their clothing, and hiding them beneath the cold earth.

Then, to top it off, he admitted that District Attorney Graham had been right – he had ruined the innocence of Alice Pitezel. He wrote that "her death was the least of the wrongs suffered at my hands."

As though recognizing that his deeds and words damned him beyond all hope of human forgiveness, Holmes refrained from offering a conventional closing word of repentance. Instead, he ended his confession with these words:

It would now seem a very fitting time for me to express regret or remorse... To do so with the expectation of even one person who has read this confession to the end believing that in my depraved nature there is room for such feelings is, I fear, to expect more than would be granted.

BY THE TIME THAT HOLMES' CHILLING FINAL CONFESSION WAS syndicated in the newspapers, his notoriety had spread quite literally around the world. Under such circumstances, it is not surprising that this spellbinding story of bloodshed and torture was a major sensation.

But there turned out to be a small problem with it -- a large part of it turned out to be wildly untrue.

Holmes could not have placed the Pitezel sisters in a trunk and gassed them to death – the house he'd rented had no gas fixtures.

Not only that, but some of the people that he named as victims in his confession came forward to announce they weren't dead. Among those were the supposedly incinerated Mr. Warner – of glass-bending fame – and Holmes' former employee, Robert Latimer. A few others died from natural causes and one perished in a train accident.

It would be D.A. Graham who offered the most likely explanation for the issues with Holmes' story. He told reporters that Holmes' confession was just like his life – a mixture of truth and falsehood. Holmes could never, he added, keep himself from lying.

Whether the lies mixed throughout Holmes' final confession were compulsive or calculated, though, they ensured that his crimes will always be shrouded in mystery, ambiguity, and rumor.

Like one pile of bones that was discovered in the cellar of the Castle that turned out to be a jumble of human and animal remains that were impossible for the police to sort out, Holmes' final statement was as much purposeful confusion as it was confession.

EVEN WITH HIS EXECUTION DATE RAPIDLY APPROACHING, Holmes remained as bold and audacious as ever. In late April – just after confessing to the murders of more than two dozen people – he applied to Pennsylvania Governor Daniel Hastings for executive clemency. Not surprisingly, the governor declined to grant it.

But Holmes was not ready to give up. For a man who claimed that his appointment with the hangman was a happy event and one that would be a release from his days and nights of torture behind bars, he seemed desperate to gain, if not a pardon, then a temporary reprieve.

On April 30, just a week before his scheduled hanging, he sent a letter to Thomas Fahy, Carrie Pitezel's Philadelphia attorney. In it, Holmes laid out a complicated financial transaction related to his Chicago property. Holmes assured Fahy that he could work out a deal with his creditors that would yield at least $2,000, which he wanted to give to Carrie. He also agreed to sell his building in Englewood and give Carrie one-third of that money, as well.

Of course, there were problems with the offer. At this point, Holmes no longer owned the Castle. It had been repossessed by the holder of its largest lien. Plus, any legal matters that needed to be handled would take several weeks to resolve. That meant that Carrie and her lawyer would have to intercede on Holmes' behalf to get the governor to delay his execution.

Carrie refused to take the bait.

So, Holmes made another bid for borrowed time, writing a letter to Detective Frank Geyer. In it, Holmes claimed that his recently published confession contained an inaccurate version of the deaths of Alice, Nellie, and Howard. He wrote that while he took responsibility for the children's deaths, he didn't kill them – an accomplice did. Holmes offered to assist Geyer with the apprehension of this mysterious person in exchange for a delay of his execution.

But like Carrie Pitezel, Geyer had no interest in Holmes' offer. He was determined to see the man hang and would do nothing to delay that fateful day.

By Wednesday, May 6, Holmes had finally run out of ideas – and run out of time.

Back in November, shortly after he received a death sentence, Holmes was asked by a reporter if he planned to seek out comfort from "spiritual advisors." Holmes had shaken his head, and declared, "I am a fatalist. Whatever is to be is to be. I have no worries about the hereafter."

A newspaper illustration of Holmes spending his final days in his prison cell.

But as the date of his execution drew nearer, a change seemed to come over him – or at least he pretended that it did. Holmes lied about everything. He never told the truth if a lie, or series of lies, would better suit his purpose. He was incapable of telling the truth – perhaps even to himself.

Regardless, Holmes made the surprise announcement that he had converted to Catholicism just days before he was to be executed. During the final week of his life, he was receiving regular visits from the Reverend Father Dailey of the Church of the Annunciation.

By the end – after the failure of his last feverish attempts to gain pardons or reprieves – he accepted the inevitable.

On the night before his execution, he sat at his writing table until just past midnight, composing letters to relatives, business associates, and the surviving family members of many of his victims. At 12:15 A.M., he put down his pen, arranged his papers into tidy stacks, and began to undress, folding his clothes with his usual care. After performing his nightly prayers, he lay down on his cot, turned his back to the light in the corridor outside his cell, and was asleep within minutes.

He slept soundly until the next morning when the day watch, a guard named John Henry, came on duty. He roused Holmes from his sleep and asked him how he felt.

Holmes considered the question before he replied, "Pretty solemn."

"Are you nervous?" the guard asked.

Holmes smiled a little, rose from his cot and stuck his hand through the bars in the door. He seemed amused, "See if I tremble."

Henry would later tell reporters that Holmes' hand was "as steady as an iron bar."

He also detailed Holmes' activities of the morning, saying that after ordering a breakfast of toast, eggs and coffee, Holmes got dressed with the care of a man who seemed to have many more years to live.

It was traditional for condemned man to go to his death in a new suit of clothes. However, Holmes refused this tradition. Instead, he put on an outfit that he had worn many times before – a light gray serge suit with lapelled vest and cutaway coat. In place of a collar and tie, he knotted a white handkerchief loosely around his neck.

By then, Samuel Rotan had arrived. The sweaty attorney looked considerably more agitated than his client. After greeting the man warmly – Holmes apparently held no hard feelings at his courtroom loss – they sat down together for an earnest talk. The subject was Holmes' burial plan. His career as a corpse-stealer had left Holmes with an abiding terror that he would end up on someone else's dissecting table.

It was not an idle fear. Several prominent physicians had already declared their interest in autopsying his brain to see what had turned him into a criminal. There was also good reason for Holmes to believe that his body might prove to be irresistibly attractive to some ghoulish huckster with plans to put it on public display. Rotan had recently been approached by one such individual, who offered him as much as $5,000 for the remains of the world-famous "Murder Demon."

Holmes had devised an elaborate scheme – news that should come as no surprise – to protect his corpse from grave robbers. He was determined that his remains would never be violated, either by science or by the curiosity of the public.

God forbid that someone might steal his corpse and articulate his skeleton to go on display.

WHILE THIS UNUSUAL CONFERENCE WAS TAKING PLACE, AN enormous crowd was gathering outside the gray walls of Moyamensing Prison. They had no hope of seeing the actual execution, though. Admission to the hanging was strictly limited to ticket holders. Requests for tickets had come in from all over the country – over 4,000 in all – but only 60 tickets had been issued and each was filled out with the name of the witness so that no one else could use it.

Most of those in the crowd outside the walls were there simply to be part of a historical event. A line of city policemen was there to keep order, but the crowd was generally well-behaved – laughing, chatting exchanging crude jokes, and buying drinks and food from enterprising vendors. A holiday atmosphere surrounded the hanging.

At 9:30 A.M., a small doorway set into the prison's great wooden gate creaked open. Clutching their tickets, the witnesses pushed and shoved their way through the crowd, then filed past the guards into the prison yard. In the end, at least 20 unauthorized individuals – relatives, friends, and cronies of prison workers – managed to get inside, bringing the total number of witnesses to at least 80 and possibly more, plus there were more than two dozen newspaper reporters and dignitaries that included Dr. N. MacDonald, a famous criminologist from Washington, D.C., Sheriff Stephen R. Mason of Baltimore, Professor W. Rasterly Ashton of Philadelphia' College, L.G. Fouse, President of Fidelity Mutual, and of course, Detective Frank Geyer, who had sworn he would be there to see Holmes swing at the end of a rope.

There were also the 12 sheriff's jurors, there to certify the time, place, and manner of death of the prisoner. The jury members included three former sheriffs and four doctors.

For 15 minutes or so, the group milled about in the brick courtyard, where executions had been carried out since the prison was built in 1771.

But this execution would be different.

Suddenly, the door to the prison opened and the sheriff's jury members were summoned to the prison office, where Sheriff Samuel M. Clement administered their oath.

The rest of the spectators continued to wait, shuffling restlessly, smoking pipes and cigars, and watching the clock. At exactly 10:00 A.M., Sheriff Clement's assistant, Mr. Grew, appeared and ordered everyone to remove their hats. He then called out to them, "Witnesses will please form a double line, jurors in front, and head towards that door."

He gestured toward the doorway he had just come through, which opened onto the main cellblock of the prison. He called out once more, "You will please preserve perfect order. And no smoking!"

Hats were removed and cigars were extinguished underfoot. The men silently arranged themselves in a double column and then the solemn procession moved into the cellblock, the soles of their shoe quietly shuffling on the stone floor.

Although it seemed wrong for such a grim place and occasion, there was sunshine streaming in from the skylight overhead, illuminating the long, whitewashed corridor with its triple-tiered cells on either side. Halfway down the corridor, the gallows loomed. It was surrounded by a group of uniformed guards. As they approached it, the witnesses broke from their orderly line and jostled for the best positions from which they could view the execution.

More than 50 men had died on those particular gallows, which dated from the 1850s. On this day, it had been moved inside the prison. Its platform, with a rail all the way around it, loomed more than eight feet above the floor. It had been painted so dark green that it looked almost black. It had a double-doored trap and a crossbar overhead from which dangled a tight length of rope. In the clear light, the spectators could count the seven turns of the hangman's knot above the circular noose.

After their struggle for the best vantage points, the witnesses fell silent and waited for the prisoner to arrive.

AFTER HIS BREAKFAST, HOLMES PICKED UP HIS PEN FOR THE LAST time and composed a brief letter of gratitude to his attorneys. He wrote to no one else.

When two priests, Fathers Dailey and MacPake, arrived a few minutes later, Holmes turned his attention to them, and they led him through a series of prayers. The two priests had just finished administering the last rites when prison superintendent Howard Perkins and his assistant, Alexander Richardson, appeared at the cell door.

Perkins spoke to the kneeling prisoner, "Are you ready?"

Holmes nodded quickly and got to his feet. Clasping a crucifix in both hands, he stepped into the corridor. With Perkins and Sheriff Clement in front, the two white-robed priests at his sides, and Richardson and attorney Samuel Rotan bringing up the rear, the procession began the last walk of Holmes' life.

Clustered around the front of the gallows, the spectators did not see the procession as it arrived on the other side. But they could hear the prayers of the priests – a mournful drone that increased in volume as they drew closer.

Footsteps could be heard on the wooden steps of the gallows as Holmes began the climb to the platform on top. A few moments later, the faces of Sheriff Clements and Superintendent Perkins could be seen above the railing. The two men stepped aside and made room for Holmes to look out toward the gathered group of men.

The witnesses later said that they were struck by the neatness of his attire: his brushed suit, creased trousers, polished shoes. Holding the crucifix in his hands, he looked almost like a clergyman about to deliver a sermon on a Sunday morning.

He made his final statement:

Gentleman, I have a few words to say. I would make no remarks at this time were it not for my feeling that by not speaking I would acquiesce in my execution by hanging. I wish to say at this instant that the extent of my misdoing in taking human life consists of killing two women. They died at my hands as the result of criminal operations. I only state this so that there shall be no misunderstanding of my words hereafter. I am not guilty of taking the lives of the Pitezel family, the three children or the father, Benjamin F. Pitezel, for whose death I am now to be hanged. This is all I have to say.

Even as he was about to meet his death, Holmes could not help but lie. Did he do it because he believed that someone might be convinced of his innocence? Probably not.

If I had to guess, I would say that he did it for sheer, perverse pleasure. He would go to his grave knowing that he had thrown one more mystery into the mix. It was essentially a complete retraction of the sworn confession that he had published only a few weeks before, which was, of course, the beauty of it. Although no witness ever recorded it, I am convinced that when Holmes then gave a small bow and turned toward the hangman's noose, he did so with a sly smile on his face.

Holmes was given a moment to embrace Samuel Rotan, who turned and hurried down the steps, clearly overcome with emotion. Holmes, meanwhile, hitched up his trouser legs to preserve the creases, and knelt briefly to pray with the two priests.

When finished, he got to his feet and handed his crucifix to Father MacPake. He then stepped over to position himself directly above the trapdoor. Assistant Superintendent Richardson leaned toward him and whispered something in his ear. Nodding, Holmes removed the white handkerchief from his neck, fastened the top button of his coat, and then held his hands out in front of him. Richardson carefully drew one of Holmes' arms behind his back, then the other. The spectators could hear the subtle click of handcuffs being snapped around his wrists. Then, Richardson took something that looked like a black satin bag and pulled it down over Holmes' head.

Holmes spoke, his voice muffled by the cloth, "Make it quick, Alex."

Richardson then slipped the noose over Holmes' head and drew it down to his neck. He lifted the black cloth so that the rope was drawn tight against his flesh. By then, Sheriff Clement and Superintendent Perkins had backed away to the edge of the platform. The priests were still kneeling in prayer at the top of the steps.

Richardson removed a white handkerchief from his pocket and gave a signal that the spectators were unable to see. Almost at once, a heavy bolt thudded, and the trapdoor crashed open.

The black-hooded figure plunged downward, bounced back up, dropped again, and then slowly spun at the end of the tightly drawn rope. The man's head was cocked gruesomely to one side. His fingers clenched, his shoulders heaved, and his feet jerked in a horrific dancing motion, as though he was walking on air.

A deputy named Saybolt gasped aloud, cried out for God, and then fainted into the arms of the man standing next to him. Several other spectators also let out choking cries and turned away.

THE HANGING OF HOLMES

The Notorious Criminal Met His Death Fearlessly.

DIED PROTESTING HIS INNOCENCE.

Just Before Plunging Into Eternity He Declared He Had No Hand in the Killing of Benjamin F. Pitezel or Any of the Pitezel Family.

PHILADELPHIA, May 8.—Herman W. Mudgett, alias H. H. Holmes, was hanged in Moyamensing prison shortly after 10 o'clock yesterday morning. It was fully a half-hour later before he was officially pronounced dead. A half-minute before he was shot into eternity he made this declaration to the solemn assemblage gathered about the scaffold:

"Gentlemen, I have very few words to say. In fact I would make no remarks at this time except that by not speaking I would appear to acquiesce in my execution. I only wish to say that the extent of my wrong doing in taking human life

As the body hung there, twitching and twisting, Dr. Benjamin F. Butcher, the prison physician, stepped onto a stool provided by a guard and placed his ear against Holmes's chest. He announced loudly: "Still beating!"

Although the force of the fall had broken his neck, and the rope had pulled so tight that it had imbedded itself in his flesh, Holmes' heart continued to beat for nearly 15 minutes.

From time to time, his body would shake, and his limbs would twitch, but eventually, the convulsions ceased.

H.H. Holmes was finally pronounced dead at 10:25 A.M. on Thursday, May 7, 1896.

JUST OVER TWO HOURS AFTER HOLMES WAS FINALLY pronounced dead, undertaker John O'Rourke arrived with a wagon at the rear door of Moyamensing Prison. In the bed of the wagon was a plain pine coffin. Within minutes, Holmes' body was bundled out of the prison and placed in the box. O'Rourke immediately returned to his house and pulled the wagon around back, where two of his assistants waited for him. On the grass was an oversized casket and five barrels of Portland cement.

The wooden box was taken from the wagon, and the big casket was loaded in its place. Then – according to Holmes' wishes – O'Rourke and his assistants poured a 10-inch layer of freshly mixed cement into the bottom of the casket. Holmes' corpse, which was still dressed in the suit he was wearing when he was hanged, was laid in wet cement and his face was covered with a silk handkerchief. More cement was poured into the box and O'Rourke packed it tightly over the body. Once the casket was filled to the top, the lid was nailed down.

O'Rourke and his men drove the heavy box to Holy Cross Cemetery in Delaware County and transferred it to a receiving vault, where it was guarded overnight by – ironically -- two Pinkerton agents.

On Friday afternoon, May 8, a crowd of 100 men, women and children watched as two dozen burly workmen hauled the cement-filled casket up a wooden ramp and onto a furniture wagon. It was driven to a double grave that had been dug to a depth of 10 feet. Samuel Rotan had purchased the plot for $24. As the casket was carefully lowered into the ground by way of a wooden slide, Father MacPake spoke a few words over it.

When the brief service was over, the gravediggers covered the casket with another layer of sand and poured fresh concrete on top of it, two feet thick. They filled the rest of the hole with dirt.

Newspaper illustration of removing Holmes' casket from the cemetery receiving vault for its placement in the specially prepared grave.

Holmes' final wish had been fulfilled. His corpse was encased in several tons of cement, sand, rocks, earth, and stone. It would take an unusually determined grave robber – armed with drills, dynamite, and a winch – to get to his remains.

Eventually, though, someone would. The producers of a proposed television show managed to get permission to remove a DNA sample from the grave. There had been a rumor that Holmes had faked his death, and the fate of the TV show was riding on it.

He hadn't. The body in the ground really was H.H. Holmes.

The grave was restored, leaving the corpse of the killer to be imprisoned there forever. But whether his malevolent spirit rested in peace was another question entirely.

NO ONE NOTICED WHEN A MAN NAMED HENRY ROGERS DIED soon after Holmes' execution. It was a miracle he'd lasted that long since Holmes had claimed that he'd murdered him in his confession back in April. But Henry wasn't dead - not then. He died soon after Holmes did from bladder cancer.

The press did take notice, though, when the next death occurred. Dr. William K. Mattern, the coroner's physician who had been one of the main witnesses at the trial suddenly dropped dead from blood poisoning.

Coroner Ashbridge, Judge Arnold, and Detective Frank Geyer all suffered life-threatening illnesses during the following year. Thankfully, all of them survived. Ashbridge would later serve as mayor of Philadelphia.

The newspapers also publicized the death of Superintendent Perkins from Moyamensing Prison. One morning, a few months after Holmes' execution, he came into the office looking exhausted. He said that he'd been suffering from insomnia. He greeted his assistant, walked into his inner office, removed a Colt pistol from his desk, and then shot himself in the head.

That's same month, a lawsuit against Holmes that had been filed by the Stock Yards Lumber Company in Chicago was officially dismissed since Holmes was dead. Soon after, the company suffered an $8,000 loss when a fire broke out in their lumberyard.

On that very same day, a fire gutted the tenth-floor office of O. LaForrest Perry, the claims manager for Fidelity Mutual. He had stepped out for only a moment and when he returned, he found his office filled with smoke. The contents of Perry's office were destroyed by the flames, except for three framed mementoes -- the original copy of Holmes' arrest warrant and two photographs of the world-famous criminal. When Perry's secretary saw the unscathed souvenirs hanging on the wall above his charred desk, she begged him to get rid of them.

By now, sensational stories had started to appear concerning the "Holmes Curse." The trial was over, and the criminal had been hanged, but he was still alive and well in the minds of the public. His infamy lived on, and many began to follow the bizarre calamities that befell some of those involved in the case. Some even suggested that Holmes' spirit remained – taking revenge on those who acted against him.

But if it was revenge Holmes was looking for, why would be target one of the few men who tried to help him?

A month after the two fires, one of the priests who prayed with Holmes before his execution and conducted a funeral service for him -- Father Henry J. MacPake -- was found dead in the yard behind St. Paul's Academy on Christian Street. His skull had been fractured, and his nose was broken. However, the coroner ruled that he had died from uremic poisoning. Complications with kidney disease caused him to pass out and his wounds were sustained in the fall. But some doubted that verdict. MacPake was only 30 and some of the witnesses at the inquest said that he had heavy bruises on his face, neck, and body. His friend Father Dailey said he'd never heard MacPake complain of any poor health except headaches.

The following day, a reporter asked Thomas Fahy, Carrie Pitezel's attorney, if he had ever felt the effects of Holmes' alleged curse. He said that he put no stock in such stories, but then grudgingly admitted that he'd nearly died from typhoid fever during the summer after Holmes was hanged.

The following year, Kate Durkee – the old friend of Myrta Holmes and who'd had many of Holmes' buildings in her name – suddenly died of heart disease.

A few years, it would be revealed that Richard Johnson, one of the men who had served as a juror for Holmes' trial, killed himself by inhaling illuminating gas.

But it was the tragic death of the jury foreman at the trial, Linford Biles, that had even some diehard skeptics wondering if there might be some truth to the talk of a curse.

One Saturday morning, Biles was awakened by a loud commotion below his bedroom window. He looked out and saw a small crowd gathered on the street. They were pointing upward and shouting something about a fire. Biles quickly dressed and hurried out onto the sidewalk. Up on his roof, he could see a bluish flame arcing into the sky Biles instantly knew the source of the flame – crisscrossing electric wires that were strung over his house had touched, sparked, and ignited the shingles on his roof. He'd had trouble with the wires, and the same thing had happened once before.

Eerily, that earlier incident had occurred on the very day that H.H. Holmes had been arrested in Boston.

Biles ran back into the house, climbed the stairs, and then eased out onto the roof, intending to somehow move the wires away from the shingles. When his daughter saw what he was doing, she woke her brother and urged him to get up on the roof and bring their father back inside before he hurt himself "fooling with" the wires.

The young man did what his sister told him. Seconds later, the spectators below heard a thumping sound on the roof – then silence. The police arrived moments later and climbed onto the roof. They found the bodies of the father and son lying side by side. The younger man was still breathing but his father – who had accidentally come into contact with the live wires – had been electrocuted. Linford Biles was dead.

OVER TIME, THE STORIES ABOUT THE HOLMES CURSE eventually faded away, banished from the pages of newspapers and living on only in the memories of those with a passion for true crime and a lingering interest in H.H. Holmes.

But not before the curse managed to claim one more victim.

On New Year's Eve 1909, two masked men burst into Novak's Saloon on Sixteenth Street in Chicago. One of the men called out for everyone to get in line and hand over the cash. It was a robbery, and they could think of it as a New Year's greeting. As the men were pulling cash out of the till and stuffing it into a burlap sack, a policeman wandered into the saloon, realized a holdup was taking place, and opened fire on the bandits.

One of the masked men was shot in the head as he ran out the back door and died soon after at St. Anthony's Hospital. According to his identification, his name was Edward Haywood.

But that wasn't his real name.

Later, the authorities learned that Haywood was Marion Hedgepeth, the train robber that Holmes met in the St. Louis jail, promised a reward, and then stiffed him. Hedgepeth's letter to Fidelity Mutual was a key part of an investigation being opened into the crimes of H.H. Holmes.

Hedgepeth's attempt to get out of prison by informing on Holmes and Jeptha Howe had been a failure, and he spent another decade in prison before being paroled in 1906.

Despite the claims that he had made about his rehabilitation to the parole board -- including that he spent each day in prison

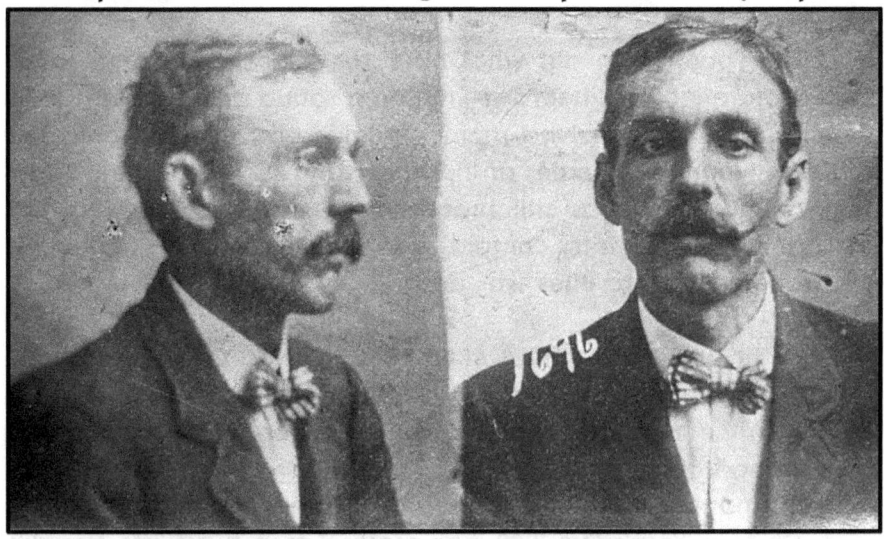

Prison and tuberculosis took a toll on the man once known as the "Handsome Bandit," but he refused to waste away in a bed somewhere. Instead, Hedgepeth wanted to go out with the proverbial bang.

reading the Bible – Hedgepeth had no interest in dying broke and starving now that he was outside prison walls.

He managed to find employment with the Pinkerton Detective Agency, of all people, but not as an agent. He became an informant for them, working under the direction of F.H. Tillotson, general manager of the agency's Kansas City office. Many of the detectives were openly distrustful of Hedgepeth, but Tillotson firmly believed he'd been rehabilitated and could be trusted.

Tillotson may have been a first-rate director but was certainly not a good judge of character. Despite his insistence that he was a new, honest man, Hedgepeth was arrested in September 1907 for blowing up a safe in Omaha, Nebraska. He was tried, found guilty and sentenced to 10 more years in prison. Two years later, though, he was released when it was discovered that he was dying from tuberculosis.

Prison and disease took a toll on the handsome bandit and while he was only in his early forties when released the second time, he looked much older. He drifted when he got out, evening up in St. Paul, where he worked for $20 a week as a cutter in a shoe factory.

But Hedgepeth decided that was no way to die. He assembled a new gang and started committing small-time robberies – like the one on New Year's Eve 1909 in Chicago.

It turned out to be the bandit's last hurrah. His corpse sat unclaimed in the morgue for a few days and then was buried in a local potter's field.

The story of the Holmes' Curse had finally reached its end.

BIBLIOGRAPHY

Anonymous – *Sold to Satan, Holmes – A poor wife's sad story*; Philadelphia, PA, Old Franklin Publishing House, 1895

Appelbaum, Stanley – *The Chicago World's Fair of 1893*; 1980

Asbury, Herbert – *Gem of the Prairie*; New York, NY, Alfred A. Knopf, 1940

Badger, R. Reid – *The Great American Fair: The World's Columbian Exposition and American Culture*, Chicago, IL, Nelson Hall, 1979

Barclay & Co. – *Holmes, the Arch-Friend or A Carnival of Crime*; 1895

Bloch, Robert – *American Gothic*, New York, NY, Simon & Schuster, 1974

Borowski, John (edited by Dismas Estrada) – *The Strange Case of Dr. H.H. Holmes*, West Hollywood, CA, Waterfront Productions, 2005

Boswell, Charles and Lewis Thompson – *The Girls in Nightmare House*, New York, NY, Fawcett, 1955

Churchill, Allan – *A Pictorial History of American Crime, 1849-1929*; New York, NY, Holt, Rinehart & Winston, 1964

Corbitt, Robert L. – *The Holmes Castle*; Corbitt & Morrison, Chicago, IL, 1895

Crighton, J.D. – *Detective in the White City: The Real Story of Frank Geyer*, Murietta, CA, RW Publishing House, 2017

Dybwad, G.L. and Joy V. Bliss – *Chicago Day at the World's Columbian Exposition*, Albuquerque, NM, The Book Stops Here, 1997

Eckert, Allan – *The Scarlet Mansion*; New York, NY, Little Brown, 1985

Franke, David – *The Torture Doctor*, New York, NY, Avon, 1975

Geyer, Frank P. – *The Holmes-Pitezel Case*; Philadelphia, PA, 1896

Horan, James D. & Howard Swiggett – *The Pinkerton Story*, New York, NY, G. Putnam & Sons, 1951

Krist, Gary – *City of Scoundrels*, New York, NY, Crown, 2012

Larson, Erik – *The Devil in the White City*, New York, NY, Crown Publishers, 2003

Lindberg, Richard C. – *Chicago by Gaslight*, Chicago, IL, Academy Chicago Publishers,1996

-------------------------- - *Chicago Ragtime*, South Bend, IN, Icarus Press, 1985
------------------------ – *Heartland Serial Killers*, 2011

Longstreet, Stephen – Chicago: An Intimate Portrait of People, Pleasures, and Power, New York, NY, David McKay & Co., 1973

Mark, Norman – *Mayors, Madams & Madmen*, Chicago, IL, Chicago Review Press, 1979

Mudgett, Herman - *H.H. Holmes – Holmes' Own Story*, Philadelphia, PA, Burk& McKetridge, 1896

Nash, Jay Robert – *Bloodletters and Badmen*, New York, NY, M. Evans, 1973

Schechter, Harold – *Depraved*, New York, NY, Pocket Books, 1994

Seltzer, Adam – *H.H. Holmes: The True History of the White City Devil*, New York, NY, Skyhorse Publishing, 2017

Sifakis, Carl – *The Encyclopedia of American Crime*, New York, NY, Facts on File,1982

Snavely, Judy Miller – *The Devil's Disciple*, Bloomington, IN, AuthorHouse, 2006

Wright, Sewell Peaslee – *Chicago Murders*, New York, NY, Duell, Sloan & Pearce, 1945

Personal Interviews and Correspondence

NEWSPAPERS

Much of my source material came from the newspapers of the day and they proved to be invaluable in writing this book, especially when it came to using quotes from the court officials, trial testimony and interviews. How accurate all the statements were is anyone's guess, but I presented them as they were offered at the time.

Keep in mind, the Holmes case was front-page news across the country and was most exhaustively covered in Chicago and Philadelphia, the two cities most closely connected to his crimes. However, I also found the New York City newspapers to be a very useful resource, especially the *New York Times*, which is a great online source. Hearst's paper, the *New York World,* also seemed to have a direct line to Holmes and as the great "yellow" paper of the day, it provided some very sensational coverage.

Boston Globe
Boston Journal
Chicago Daily News
Chicago Evening Journal
Chicago Herald
Chicago Inter Ocean
Chicago Record
Chicago Times-Herald
Chicago Tribune
Fort Worth Daily Gazette
Galveston Daily News
Indianapolis News
New York Herald
New York Times
New York World
Philadelphia Inquirer
Philadelphia Press
Philadelphia Public Ledger
Philadelphia Record
Philadelphia Times
St. Louis Globe-Democrat
Syracuse Journal
Toronto Daily Globe & Mail

www.ingramcontent.com/pod-product-compliance
Lightning Source LLC
Chambersburg PA
CBHW070949160426
43193CB00012B/1814